MW01014559

Tupolev Tu-160

SOVIET STRIKE FORCE SPEARHEAD

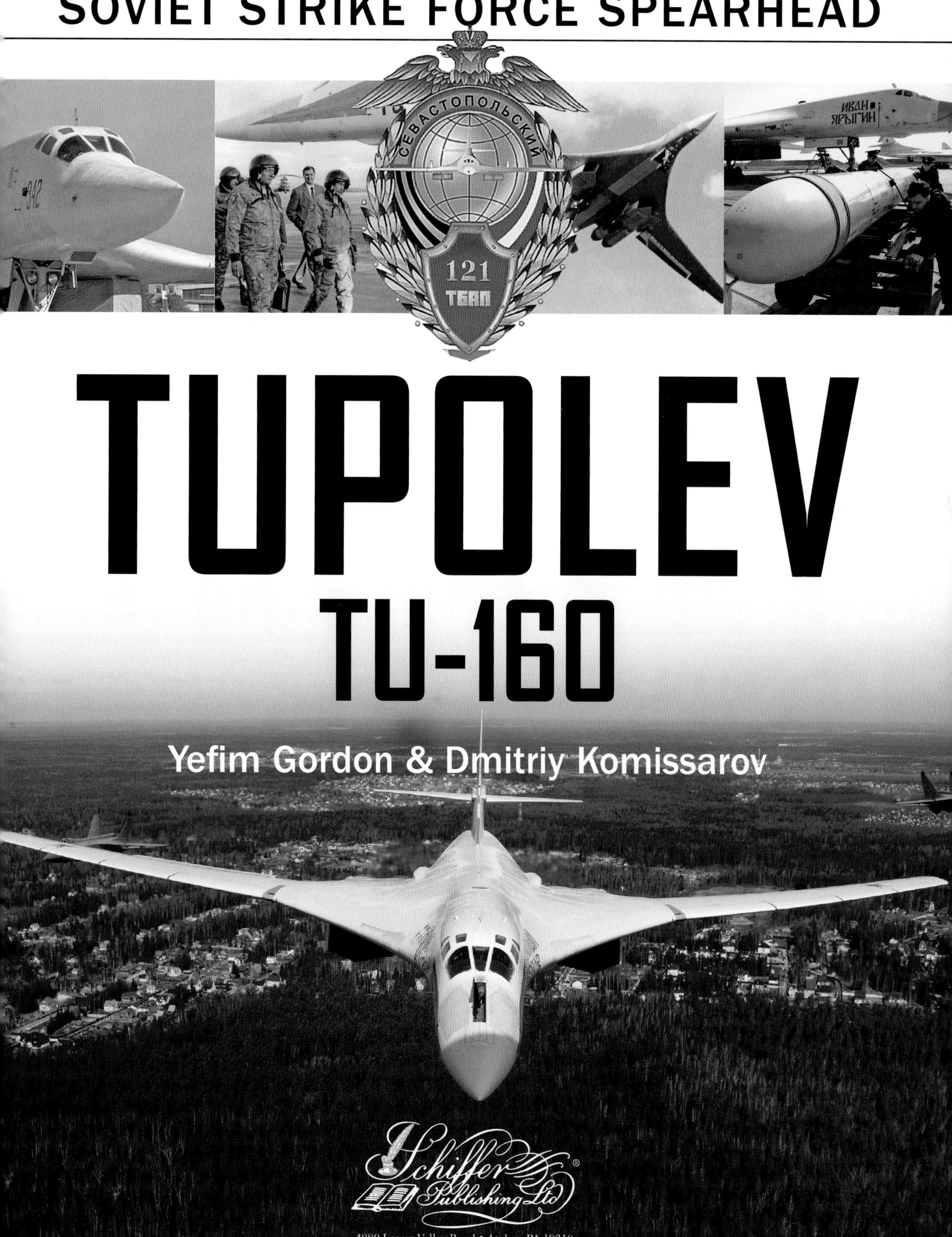

TUPOLEV TU-160

Yefim Gordon & Dmitriy Komissarov

Schiffer Publishing Ltd
4880 Lower Valley Road • Atglen, PA 19310

Library of Congress Control Number: 2016944625

Designed by Polygon Press Ltd., Moscow

ISBN: 978-0-7643-5204-1
Printed in China

Published by Schiffer Publishing, Ltd.
4880 Lower Valley Road
Atglen, PA 19310
Phone: (610) 593-1777; Fax: (610) 593-2002
E-mail: Info@schifferbooks.com
Web: www.schifferbooks.com

Other Schiffer Books by the Author:
Tupolev Tu-4 (978-0-7643-4797-9)
Tupolev Tu-144 (978-0-7643-4894-5)

Other Schiffer Books on Related Subjects:
Stalin's Eagles (978-0-7643-0476-7)
*MiG-29 Flight Manua*l (978-0-7643-1389-9)

Contents

Acknowledgments

This book is illustrated with photos by Yefim Gordon, Aleksandr Bel'tyukov, Sergey Burdin, Artur Gasparyan, Mikhail Gribovskiy, Yevgeniy Kazyonnov, Dmitriy Karpov, Dmitriy Komissarov, Vladimir Koval'chuk, Sergey Krivchikov, Marina Lystseva, Sergey Lutsenko, Aleksey Mikheyev, Andrey Nesvetayev, Dmitriy Pichugin, Sergey Popsuyevich, Sergey Sergeyev, the late Sergey Skrynnikov, Vyacheslav Timofeyev, Ferdinand C. W. Käsmann, Ivan Nesbit, as well as from the archives of the Tupolev PLC, the Kazan' Aircraft Factory (KAPO), the Sukhoi Holding Co., the Myasishchev EMZ, the ITAR-TASS News Agency, the Royal Norwegian Air Force, the UK MoD and the archive of Yefim Gordon.

The authors wish to express special thanks to Yevgeniy Kazyonnov, who supplied excellent photos, Vladimir Rigmant, who gave consultations on the Tu-160's development history and Pavel Sineokiy, who provided some valuable materials.

The authors have also used the following web sources: www.gelio.livejournal.com, www.russianplanes.net, www.spotters.net.ua, www.militaryrussia.ru, www.testpilot.ru, www.rg.ru.

Line drawings by Nikolay Gordyukov, Viktor Mil'yachenko, Vyacheslav Zenkin and the Tupolev PLC.

Colour artwork by Sergey Ignat'yev, Viktor Mil'yachenko and Andrey Zhirnov.

Russian Air Force personnel form the number "100" to mark the centennial of the Long-Range Aviation. The service's main types are present here – its flagship, the Tu-160, followed by the Tu-95MS strategic bomber, the Tu-22M3 heavy bomber and the IL-78M tanker.

Introduction

It is a generally known fact that the Soviet Union and the United States were allies during the Second World War. Soon after the end of the hostilities, however, Europe found itself divided according to the strategic interests of the two superpowers and co-operation gave way to confrontation. The North Atlantic Treaty Organisation (NATO) was formed in 1949, followed in 1955 by its Soviet counterpart, the Warsaw Pact military bloc. The two were in a perpetual stand-off in the more than three decades that followed; more than once the Cold War going on between the East and the West looked set to escalate into a full-blown "hot" war – the Third World War. In short, the Soviet Union and the United States were, as a line from an early 1980s song went, "cowboys and Indians of today."

Spurred by politicians and generals on both sides of the "Iron Curtain," the arms race took a heavy toll on the economies of the Soviet bloc nations which would not be outdone by the West in anything – particularly in defence matters. On the other hand, the confrontation between the East and the West became a catalyst which accelerated military technology development considerably, especially as far as missile and aircraft design was concerned. For many years it was a neck-and-neck race; now and then one of the superpowers would gain a lead and the opposing side would then strive to catch up. For instance, in the late 1950s and early 1960s the Soviet Union led the way in intercontinental ballistic missile (ICBM) development, whereas the USA placed its bet on strategic bombers. The military balance of power between the two nations (and the two military blocs at large) remained virtually until the early 1990s – that is, until the demise of the Soviet Union.

Quite often the decisions on the development of new weapons systems taken by the Soviet political and military elite were out of touch with reality, not correlating with the nation's economic capabilities and running contrary to common sense. On the other hand, Soviet designers were quite a match for their Western col-

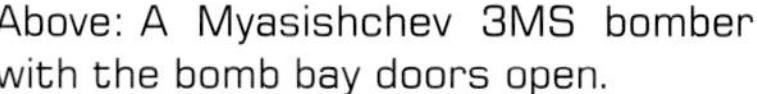

Above: A Myasishchev 3MS bomber with the bomb bay doors open.

Above right: The sole example of the Myasishchev M-50 supersonic bomber with the tactical code "023 Red" it wore during trials. Again, the bomb bay doors are open.

Right: "101 White," the sole example of the Sukhoi T-4 missile strike/strategic reconnaissance aircraft to fly. The hinged nose visor is raised to cruise position.

An operational Tupolev Tu-95MS missile strike aircraft in cruise flight.

leagues (and often excelled them), and their creative endeavours were mostly hampered by political decisions and the myopic views of the nation's whimsical leaders.

The field of strategic bomber design is a prime example. The Moscow-based OKB-156 design bureau led by General Designer Andrey Nikolayevich Tupolev (*opytno-konstrooktorskoye byuro* – experimental design bureau; the number is a code allocated for security reasons) was the national leader in heavy aircraft design; yet, despite being highly advanced (in fact, ahead of their time), many of the aircraft developed there never got further than the drawing board. The same was true for many projects evolved by such design bureaux as OKB-23 (headed by Vladimir Mikhaïlovich Myasishchev), OKB-938 (headed by Robert Lyudvigovich Bartini at the time) and OKB-51 (headed by Pavel Osipovich Sukhoi). The Soviet Union was actively pursuing missile programmes (especially in the years when Nikita S. Khrushchov with his famous 'missile itch' was ruling the country), and manned combat aircraft were out of favour. Few strategic bombers were destined to reach the hardware stage, and even fewer were to complete their test programmes – not because they showed disappointing performance, mind you; on the contrary, they were much too advanced and thus were considered a threat by the ICBM lobby!

In keeping with this policy all work on the Myasishchev M-50 and M-52 strategic bombers (NATO reporting name *Bounder*) was terminated in the early 1960s and the Myasishchev OKB itself was dissolved – for the second time in its history (fortunately to be reborn in 1967). The Sukhoi T-4 Mach 3 missile strike/reconnaissance aircraft with an advanced all-titanium airframe (in-house designation *izdeliye* 100), which first flew on August 22, 1972 and showed encouraging results, was similarly victimised in 1974 after making only ten flights – thanks largely to the efforts of Andrey N. Tupolev, who perceived it as an unwelcome competitor to his own designs. (*Izdeliye* [product] such-and-such is a term often used for coding Soviet/Russian military hardware items.)

Thus, while possessing a large nuclear fist in the form of ICBMs, by the mid-1970s the Soviet Union had only a small strategic bomber arm equipped with Tupolev Tu-95 *Bear* and Myasishchev M-4 *Bison-A* and 3M (3MS and 3MN) *Bison-B* bombers. These obsolescent subsonic aircraft stood no chance against the well-equipped, modern air defences of the 'potential adversary' (that is, NATO). Conversely, the Americans consistently developed and refined the aviation component of their nuclear attack force.

It was not until 1967, three years after Khrushchov's removal from power which changed the fortunes of the Soviet aircraft makers, that the Soviet military turned their attention to the much-neglected strategic bomber arm of the Soviet Air Force (VVS – *Voyenno-vozdooshnyye seely*). This change of heart was prompted by the USA's decision to launch the AMSA (Advanced Manned Strategic Aircraft) programme which emerged as the Rockwell International B-1 bomber. the Soviet government responded by ordering the development of a new multi-mission, multi-mode strike aircraft possessing intercontinental range; this effort culminated in the now world-famous Tu-160 bomber/missile strike aircraft. This book tells the story of how this advanced Soviet weapons system was born amid a lot of strife and devious schemes.

Chapter 1

The Great Contest: You Win Only to Lose

On November 28, 1967, the Soviet Union's Council of Ministers (that is, government) issued directive No.1098-378 ordering the commencement of design work on what was referred to as a "strategic intercontinental aircraft"; this was, in western terminology, a request for proposals (RFP). The design bureaux participating in the tender for the new strategic bomber were required to develop a weapons platform possessing outstanding performance. Suffice it to say that cruising speed at 18,000 m (59,060 ft) was stipulated as 3,200-3,500 km/h (1,987-2,174 mph); the required range in this mode was 11,000-13,000 km (6,830-8,075 miles). Maximum range in high-altitude subsonic cruise and at sea level was to be 16,000-18,000 km (9,940-11,180 miles) and 11,000-13,000 km respectively.

The aircraft was to be capable of operating in visual meteorological conditions (VMC) and instrument meteorological conditions (IMC), in daytime and at night, in any latitudes. It was to be able to complete its objective in a strong air defence and electronic countermeasures (ECM) environment, destroying the target with conventional or nuclear ordnance. In a nuclear war scenario, the aircraft's targets included political centres and military headquarters/command posts, defence industry centres, nuclear weapon depots, bomber and military airlift aviation bases, ballistic missile sites, naval task forces and single ships of importance, concentrations of enemy reserves, dams and power stations. In a conventional warfare scenario the targets were much the same, plus vulnerable targets such as oil wells and refineries, fuel dumps, chemical plants and the like. If key targets were destroyed by their own strategic missile forces or missile submarines, the aircraft's mission was to assess the results and take out whatever targets were left. Its high speed and the ability to launch the missiles from out of range of the target's air defences rendered it less vulnerable than conventional strike aircraft.

An artist's impression of the Tu-160M from the jacket of the PD project materials submitted for the contest.

General Designer Andrey N. Tupolev, head of OKB-156, in the late 1960s when the work on the Tu-160 started.

The armament was to vary according to the nature of the mission, consisting of air-to-surface missiles – four Kh-45 ***Molniya*** (Lightning) long-range hypersonic missiles or 24 Kh-2000 supersonic missiles – or free-fall and guided bombs. The specified maximum weapons load was 45,000 kg (99,200 lb).

A few words must be said here about the missiles. The Kh-45 had started life as the Kh-33 missile designed in house by the Sukhoi OKB as the T-4's principal weapon, but in keeping with Council of Ministers directive No.119-4440 issued on December 3, 1963, the project was transferred to a specialised missile design bureau – OKB-2-155 headed by Aleksandr Ya. Bereznyak, which reworked it considerably. This entity based in the town of Doobna (Moscow Region), a branch office of the OKB-155 "fighter maker" design bureau headed by Artyom I. Mikoyan, later became MKB ***Ra**duga* (*ma**shi**nostro**i**tel'noye kon**strook**torskoye by**u**ro* – "Rainbow" Machinery Design Bureau named after Aleksandr Ya. Bereznyak). It is now part of the Tactical Missiles Corporation, or KTRV (*Korpo**rah**tsiya 'Tak**ti**cheskoye ra**ket**noye vo'oru**zhe**niye'*).

The Kh-45, which initially was likewise regarded as the T-4's main weapon, had a conventional layout with cruciform wings and aft-mounted cruciform rudders (the tail-first and tailless versions of the original project had been discarded). The low aspect ratio wings of trapezoidal planform were sharply swept, while the large all-movable rudders placed immediately downstream had a pentagonal shape, with negative sweep on the root portion of the leading edge to create a sort of dogtooth. Because the missile was to cruise at speeds up to Mach 7, the airframe was largely made of high-strength stainless steel and titanium alloys. Two specially developed grades of glassfibre reinforced plastic (GRP) were used for the radome to provide the required strength and resistance to erosion during sustained supersonic flight and lengthy external carriage at up to Mach 3.2.

Unlike the Kh-33, which was to have a solid-propellant rocket motor, the Kh-45 was powered by a single-chamber liquid-propellant rocket motor – the S5.57 developed in 1971–72 by KB Khimmash (*Kon**strook**torskoye by**u**ro khi**mi**cheskovo ma**shi**no-stro**ye**niya* – the Chemical Machinery Design Bureau named after Aleksey M. Isayev) which specialises in such powerplants. This variable-thrust rocket motor ran on special TG-02 fuel (***top**livo ghipergo**li**cheskoye* – hypergolic or self-igniting fuel), a 50/50 mixture of xylidine and triethylamine which self-combusted when coming into contact with AK-27M oxidiser (AK = *a**zot**naya kis**lo**ta* – nitric acid).

The Kh-45 had been conceived as a long-range air-to-ground and anti-shipping missile. Hence it came with a choice of warheads – the original nuclear warhead, which could be used against a large ground target or a naval task force, was later supplemented with a conventional shaped-charge/high-explosive warhead designed to burn its way through a ship's decks. The missile was to be guided to a target with known co-ordinates by a *Tsen**trahl'*** (Central unit) gyro inertial navigation system with a digital processor and radio command mid-course correction; the anti-shipping version additionally featured a *Gar**poon*** (Harpoon) active radar homing seeker head for terminal guidance.

The missile had a length of 9.9-10.8 m (32 ft $5^{49}/_{64}$ in to 35 ft $5^{13}/_{64}$ in), a wing span of 2.0 m (6 ft $6^{47}/_{64}$ in) and a body diameter of 0.8 m (2 ft $7^{1}/_{2}$ in); some sources state the wing span as 2.4 m (7 ft $10^{31}/_{64}$ in). The launch weight was variously reported as 4,500 or 5,000 kg (9,920 or 10,020 lb), including a 500-kg (1,102-lb) warhead; some sources give the warhead weight as 1,000 kg (2,204 lb), depending on the version, which explains the discrepancy. The Kh-45 was to fly at altitudes in excess of 20,000 m (65,620 ft) and speeds of 7,000-9,000 km/h (4,347-5,590 mph), following a ballistic trajectory and then levelling out shortly before the terminal dive onto the target. Maximum range was 1,000-1,500 km (621-931 miles) for the INS-only version and 500-600 km (310-372 miles) for the anti-shipping version with the combined guidance system.

The Kh-2000 was likewise a product of MKB Raduga. This was to be an even heavier aeroballistic missile with a cruising speed of Mach 3-3.5; it was to have a thermonuclear warhead, hence the sometimes quoted designation Kh-2000T for *termo-**ya**dernyy* [*za**ryad***] – thermonuclear charge. Dimensionally the Kh-2000 was similar to the Kh-45, with a length of 9.8 m (32 ft $1^{53}/_{64}$ in), a wing span of 2.1 m (6 ft $10^{43}/_{64}$ in) and a body diameter of 1 m (3 ft $3^{25}/_{64}$ in), but the launch weight was 6,500 kg (14,330 lb) and

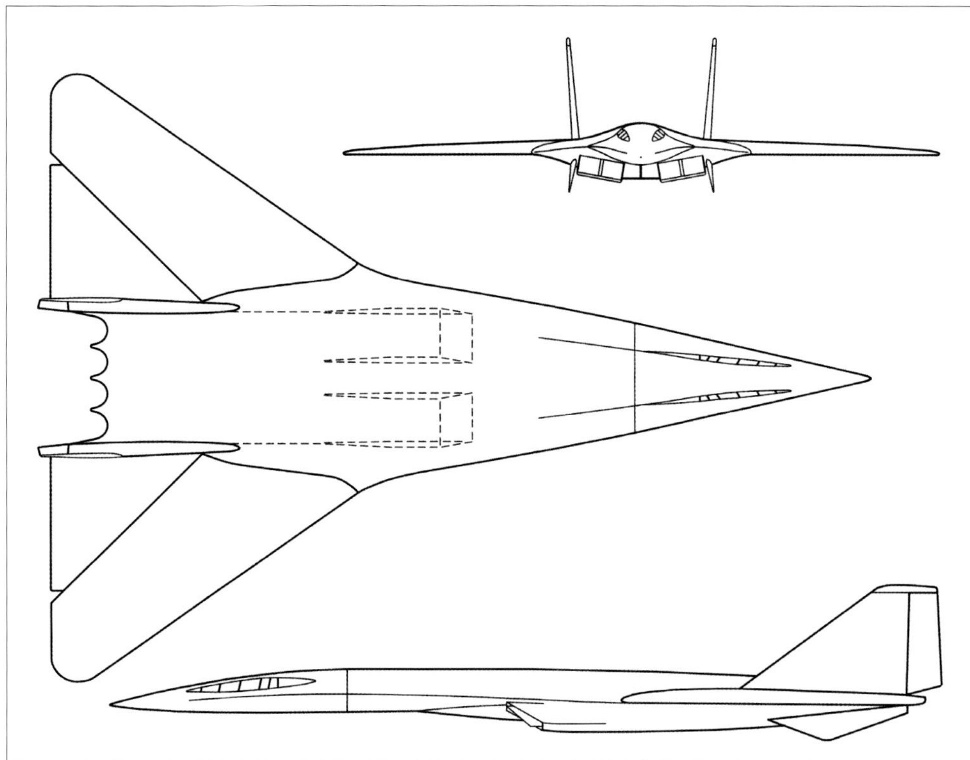

Right: A three-view drawing of the very first VG-wing "aircraft 160" project (sometimes called "160IS").

Below: A wooden desktop model of the same aircraft. The "manufacturing break" aft of the flight deck was probably there to allow an alternative version of the nose section to be fitted.

the range was 1,500 km. That said, the figure of 24 Kh-2000 missiles in the CofM directive appears impossible – this would amount to a total weight of 156,000 kg (343,920 lb)!

The Sukhoi OKB and the Myasishchev OKB were the first to take on the task; the Tupolev OKB was not in a position to join the contest at this stage, having other irons in the fire. Consider this: the Tu-144 *Charger* supersonic transport (in its original ogival-wing form known as *izdeliye* 044), the Tu-154 *Careless* three-turbofan medium-haul airliner, the Tu-22M *Backfire-A* medium bomber with variable-geometry (VG) wings and the Tu-142 *Bear-F* shore-based long-range anti-submarine warfare (ASW) aircraft were all under development at the time, entering flight test on December 31, 1968, October 3, 1968, August 30, 1969, and June 18, 1968, respectively. The Tupolev OKB sure had more than enough current projects to take care of! Thus it merely kept a tab on the new heavy bomber contest until 1970.

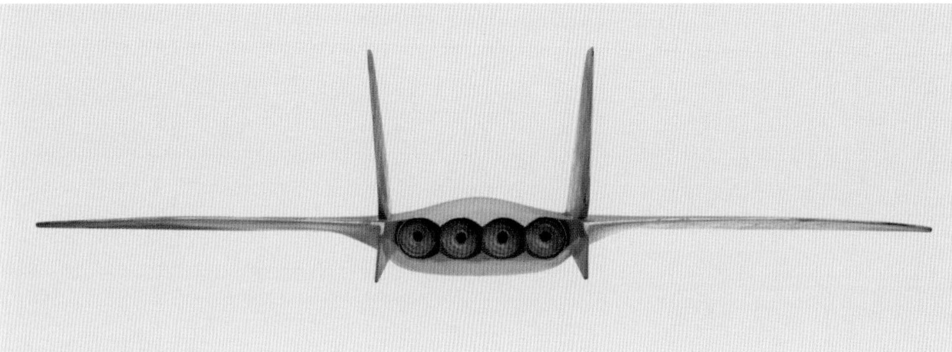

Left: Front view of the "160IS" model showing the paired air intakes and the rhomboid cross-section of the forward fuselage.

Below left: This rear view shows the engines placed close together.

Bottom left: The Tu-144 style centrebody between the air intakes housed the nose gear unit, with the weapons bay aft of it.

Bottom: A side view showing the drooped nose section and the shape of the ventral fins.

Opposite page: Two more views illustrating the aircraft's planform.

Actually, in 1969 the Tupolev OKB did begin the first project studies of such an aircraft.

Tupolev 'aircraft 160' ('aircraft 156' – first use of designation; 'aircraft 160IS', *izdeliye* K) strategic bomber/missile strike aircraft (project)

Until 1970, the top executives of the Tupolev OKB attended all government meetings having to do with the new bomber strictly as observers. (Of course, one may justly say these observers were not wholly impartial; they listened carefully and drew a few conclusions to be used later in their own bomber design efforts!) The OKB was heavily burdened with current programmes, hence its leaders did not want to bite off more than they could chew, even though the

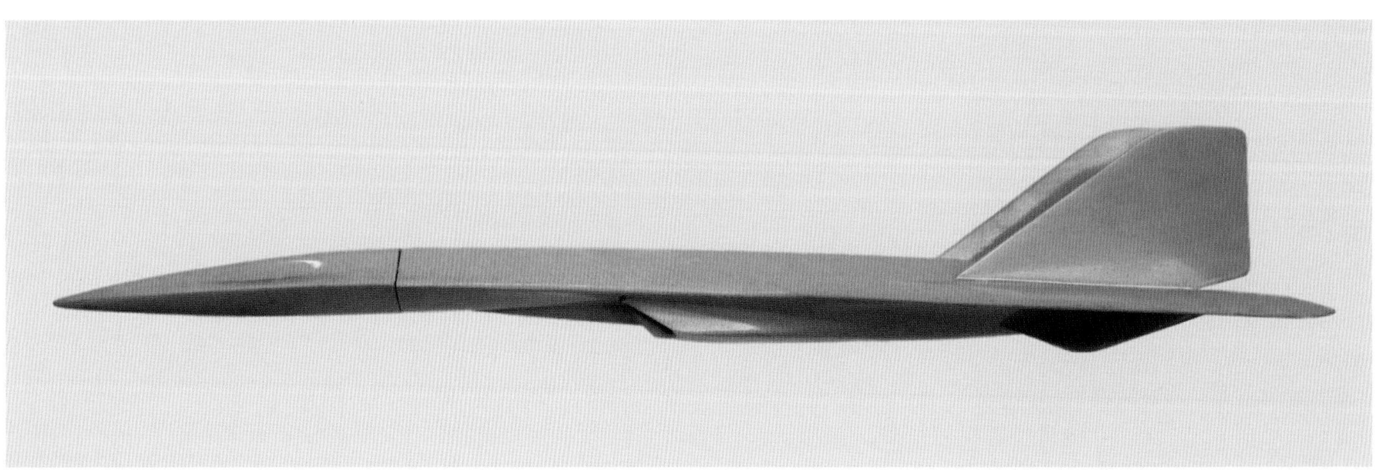

advanced multi-mode strategic strike aircraft programme fitted well into the OKB's traditional line of work.

Yet, after carefully analysing the programme's actual state and prospects, assessing its own capabilities and those of its competitors OKB-156 did indeed embark on a new strategic bomber project, using the preliminary specifications of 1967 as a starting point. This work was performed by the design bureau's Section K (responsible for unmanned aerial vehicles) under the overall co-ordination of Aleksey A. Tupolev, the General Designer's son, who subsequently became head of the OKB when Andrey N. Tupolev passed away in 1972. Later, overall project responsibility passed to Valentin I. Bliznyuk; he was a seasoned designer who had participated in the development of the OKB's first supersonic UAVs – the "121" (Tu-121) surface-to-surface missile and the closely related "123" (Tu-123) reconnaissance drone, a.k.a. DBR-1 ***Yastreb*** (Hawk), then the stillborn "135" (Tu-135) strategic bomber/missile strike aircraft, and finally the Tu-144 SST. A major contribution to the early project studies was made by Aleksandr L. Pookhov who now supervises the Tu-144LL SST technology research aircraft programme and the creation of Russia's second-generation SST, the Tu-244.

Initially known as "aircraft 156," the bomber was soon redesignated "aircraft 160" (Tu-160). Some documents referred to it as *izdeliye* K (presumably thus named after the OKB's Section K). As for the "aircraft 156" (Tu-156) designation, it was later reused for a projected four-turbofan airborne early warning and control system (AWACS) aircraft – a "clean sheet of paper" design strongly reminiscent of the Boeing E-3 Sentry that lost out to the Ilyushin/Beriyev A-50 *Mainstay-A* based on the Ilyushin IL-76 *Candid-B* military transport – and, later still, reused again for a derivative of the Tu-154 using cryogenic fuel (liquid natural gas), which likewise remained unbuilt. Gener-

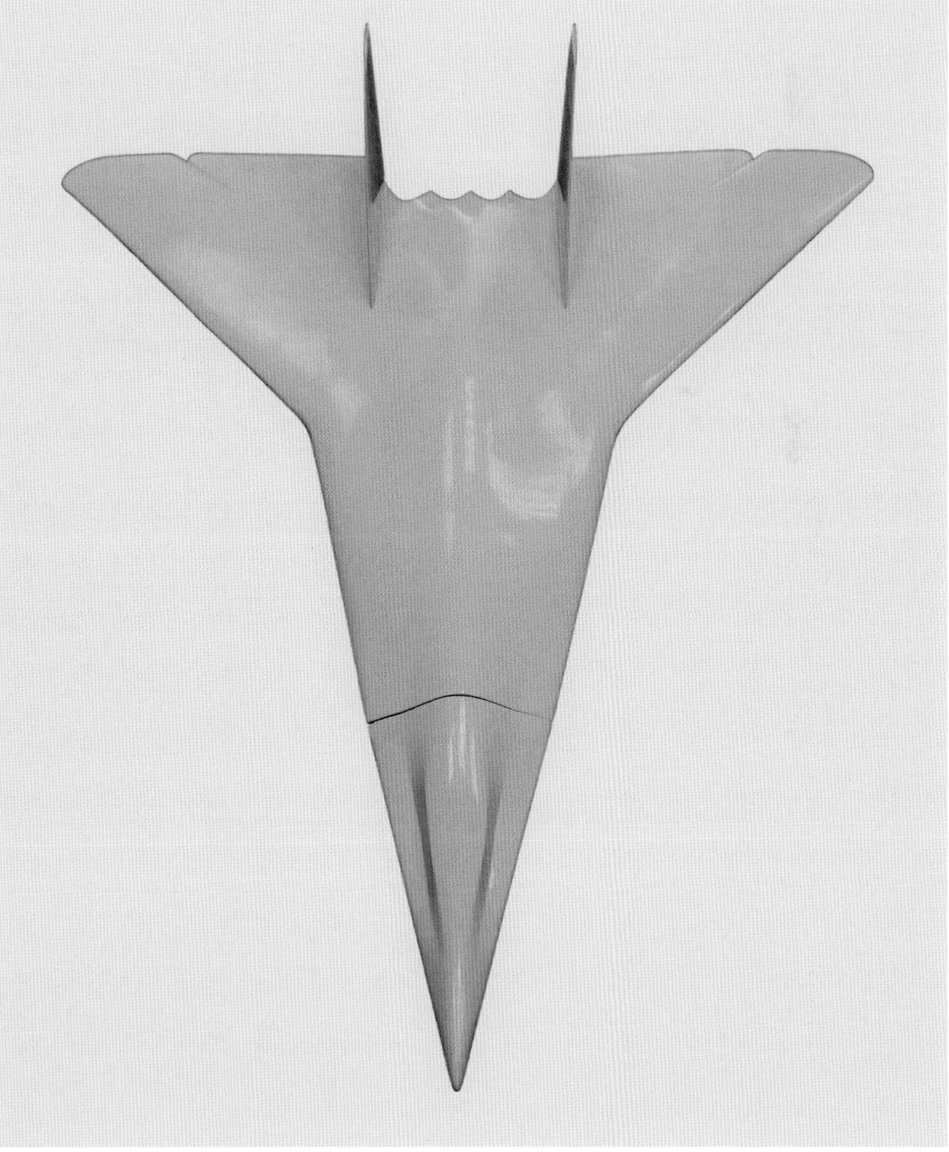

ally speaking, reusing project designations was common practice at the Tupolev OKB.

Initially the Tupolev OKB developed the *izdeliye* K unbidden, and information about it was distributed on a 'need to know' basis – only a very small group of people working at the OKB itself and the Ministry of Aircraft Industry (MAP – *Ministerstvo aviatsionnoy promyshlennosti*) knew about the project. Therefore the designers were given a free hand as far as the choice of aerodynamic layout and specific design features were concerned. They decided not to reinvent the wheel, relying heavily on the unique engineering experience gained when designing the Tu-144. This served as the basis for the initial project version of Tupolev's multi-mode strike aircraft – an aircraft which differed markedly in its design from both Sukhoi's T-4MS and Myasishchev's M-18/M-20 described below.

The extremely high demands posed by the Council of Ministers directive of November 28, 1967, meant that the engineers were facing a Mission Impossible. Therefore initially the Tupolev OKB engineers decided to select the specified maximum speed and maximum-range cruising speed as the main performance targets and take it from there. It should be noted that, concurrently with the bomber project, Section K conducted research on ways of further developing supersonic transports; this research later laid the foundation of the SPS-2 programme (*sverkhzvookovoy passazheerskiy samolyot*, SST) – the future Tu-244 project. It is quite logical therefore that part of this research should go into the Tu-160 programme – specifically, the general arrangement. Hence initially the bomber shared the tailless delta layout used by the SPS-1 (Tu-144) and SPS-2 (Tu-244).

As an aside, research and development data accumulated under the next-generation SST programme showed that in theory it was possible to obtain a lift/drag ratio of 7-9 in supersonic cruise and as much as 15 in subsonic cruise. This, coupled with advanced fuel-efficient engines, made reaching the specified range target – or at least approaching it – a realistic prospect. At any rate, some of the Tu-244 project documents (dated 1973) show that with turbojet engines having a specific fuel consumption (SFC) of 1.23 kg/kgp·hr (lb/lbst·hr) in supersonic cruise mode the airliner was expected to have a maximum range of 8,000 km (4,970 miles). Given adequate engine power, the tailless delta layout ensured the required speed and many other target performance figures.

The main problems inherent in this layout were associated with the need to use new structural materials and technologies enabling sustained cruise flight at high temperatures (caused by kinetic heating at high Mach numbers). Seeking to reduce the technical risks involved, the Tupolev OKB decided to restrict the new bomber's cruising speed to Mach 2.3, which was somewhat less than the competitors' figures.

One of the key requirements was long range over a complex mission profile involving air defence penetration at high altitude in supersonic mode (a so-called "hi-hi-hi" mission profile) or at low altitude in subsonic mode (a "hi-lo-hi" profile). Target approach was to be performed in subsonic cruise at optimum altitude. Another (albeit less critical) requirement was good field performance allowing the bomber to operate from relatively short runways. Combining these virtues in a single aircraft was no simple task. An acceptable balance of subsonic and supersonic performance could only be obtained by utilising variable-geometry wings and unconventional compound engines operating as turbofans in subsonic mode and as pure turbojets in supersonic mode.

An aerodynamics comparison of the fixed-sweep and variable-geometry versions made when the optimum layout was being defined revealed that the VG version had a 20-50% better lift/drag ratio at subsonic speeds. In supersonic cruise with the wings at maximum sweep the L/D ratio was virtually equal to that of the fixed-sweep aircraft.

An inherent major shortcoming of 'swing-wing' aircraft is the increase in empty weight caused by the massive wing pivots and actuators. Calculations showed that if this assembly made up more than 4% of the empty weight, the weight penalty negated all the advantages conferred on a heavy bomber by the variable-geometry wings. Assuming the powerplant was identical, a heavy VG-wing aircraft offered approximately 30-35% longer range at medium altitude and 10% longer range at low altitude than a conventional fixed-sweep aircraft when flying at subsonic speeds. In supersonic cruise at high altitude the range was about equal but again a "swing-wing" heavy aircraft gained an advantage of approximately 15% at low altitude. VG-wing aircraft also had better field performance.

Choosing the correct cruise Mach number was an important aspect of a supersonic heavy bomber's design process. Theoretical and aerodynamic research was undertaken to compare the range of a "swing-wing" heavy aircraft at two different cruising speeds, Mach 2.2 and Mach 3.0. The results were unmistakable: reducing the cruising speed to Mach 2.2 enhanced range considerably thanks to a lower SFC and a better lift/drag ratio. Besides, the airframe of a bomber designed to cruise at Mach 3 would include a large proportion of titanium alloys, which increased unit costs and created additional technological problems, as titanium is difficult to machine and weld.

In the original version of the "160" project the Tupolev OKB also assessed the VG layout. Hence the first version of the project was sometimes referred to as the "160IS," the suffix standing for *izmenyayemaya strelovidnost'* – variable sweep. This layout offered certain advantages but imposed a weight penalty and complicated the design considerably.

Information on the "160IS" is scarce – not least because the first VG version was dropped at an early stage. Just about the only pictorial evidence is a desktop model painted white overall and not revealing much in the way of detail. The aircraft had a so-called integral or blended wing/body (BWB) layout, the forward fuselage (or rather lifting body), having a shallow quasi-rhomboid cross-section; sharp chines ran from just aft of the nose radome to a point at about two-thirds of the fuselage length, the leading-edge sweep being constant and very strong. Judging by the shape of the nose, the aircraft obviously had a drooping nose visor to improve the pilots' view on take-off and landing, just like on the Tu-144.

Further downstream the leading-edge sweep diminished to about 45° with the wide-chord outer wings at maximum sweep; unfortunately no pictures are available to show the wings at minimum sweep. Large delta-shaped slab stabilisers were located further aft, with just a hint of a gap between them and the fully swept outer wings. The wingtips were rounded and the trailing edge was at 90° to the aircraft's longitudinal axis, coinciding with the stabilators' trailing edge; the result looked like a huge double delta, and in fact the VG wings were not obvious at all.

The vertical tail consisted of widely spaced twin fins and rudders which had a basically trapezoidal shape similar to that of the Tu-144's vertical tail. The fins were very slightly canted outward.

The powerplant consisted of four turbojet or turbofan engines of an unspecified type – possibly Kuznetsov NK-144 two-spool afterburning turbofans with a take-off rating of 17,500 kgp (38,580 lbst) in maximum afterburner, a minimum-afterburner cruise rating of 3,970 kgp (8,750 lbst) and a dry cruise rating of 3,000 kgp (6,610 lbst). In common with the 'first-generation' Tu-144 prototype (*izdeliye* 044) all four engines were housed side by side in a common nacelle placed under the wing centre section trailing edge. The air intakes were arranged in pairs with the nose gear fairing between the pairs; the nozzles were located between the fins, with "pen nib" fairings in between. This arrangement allowed the slanting shock waves generated in supersonic cruise to be utilised for improving the lift/drag ratio. However, it also led to excessive pressure loss in the long inlet ducts; moreover, individual adjustment of the intake ramps could have an adverse effect on the neighbouring intakes. Finally, placing the engines so close together entailed a risk of the neighbouring engines being put out of action, should one of the engines suffer an uncontained failure or fire. This is one of the reasons why the engines were moved apart in pairs on the production "second-generation" Tu-144 (*izdeliye* 004).

The model does not show how the armament was to be carried. However, judging by the wide fuselage one might assume that the missiles were to be carried internally, like in the next project version (see Tu-160M below).

However, when the "160IS" project was submitted to General Designer Andrey N. Tupolev for approval, he axed it – probably believing that VG wings constituted too much of a technological risk and imposed an unacceptable weight penalty, reducing the payload/weight ratio to such an extent that the required performance could not be achieved. ("Old Man Tupolev," as he was informally referred to, was known for his rather conservative views on some aspects of aircraft design.) Therefore Andrey N. Tupolev chose not to submit the "160IS" for the contest; instead, he took the decision to use the existing Tu-144 SST as a basis for further work on the multi-mode supersonic strategic aircraft. His reasoning was that taking the Tu-144 as the starting point would ensure maximum commonality, minimise risks and cut costs.

Proceeding from the November 28, 1967, directive and the provisional operational requirement issued by the VVS, the Sukhoi and Myasishchev design bureaux had completed their preliminary design (PD) projects in the early 1970s. In their ultimate form, both contenders were four-turbojet aircraft with VG wings but utilised completely different aerodynamic layouts.

The Contest: The Sukhoi OKB's Bid

Changing requirements led the Sukhoi OKB to start reworking the T-4 *sans suffixe* (*izdeliye* 100) before it had even flown. The original T-4 was a single-mode aircraft optimised for high-altitude supersonic cruise and delivering missile attacks while staying out of reach of the enemy's air defences. Yet, the latter were becoming increasingly sophisticated and the chances of surviving a mission in hostile airspace by relying on speed and altitude alone were becoming negligible. A study undertaken by the Central Institute of the Soviet Air Force showed that 75-80% of the aircraft in a strike force attacking NATO targets in Europe would be shot down. A new approach was needed – a multi-mode aircraft capable of low-level air defence penetration.

Therefore, as a first step, as early as 1969, the OKB started work on a two-mode strategic bomber bearing the designation T-4M (*modifitseerovannyy* – modified), or *izdeliye* 100I. While striving to retain as much as possible of the existing structure, systems and manufacturing technologies, the designers reworked the aircraft considerably and scaled it up somewhat. Most notably, the T-4M still had a tail-first layout but the fixed-geometry double-delta wings with a leading-edge sweep of 75°44' inboard and 60°17' outboard gave way to VG wings (hence the I suffix standing for *izmenyayemaya* [*strelovidnost'*] – variable sweep). At maximum sweep (in high-speed cruise mode) the wings had constant 72° leading-edge sweep; at minimum sweep (in take-off/landing mode) the high aspect ratio outer wings had 15° leading-edge sweep. The cropped-delta canard foreplanes aft of the flight deck for pitch control and the single trapezoidal vertical tail were considerably enlarged. The main gear units had larger bogies with 12 wheels each instead of eight (three rows of four instead of two rows) to cater for the higher weight. The powerplant consisting of four 16,000-kgp (35,270 lbst) Kolesov RD36-41 afterburning turbojets located side by side in a rectangular-section ventral nacelle with a V-shaped front end was retained. The crew was expanded to three – two pilots and navigator/weapons systems operator (WSO) – by adding a co-pilot; this was made possible by the larger fuselage diameter (the T-4's hinged nose visor closing the flight deck windshield completely when raised to cruise position was retained).

However, the designers soon realised it was a bad idea; this approach led to an increase in the bomber's overall dimensions and structural weight while still leaving no room at all for weapons stowage. Like the T-4 *sans suffixe*, the T-4M carried its weapons load externally (in this case, under the engine package); this limited the warload to two Kh-45 missiles – same as on the predecessor, which was not enough. (True, some sources mention an external load option of eight Kh-2000 missiles, but this appears impossible for the reasons stated earlier.) After considering 32 consecutive PD project configurations the OKB terminated further development of the T-4M and had to seek other solutions.

The general arrangement of the future bomber had to meet the following main criteria. The internal volume had to be maximised while keeping the surface area (and hence drag) to a minimum. The weapons bays had to be capacious enough to accommodate the required range of armament. The structure had to be as stiff as possible to permit high-speed ultra-low-level operations. (This flight mode, which increased the chances of penetrating the enemy's air defences, placed high demands on structural strength because in low-level flight turbulence might occur and terrain avoidance manoeuvres may be needed.) The powerplant had to be located externally so as to facilitate eventual re-engining (that is, buried engines were ruled out because integrating new engines might require drastic structural changes). Finally, the layout had

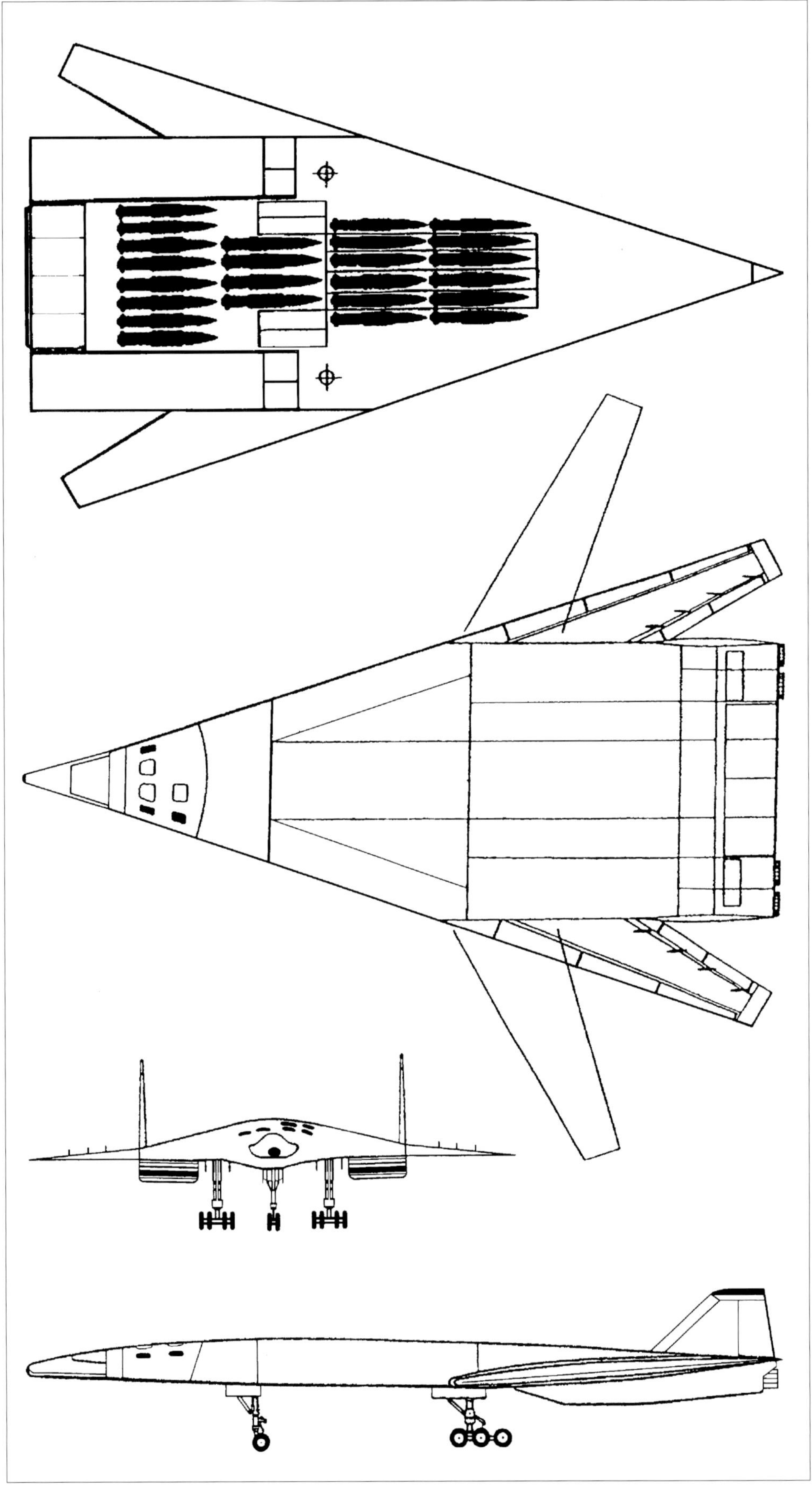

to offer the potential of continuously improving the aircraft's performance and handling.

Hence in 1969, the Sukhoi OKB started work on the **T-4MS** (*izdeliye* 200) two-mode bomber, the S suffix meaning *strategicheskiy* (strategic). Despite the similar-sounding designation, this was an altogether new aircraft, as the product code suggests. It was this project that was submitted for the contest.

The designers still paid special attention to ensuring maximum technological and component commonality with the T-4 *sans suffixe*, keeping the predecessor's systems and equipment, structural materials, detail design features and the manufacturing technologies mastered during the T-4 programme. Among other things, the four RD36-41 afterburning turbojets were retained at the initial stage (the so-called Stage A). They were to be replaced by K-101 afterburning variable-cycle engines rated at 20,000 kgp (44,090 lbst) each for take-off during Stage B. Developed by the same OKB-36 in Rybinsk, alias RKBM (***Ryb****inskoye* ***k****onstrooktorskoye* ***b****yuro* ***m****otorostroyeniya* – Rybinsk Engine Design Bureau), the K-101 operated as a turbofan in subsonic cruise and as a pure turbojet in acceleration/supersonic cruise mode when the bypass duct was shut off; the afterburner was in the bypass duct. Some sources, however, refer to the T-4MS's engine type as K-1012. The fuel tanks were housed in the fuselage between the engines.

Originally the T-4MS had a conventionally built airframe but this was rejected in favour of a BWB design where the fuselage contributes a large amount of lift. Sukhoi OKB engineers decided that a 'flying wing' BWB layout would meet the demands described above. A while earlier, their colleagues at the Tupolev OKB had arrived at the same conclusion. Like the Tupolev OKB in the aforementioned 'aircraft 160IS' project, the Sukhoi OKB proposed variable-geometry wings with movable outer portions of relatively small

Opposite: A provisional four-view of the Sukhoi T-4MS (*izdeliye* 200). The lower view shows the 24 unidentified missiles (similar in size to the Kh-15 but having wings, unlike the latter model) carried externally in maximum payload configuration.

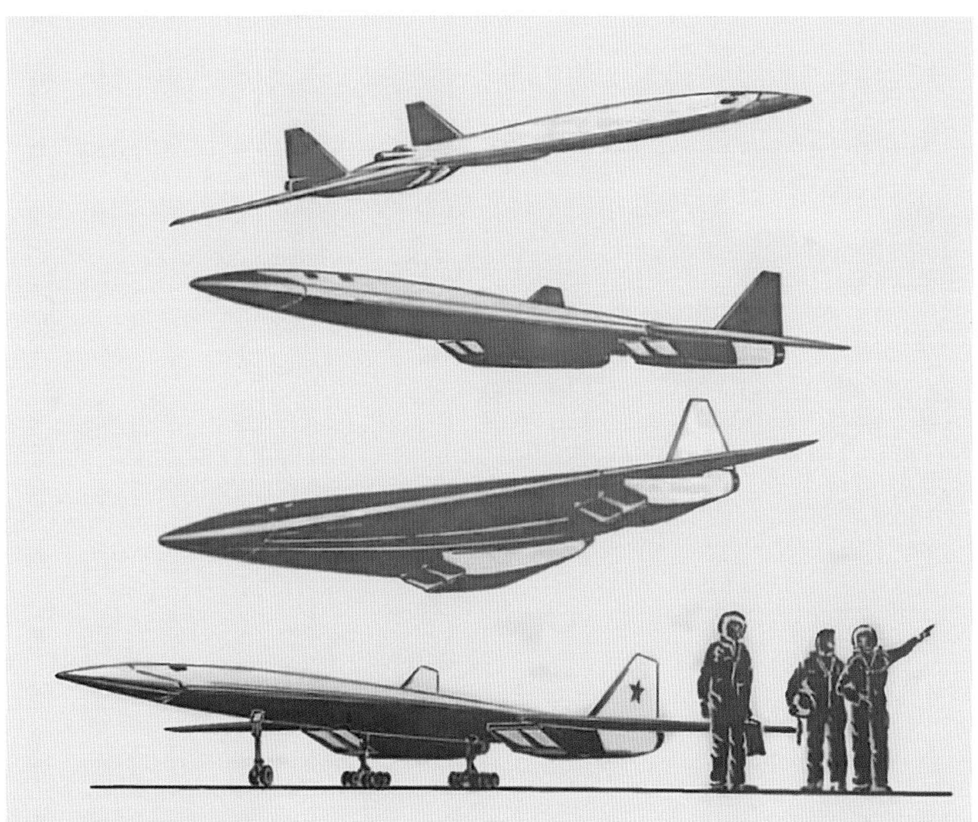

Right: Artist's impressions of the T-4MS from the PD project submitted for the contest.

Overleaf: A desktop model showing the final configuration of the T-4MS with three different wing settings for take-off/landing, subsonic cruise and a supersonic dash.

Project specifications of the Sukhoi T-4MS

Powerplant:	
Stage A	4 x Kolesov RD36-41
Stage B	4 x RKBM K-101
Engine thrust:	
Stage A	4 x 16,000 kgp (4 x 35,270 lbst)
Stage B	4 x 20,000 kgp (4 x 44,090 lbst)
Thrust/weight ratio at take-off power:	
Stage A	0.38
Stage B	0.47
Wing loading for overall wing area	335 kg/m² (68.6 lb/sq ft)
Length overall	41.2 m (135 ft 2 in)
Height on ground	8.0 m (26 ft 3 in)
Wing span:	
centre section	14.4 m (47 ft 2 30/32 in)
at minimum sweep (30°)	40.8 m (133 ft 10 19/64 in)
at maximum sweep (72°)	25.0 m (82 ft 1/4 in)
Landing gear track	6.0 m (19 ft 8 7/32 in)
Landing gear wheelbase	12.0 m 39 ft 4 14/32 in)
Overall wing area:	
at maximum sweep	482.3 m² (5,186 sq ft)
at minimum sweep	506.8 m² (5,449 sq ft)
Inner wing area	409.2 m² (4,400 sq ft)
Outer wing area:	
at minimum sweep	97.5 m² (1,048 sq ft)
at maximum sweep	73.1 m² (786 sq ft)
Inner wing leading edge sweep	72°
Outer wing leading edge sweep:	
at minimum sweep	30°
at maximum sweep	72°
Aspect ratio with respect to overall wing area:	
at minimum sweep	3.3
at maximum sweep	1.14
Empty weight	123,000 kg (271,160 lb)
Maximum take-off weight	170,000 kg (374,780 lb)
Normal take-off weight	170,000 kg (374,780 lb)
Internal fuel load	97,000 kg (213,845 lb)
Weapons load:	
normal (internal)	9,000 kg (19,840 lb)
maximum (internal bay and external hardpoints)*	45,000 kg (99,200 lb)
Maximum speed:	
at sea level	1,100 km/h (683 mph)
at altitude	3,200 km/h (1,987 mph)
Cruising speed:	
above 18,000 m (59,000 ft)	3,000-3,200 km/h (1,863-1,987 mph)
at medium altitude	800-900 km/h (497-559 mph)
at sea level	850 km/h (528 mph)
Maximum range with K-101 engines at cruising speed with normal warload, internal fuel only:	
above 18,000 m (59,000 ft)	9,000 km (5,590 miles)
at medium altitude	14,000 km (8,695 miles)
Take-off run	1,100 m (3,610 ft)
Landing run	950 m (3,120 ft)
Crew	3
Armament:	
long-range air-to-surface missiles	4 x Kh-45
short-range air-to-surface missiles	24 x Kh-??
bombs (total weight)	45,000 kg (99,200 lb)

* with a partial fuel load

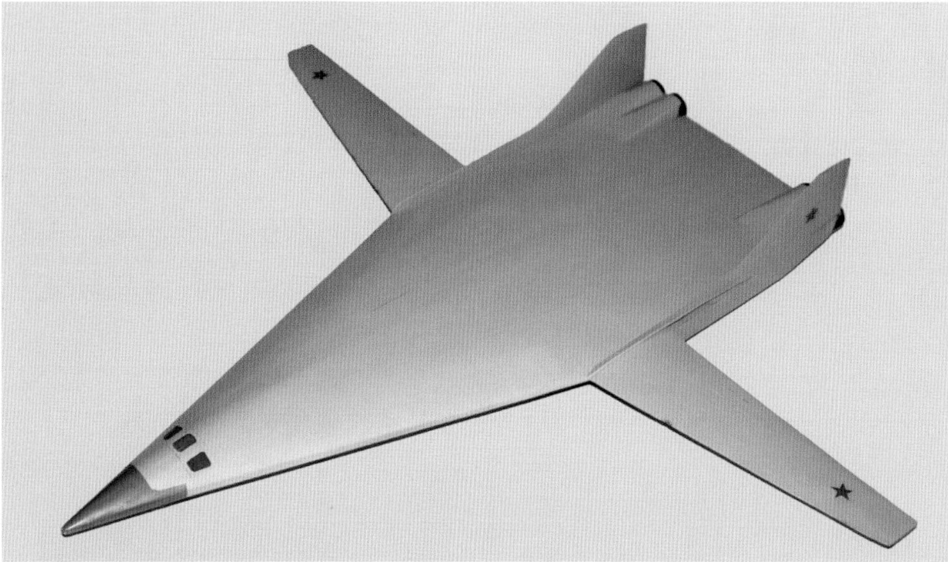

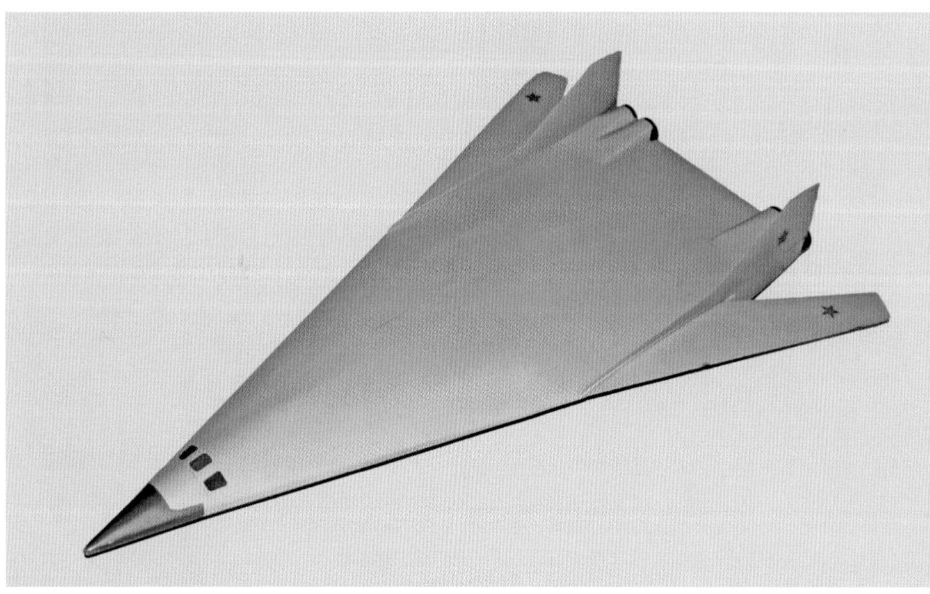

area. This tailless "swing-wing" layout was probably unique in the world aircraft design practice.

Known in-house as "version 2B,"the BWB tailless variable-geometry layout was developed by engineer Leonid I. Bondarenko in August 1970. In due course it was approved by the OKB's PD section chief Oleg S. Samoylovich, then by the T-4MS's chief project engineer Naum S. Chernyakov and finally by General Designer Pavel O. Sukhoi, serving as the basis for the advanced development project.

In its final form the aircraft had constant 72° leading-edge sweep at maximum sweep, appearing as an almost pure delta shape in plan view; at minimum sweep the small movable outer wings were swept back 30°. Both the fuselage (or rather lifting body) and the outer wings with full-span leading-edge slats and flaps utilised the TsAGI SR-15 airfoil with a thickness/chord ratio of 6% and 11-7% respectively. The engines were placed in pairs at the sides of the rear fuselage in boxy nacelles, breathing through two-dimensional air intakes with horizontal airflow control ramps and vertical splitters. A four-section elevon occupied the entire trailing edge of the lifting body between the Nos. 2 and 3 engine nozzles. Small all-movable vertical tails were placed above the outer sides of the engine nacelles. Roll control was by means of unique spoilers mounted on turntables on the wing upper surface that were mechanically linked to the fuselage so that the spoilers remained at 90° to the fuselage axis at all times.

Again, the T-4MS had a crew of three, with two pilots in the front row and the navigator/WSO sitting behind the captain on the left. The extreme nose was occupied by a large radome and an avionics bay; unlike the T-4/T-4M, there was no drooping nose visor. Drawings and models of the T-4MS suggest the forward view from the flight deck must have been very limited.

The tall landing gear comprised a forward-retracting twin-wheel nose

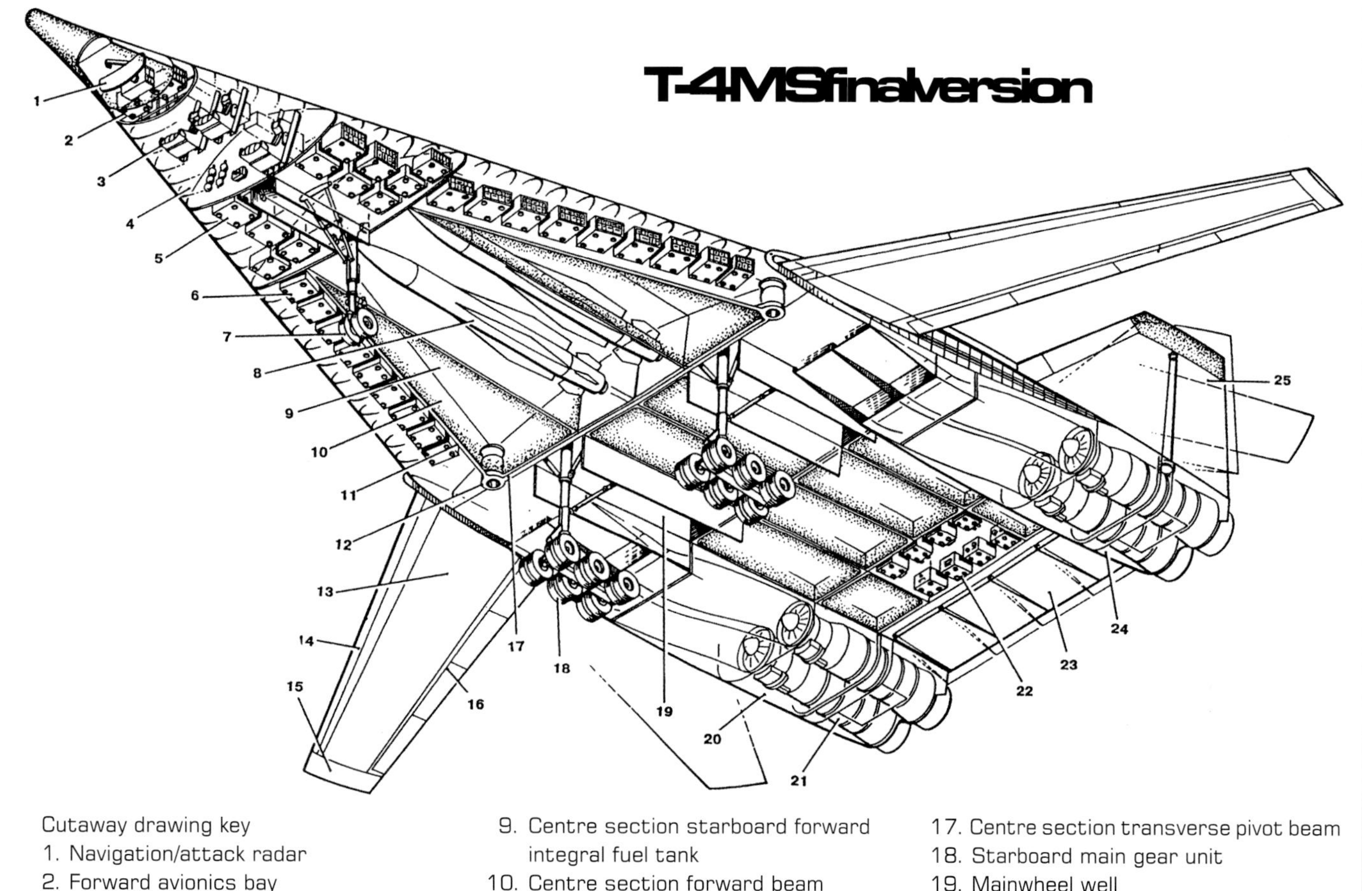

Cutaway drawing key
1. Navigation/attack radar
2. Forward avionics bay
3. Co-pilot's ejection seat
4. Flight deck
5. Centre avionics bay
6. Equipment bays in wing centre section
7. Nose gear unit
8. Kh-45 missiles in weapons bay
9. Centre section starboard forward integral fuel tank
10. Centre section forward beam
11. Equipment module
12. Wing pivot
13. Movable outer wing
14. Starboard leading-edge slat
15. Wingtip fairing
16. Starboard flap
17. Centre section transverse pivot beam
18. Starboard main gear unit
19. Mainwheel well
20. Starboard engine nacelle
21. No.4 engine
22. Rear avionics bay
23. Elevon section
24. Rear section of engine nacelle
25. Port all-movable fin

unit and aft-retracting main units with 12-wheel bogies which somersaulted aft through 180° during retraction to lie in the fuselage just inboard of the air intakes. The main armament – two Kh-45 or Kh-2000 missiles – was carried in a weapons bay between the nosewheel and mainwheel wells which was wide enough to accommodate two missiles side by side. In high gross weight configuration, two more Kh-2000s were to be carried externally. Some drawings depict the aircraft with no fewer than 24 missiles (erroneously referred to as Kh-2000s; these were similar in size to the Kh-15 but differed from it in having wings) carried internally and externally in four rows – six-abreast in rows 1 and 2, four-abreast in row 3 (between the mainwheel wells) and eight-abreast in row 4 (between the engine nacelles).

Wind tunnel tests at the Central Aerodynamics & Hydrodynamics Institute named after Nikolay Ye. Zhukovskiy (TsAGI – *Tsen**trahl'**nyy **ae**ro-**ghid**rodina**miche**skiy insti**toot***) showed that the chosen layout offered a high lift/drag ratio in both subsonic and supersonic modes. Actually, "high" is a poor description; the results were truly fantastic – a lift/drag ratio of 17.5 at Mach 0.8 and 7.3 at Mach 3.0. The BWB layout also took care of aeroelasticity problems. The limited area of the movable outer wings, coupled with the stiff structure of the lifting body, enabled high-speed flight in turbulent conditions at low altitude.

Work on defining and refining the PD project of the T-4MS (*izdeliye* 200) to the degree when it could be submitted for the tender continued for the greater part of 1971. Lots of wind tunnel models were manufactured that year, allowing different versions of the wing centre section/fuselage, outer wings, vertical and horizontal tail to be tested in TsAGI's wind tunnels. The tests showed that the T-4MS was catastrophically unstable because the centre of gravity shifted too radically when wing sweep was altered. Chief project engineer Naum S. Chernyakov decided to alter the layout. As a result, several project versions emerged featuring an extended nose and additional (conventionally placed) horizontal tail surfaces; one of them (version 8) had a needle-sharp nosecone.

The configuration selected eventually featured an extended forward fuselage with an extremely streamlined flight deck canopy so that the upper fuselage contour was virtually unbroken; apart from this, there were no changes as compared to the original project. The T-4MS project was completed in September 1971.

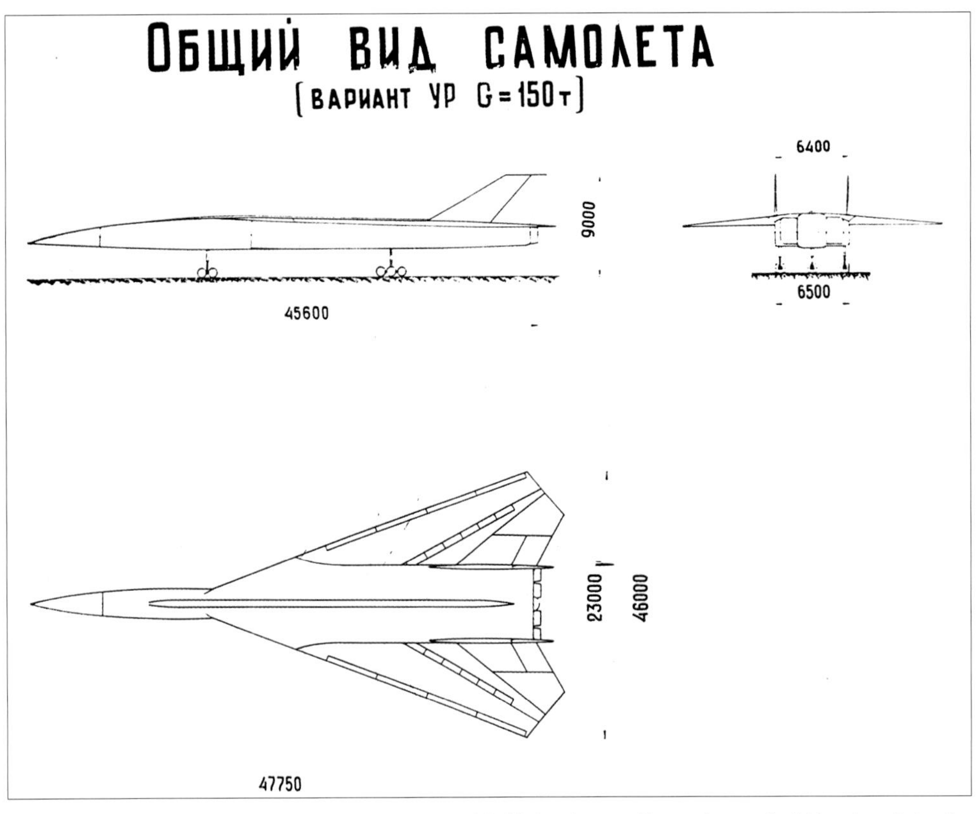

Above and below: PD project drawings of the M-20 in the configuration called Version 1 in the text.

Opposite page: PD project drawings of the M-20 in the configurations called Version 3 (above) and Version 2 (below).

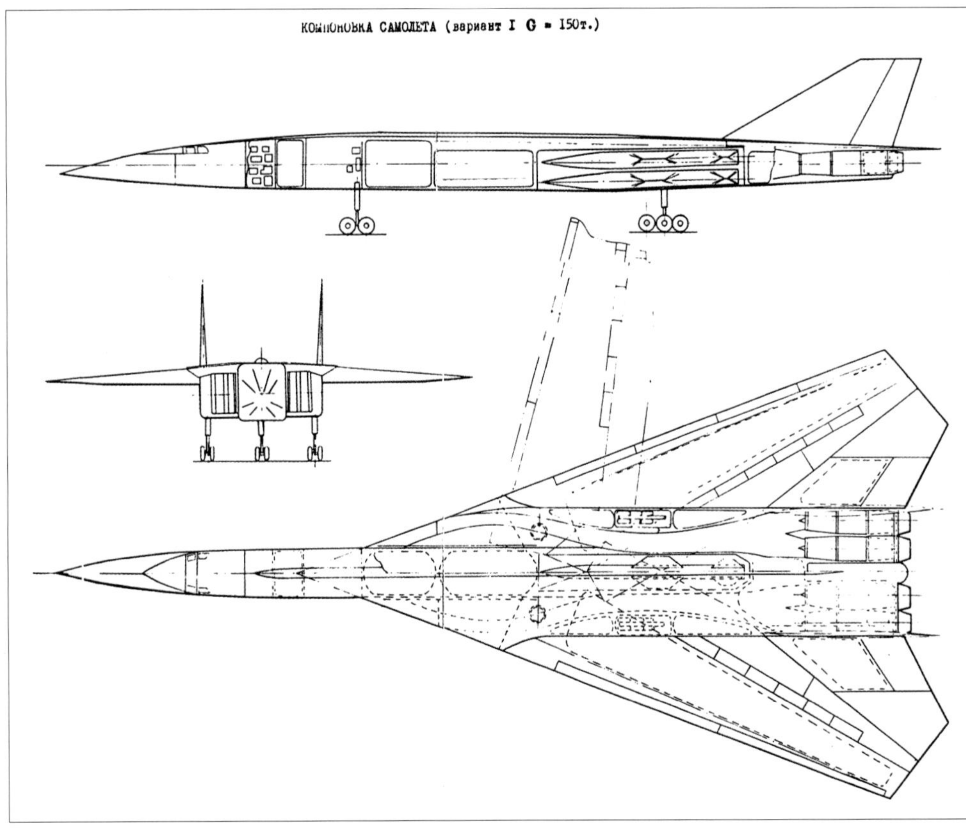

The Contest: The Myasishchev OKB's Bids

Now we will turn our attention to the competitor. The Myasishchev OKB (which, as already mentioned, had just been reborn in 1967) received orders from MAP to develop a PD project of a strategic multi-mode missile carrier as far back as 1968. This was to be a multi-mission strike aircraft with three distinct operational configurations. Actually, the OKB was officially known as the Myasishchev EMZ (*Eksperimentahl'nyy mashinostroitel'nyy zavod* – experimental machinery plant), since it was based at a small prototype manufacturing facility in Zhukovskiy.

The EMZ design team set to work with a will, ignited by the enthusiastic approach of its leader, Vladimir M. Myasishchev. The project submitted for Stage 1 of the contest was the **M-20** multi-mode bomber/missile strike aircraft known in house as *tema dvadtsat'* ("subject 20"). The basic strike/reconnaissance configuration was intended for attacking remote targets of strategic importance with nuclear-tipped missiles or bombs and performing strategic reconnaissance. The second configuration was a counter-air version designed to seek and destroy transport aircraft flying transoceanic routes and airborne early warning (AEW) aircraft. Finally, the third version was a long-range ASW aircraft intended to seek and destroy submarines at up to 5,000-5,500 km (3,105-3,420 miles) away from base. The aircraft's maximum range in subsonic cruise was specified as 16,000-18,000 km (9,940-11,180 miles).

As was often the case with the Myasishchev OKB, a host of project configurations was considered. Four configurations designated M-20-I, M-20-II, M-20-III and M-20-IV are known to have existed, each of them, in turn, having several versions. The following numeration of the versions is solely for the reader's convenience and does not reflect the order in which they appeared – the versions are numbered arbitrarily.

One of the versions – we will call it **Version 1** – had a rectangular-section fuselage with a hinged nose visor, shoulder-mounted VG wings, high-set slab stabilisers (stabilators) which formed a single shape with the wings when the latter were at maximum sweep, in similar manner to the General Dynamics F-111 bomber, and sharply swept twin fins and rudders. All four engines were buried in the rear fuselage in horizontal pairs, breathing through two-dimensional lateral air intakes with inlet ducts that curved around the weapons bay in an S shape. The bay was so narrow that the two Kh-45 missiles had to be carried above one another. The landing gear comprised a four-wheel nose bogie and six-wheel main bogies with three pairs of wheels; all three units retracted forward, the main bogies stowing upside down outboard of the inlet ducts. The aircraft was 47.75 m (156 ft 7⁵⁹⁄₆₄ in) long, with a fuselage length of 45.6 m (149 ft 7⁹⁄₃₂ in), and 9 m (29 ft 6²¹⁄₆₄ in) high when parked, with the fin tips 6.4 m (21 ft) apart; the wing span was 46 m (150 ft 1¹³⁄₁₆ in) at minimum sweep and 23 m (75 ft 5³³⁄₆₄ in) at maximum sweep. The take-off weight was 150,000 kg (330,700 lb).

Version 2 had low-set VG wings with a leading-edge kink on the fixed portions – that is, sharply swept leading-edge root extensions (LERXes), low-set stabilators (which again matched up with the wings at maximum sweep), a single sharply tapered trapezoidal vertical tail with a huge rudder, and a common engine nacelle (with a V-shaped front end in plan view) which also housed the weapons bay. The four engines were located side by side near the rear end of the fuselage, the inlet ducts curving around the bay in which two missiles were carried in a vertically staggered pair. The landing gear consisted of five aft-retracting four-wheel bogies; the nose gear positioned ahead of the nacelle shortened during retraction, while the main units were arranged in tandem pairs. The take-off weight was 250,000 kg (551,150 lb).

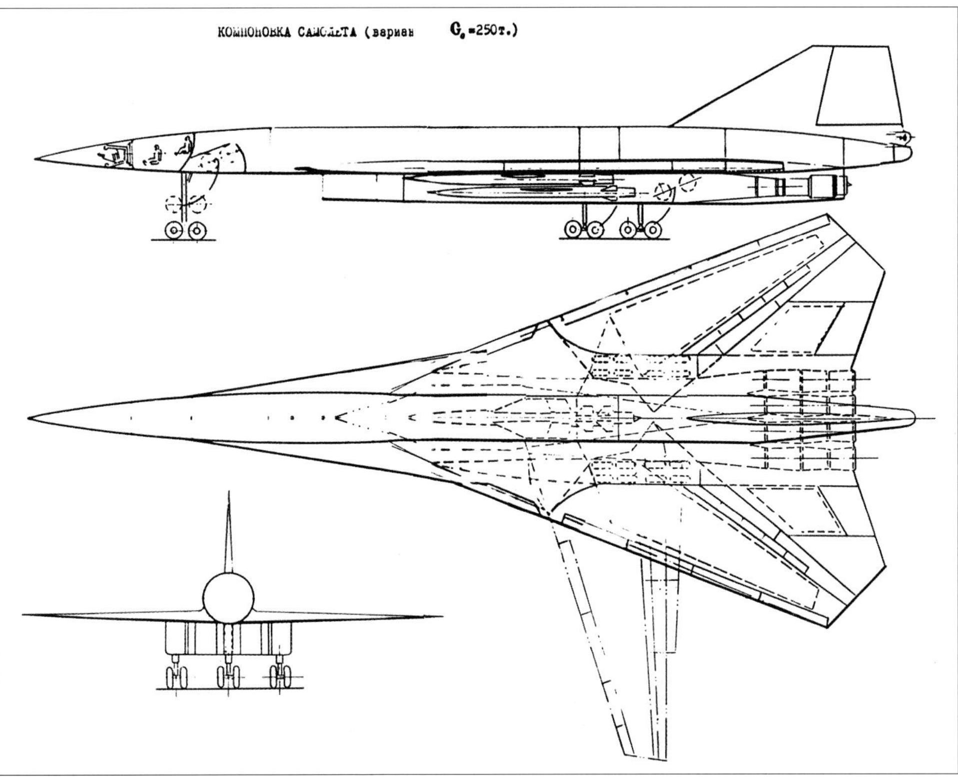

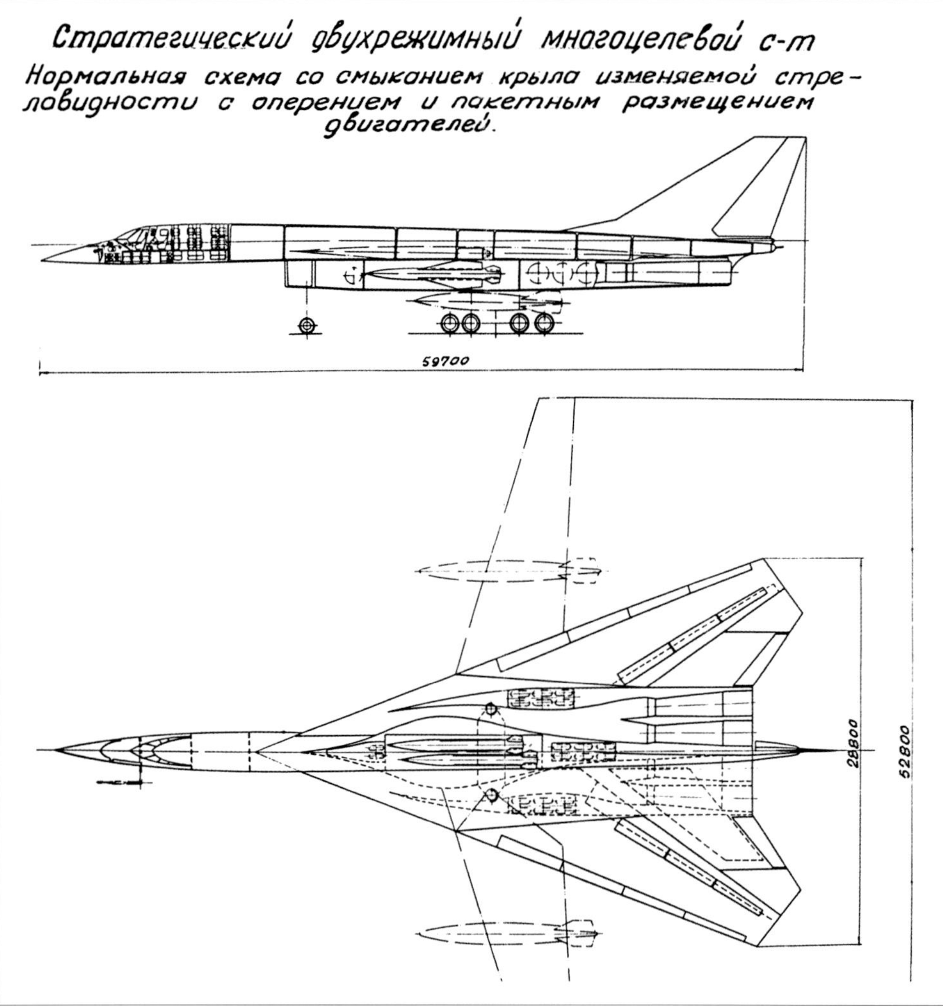

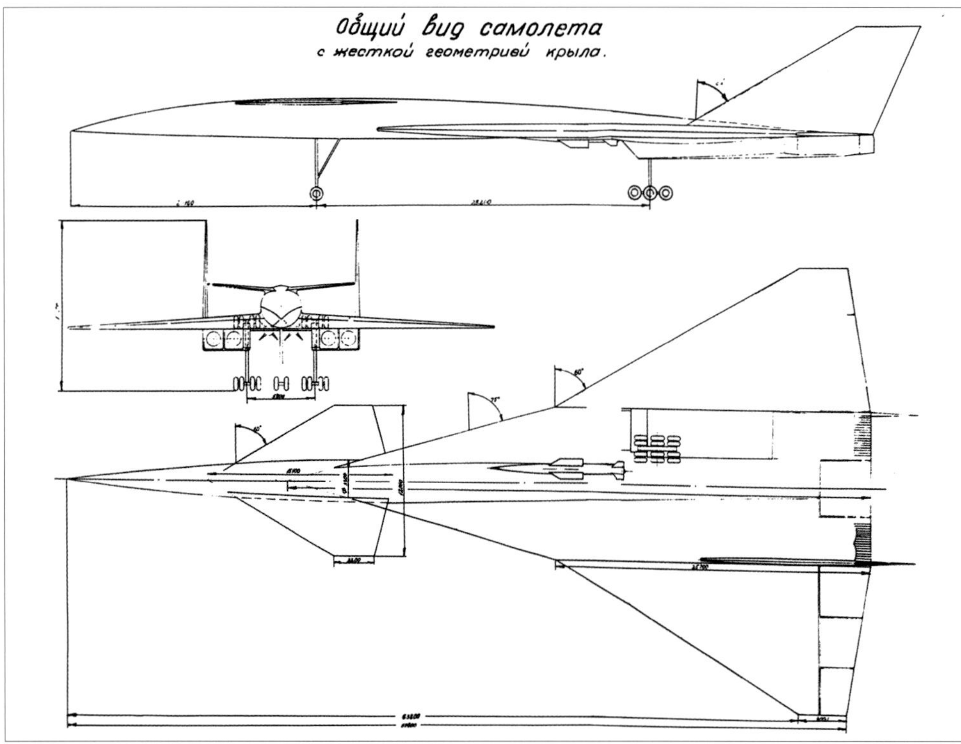

Version 3 was basically similar to the one above, but the engine nacelle was extended forward so that the nose gear unit stowed in the intake splitter; there was also a fifth main gear unit with an eight-wheel bogie (two rows of four wheels)! The take-off weight was 300,000 kg (661,400 lb). **Version 4** looked similar to this one, featuring drop tanks under the movable outer wings; the landing gear had a twin-wheel nose unit and three main units with four-wheel bogies. A retractable L-shaped in-flight refuelling (IFR) probe was located on the port side of the nose. The aircraft was 59.7 m (195 ft $10^{25}/_{64}$ in) long, with a wing span of 52.8 m (173 ft $2^{47}/_{64}$ in) at minimum sweep and 28.8 m (94 ft $5^{55}/_{64}$ in) at maximum sweep.

Version 5 of the M-20 grossing at 325,000 kg (716,500 lb) had six engines in a common nacelle under the rear fuselage, a tail-first layout with delta wings and retractable (!) cropped-delta canards. The four main gear bogies were conventional, but the nose bogie had a Y-shaped frame with three pairs of wheels – one at the front and two at the rear. The two missiles were semi-recessed in the fuselage because there was no room for a proper weapons bay!

Version 6 had low-set double-delta wings with 75° leading-edge sweep inboard and 60° outboard, huge high-set trapezoidal canards (also with 60° leading-edge sweep), twin tails and four engines located in pairs in rectangular-section conformal nacelles under the wings. The landing gear comprised a twin-wheel nose unit and 12-wheel main bogies stowing in the thin wings. Again, the two missiles were semi-recessed side by side in the fuselage.

Version 7 (some sources call it M-20-6) grossing at 300,000 kg (661,390 lb) was again a low-wing

Above left: The M-20 in the configuration called Version 4 here.

Left: The M-20 in Version 6. Note the side-by-side semi-recessed missile carriage.

aircraft but had a tailless-delta layout with a large, sharply swept fin and rudder. The five-spar wings with about 60° leading-edge sweep had large cigar-shaped fairings at the tips and were equipped with a laminar flow control (LFC) system, and the trailing edge was entirely occupied by two-section flaps and large one-piece ailerons. The fuselage had a circular cross-section up to the wing leading edge, the long pointed nose ahead of the four-man flight deck featuring a drooping visor. Further aft the cross-section became rectangular with rounded corners, narrowing towards the rear.

Four afterburning turbofans rated at 22,000 kgp (48,500 lbst) for take-off were buried in the rear fuselage in a square arrangement (that is, two vertical pairs side by side). The engines were to be developed by OKB-276 based in Kuibyshev (now renamed back to Samara) and headed by Nikolay D. Kuznetsov. Each pair of engines was fed by a narrow two-dimensional intake with a boundary layer splitter plate and a vertical airflow control ramp, the inlet duct being divided by a horizontal splitter ahead of the engines. The inlet ducts curved around a long weapons bay housing two missiles in tandem. The tall landing gear (apparently with telescopic struts) comprised a forward-retracting four-wheel nose bogie and 12-wheel main bogies (three rows of four wheels) somersaulting forward to stow in the wing roots between the second and third spars.

Version 8 was perhaps the most unusual. Basically it shared the fuselage, nose gear unit and engine placement/intake design of Version 7 (except for the shorter, fixed-geometry nose with a stepped windscreen and a fixed IFR probe offset to port). However, it had a tailless high-wing

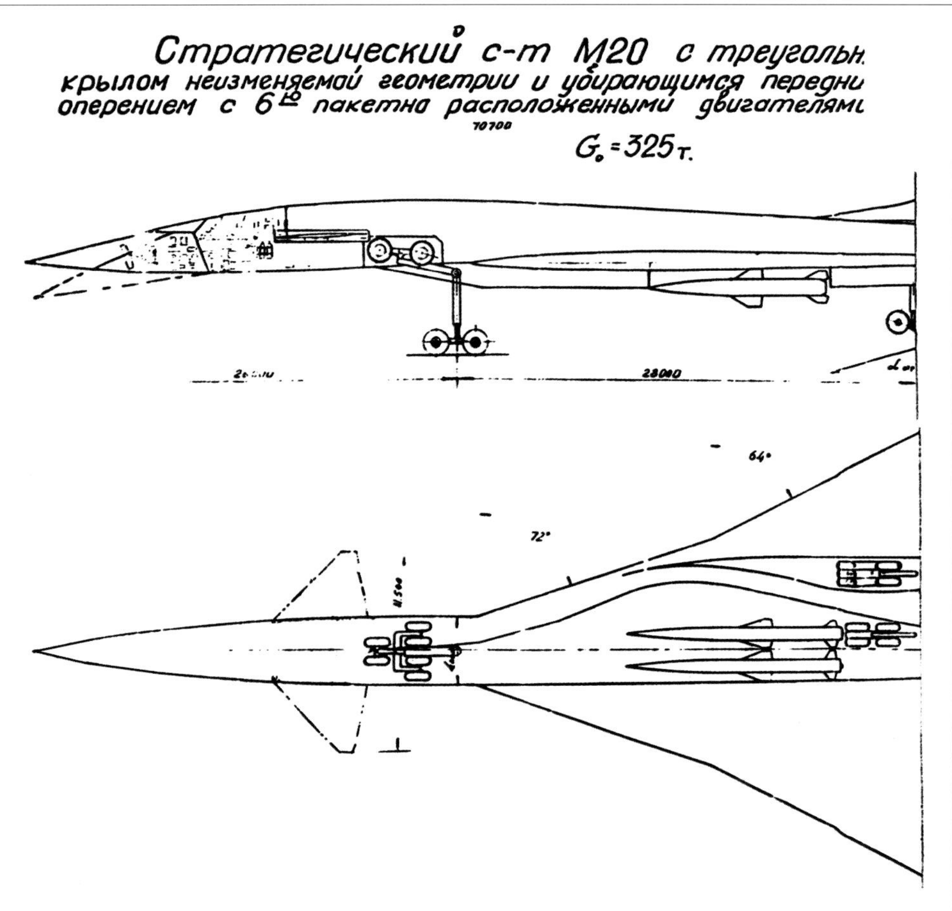

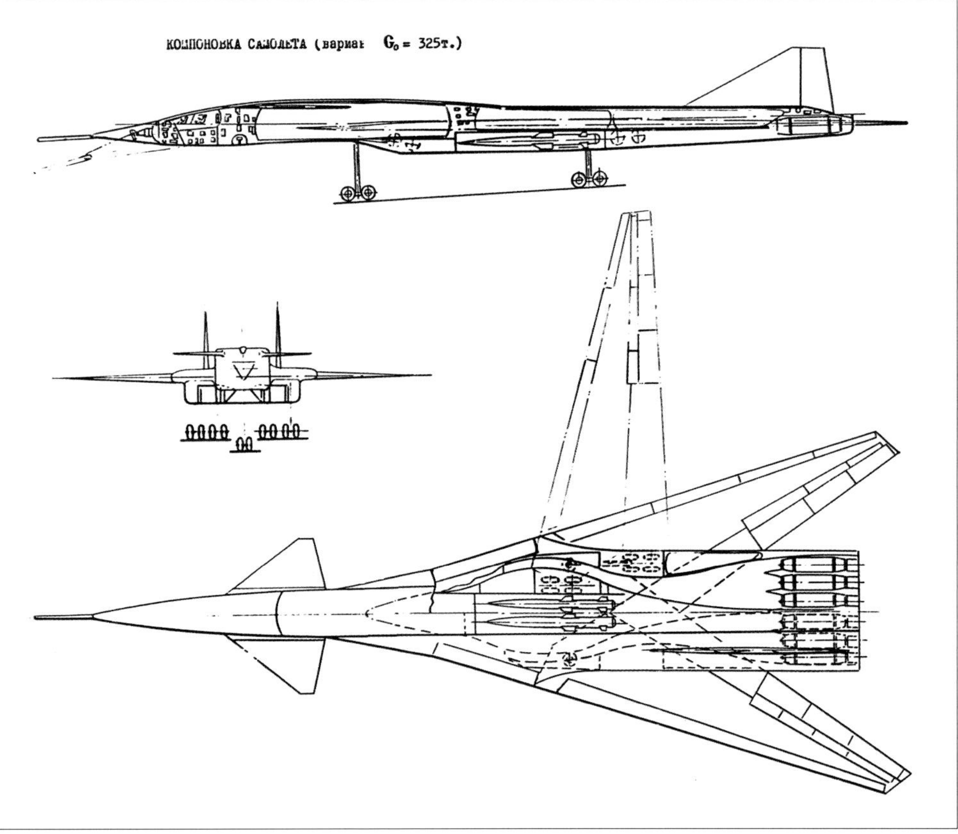

Above right: An unfortunately incomplete drawing of the M-20's Version 5 with retractable canards.

Right: "Squarehead" version 15 of the M-20; note the serpentine inlet ducts.

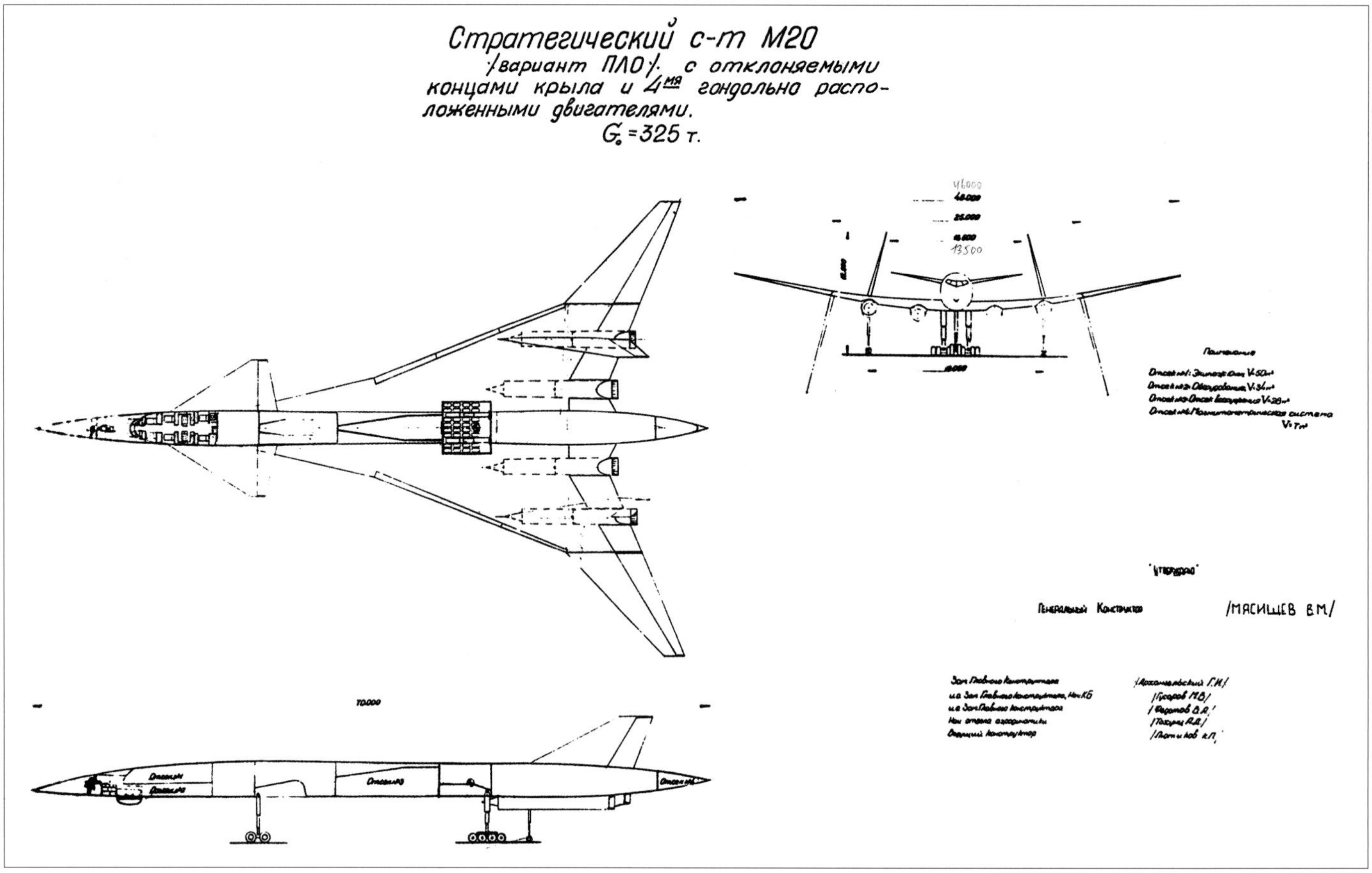

Стратегический с-т М20
/вариант ПЛО/. с отклоняемыми концами крыла и 4 мя гондольно расположенными двигателями.
G_0 =325 т.

46000

13500

70.000

"Утверждаю"

Генеральный Конструктор /МЯСИЩЕВ В.М./

/Архангельский Г.Н./
/Гусаров М.В./
/Федотов Б.А./
/Тохунц А.Д./
/Литвинов К.П./

Многорежимный стратегический с-т М20
с отклоняемыми концами крыла и 4мя гондольно расположенными двигателями.
G_0 = 325 т.

53
27

72 000

24 000

"Утверждаю"

Генеральный конструктор

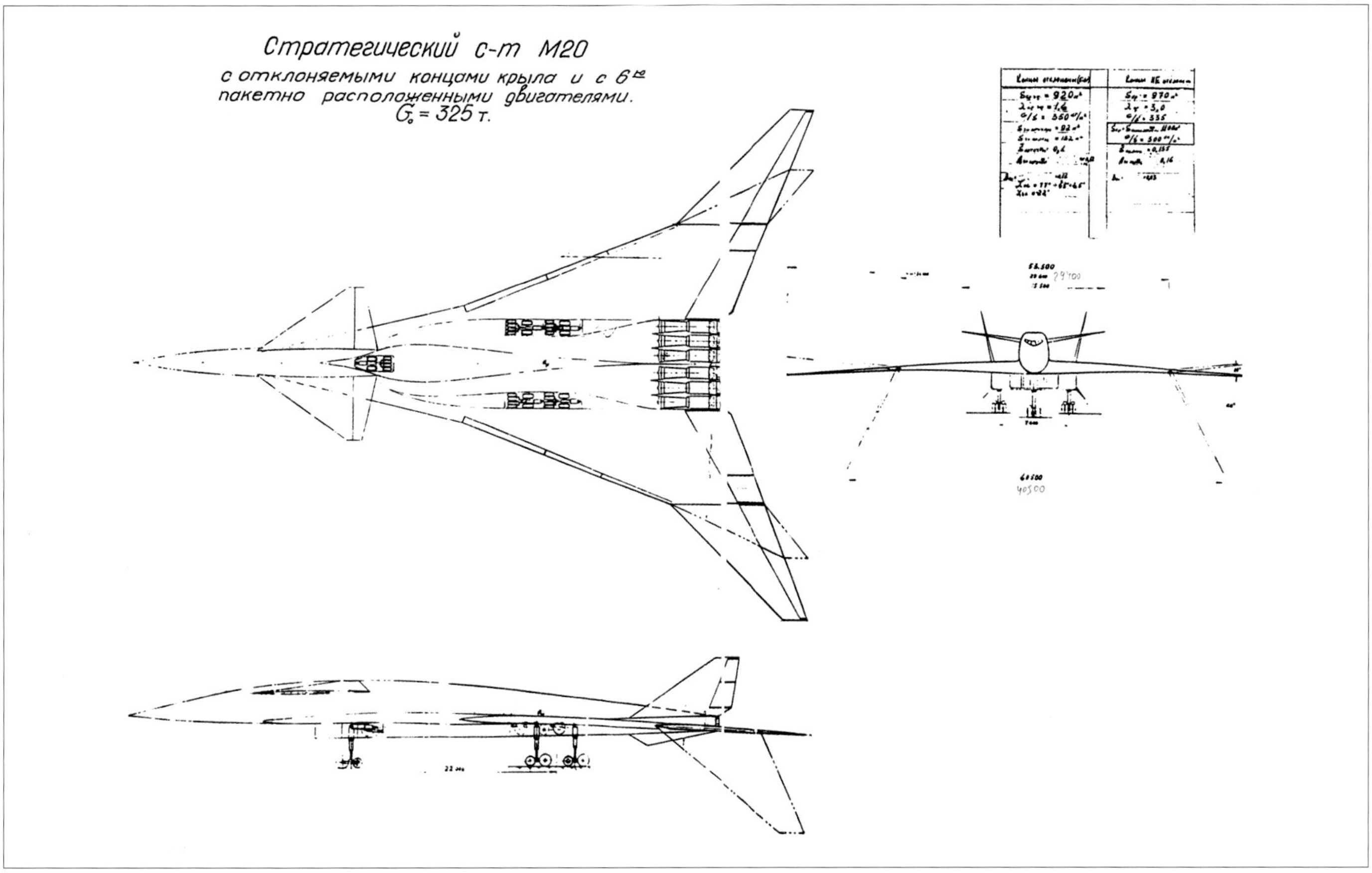

Стратегический с-т М20
с отклоняемыми концами крыла и с 6-ю пакетно расположенными двигателями.
G_0 = 325 т.

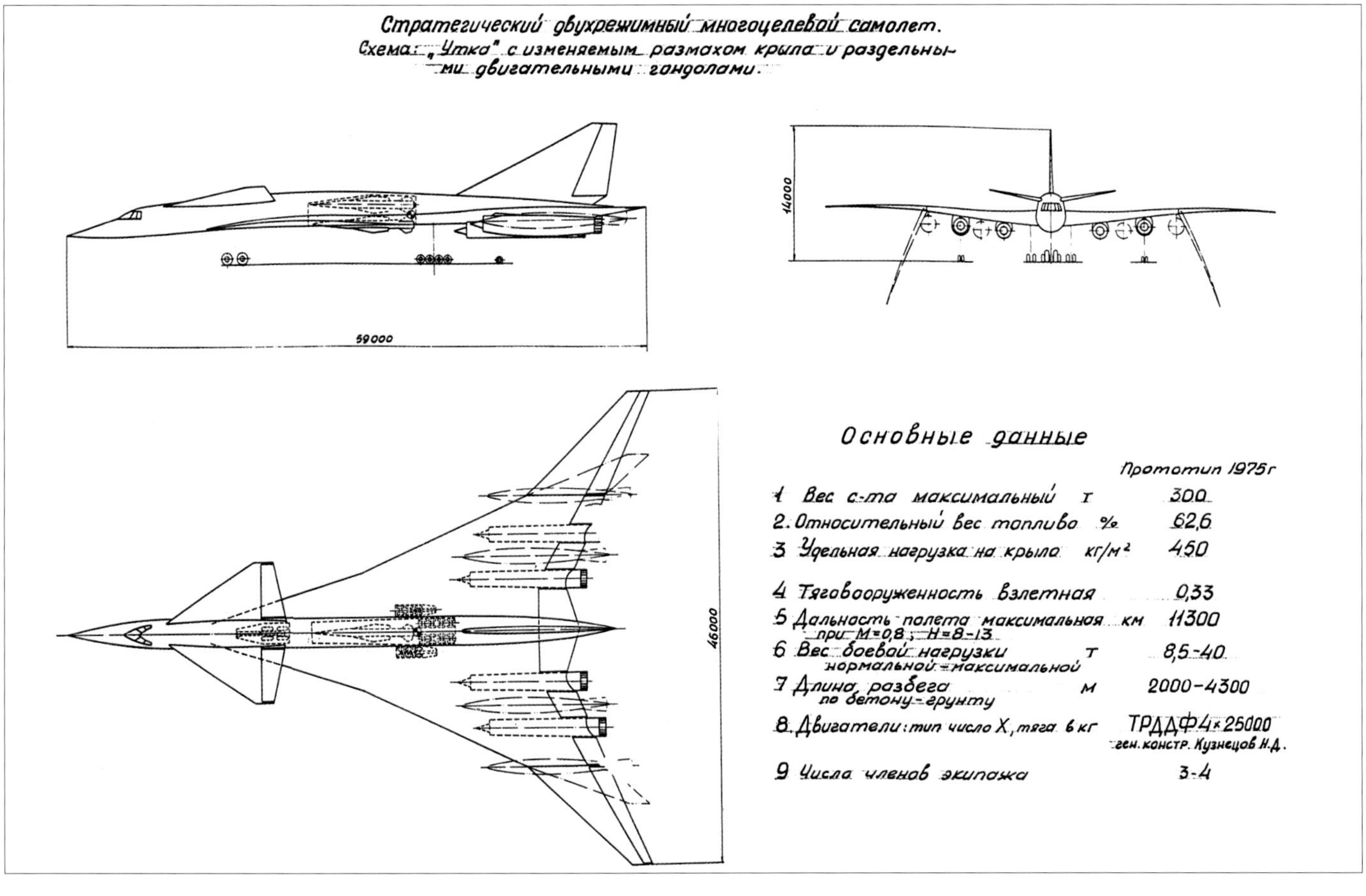

Стратегический двухрежимный многоцелевой самолет.
Схема: „Утка" с изменяемым размахом крыла и раздельными двигательными гондолами.

14000

59000

46000

Основные данные

		Прототип 1975г
1	Вес с-та максимальный т	300
2.	Относительный вес топлива %	62,6
3	Удельная нагрузка на крыло кг/м²	450
4	Тяговооруженность взлетная	0,33
5	Дальность полета максимальная км при М=0,8; Н=8-13	11300
6	Вес боевой нагрузки т нормальной-максимальной	8,5-40
7	Длина разбега м по бетону-грунту	2000-4300
8.	Двигатели: тип число Х, тяга в кг	ТРДДФ4×25000 ген. констр. Кузнецов Н.Д.
9	Числа членов экипажа	3-4

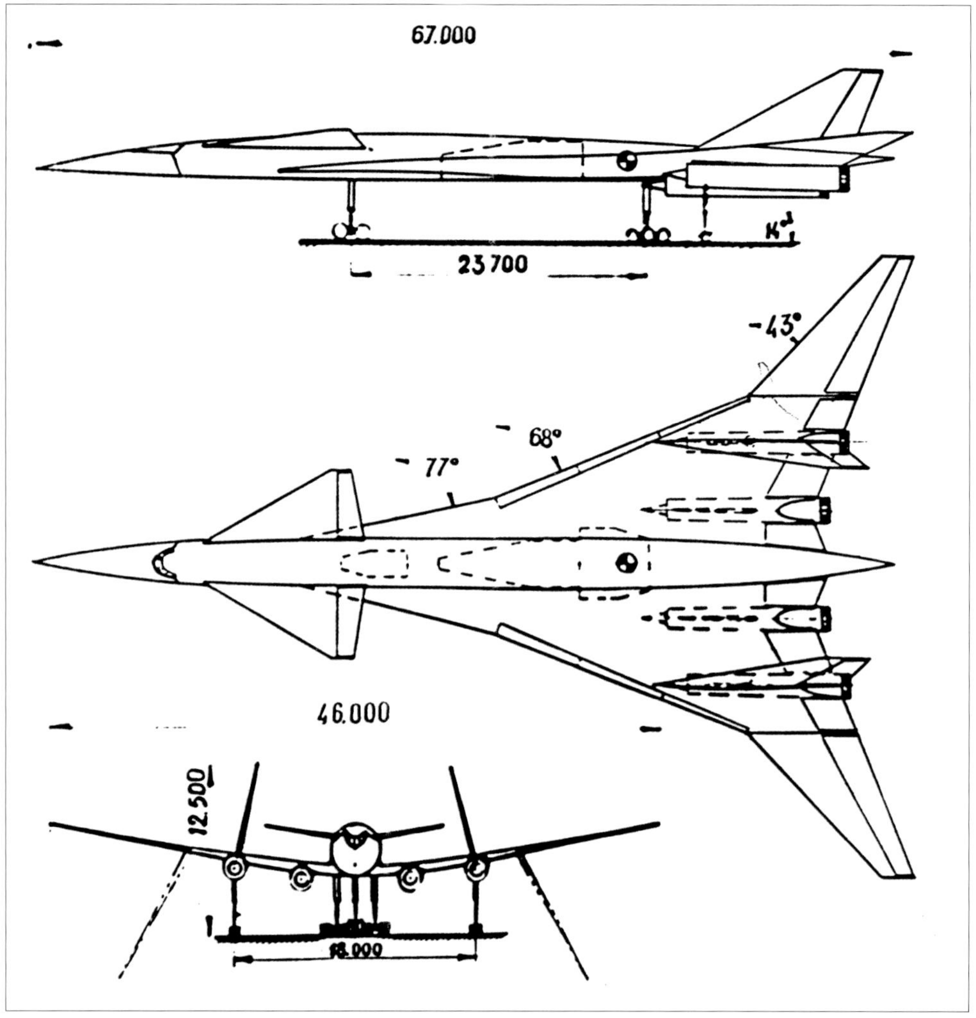

Page 24, above: The M-20 in Version 9B – an ASW aircraft with a search radar in an undernose radome and 16-wheel (four-axle) main gear bogies to absorb the higher gross weight.

Page 24, below: The M-20 in Version 10. The vertical tails are omitted in the plan view, only the drooped position of the outer wings being shown.

Page 25, above: The M-20 in Version 11 looking like an overfed XB-70.

Page 25, below: The M-20 in Version 12. Note the banana-like curvature of the fuselage and the four drop tanks under the wings (two of them are under the hinged portions).

Left and right: The M-20 in Version 9A, the lower weight allowing the use of 12-wheel (three-axle) main gear bogies. Again, the mainwheels are rather smaller than the nosewheels.

Below: The M-20 in Version 13 which resembled the Sukhoi T-4I. The legend reads "Multi-mode strategic bomber."

Below right: The M-20 in Version 14A with drop tanks fitted under the wing gloves.

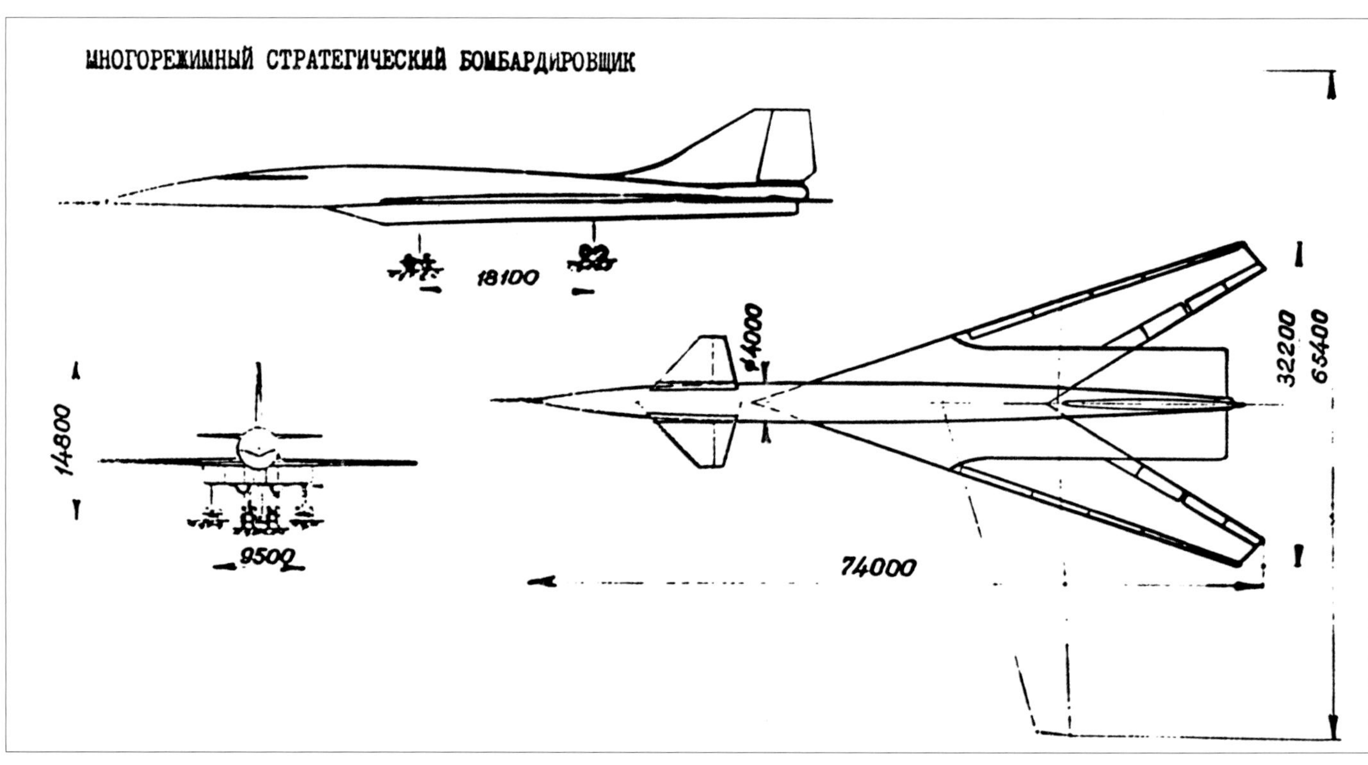

layout, the anhedral wings having a kinked leading edge. Large pointed fairings were grafted onto the wing underside at the kink, protruding beyond the leading edge; they carried the outward-canted twin vertical tails and housed two of the three main gear units (the third was located on the centreline between the weapons bay and the engine bay). All three had eight-wheel bogies with four tandem pairs of wheels (!). In addition to the two Kh-45 missiles carried internally in tandem, a further two could be carried on canted pylons low on the centre fuselage sides; alternatively, two drop tanks could be suspended under the fuselage inboard of these pylons.

The aircraft was 63.8 m (209 ft 3[13]/[16] in) long and 14.0 m (45 ft 11[3]/[16] in) high, with a wing span of 44.8 m (146 ft 11[49]/[64] in). The TOW was 300,000 kg, the fuel accounting for 57.9% of this figure; the normal and maximum weapons load was 8,500 kg (18,740 lb) and 40,000 kg (88,180 lb) respectively. The bomber was to have a wing loading of 434 kg/m² (89 lb/sq ft), a thrust/weight ratio of 0.3 and a maximum range of 14,300 km (8,890 miles) when cruising at Mach 0.8 and

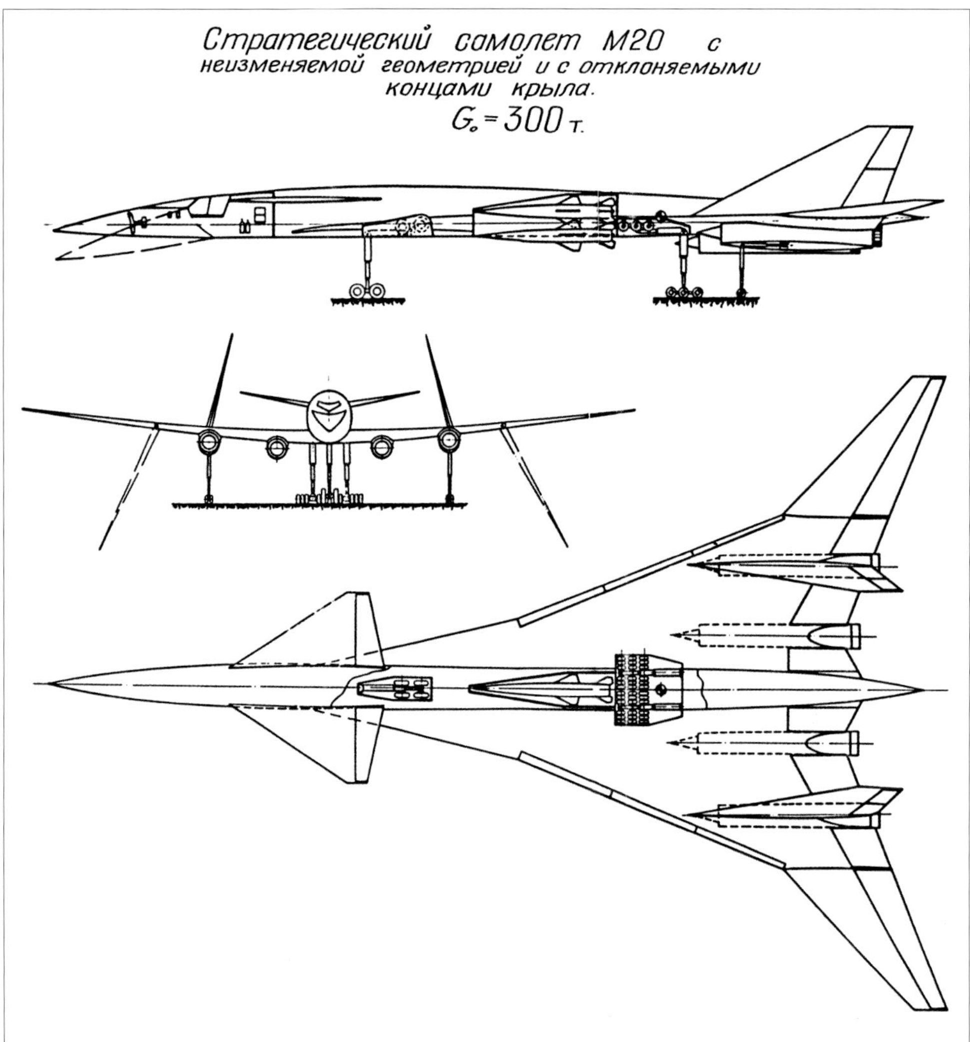

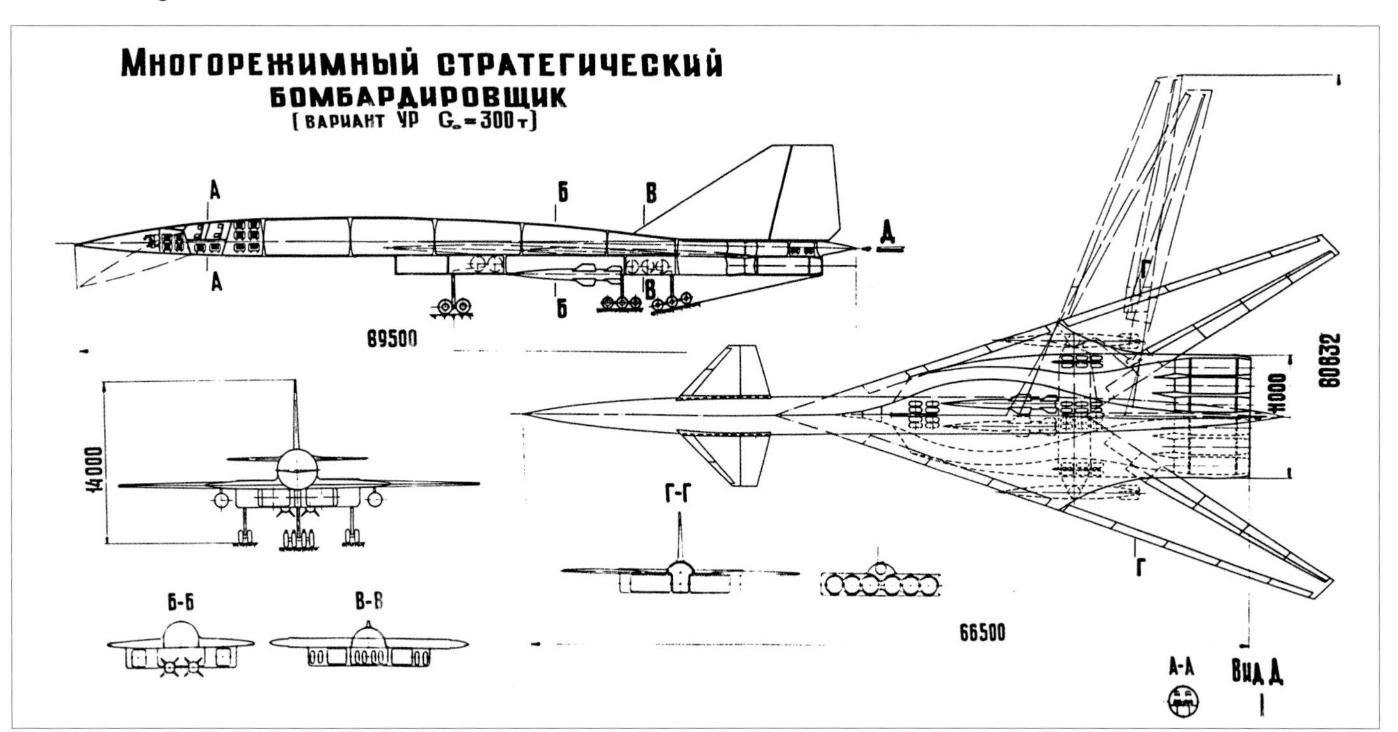

Многорежимный стратегический самолет М20
с УЛО.
G_o = 300 т.

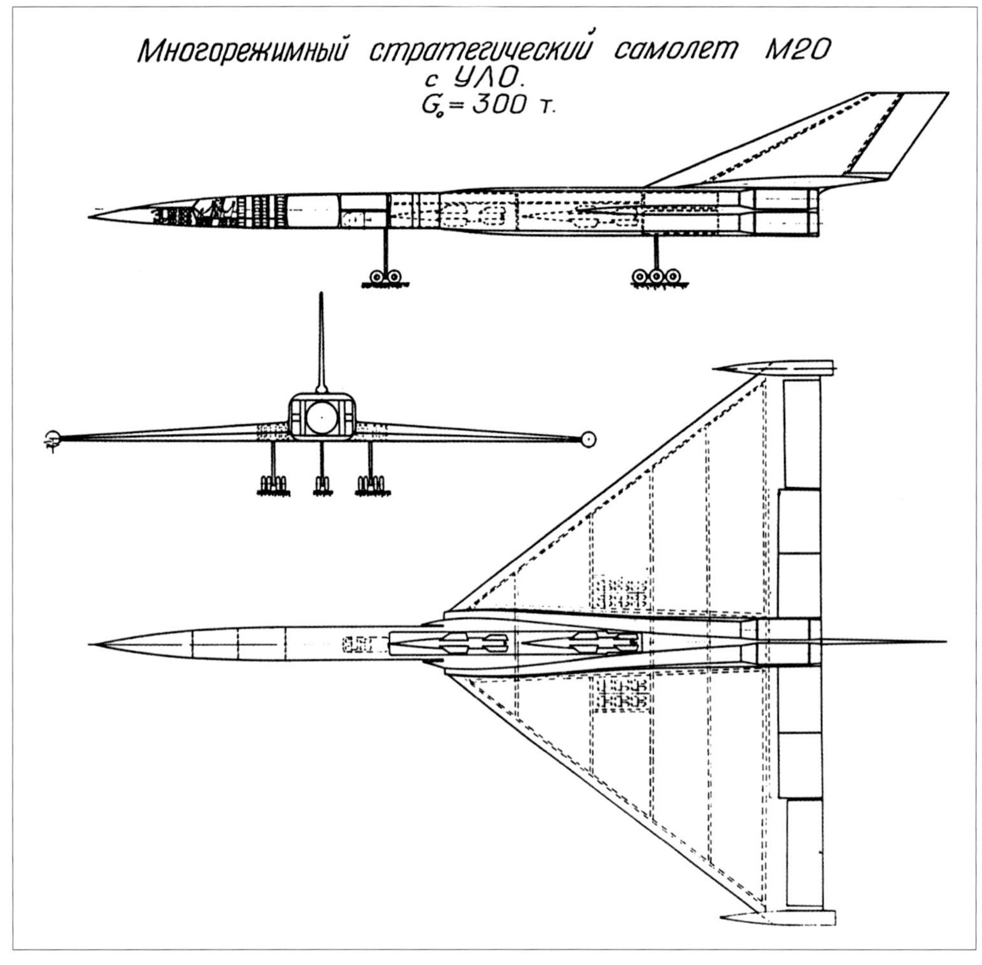

Left: The M-20 in Version 7 featuring wings with laminar flow control (LFC). Note the tandem missile carriage. The vertical tail may appear oversized in side elevation, but not when you compare it with the size of the wings.

Below: Version 17 of the M-20, described on the drawing as a "multi-mode strategic aircraft with separately placed engines." Despite the deep oval-section fuselage, the lower missile could only be carried semi-recessed.

Right: Version 18 of the M-20 had an all-movable horizontal tail, revised wings, a revised landing gear and more stagger to the engine nacelles.

Below right: Version 8 (described as a "strategic two-mode multi-role aircraft") was probably the most unusual one. Like Version 7, it was to feature LFC. Note the four-axle main gear bogies and the external stores options of two extra Kh-45 missiles or two drop tanks.

Page 30: The M-20 in Version 14B.

Page 31: The M-20 in Version 16.

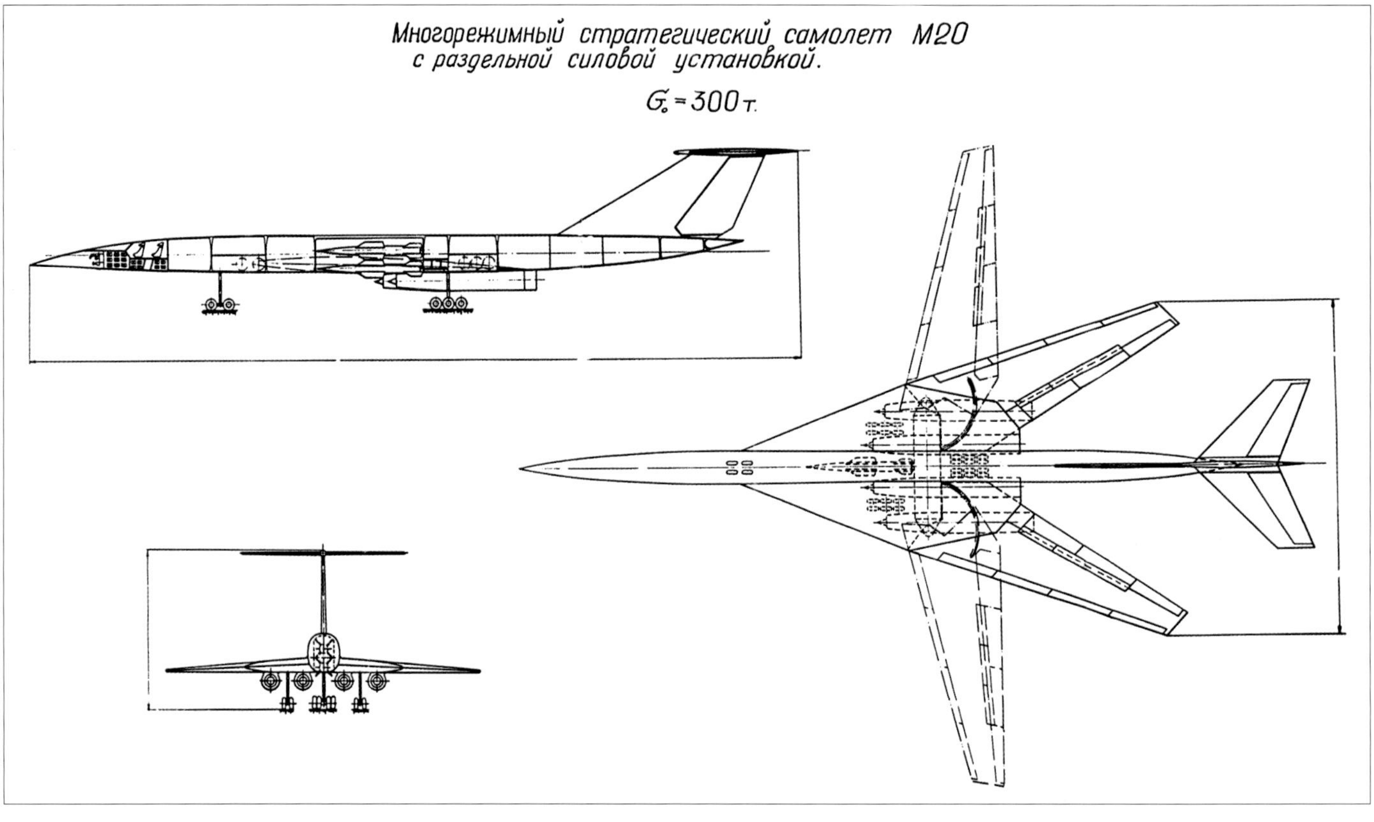

Многорежимный стратегический самолет М20
с раздельной силовой установкой.
G_o = 300 т.

Стратегический двухрежимный многоцелевой с-т

Нормальная схема с изменяемой стреловидностью крыла и раздельными двигательными гондолами

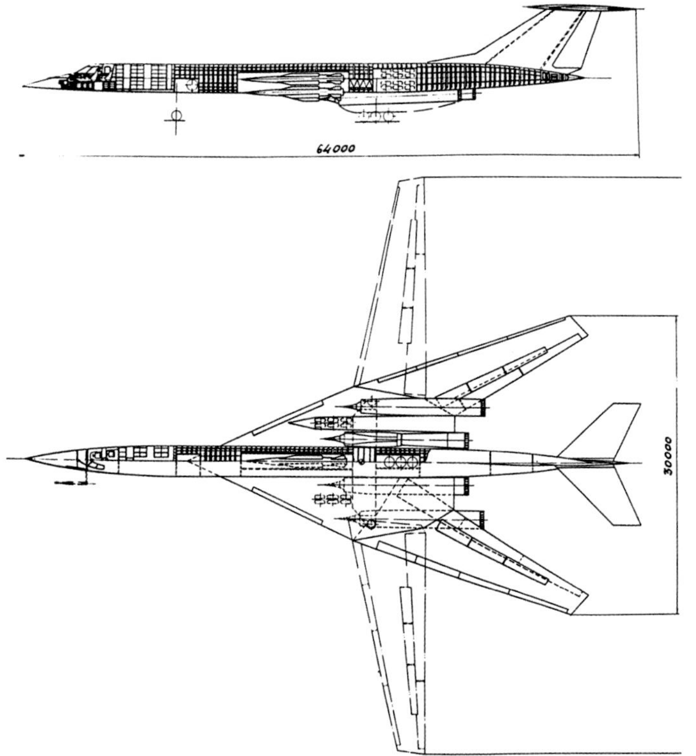

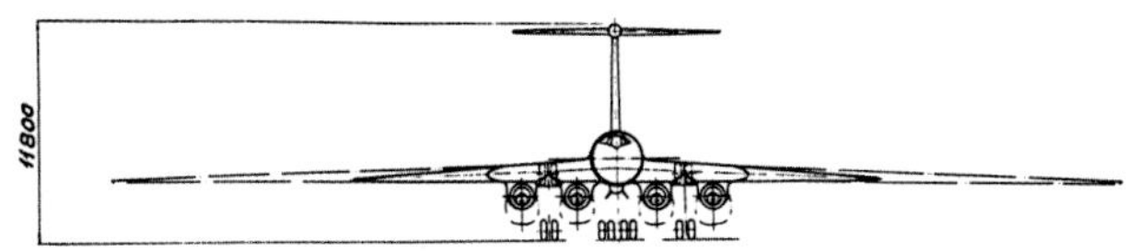

Основные данные

		Прототип 1975 г
1. Вес с-та максимальный	т	300
2. Относительный вес топлива	%	57,9
3. Удельная нагрузка на крыло при $X_{пк}$ = 13°	кг/м²	608
4. Тяговооруженность взлетная		0,3
5. Дальность полета максимальная при M = 0,8; H = 8 - 13.	км	14200
6. Вес боевой нагрузки нормальной — максимальн.	т	8,5-40
7. Длина разбега по бетону — грунту	м	1600-3000
8. Двигатели: тип, число X, тяга в кг		ТРДДФ4 × 22000 ген. конст. Кузнецов Н.Д.
9. Число членов экипажа		3-4

Стратегический двухрежимный многоцелевой самолет.

Схема: „бесхвостка" с системой управления ламинарным обтеканием и пакетным размещением двигателей.

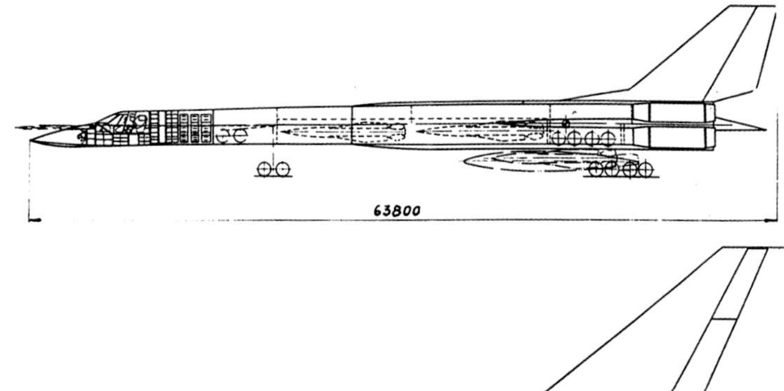

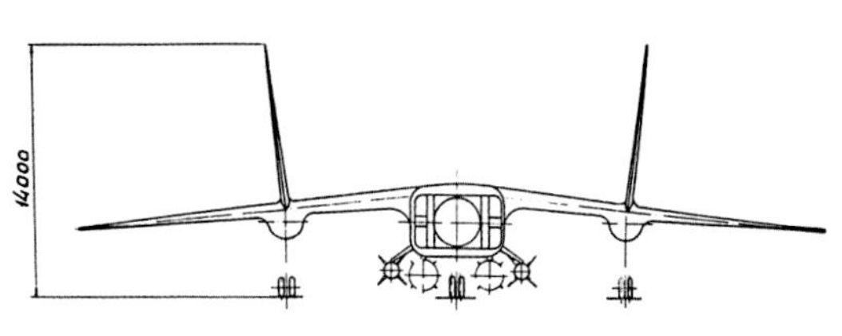

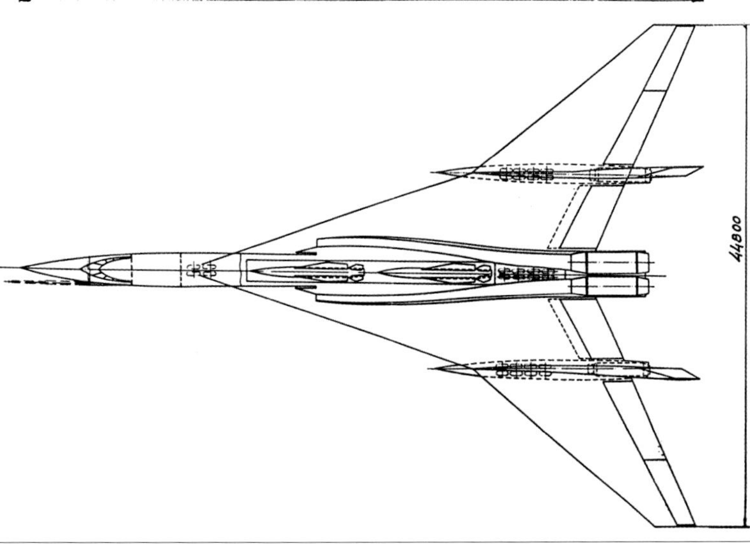

Основные данные

		Прототип 1975 г
1. Вес с-та максимальный	т	300
2. Относительный вес топлива	%	58,2
3. Удельная нагрузка на крыло при $X_{пк}$ =	кг/м²	434
4. Тяговооруженность взлетная		0,3
5. Дальность полета максимальная при M = 0,8; H = 8 - 13	км	14300
6. Вес боевой нагрузки нормальной — максимальной	т	9,5-40
7. Длина разбега по бетону — грунту	м	2000-4300
8. Двигатели: тип, число X, тяга в кг		ТРДДФ4 × 22000 ген. конст. Кузнецов Н.Д
9. Число членов экипажа		3-4

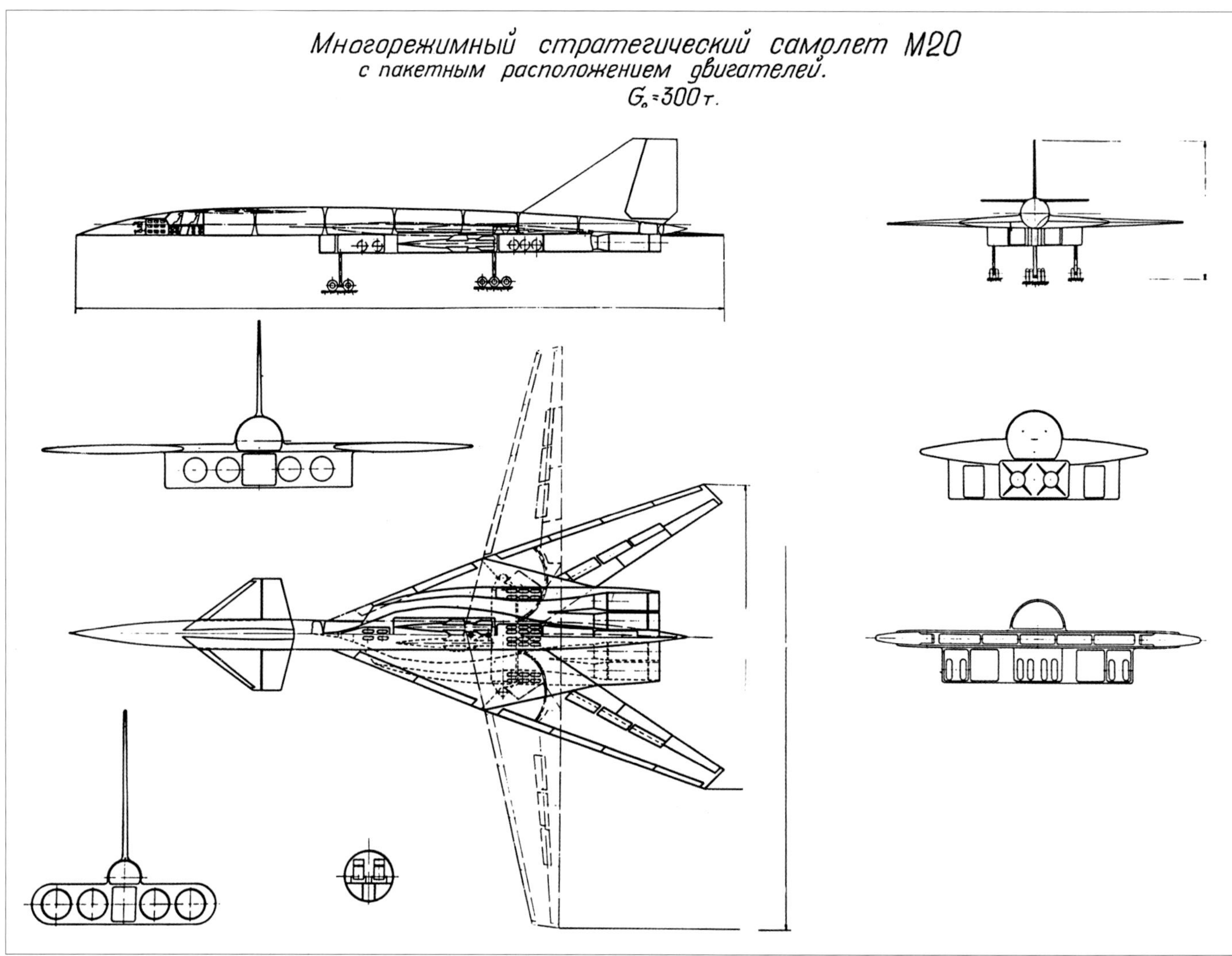

8,000-13,000 m (26,250-42,650 ft). The take-off run was to be 2,000 m (6,560 ft) on paved runways and 4,300 m (14,110 ft) on unpaved runways (the possibility of operating strategic bombers from dirt airstrips at forward operational locations was contemplated then).

Version 9A having the same take-off weight had a tail-first layout with a circular-section fuselage (again featuring a drooping visor), *very* compound-delta wings (this is the only fitting description), the leading-edge sweep changing from 77° on the LERXes (which began ahead of the canards' trailing edge) to 68° on the inboard wing sections to 43° on the outer wings. The inboard wing sections featured leading-edge slats. The trailing edge was also kinked, the flaps (which were divided into three sections on each side by the four individual engine nacelles) having negative trailing-edge sweep on the innermost sections. The high aspect ratio outer wings, which carried the ailerons, were designed to fold downward (just like on the North American XB-70 Valkyrie bomber) for high-speed cruise, the wing folding joints being well outboard of the engines; apparently this feature served the same purpose as on the American bomber, being used for longitudinal trim at high speed. The large canards of trapezoidal planform with 53° leading-edge sweep were shoulder-mounted, having strong dihedral and inset elevators. The sharply swept trapezoidal vertical tails (with inset rudders) were positioned above the outer engine nacelles and strongly canted inwards. The widely spaced engine nacelles had a circular cross-section and sharp-lipped axisymmetrical air intakes with shock cones. The landing gear (apparently with telescopic struts) consisted of an aft-retracting four-wheel nose bogie, two 12-wheel main bogies (three rows of four small wheels) side by side just aft of the CG retracting forward into the centre fuselage and twin-wheel outrigger struts retracting aft into the undersides of the outer engine nacelles; the maximum rotation angle was 14°. The weapons bay located immediately ahead of the mainwheel well accommodated two missiles above one another.

The aircraft was 67.0 m (219 ft 9 51/64 in) long, with a maximum wing span of 46.0 m (150 ft 11 1/32 in), a distance of 26.0 m (85 ft 3 5/8 in) between the wing folding joints, a canard span of 13.5 m (44 ft 3 1/2 in) and a height of 12.5 m (41 ft 0 1/8 in). The landing gear track at the outrigger struts was 18.0 m (59 ft 0 21/32 in) and the wheelbase at the centres of the main gear bogies was 23.7 m 77 ft 9 5/64 in).

Version 9B was an ASW derivative with a search radar in a teardrop radome aft of the flight deck and 16-wheel (!) main gear bogies (four rows of four small wheels). The overall length was increased to 70.0 m (229 ft 7 29/32 in) and the TOW to 325,000 kg (716,500 lb).

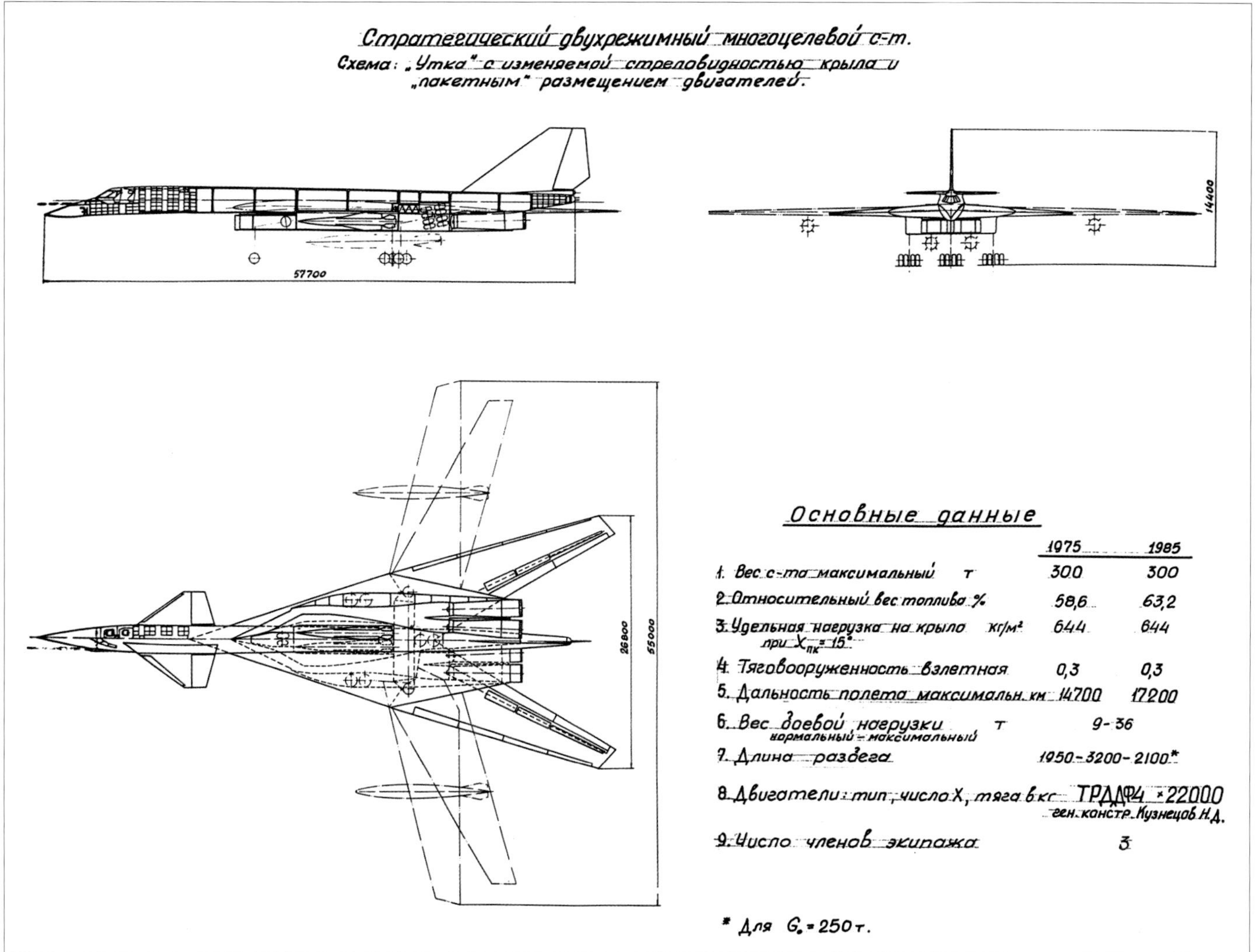

Version 10 was similar in layout to Version 9A/B but the wing LERXes had less sweep (72°), the smaller vertical tails were moved outward to the wing folding joints and canted outward instead of inward. The main gear units were moved outward as well, retracting into the wings between the engine nacelles and having eight-wheel bogies with two rows of four wheels. This aircraft was larger, with a length of 72.0 m (236 ft 2 41/64 in), a maximum wing span of 53.5 m (175 ft 6 19/64 in), a distance of 29.4 m (96 ft 5 31/64 in) between the wing joints, a canard span of 15.5 m (50 ft 10 15/64 in), a landing gear track of 15.0 m (49 ft 2 35/64 in) and a wheelbase of 26.0 m (85 ft 3 5/8 in). The TOW was again 325,000 kg.

Version 11 – also grossing at 325,000 kg – was similar to the XB-70, copying its layout almost completely, except for the "very compound-delta" wings (which, like the canards, were similar to Version 9). The powerplant consisted of six engines located side by side at the rear of a common boxy nacelle with a V-shaped front end in plan view. The two-dimensional air intakes were divided into two groups by a splitter with vertical airflow control ramps, which accommodated the nosewheel well and the weapons bay housing two missiles above one another; the inlet ducts curved in an S shape around this bay and the mainwheel wells. The outward-canted twin tails with inset rudders were placed at the sides of the engine nacelle. The landing gear comprised an aft-retracting nose unit and tandem pairs of main units retracting forward into the engine nacelle. Each unit had a six-wheel bogie of unusual Y-shaped design with two large wheels at one end and two pairs of small wheels side by side at the other end facing the direction of retraction; during retraction the bogie turned around the oleo, remaining horizontal so that the larger wheels flanked the oleo in the stowed position. The hinged outer wings could be deflected 10° up or 40° down from the neutral position, in the latter case reducing the wing span from a maximum of 56.5 m (185 ft 4 13/32 in) to 40.5 m (132 ft 10 31/64 in) and the wing area from 970 to 920 m² (from 10,441 to 9,902.8 sq ft); the canard span was again 15.5 m.

Version 12 shared the wings, canards and engine placement of Version 9A but had a single large trapezoidal vertical tail; the circular-section fuselage (with no drooping visor this time) was curved upward like a banana. The two Kh-45 missiles were carried above one another in the weapons bay amidships, the lower one being semi-recessed. Due to a shortage of space for internal fuel the aircraft carried four huge drop tanks under the hinged outer wings and between the engine nacelles. The landing gear consisted of an aft-retracting four-wheel nose bogie, two eight-wheel main bogies (with four tandem pairs of wheels) side by side

A desktop model of the M-20 in Version 16. The top and centre photos show the wings at the intermediate (subsonic cruise) setting. Note the three-cannon tail barbette and the rudder cut away to give an adequate field of fire.

retracting directly upward into the centre fuselage, two six-wheel main bogies (with three tandem pairs of wheels) retracting forward into the wing roots and twin-wheel outrigger struts retracting aft into the outer engine nacelles.

The aircraft, which was expected to fly in 1975, was 59.0 m (193 ft 6$^{53}/_{64}$ in) long and 14.0 m (45 ft 11$^{3}/_{16}$ in) high, with a maximum wing span of 46.0 m (150 ft 11$^{1}/_{32}$ in). The maximum TOW was 300,000 kg (661,390 lb), with a fuel share of 62.6%; the four Kuznetsov afterburning turbofans rated at 25,000 kgp (55,115 lbst) gave a take-off thrust/weight ratio of 0.33. The normal and maximum weapons loads were 8,500 kg (18,740 lb) and 40,000 kg (88,180 lb) respectively. The wing loading was 450 kg/m^2 (92.26 lb/sq ft). The M-20 was to have a take-off run of 2,000 m (6,560 ft) on paved runways and 4,300 m (14,110 ft) on unpaved runways.

Version 13 again had a tail-first layout and a "Valkyriesque" six-pack of engines with the same type of air intake, but here the similarity ended. In fact, the aircraft was closer to the Sukhoi T-4I, having low-set VG wings of high aspect ratio (with five-section leading-edge slats, three-section flaps and two-section ailerons) and a single trapezoidal vertical tail with negative sweep on the trailing edge; the canards had less sweepback and taper; the circular-section fuselage of 4.0 m (13 ft 1$^{31}/_{64}$ in) diameter had a drooping nose visor. The landing gear featured five four-wheel bogies – an aft-retracting nose unit and four-abreast main units, the inner pair retracting forward and the outer pair aft. The two missiles were carried side by side in a semi-recessed position. the aircraft was 74.0 m (242 ft 9$^{25}/_{64}$ in) long and 14.8 m (48 ft

$6\frac{43}{64}$ in) high, with a landing gear track of 9.5 m (31 ft $2\frac{1}{64}$ in) and a wheelbase of 18.1 m (59 ft $4\frac{39}{64}$ in); the wing span was 65.4 m (214 ft $6\frac{51}{64}$ in) at minimum sweep and 32.2 m (105 ft $7\frac{23}{32}$ in) at maximum sweep.

Version 14A was similar outwardly, except for the eight-wheel nose gear bogie (two rows of four wheels) and the three main gear units, the outer pair with six-wheel bogies (three tandem pairs of wheels) retracting aft and the centreline unit with a 12-wheel bogie being located farther aft to retract forward. Provisions were made for carrying two drop tanks under the wing gloves to extend range. The dimensions were also different, with a length of 69.5 m (228 ft $0\frac{7}{32}$ in), a height of 14.0 m (45 ft $11\frac{3}{16}$ in) and a wing span of 60.632 m (198 ft $11\frac{5}{64}$ in) at minimum sweep. The TOW was 300,000 kg.

Version 14B differed mainly in that the six engines were substituted by four more powerful engines. Also, the missiles were now carried internally (not semi-recessed).

Version 15 was also similar to Version 13 but the forward fuselage had a rectangular cross-section and the nose contour was stepped, despite the drooping nose visor. Also, the aircraft had Valkyrie-style twin tails and all-movable canards. The wings were equipped with four-section slats, three-section flaps and three-section spoilers (used for roll control); the inboard ends of the outer wing trailing edges overlapped inside the fuselage at maximum sweep. Again, the missiles were carried internally side by side.

Version 16 again had a tail-first layout with low-set VG wings having three sweep settings, fixed canards with inset elevators, a single vertical tail and four 22,000-kgp (48,500-lbst) Kuznetsov afterburning turbofans side by side in a common nacelle, with the weapons bay (accommodat-

Three more views of the same model with the wings fully swept back. The three eight-wheel main gear bogies are visible here.

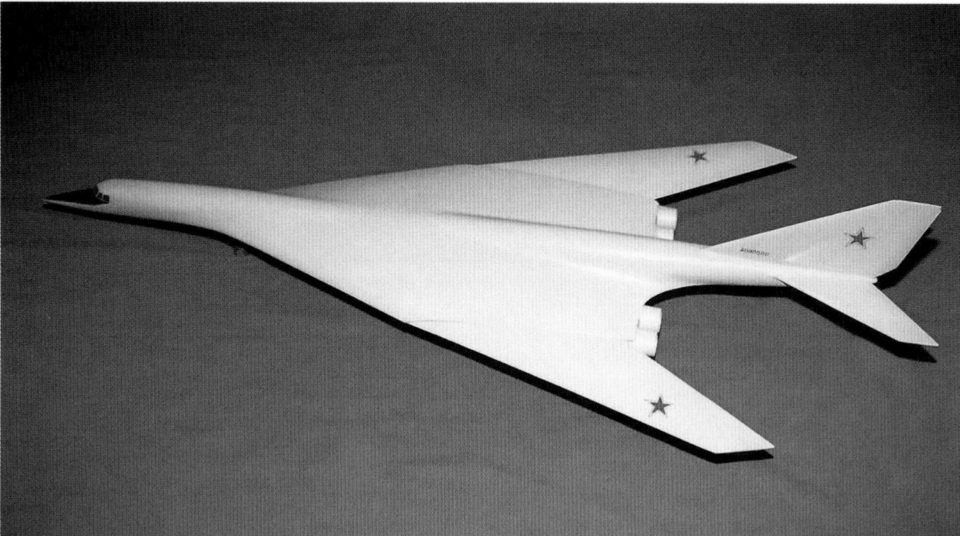

This page and opposite page: A model showing the ultimate project version of the Myasishchev M-18. Note the raked wingtips and the sharply swept tail with low-set dihedral tailplanes.

ing two missiles internally side by side) between the inlet ducts. The fixed-geometry fuselage nose had a stepped windscreen. The twin-wheel nose gear unit retracted aft; the three main units had eight-wheel bogies (two rows of four wheels) which tilted with the axles vertical before retraction, the outer units retracting forward to stow outside the inlet ducts (the wheels lying horizontally), while the centreline unit retracted aft, stowing aft of the wing pivot carry-through structure with the axles in an inclined position. The aircraft was to carry four drop tanks – two under the fuselage and two under the outer wings; the project drawing does not indicate if the outer wing drop tank pylons pivoted as the wings moved (as on the Sukhoi Su-24 *Fencer* tactical bomber) or they were to be jettisoned before the wings could move, as on the Mikoyan MiG-23 *Flogger* fighter. The aircraft had a crew of three.

In this configuration, the M-20 was 57.7 m (189 ft $3\frac{21}{32}$ in) long and 14.4 m (47 ft $2\frac{30}{32}$ in) high, with a wing span of 55.0 m (180 ft $5\frac{23}{64}$ in) at minimum sweep and 26.8 m (87 ft $11\frac{7}{64}$ in) at maximum sweep. It had a TOW of 300,000 kg, a wing loading of 644 kg/m² (132 lb/sq ft), a thrust/weight ratio of 0.3, a normal weapons load of 9,000 kg (19,840 lb) and a maximum weapons load of 36,000 kg (79,370 lb). As of 1975 the M-20 was to have a fuel share of 58.6% of the TOW and a take-off run of 1,950-3,200 m (6,400-10,500 ft); by 1985 this was to improve to 63.2% and 2,100 m (6,80 ft) respectively with a 250,000-kg (551,160-lb) TOW.

Version 17 was very different, utilising a conventional layout with low-set VG wings and a sharply swept T-tail with inset control surfaces. The fuselage had an oval cross-section with the longer axis vertical, the nose having a pointed profile with a blended windscreen. The weapons bay accommodated two Kh-45 missiles above one another ahead of the wing pivot carry-through structure, the lower missile being semi-recessed. The outer wings featured four-section leading-edge slats, three-section flaps, one-piece ailerons and three-section spoilers. The four 22,000-kgp Kuznetsov afterburning turbofans were housed in individual cylindrical nacelles located close together under the wing gloves so that the sharp-lipped axisymmetrical intakes with shock cones were aft of the wing leading edge. Again, there were four landing gear struts; the four-wheel nose gear bogie and the 12-wheel centreline main gear bogie retracted aft while the outer main units with six-wheel bogies (three pairs of wheels in tandem) stowed in the wing gloves between the engines, the wheels remaining vertical in all cases. The TOW was again 300,000 kg.

Version 18 was similar to the previous one but the fuselage nose had a stepped windscreen and a retractable L-shaped IFR probe on the port side. The wings now had leading-edge slats on the fixed inboard portions as well, and the outer wings had two-section flaps; also, they no longer obscured the outer engines' nozzles at maximum sweep. The tail unit was also revised – the fin had a small root fillet, while the horizontal tail was all-movable (a feature seldom seen on a T-tail aircraft). The nose gear unit had twin wheels, while the centreline main gear bogie now tilted before retraction, stowing with the wheel axles vertical. The aircraft was 64.0 m (209 ft 11$^{11}/_{16}$ in) long and 11.8 m (38 ft 8$^{9}/_{16}$ in) high; wing span at maximum sweep was 30.0 m (98 ft 5$^{7}/_{64}$ in). The TOW was 300,000 kg, with a fuel share of 57.9%; the normal and maximum weapons load was 8,500 kg (18,740 lb) and 40,000 kg (88,180 lb) respectively. The bomber was to have a wing loading of 608 kg/m^2 (124 lb/sq ft) at 13° minimum sweep, a thrust/weight ratio of 0.3, a maximum range of 14,200 km (8,820 miles) when cruising at Mach 0.8 and 8,000-13,000 m (26,250-42,650 ft); the take-off run was to be 1,600 m (5,250 ft) on paved runways and 3,000 m (9,840 ft) on unpaved runways.

After the preliminary design work on the M-20 had been completed, General Designer Vladimir M. Myasishchev succeeded in getting his design bureau entered into the tender for the supersonic strategic missile carrier. MAP orders to this effect were issued on September 15, 1969 (No.285), September 17, 1970 (No.134) and October 9, 1970 (No.321). The Myasishchev EMZ started work on a new project – the **M-18** strategic missile strike aircraft or ***tema*** *vosem**nadsat'*** ('subject 18'). Despite the lower designation, this was a later project that evolved in parallel with the M-20.

On February 15, 1971, Myasishchev delivered a report to the assembled representatives of various research establishments and OKBs, describing the progress the EMZ had made on the programme jointly with TsAGI and several research institutes within the frameworks of the Ministry of Defence, Ministry of Electronics Industry and Ministry of Defence Industry. In his report he pointed out that the general operational requirement (GOR) for the new bomber specified an increase in warload over aircraft then in service with the Soviet Air Force by a factor of 1.8, which led to a higher all-up weight. The GOR also demanded the provision of special equipment facilitating the penetration of air defences (this obviously means ECM equipment for jamming enemy AD radars

– *Auth.*), an improvement in thrust/weight ratio over existing aircraft by a factor of at least 1.5-1.7 (due to the need to be capable of operating from Class 1 unpaved airstrips) and a cruising speed of 3,000-3,200 km/h (1,863-1,987 mph). Class 1 means a runway length of 3,250 m (10,660 ft). All of this, according to Vladimir M. Myasishchev's own calculations and those of his staff, reduced the aircraft's range by 28-30%.

The OKB undertook a lot of research and development work under the strategic multi-mission strike aircraft programme; much of it was performed jointly with TsAGI. This included up to 1,200 hours of computer analysis of different airframe layouts; much effort was spent on flight dynamics and controllability studies in various flight modes. The size and weight of the aircraft were optimised, proceeding from different all-up weights (ranging from 150 to 300 tons/from 330,690 to 661,375 lb) and dimensions. Heat transfer and heat rejection quotients were studied in TsAGI's T-33 wind tunnel, using models.

The airframe's structural strength and stiffness characteristics were explored for different aerodynamic layouts and structural materials; among other things, this required the use of the wind tunnels at the Siberian Aviation Research Institute (SibNIA – ***Si**beerskiy* *naoch**no-issled**ovatel'skiy* *insti**toot*** *avi**ahtsii'***) in Novosibirsk, in addition to TsAGI's T-203 wind tunnel. The layouts and weights of the aircraft's principal systems (flight control system, avionics, landing gear, armament, engines and so on) were studied and the best ones selected. Detail design of the wings, fuselage landing gear and powerplant commenced at the same time.

The Myasishchev EMZ studied several general arrangements concurrently while working on the M-18 and M-20 projects. The engineers started with the conventional layout, then tried the canard (tail-first) layout. The following options were considered, among other things:

• a conventional layout with variable-geometry wings and twin tails or a single vertical tail;

• a conventional layout with variable-geometry wings and a T-tail;

• a tail-first layout with delta wings and delta foreplanes;

• a tail-first layout with variable-geometry wings;

• a tail-first layout featuring compound leading-edge sweep and drooping outer wings (as used on the XB-70);

• a tailless delta layout.

The result of this research was a firm conviction that the future multi-mission strategic strike aircraft should have VG wings. The main difference between the two Myasishchev projects was that in the M-20 project the tail-first layout prevailed, whereas most versions of the M-18 project utilised a conventional layout.

Vladimir M. Myasishchev directly supervised the development of the multi-mission strike aircraft. Many other prominent designers of the recreated OKB were also heavily involved in the M-18/M-20 programme; these included Deputy General Designer G. I. Arkhangel'skiy, acting Deputy General Designer M. V. Gusarov, acting Deputy General Designer V. A. Fedotov, aerodynamics section chief A. D. Tokhoonts and many others. K. P. Lyutikov was appointed chief project engineer. Responsibilities were distributed as follows: Tokhoonts was responsible for the general arrangement, internal layout, aerodynamics and powerplant; Fedotov supervised all structural strength work, introduction of new materials and detail design. Another man, N. M. Glovatskiy, was in charge of prototype manufacturing, acting as chief engineer of the OKB's impressive experimental production facility at the same time.

The general arrangements were selected with two options in mind: an aircraft with a take-off weight around 150,000 kg (330,690 lb) equipped with an IFR system or a much larger aircraft with a TOW of 300-325 tons (661,375-716,490 lb) and no provisions for IFR. The powerplant was selected accordingly; a 150-ton aircraft would be powered by four engines delivering 12,000 kgp (26,455 lbst) each, whereas the heavy version required engines in the 22,000-25,000 kgp (48,500-55,115 lbst) thrust class. The Kuznetsov OKB was chosen as the engine supplier.

The crew consisted of three or four persons. The wing area ranged from 670 to 970 m^2 (7,204 to 10,430 sq ft), depending on the take-off weight. The principal offensive armament was to consist of two heavy air-to-surface missiles. There was no defensive armament.

In general arrangement and specific design features the final version of the M-18, which was submitted for Stage 2 of the tender, closely paralleled the Rockwell International B-1, featuring a low-wing BWB layout with variable-geometry wings. The forward fuselage featured a sharply pointed fixed-geometry nosecone and a V-shaped stepped windscreen; the four-man forward-facing flight deck was followed by an avionics bay, the nosewheel well and the single weapons bay ahead of the wing pivot carry-through box, with fuel tanks aft of it. At maximum sweep the wings had constant leading-edge sweep from root to tip. Unlike the American bomber, the tail unit was conventional with a sharply swept trapezoidal vertical tail and low-set dihedral stabilisers, not cruciform. As on the B-1, the engines were housed in side-by-side pairs under the inner wings in conformal nacelles having V-shaped front ends in plan view; the two-dimensional air intakes had vertical airflow control ramps. The aft-retracting twin-wheel nose gear unit was located well aft; the four main units had four-wheel bogies, two of which retracted forward into the engine nacelles to lie in narrow bays between the inlet ducts so that the axles were disposed vertically, while the other two retracted aft to stow between the nacelles, the wheels remaining vertical. The two Kh-45 missiles were accommodated side by side in the weapons bay. Information on the aircraft's dimensions and weight is sketchy; most sources quote a length of about 44 m (144 ft $4\frac{9}{32}$ in), a wing span of about 42 m (137 ft $9\frac{17}{32}$ in) at minimum sweep, a height of about 10 m (32 ft $9\frac{45}{64}$ in) and a TOW of about 150,000 kg (330,690 lb).

The M-18 was considered to be – and promoted as – the more promising of the two Myasishchev projects (perhaps the truth is that it was simply a safer option, being less innovative than the M-20). Way ahead of all other aspects of detail design, work started on the most crucial element of the airframe – the wing pivots; the novel design of these units underwent structural and dynamic testing on a scale model at TsAGI. Nine test rigs and two flying testbeds were involved in the development of the M-18. The result of this massive effort was a 10% reduction in the aircraft's weight.

As already mentioned, the multi-mission, multi-mode strike aircraft projects developed by the Sukhoi and Myasishchev bureaux envisaged the strategic bomber/missile carrier role as the main one, with provisions for later adaptation for the high-altitude reconnaissance or ASW roles.

After the Air Force had formulated a GOR for an advanced multi-mode strategic strike aircraft in 1969, the Soviet government decided that multiple design bureaux should compete for the order and a deadline for project submission should be set for all participants of the tender. This time the Tupolev OKB was 'invited' along with Sukhoi and Myasishchev, since Tupolev was the Soviet Union's top authority in heavy bombers and possessed the greatest expertise in this field.

The Contest: The Tupolev OKB's Bid (Tu-160M – first use of designation, *izdeliye* L)

In 1970, working in close co-operation with TsAGI and other research organisations, the Tupolev OKB finally joined the contest with a further multi-mode strategic bomber project under the provisional designation **Tu-160M** – the first aircraft thus designated (aka *izdeliye* L). Two roles were envisaged – a missile strike aircraft armed with various types of air-to-surface missiles for various missions and a strategic reconnaissance aircraft; hence the M suffix apparently stood for ***mnogotselevoy*** (multi-role), not *mod-ifitseerovannyy*. The in-house product code was probably just the next letter in the alphabetical sequence after the aforementioned *izdeliye* K. Several project versions were developed in 1970-72; these were known as Tu-160M-1 ("L-1"), Tu-160M-2 ("L-2") etc.

The project materials stated that the aircraft was intended both for nuclear strikes against strategic objectives on transoceanic theatres of operations and for conventional strikes on TOs adjacent to the Soviet borders, as well as for strategic reconnaissance. Furthermore, the possibility of developing an over-the-horizon targeting version providing guidance for sea-launched missiles (a successor to the Tu-95RTs *Bear-D*), an ASW version and a so-called "raider" intended for disrupting the enemy's airlift and aerial resupply operations was also mentioned.

After assessing the merits and shortcomings of the various aerodynamic and structural layouts the OKB selected a tailless delta layout which drew heavily on the Tu-144's design. Calculations showed that the most promising one was a tailless-delta aircraft utilising the BWB layout.

The Tu-160M was shorter than the Tu-144 but had a much longer wing span and greater wing aspect ratio. The bomber's wing area was only marginally greater if the LERXes were disregarded, but the increase in overall wing area was much greater. At a glance the double-delta wings with cropped tips appeared to have a similar planform to that of the production Tu-144; however, again the LERXes ran the full length of the forward fuselage, which had the same quasi-rhomboid cross-section with sharp chines as the "aircraft 160IS" (as opposed to the conventionally designed Tu-144 with a circular-section fuselage and the LERXes beginning well aft). The leading-edge sweep angles were also different – 78° on the LERXes and 50° on the outer wings versus 76° and 57° respectively for the Tu-144. The same TsAGI P-109S high-speed airfoil as on the Tu-144 was used for the outer wings and a special TsAGI airfoil for the LERXes. The trailing edge was occupied almost entirely by four-section elevons which had a travel limit of ±22°30'. A major difference from the Tu-144 was that the LERXes and outer wings featured leading-edge flaps increasing the lift/drag ratio to 15.2 at Mach 0.94 and 9.0 at Mach 2.35; the Tu-144 had no leading-edge devices.

The trapezoidal vertical tail was outwardly similar to that of the Tu-144, having the same leading-edge sweep of 50°, no trailing-edge sweep and a two-section rudder. The latter had a travel limit of ±24°30'.

The airframe structure made maximum possible use of the design features and manufacturing technologies developed for the Tu-144. Similarly to the latter, the forward fuselage incorporated a drooping nose visor ahead of the flight deck – even the glazing shape was the same, with narrow lateral windows offering very little in the way of forward visibility when the visor was up. This visor incorporated a large radome for a navigation/attack radar

Top right: A desktop model of the Tu-160M. This lower view illustrates the convex fuselage underside between the engine nacelles (in the area of the weapons bay).

Above right: This aspect of the same model illustrates the blended wing/body layout and the sharp chines running all the way to the tip of the nose.

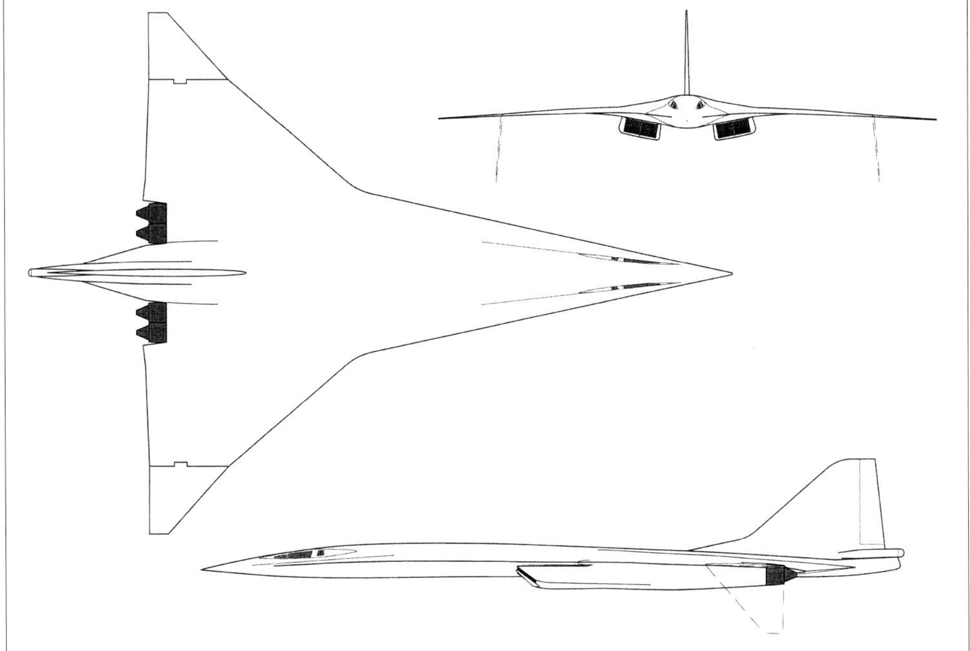

Right: A three-view of the Tu-160M in the version with drooping wingtips.

САМОЛЕТ Ту-160М

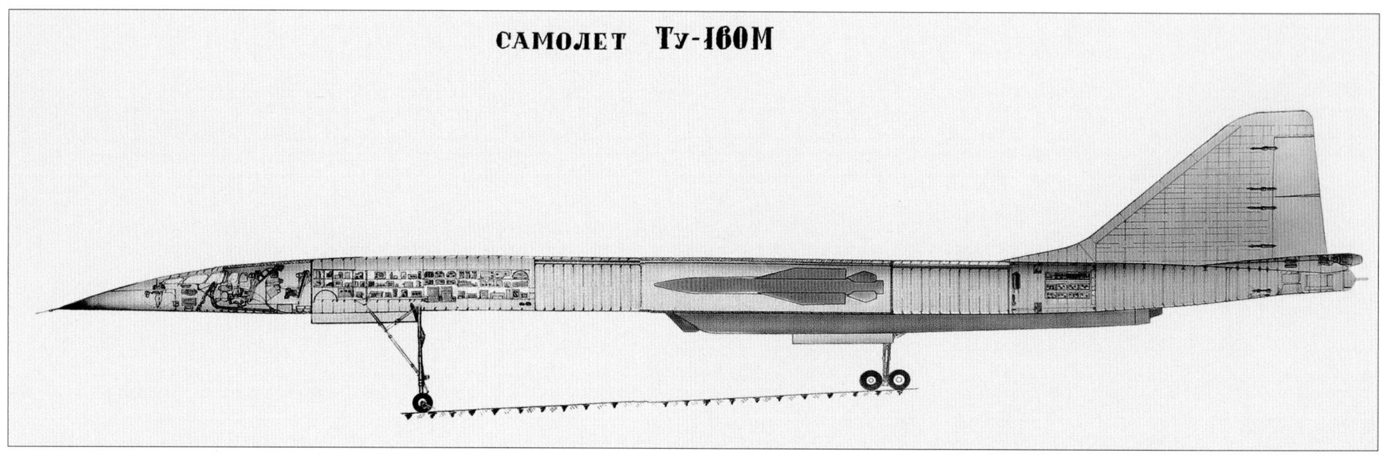

Above: A cutaway drawing of the Tu-160M from the PD project documents, showing the fuel tanks fore and aft of the weapons bay.
Below: The Tu-160M structural design layout from the project documents. The dark grey areas show the titanium components; the arrows indicate the manufacturing breaks.

Right: The Tu-160M's fuel system layout; note the retractable IFR probe to port. The dark-coloured tanks are trim and service tanks.
Below right: A three-view of the Tu-160M from the PD project documents.

replacing the airliner's weather radar. The flight deck seated a crew of four (the captain and co-pilot at the front, the navigator/WSO and the radio operator behind them). All crew members faced forward, sitting on upward-firing KT-1 ejection seats. The latter were developed in house, as was common in the Soviet Union at the time (KT stood for [*kata**pool'**tnoye*] ***kres**lo* ***Too**poleva* – Tupolev ejection seat) and were borrowed from the Tu-22M. At a later stage, each crew member was to have his own jettisonable pressurised capsule that would ensure survival in a high-altitude/high-speed ejection and remain afloat in the event of a splashdown.

КОНСТРУКТИВНО - СИЛОВАЯ СХЕМА ПЛАНЕРА
I-I
II-II
III-III
IV-IV
V-V
РАЗЪЕМ

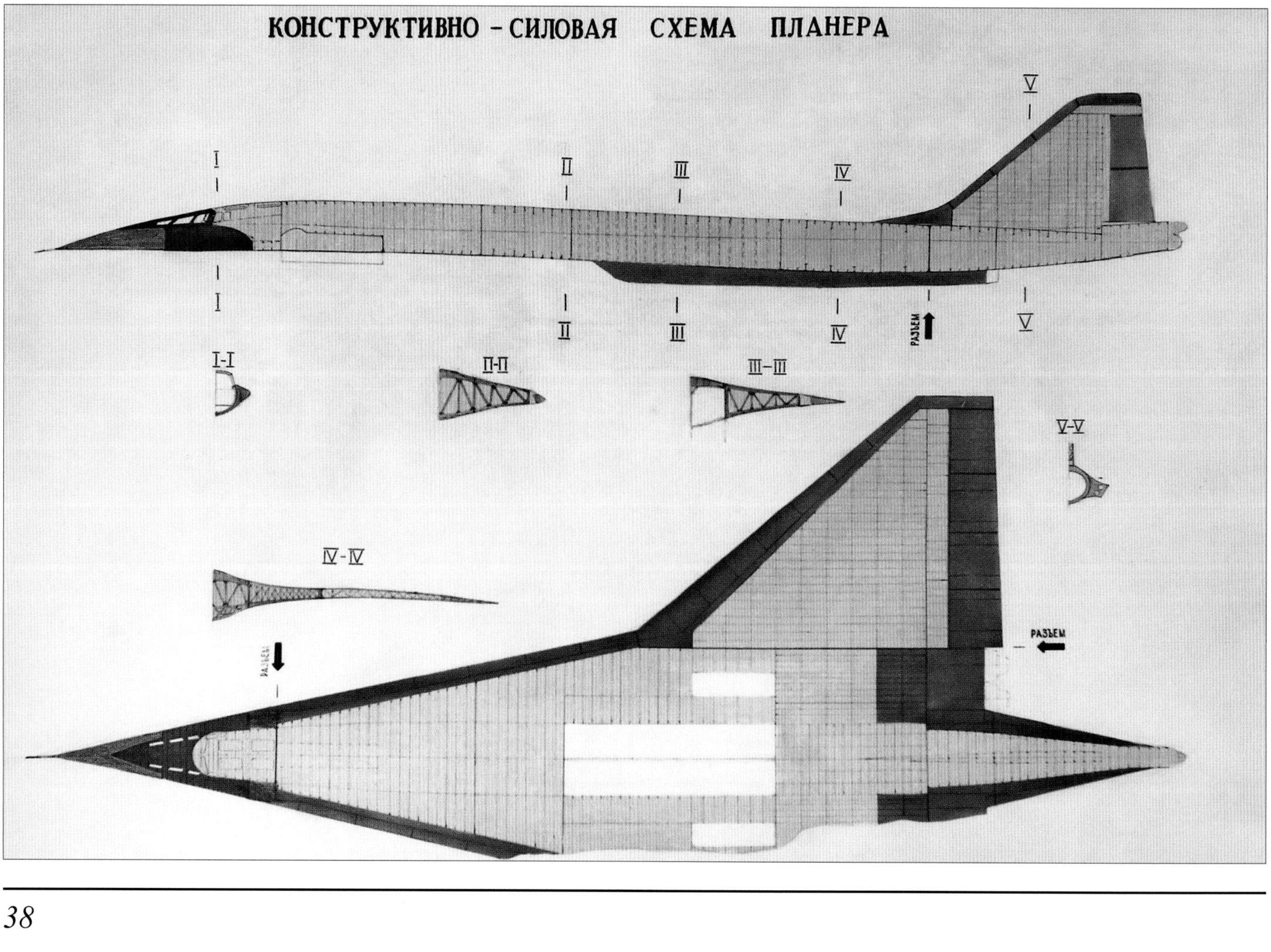

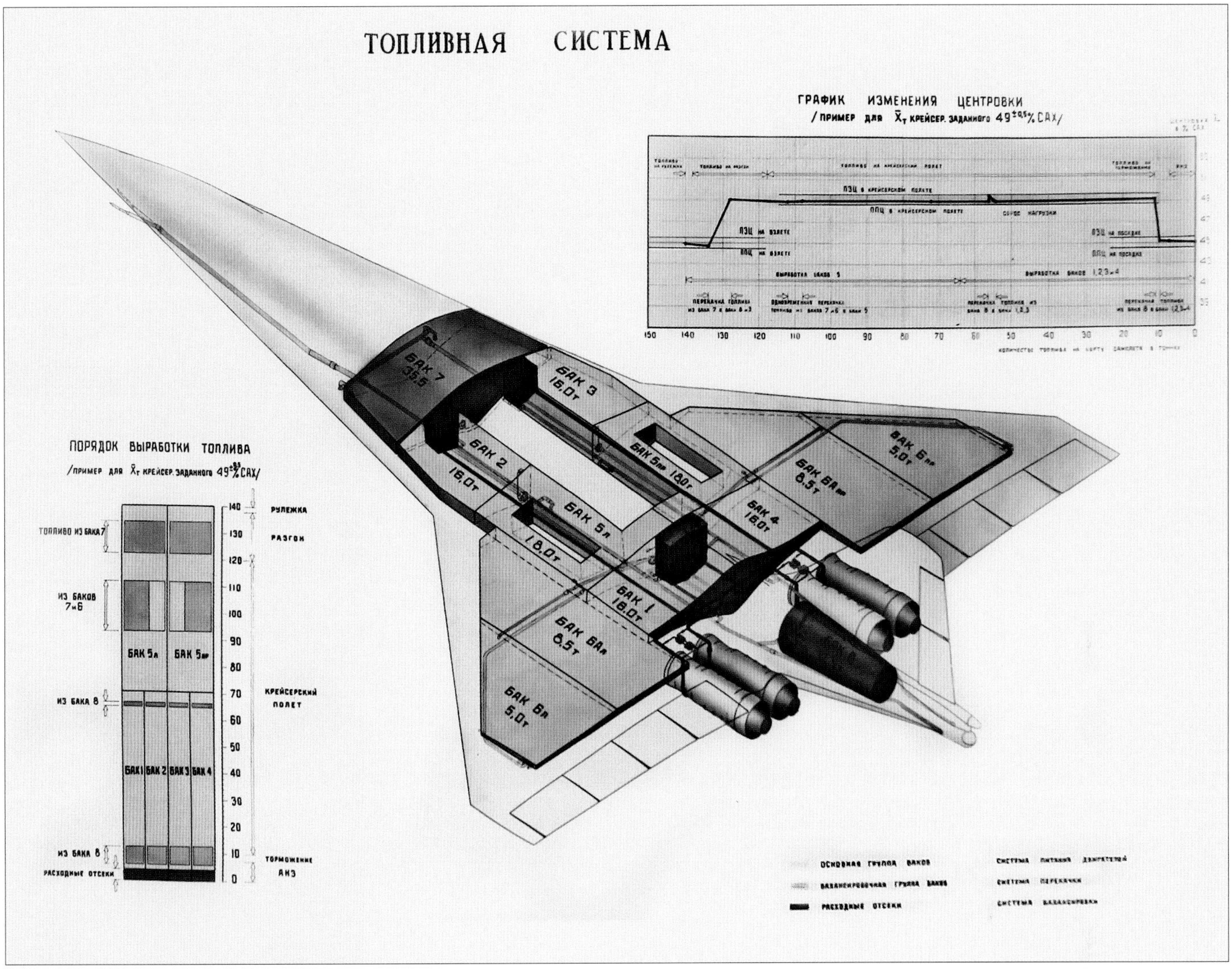

ТОПЛИВНАЯ СИСТЕМА

ГРАФИК ИЗМЕНЕНИЯ ЦЕНТРОВКИ

ПОРЯДОК ВЫРАБОТКИ ТОПЛИВА

БАК 7 36.5

БАК 3 16.0т

БАК 2 16.0т

БАК 5пр 18.0т

БАК 5л 18.0т

БАК 1 16.0т

БАК 4 16.0т

БАК 6Апр 8.5т

БАК 6пр 5.0т

БАК 6Ал 8.5т

БАК 6л 5.0т

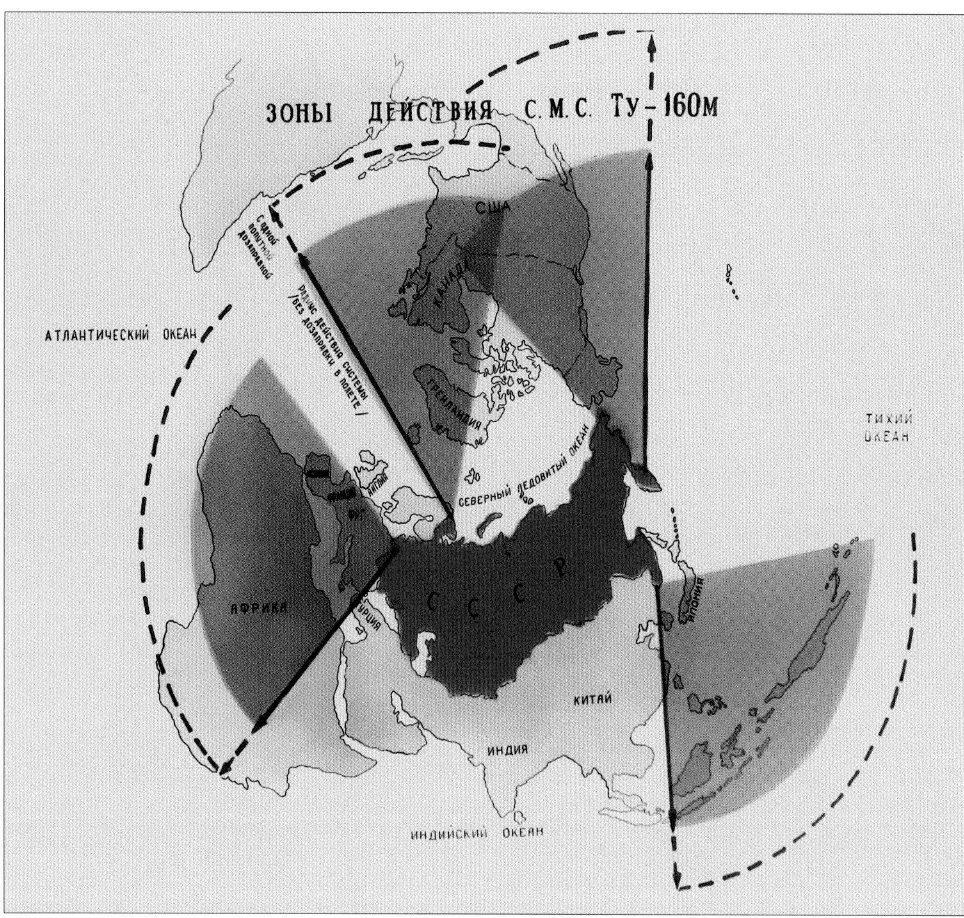

Above: A diagram from the PD project documents showing the Tu-160M's combat radius on internal fuel (coloured sectors) and with one fuel top-up (hatched lines).
Below: A diagram showing the aircraft's flight profiles (altitude/speed/range) with a 230-ton (507,050-lb) TOW.

Opposite page: Drawings and tables from the project documents illustrating the Tu-160M's missile load and bomb load options in normal payload and maximum payload configurations.

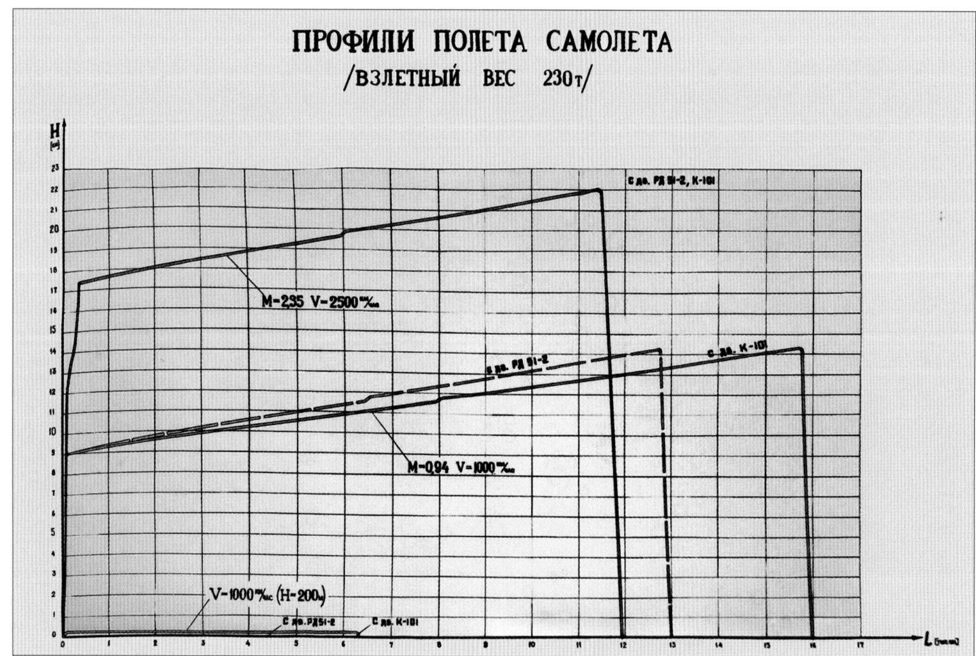

The flight deck was followed by a large forward avionics bay with the nosewheel well underneath it. Further aft was the weapons bay surrounded by fuel tanks on all sides, a small rear avionics bay and the rear fuselage tank situated below the base of the fin. The weapons bay was unusually wide and accommodated two Kh-45 or Kh-2000 missiles side by side; this allowed the length of the bay to be minimised, leaving more internal volume available for fuel. It also made for a robust and stiff structure. The missiles were separated by a longitudinal bulkhead which doubled as a centreline keel beam, increasing the stiffness of the centre fuselage structure. The rear fuselage appeared shorter than on the airliner and housed avionics and equipment bays. The flight deck section, the rear fuselage (together with the vertical tail) and the outer wings were detachable.

The primary structural material was AK4 aluminium alloy (*alyuminiy kovochnyy* – aluminium optimised for forging), which accounted for 55% of the structural weight. The drooping nose visor, the wing and fin leading edges, and the control surfaces, which were subjected to the greatest kinetic heating in supersonic flight, were made of titanium alloy making up 33.5% of the structural weight; using a higher share of titanium was deemed inexpedient on cost grounds. Steel accounted for 9% and other metals and non-metallic materials made up the remaining 2.5%.

The landing gear was taken virtually wholesale from the airliner, with an exceptionally tall forward-retracting twin-wheel nose unit and short main units with eight-wheel bogies (two rows of four wheels) retracting forward into the nacelles. (Actually the bogie had four wheels but each wheel was exceptionally wide, with two tyres mounted side by side.) Prior to retraction the bogies tilted into a vertical position, inboard ends uppermost, to stow in narrow wheel wells between the inlet ducts of each pair of engines so that the wheels were vertical but at 90° to the direction of flight.

РАКЕТНОЕ ВООРУЖЕНИЕ УДАРНОГО ВАРИАНТА

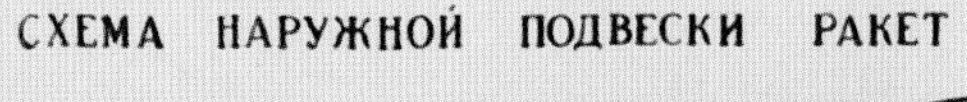

БОЕВАЯ НАГРУЗКА

НОРМАЛЬНЫЙ ВАРИАНТ				вариант	
вариант	наименование	кол-во на самолет	общий вес /т/	количество	общий вес /т/
I	Х - 45	2	8,4	4	16,8
II	Х - 2000Т	1	6,5	4	26
III	ТУС - 2	4	8	8	16

ПОДВЕСКА РАКЕТ ВО ВНУТРЕННИХ ОТСЕКАХ

Х - 45

Х - 2000т

ТУС-2

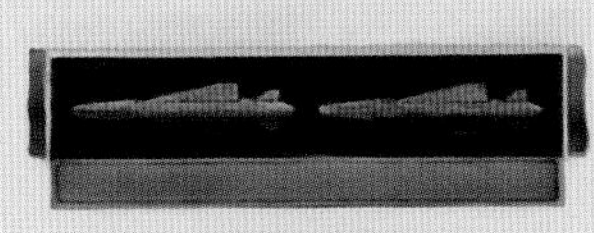

БОМБОВОЕ ВООРУЖЕНИЕ УДАРНОГО ВАРИАНТА

СХЕМА НАГРУЖЕННОЙ ПОДВЕСКИ БОМБ

№№ вариантов	НАИМЕНОВАНИЕ БОМБ	НОРМАЛЬНЫЙ ВАРИАНТ		ПЕРЕГРУЗОЧНЫЙ ВАРИАНТ		
		количество	общий вес /т/	количество во внутренних отсеках	количество на наружной подвеске	общий вес /т/
I	ФАБ - 250	36	9	120	36	39
II	ФАБ - 500	18	9	80	10	45
III	ФАБ - 1500	6	9	24	6	45
IV	ФАБ - 3000	3	9	8	6	42

ПОДВЕСКА БОМБ ВО ВНУТРЕННИХ ОТСЕКАХ

ФАБ-250

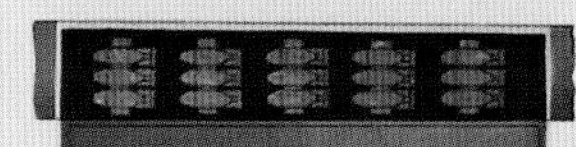

ФАБ-500

ФАБ-1500

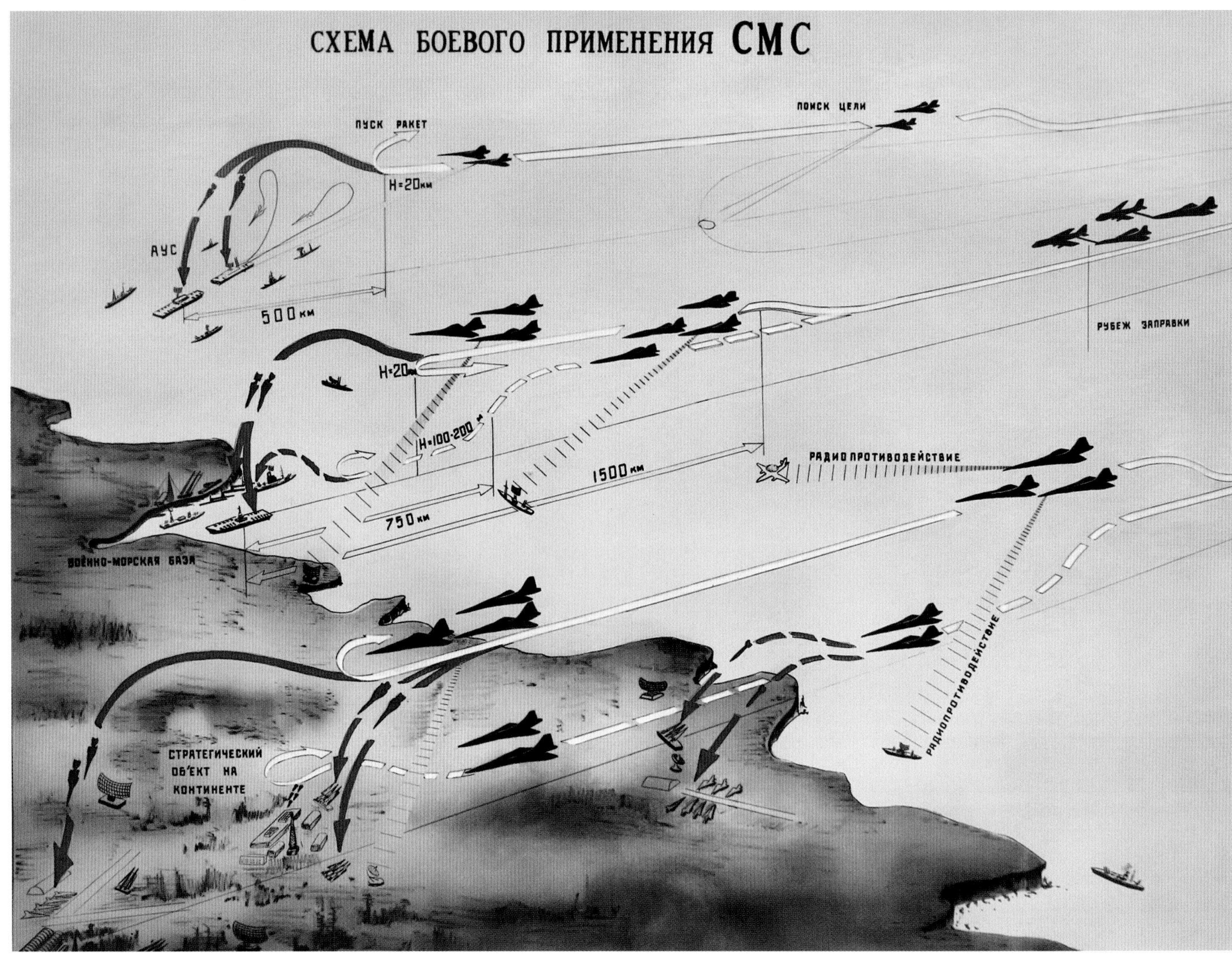

One difference was that that all wheels were of the same size and slightly larger than the Tu-144's – 1,000 x 450 mm (39.37 x 17.71 in) versus the airliner's 960 x 300 mm (37.79 x 11.81 in) nosewheels and 950 x 400 mm (37.40 x 15.74 in) mainwheels. Also, the bomber had a shorter wheelbase but a wider wheel track. A brake parachute with an area of 50 m² (538.2 sq ft) was provided to reduce the landing run.

At the initial stage the Tu-160M was to be powered by RD51-2 turbojets. These engines had a take-off thrust of 23,800 kgp (52,470 lbst); the SFC was 0.9-0.91 kg/kgp·hr in subsonic cruise at a rating of 3,500-4,000 kgp (7,720-8,820 lbst), increasing to 1.23-1.3 kg/kgp·hr in supersonic cruise at a rating of 5,000-6,000 kgp (11,020-13,230 lbst). Later the cruise SFC in subsonic mode was to be reduced to 0.75-0.77 kg/kgp·hr

It should be noted that the designation RD51-2 stated in the PD project documents is rather puzzling because it does not correlate with any of the Soviet aero engine design bureaux (after all, OKB-51 was the Sukhoi OKB, which is definitely not an engine maker, and OKB-2 was not an engine maker either!). However, the drawings in the PD project show nozzles strongly reminiscent of the Kolesov (RKBM) RD36-51A single-spool non-afterburning turbojet with its distinctive translating centrebody in the shape of a cropped cone; these engines powered the Tu-144D – the late-production version of the *Charger* (the D stood for ***[novyye] dvigateli*** – [new] engines). Therefore, it stands to reason that the mysterious RD51-2 was an uprated afterburning derivative of the 20,000-kgp (44,090-lbst) RD36-51A which never materialised.

Later still, the bomber was to be re-engined with RKBM K-101 variable-cycle engines having an SFC of 0.67-0.72 kg/kgp·hr in subsonic cruise at Mach 0.8, 1.23-1.35 kg/kgp·hr (dry) or 1.45 kg/kgp·hr (reheat) in supersonic cruise at Mach 2.2, and 1.05 kg/kgp·hr (dry) or 1.2 kg/kgp·hr (reheat) at take-off power. The engine nacelles were very similar to those of the production Tu-144, featuring two-dimensional air intakes with horizontal airflow control ramps and auxiliary blow-in/spill doors. However, the nacelles were moved outward to make room for the weapons bay.

The fuel system with a total capacity of 175.000 litres (38,500 Imp gal) consisted of 12 integral tanks, eight of which were housed in the fuselage, and four service tanks. The numeration was rather puzzling; the No.7 fuselage tank was foremost (in the LERXes ahead of the weapons bay), followed by the Nos. 2 (port) and 3 (starboard) tanks flanking the front half of the bay, the Nos. 5L (port) and 5R (starboard) tanks flanking the rear half of the bay (with integrated mainwheel wells), the Nos. 1 (port) and

4 (starboard) tanks aft of the bay, with the unnumbered service tanks in between, and the No.8 rear fuselage tank which, like No.7, was a trim tank. Four further tanks – Nos. 6L/6R outboard and Nos. 6AL/6AR inboard – were located in the wing torsion box. The Tu-160M had IFR capability with a fully retractable IFR probe at the front of the port LERX; a fuel jettison system was provided, with outlets on the underside of the tailcone.

The control system featured electrohydraulic actuators, two for each control surface segment, and an automatic flight control system (AFCS) with a stability augmentation feature. The hydraulic system with a nominal pressure of 280 kg/cm² (4,000 psi) consisted of four separate subsystems. The 200 V/400 Hz AC main electric system was served by four 60-kVA GT-60M48U engine-driven alternators with constant-speed drives. 28 V DC power was supplied by rectifiers.

Another version of the Tu-160M was very similar but had wings of even greater span and area. The elevons terminated well inboard of the wingtips, which were hinged and could be drooped hydraulically in similar manner to the XB-70.

The Tu-160M's main weapons in normal payload configuration were two Kh-45 missiles with a total weight of 8,400 kg (18,520 lb) or one Kh-2000T missile weighing 6,500 kg (14,330 lb). If the air defences in the target area had been suppressed it was possible to use TUS-2 TV-guided missiles (*televizi**on**nyy oopravl**ya**yemyy snar**ya**d*) with a conventional warhead against small ground targets or maritime surface targets requiring high accuracy. The TUS-2, which as it turned out was never built, was to have a launch weight of 2,000 kg (4,410 lb; also quoted as 1,700 kg/3,750 lb), a length of 5 m (16 ft 4⁵⁵⁄₆₄ in), a wing span of 1.7 m (5 ft 6⁵⁹⁄₆₄ in), a body diameter of 1.4 m (4 ft 7⁷⁄₆₄ in) and a maximum range of 12 km (7.45 miles). Four such missiles were to be carried, with a total weight of 8,000 kg (17,640 lb).

In maximum payload configuration the number of missiles was four Kh-45s (16,800 kg/37,040 lb), or four Kh-2000s (26,000 kg/57,320 lb), or eight TUS-2s (16,000 kg/35,270 lb). There were also plans to develop the Kh-200 short-range air-to-surface missile for the new Soviet multi-mode strategic aircraft; this was to be broadly comparable to the Boeing AGM-69 SRAM which had been fielded by the US Air Force in 1972.

Additionally, the Tu-160M could carry free-fall bombs internally on bomb cassettes for bombs of up to 1,500-kg (3,310-lb) calibre or BD-4 racks (***bah**lochnyy der**zhah**tel'* – beam-type [bomb] rack for Group 4 ordnance, which means up to 3,000-kg/6,610-lb calibre). 1,500-kg FAB-1500 bombs (*foo**gahs**naya avia**bom**ba* – high-explosive bomb) were carried two abreast in each bay in three rows, two per cassette; smaller sizes – 250-kg (551-lb) FAB-250s and 500-kg (1,102-lb) FAB-500s – were carried three-abreast on five rows of cassettes, with as many as five per cassette. If that was not enough, more bombs could be carried externally on rather untidy-looking MBD3-U9-68 multiple ejector racks (MERs), two of which were fitted on each side outboard of the engine nacelles; each MER could take nine 250-kg bombs or six 500-kg bombs. The designation means *mnogozam**ko**vyy **bah**lochnyy der**zhah**tel', oonifit**see**rovannyy* – multi-shackle beam-type rack for Group 3 ordnance (up to 500 kg calibre), standardised, nine-bomb version, 1968 model.

The normal bomb load of 9,000 kg (19,840 lb) could consist of three 3,000-kg FAB-3000 bombs, or six FAB-1500s, or eighteen FAB-500s, or thirty-six FAB-250s. In high gross weight configuration the Tu-160M could take 14 FAB-3000s (eight internally and six externally) for a total load of 42,000 kg (92,590 lb), or 30 FAB-1500s (24 + 6), or 90 FAB-500s (80 + 10) for a total maximum load of 45,000 kg (99,210 lb) in both cases, or as many as 156 FAB-250s (120 + 36) for a total load of 39,000 kg (85,980 lb).

On naval theatres of operations the Tu-160M could be used for setting up minefields. In that case the weapons load could com-

Opposite page: A drawing showing the Tu-160M's combat tactics. The pair cruise at 20,000 m (65,620 ft), attacking a carrier task force at 500 km (310 miles) range. The quartet refuel, then set up active ECM for radar picket ships and AD radars at up to 1,500 km (931 miles) range before attacking a naval base (one aircraft descends to 100-200 m/330-660 ft). The nearest group splits to attack strategic targets on the continent, some of the aircraft jamming picket ships and AWACS aircraft to enable air defence penetration.

Previous page: This model demonstrates the other project version of the Tu-160M (with longer wing span and drooping wingtips in the manner of the XB-70). Only one wingtip is shown drooped; of course the aircraft was not meant to fly in such a lop-sided configuration!

The photos on this page show the same model with both wingtips drooped. Actually the model gives a false impression – the wingtips were to be angled down, not vertical. The front view illustrates the rhomboid cross-section of the fuselage and the resulting canted position of the engine nacelles.

prise up to 80 UDM-500, IGDM-500 or ADM-500 naval mines for a total weight of 42,000 kg (92,590 lb), or 24 mines of other types – RM-1 or APM (totalling 20,400 kg/44,970 lb), UDM (32,400 kg/71,430 lb), *Ser**pey*** (31,200 kg/68,780 lb), ***Lee**ra* (Lyre, 23,400 kg/51,590 lb), IGDM or AMD-2M (25,320 kg 55,820 lb) or UDM-5 (26,400 kg/58,200 lb).

(Note: AMD = *aviatsi**on**naya* ***mee**na* ***don**naya* – air-dropped bottom mine; IGDM = *indooktsi**on**no-**ghid**rodina**mich**eskaya* ***don**naya* ***mee**na* – bottom mine with a combined induction/hydrodynamic detector. As for the nonsensical word Serpey, it is nothing more than an accidental anagram of the intended codename *Per**sey*** (Perseus). Quite simply, a typist had made an error when typing out the document clearing the weapon for service, and no-one had taken the responsibility to set it straight, believing that, "the Powers That Be know better!")

For self-defence the Tu-160M was provided with a remote-controlled tail barbette mounting a 30-mm (1.18 calibre) cannon, with a ***Ghe**liy* (Helium) gun ranging radar in a cigar-shaped fairing above it. The barbette was located at the rear extremity of the fuselage (occupying the place of the Tu-144's brake parachute bay, which had to be relocated further forward); its field of fire was ±45° in azimuth and +40°/–30° in elevation. Additionally, the Tu-160M was to have a comprehensive active/passive ECM and infrared countermeasures (IRCM) suite for individ-

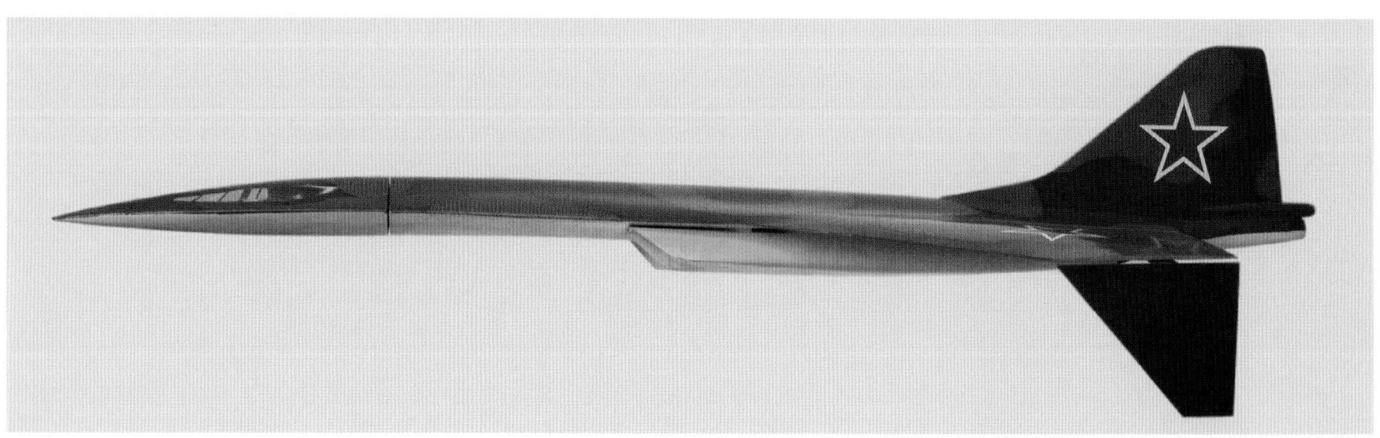

Overleaf: A drawing from the PD project documents showing the reconnaissance version of the Tu-160M carrying two DSBR (Voron) air-launched strategic reconnaissance drones under the wings. The table gives the drone's brief specifications.

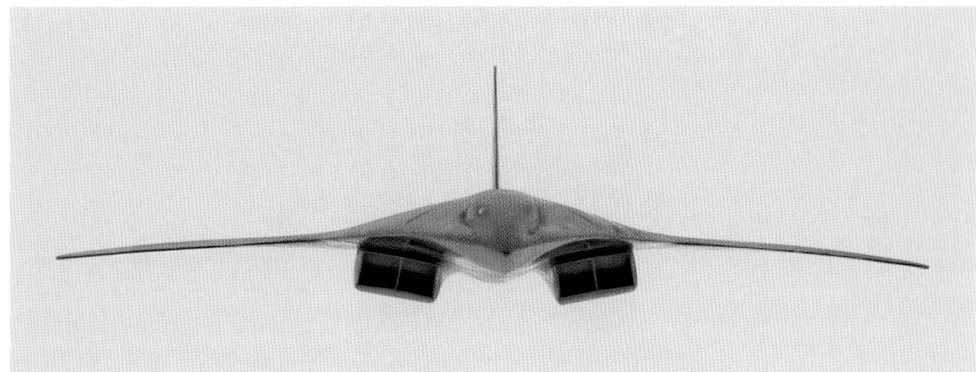

Right and centre right: Front and rear views of the Tu-160M model depicted on page 37, showing the shorter wing span.

Below right: This view shows the centrebodies in the engine nozzles, the tail cannon barbette and its ranging radar.

Below: A side view of the same model illustrating the slender silhouette.

ual and group protection in a bomber formation. This included an SPS-161 *Gher**ahn'**-F* (Geranium) active jammer (***stahn**tsiya **po**me**kh**ovykh sig-**nah**lov* – interference emitter), a *Ro**mash**ka* (Daisy) infrared missile warning system, chaff dispensers, IRCM flare launchers and a ***Li**liya* (Lily) signals intelligence pack. (*Sic* – the latter was listed in the defensive avionics suite section of the project materials for some reason.)

The targeting equipment included a PMN navigation/attack radar with a 600-km (372-mile) detection range in the nose radome and an OPB-17 optical bomb sight (*op**ti**ch**es**kiy prit-**sel** bombar**di**ro**vo**chnyy*) linked to the radar, which had a field of view of ±30° (left/right), 88° forward and 15° aft from the vertical. The Tu-160M

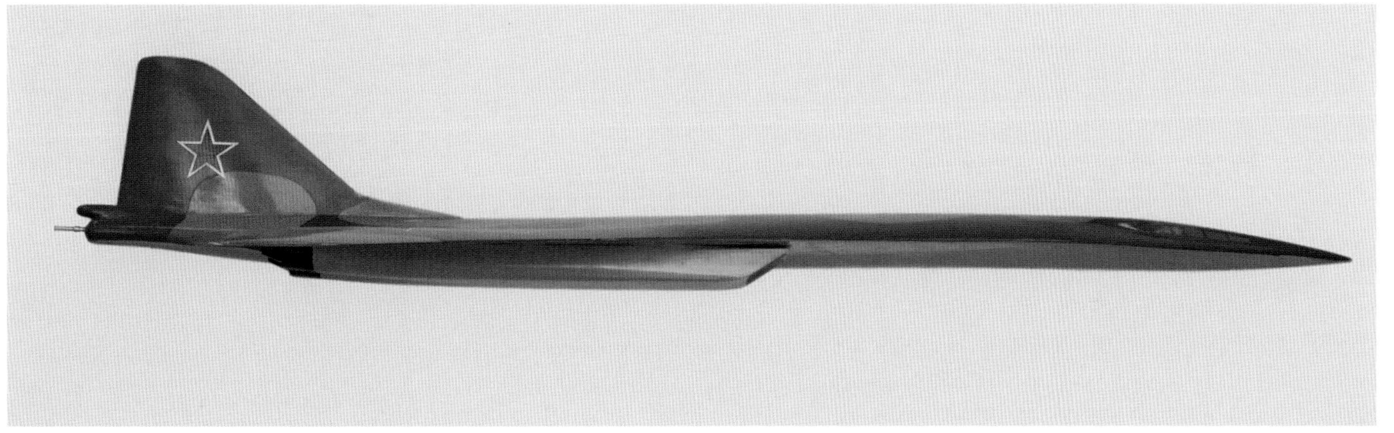

was also fitted as standard with equipment enabling it to reconnoitre targets of opportunity – namely an SRS-9 ***Virazh*** (Banked turn) signals intelligence pack (***stahntsiya razvedki svyazi*** – SIGINT set) and an Alpha radiation reconnaissance (RINT) suite capable of measuring radiation levels of 5-500 R/h. The SRS-9 detected emitters with a wavelength range of 0.8-300 cm within a sector measuring 30° in azimuth and 45° in elevation. The Alpha suite comprised a Gamma module measuring – you've guessed it – gamma radiation levels at the aircraft's own altitude and a *Vizeer* (Sighting device) module recording radiation levels on the ground.

The bomber was equipped with an NK-160 navigation suite (*navigatsionnyy kompleks*) serving the purposes of navigation and weapons application, as well as with a celestial compass. The suite included two BTsVM-72 digital processors (*bortovaya tsifrovaya vychislitel'naya mashina*), an INS (comprising three IS-I-72 inertial gyros), a DISS-II-72 *Gorizont* (Horizon) Doppler speed/drift sensor (*doplerovskiy izmeritel' skorosti i [oogla] snosa*), an RSDN-72 *Yantar'* (Amber) long-range navigation system (*rahdiotekhnicheskaya sistema dahl'ney navigahtsii* – LORAN), an Alpha-D LORAN, an RSBN-72G short-range radio navigation system (*rahdiotekhnicheskaya sistema blizhney navigahtsii* – SHORAN) and the like. The flight deck featured a PPI-II-72A head-up display (*pritsel'no-pilotazhnyy indikahtor* – 'aiming/flying sight', that is, HUD), an INTO navigation/tactical situation display (*indikahtor navigatsionno-takticheskoy obstanovki*) and other instruments. The latest identification friend-or-foe (IFF) system aptly called *Parol'* (password) was fitted.

Three mission profiles were possible. In Option 1 the entire mission would be flown in subsonic cruise mode. Option 2: after take-off the Tu-160M would climb to 9,000 m (29,530 ft) and cruise towards the target in subsonic mode at 1,000 km/h (621 mph), gradually climbing to 11,000 m (36,090 ft). About 5,500 km (3,420 miles) from the base the aircraft would climb to 20,000 m (65,620 ft) and go supersonic, accelerating to 2,500 km/h (1,552 mph) in order to avoid being engaged by the enemy air defences (including interceptors). After approaching within 500 km (310 miles) of the target the aircraft would launch the missile(s), make a U-turn and head for home, decelerating and descending to subsonic cruise altitude at about the same distance from the base. Meanwhile, the missile climbed to more than 30,000 m (98,430 ft) and cruised before commencing the terminal dive onto the target at 50 km (31 miles) range.

Option 3: after approaching within a certain range of the target the Tu-160M would descend to low altitude (100-200 m/330-660 ft) for air defence penetration at 1,000 km/h, minimising detection and intercept time. As it approached the target, the defensive avionics (ECM/electronic support measures) suite would be activated, operating ever more intensively as the Tu-160M penetrated deeper into the air defence zone. In the event of a concerted attack by several such aircraft the formation would create a strong ECM environment, reducing the risk of engagement by the enemy air defence assets.

According to the OKB's calculations, with a production run of 100 the Tu-160M would have a unit cost of 11 million roubles (in the day's prices). Increasing the number to 200 aircraft would lower the unit cost to 9 million. To put these figures into perspective, the average wages in the Soviet Union in the mid-1970s were 130 roubles.

The strategic reconnaissance version of the Tu-160M was intended to operate in the interests of the Soviet Supreme High Command and the commands of various armed services. The aircraft had a comprehensive suite of photo reconnaissance (PHOTINT) and electronic intelligence (ELINT) equipment.

In daytime PHOTINT configuration the aircraft was equipped with an AFA-70/M camera (***aerofotoapparaht*** – aerial camera), AT/10 and 2AT/10 topographic cameras, a PA-1 low-altitude camera, a Temp (Tempo, or Pace) thermal imager with a resolution of 2-3°C covering a swath whose width was equal to the flight altitude, a Shpil'-2M (Spire) laser line scan system, and Koob-3M (Cube) and SRS-11 Koob-4 detailed SIGINT packs. The latter could detect emitters with a wavelength range of 2.95-32.4 m and 30-300 m respectively at a range equalling up to seven times the flight level and determine their location with an error margin of ±5°. The Koob-3M (*izdeliye* 3M) and Virazh SIGINT sets were identical to those used on the Mikoyan MiG-25RBV *Foxbat-D* reconnaissance aircraft.

The first three types of camera covered a strip whose width was 4.6 times the flight altitude and whose length was 3,000 km (1,863 miles), the resolution being 0.4-0.6 m (1 ft 3 3/4 in to 1 ft 11 5/8 in) for the AFA-70/M producing 30 x 30 cm (11 13/16 in x 11 13/16 in) exposures and 5-7 m (16 ft 4 55/64 in to 22 ft 11 19/32 in) for the AT/10 and 2AT/20 producing 18 x 18 cm (7 29/32 in x 7 29/32 in) exposures. The PA-1 had a focal length of 28 mm and covered a 120-km (74.5-mile) strip whose width was ten times the flight altitude, with a resolution of 0.3-0.6 m (11 13/16 in to 1 ft 11 5/8 in). During overwater operations in the interests of the navy the AFA-70/M was replaced by an AFA-72 camera. The Temp had a working spectrum range of 3.8-5.6 micron in the daytime and 1.8-5.6 micron at night. The Shpil' covered a 1,000-km (621-mile) strip whose width was three times the flight altitude, with a resolution of 0.4m (1 ft 3 3/4 in).

The night PHOTINT configuration differed only in the camera fit comprising the Shpil' scanner and the 2NA-100 camera, the latter having a film capacity of 30 exposures measuring 30 x 30 cm. The OPB-17 optical bomb sight was used for aiming the cameras.

The aircraft could be equipped with a special pressurised capsule with a camera in the weapons bay. This was manned by an operator whose job was to retrieve the exposed film from the camera, develop it in an on-board automated minilab, examine it on a

Tu-160M project specifications

Length overall (including pitot)	57.145 m (187 ft 5 5/164 in)
Wing span	35.2 m (115 ft 5 53/64 in)
Wing aspect ratio:	
with LERXes	1.905
less LERXes	2.398
Wing taper:	
with LERXes	12.55
less LERXes	6.803
Height on ground	11.85 m (38 ft 10 17/32 in)
Landing gear track	8.5 m (27 ft 10 41/64 in)
Landing gear wheelbase	17.8 m (58 ft 4 25/32 in)
Wing mean aerodynamic chord (MAC)	26.23 m (86 ft 0 43/64 in)
Wing area:	
with LERXes	650 m² (6,996.54 sq ft)
less LERXes	516.7 m² (5,561.71 sq ft)
Overall area in plan view	667 m² (7,179.53 sq ft)
Wetted area	1,520 m² (16,361 sq ft)
Aggregate elevon area	50.5 m² (543.58 sq ft)
Vertical tail height above fuselage	6.32 m (20 ft 8 1/64 in)
Vertical tail aspect ratio	0.9
Vertical tail MAC (less dorsal fin)	7.85 m (25 ft 9 3/64 in)
Vertical tail area:	
with dorsal fin	44.5 m² (478.99 sq ft)
less dorsal fin	n.a.
Rudder area	10.27 m² (110.55 sq ft)
Engine nacelle length	18.5 m (60 ft 8 11/32 in)
Engine nacelle cross-section area	2 x 5.3 m² (2 x 57.05 sq ft)
Air intake cross-section area	4 x 1.55 m² (4 x 16.68 sq ft)
Operating empty weight	83,300 kg (183,640 lb)
Equipment weight	4,500 kg (9,920 lb)
Take-off weight:	
normal	n.a.
maximum	230,000 kg (507,050 lb)
Fuel load	137,800 kg (303,790 lb)
Payload	8,400/500 kg (18,520/1,100 lb) [1]
Unstick speed	362.5 km/h (225 mph)
Cruising speed:	
supersonic cruise	2,500 km/h (1,552 mph)
subsonic cruise	1,000 km/h (621 mph)
Approach speed	294 km/h (225 mph)
Normal cruise altitude:	
supersonic cruise	16,000-22,000 m (52,490-72,180 ft)
subsonic cruise	10,000-15,000 m (32,080-49,210 ft)
Air defence penetration altitude	100-200 m (330-660 ft)
Combat radius:	
on internal fuel	7,500 km (4,658 miles)
with one refuelling (outbound leg)	9,500 km (5,900 miles)
Maximum range:	
subsonic cruise (Mach 0.94)	13,000/16,000 km (8,074/9,937 miles) [4]
supersonic cruise (Mach 2.35) [2]	12,000 km (7,453 miles)
air defence penetration [3]	4,500/6,300 km (2,795/3,913 miles) [4]
Endurance:	
on internal fuel	12 hrs 30 min
with one refuelling (outbound leg)	16 hrs 30 min
Take-off run	1,340 m (4,400 ft)
Take-off distance to h=25 m (82 ft)	1,840 m (6, 040 ft)
Landing run	1,390 m (4,560 ft)
Required runway length	1,985 m (6,510 ft)

Notes:

1. Offensive weapons/cannon ordnance
2. Composite flight profile with a high-altitude stretch flown at Mach 2.35 or 2,500 km/h (1,552 mph)
3. Composite flight profile with a stretch flown at 100-200 m (330-660 ft) and Mach 0.9 or 1,000 km/h (621 mph)
4. With RD51-2 engines/with K-101 engines

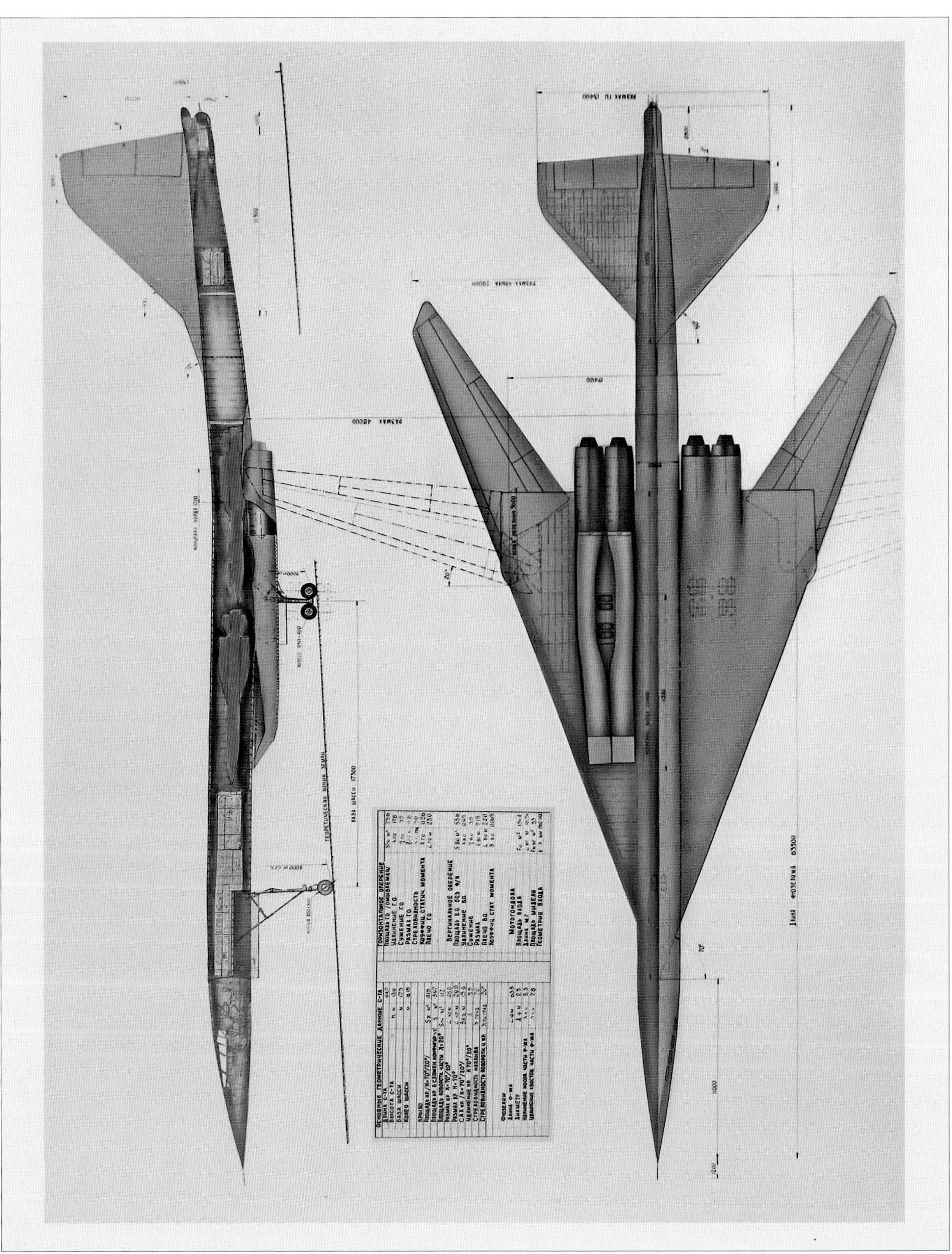

A drawing from a supplement to the Tu-160M's PD project showing a VG-wing derivative which had no proper designation. Note the outsize tail surfaces with inset rudder and elevators, the conventional wing gloves and the tandem carriage of the Kh-45 missiles.

lighted viewing table and report the results pronto so that the radio operator could relay them to ground command centres. Thus, intelligence could be analysed and reported within just 15-20 minutes, allowing the Tu-160M to reconnoitre several objectives in a single sortie. The camera was to have a focal length of 500 mm and contain 30 m (98 ft) of film, producing 30 x 30 cm exposures with a resolution of 1-2 m (3 ft 3⅜ in to 6 ft 6⁴⁷⁄₆₄ in).

In a different reconnaissance configuration the Tu-160M was to carry a pair of ***Voron*** (Raven) Mach 3 reconnaissance drones under the wings for reconnoitring heavily defended areas that were too dangerous for manned aircraft. The Voron, a.k.a. DSBR (***d****ahl'niy* ***s****amolyot* ***b****espilotnoy* ***r****azvedki* – long-range unmanned reconnaissance aircraft; no numeric OKB designation is known), was a look-alike of the Lockheed D-21 (GTD-21B) drone which shared certain design features with the famous Lockheed SR-71 Blackbird Mach 3 reconnaissance aircraft; in fact, it looked like a scaled-down SR-71 engine nacelle with wings. In 1968 or 1969 a crashed example lost over Vietnam was transferred to the Soviet Union by the North Vietnamese authorities and subjected to detailed analysis with the participation of the leading Soviet aircraft, electronics and defence industry enterprises, including the Tupolev OKB. On 19th March 1971 the Council of Ministers Presidium's Commission on Defence Industry Matters (VPK – ***V****oy-enno-****p****romyshlennaya* ***k****omissiya*) issued ruling No.57, prescribing the Tupolev OKB to develop a Soviet analogue of the D-21, making use of indigenous structural materials, engines and equipment. The drone's provisional name Voron very probably derived from the fact that the D-21 was flat black overall, being covered with a special heat-dissipating paint.

As one might imagine, the Voron was extremely similar in appearance to the D-21 – right down to the two pitot booms flanking the circular air intake with its conical centrebody (shock cone). The main external difference lay in the shape of the wings which were close to a pure delta planform, whereas those of the D-21 had large curved LERXes similar in shape to the SR-71's nose chines. As was the case with the American drone, the cameras and their film cassettes were to be housed in a special capsule which was ejected and retrieved after the drone had passed over the target. (Incidentally, this technology was nothing new to the Tupolev OKB; on the Tu-123 Yastreb supersonic reconnaissance drone built in quantity for the Soviet Air Force the entire forward fuselage housing the cameras was jettisoned and parachuted to safety over territory held by friendly troops.)

The Voron was to be powered by a 1,350-kgp (2,975-lbst) RD-012 supersonic ramjet and accelerated to ramjet ignition speed by a massive solid-propellant rocket booster attached to the underside and delivering an awesome 47,500 kgp (104,720 lbst). Dry weight was estimated as 3,450 kg (7,605 lb) and own launch weight as 6,300 kg (13,890 lb), increasing to 14,120 kg (31,130 lb) with the rocket booster; some Tupolev OKB documents give the launch weight less booster as 6,000-7,000 kg (13,230-15,430 lb). Overall length was 13.06 m (42 ft 10¹¹⁄₆₄ in), wing span was 5.8 m (19 ft 0¹¹⁄₃₂ in) and height was 2.08 m (6 ft 9⁵⁷⁄₆₄ in); wing area was 37.0 m² (397.85 sq ft). The drone was designed to cruise at 3,500-3,800 km/h (2,170-2,360 mph) and an altitude of 23,000-27,000 m (75,460-88,580 ft); maximum range was 4,600 km (2,855 miles).

The intention was to launch the drone over international waters, so that after completing the photo run the Voron would head to a "friendly nation" for recovery; for example, the drones were to reconnoitre strategic targets in the continental USA and land on Cuba! However, the Voron was destined never to enter production and service.

The shape and design of the BWB/tailless-delta version were a logical continuation of the ideas that went into the Tu-144. The chosen wing shape based on TsAGI's recommendations ensured the Tu-160M its intended multi-mode capability (subsonic cruise, low-level air defence penetration and high-altitude supersonic cruise).

The PD project of the Tu-160M was completed in 1972 and submitted to the Soviet Air Force's Scientific & Technical Committee, a body which evaluated projects of new hardware before detail design could begin and the first metal could be cut. Concurrently the committee assessed the T-4MS and M-18 projects.

That was not all. At the recommendation of TsAGI the Tupolev OKB brought out an alternative VG-wing version of the Tu-160M project in November 1971, as a supplement to the PD project. This aircraft, which did not even have a proper project designation (it was referred to in the supplement simply as "variable-geometry aircraft"), was much less related to the Tu-144; indeed, it looked more like the M-18 in its definitive version – except that it had a conventional (non-BWB) design. Nevertheless, it did share some of the Tu-160M's features, such as the drooping nose visor, the engine nacelle/air intake design with horizontal airflow control ramps, and the landing gear design (all three units retracted forward, the main bogies still stowing vertically in the engine nacelles) which gave the aircraft a strong nose-up ground angle.

As compared to the Tu-160M the VG-wing version had a much more slender fuselage (its fineness ratio was similar to that of the Tu-144), conventional tail surfaces with low-mounted stabilisers and a shorter landing gear wheelbase. The rear fuselage curved upwards like a banana at the inner wing trailing edge – not only to increase the rotation angle and prevent a tailstrike but also to raise the horizontal tail, keeping it out of the wing upwash and the influence of the exhaust jets. The flight deck was followed by a long forward avionics/equipment bay, an even longer weapons bay, a fuel tank and a short rear avionics/equipment bay.

The multi-spar wing centre section carried the engine nacelles and accommodated most of the fuel. The outer wings, which apparently were of three-spar design, had a high aspect ratio and raked tips that were not parallel to the fuselage axis at either minimum or maximum sweep; their entire trailing edge was occupied by two-section flaps and ailerons. Typically of "swing-wing" aircraft, the inboard portions of the flaps fitted inside the open-ended trailing-edge portions of the fixed inner wings – the so-called wing gloves – as the wings moved. When fully swept back for high-speed cruise, the wings had constant 72° leading-edge sweep

Provisional specifications of the unnamed VG-wing 'proto-Blackjack'	
Length overall	64.7 m (212 ft 3 15/64 in) *
Fuselage length	63.5 m (208 ft 4 in)
Wing span:	
minimum sweep (20°)	48.0 m (157 ft 5 49/64 in)
maximum sweep (72°)	29.0 m (95 ft 1 47/64 in)
Wing centre section span	17.4 m (57 ft 10 25/64 in)
Wing chord:	
root	23.4 m (76 ft 9 17/64 in)
centre section limits	5.6 m (18 ft 4 15/32 in)
tip	1.7 m (5 ft 6 59/64 in)
Wing MAC	15.9 m (52 ft 1 63/64 in)
Horizontal tail span	7.15 m (23 ft 5½ in)
Horizontal tail chord:	
root	8.23 m (27 ft 0 1/64 in)
tip	2.4 m (7 ft 10 49/64 in)
Height on ground	13.0 m (42 ft 7 13/16 in)
Landing gear track	6.15 m (20 ft 2⅛ in)
Landing gear wheelbase	17.3 m (56 ft 9 7/64 in)
Wing area:	
at minimum sweep	418 m² (4,499.31 sq ft)
at maximum sweep	397 m² (4,237.27 sq ft)
movable outer wings	112 m² (1,205.56 sq ft)
Vertical tail area (less fin fillet)	53.6 m² (576.95 sq ft)
Horizontal tail area	75.6 m² (813.75 sq ft)

* Nose visor raised/excluding pitot

from root to tip, the straight leading edge being broken only by small curved sections near the wing pivots sealing the gap with the wing gloves; at minimum sweep (in take-off/landing configuration) the outer wings had a leading-edge sweep of 20°. The wing aspect ratio at minimum sweep was 5.5.

The trapezoidal vertical tail featuring a two-section inset rudder had 45° leading-edge sweep, a small root fillet with 72° leading-edge sweep, an aspect ratio of 0.95 and a taper of 3.5. The very large horizontal tail of similar planform with two-section inset elevators had 50° leading-edge sweep, an aspect ratio of 12.8 and a taper of 3.5.

The offensive and defensive armament was the same as on the previous version; however, because of the narrow fuselage the two Kh-45 missiles were carried in tandem in the long weapons bay. The latter had only one pair of doors 11.2 m (36 ft 8 15/16 in) long ahead of the wing carry-through box – obviously in order to avoid weakening the fuselage structure too much. This suggests that the second missile was to slide forward into launch position after the first one had been launched.

According to TsAGI estimates, the 'swing-wing' version had a 15% smaller wetted area of 1,410 m² versus 1,650 m² (15,161 sq ft versus 17,741 sq ft) and a 2% greater cross-section area of 21.8 m² versus 21.3 m² (234.65 sq ft versus 229.27 sq ft), and the lift/drag ratio was broadly comparable to that of the delta-wing version, reaching 17-18 at Mach 0.8 and 7.5 at Mach 2.5-3.0. However, the most expedient operational modes were subsonic cruise at 850-1,000 km/h (527-621 mph) or Mach 0.8-0.94.

A weight comparison of the double-delta wing Tu-160M and the VG-wing version

	Tu-160M	VG-wing version
Airframe (total), kg (lb)	48,200 (106,260)	70,700 (155,860)
Wings and fuselage, kg (lb)	31,800 (70,105)	52,500 (115,740)
Vertical tail, kg (lb)	1,200 (2,645)	3,000 (6,610)
Landing gear, kg (lb)	7,200 (15,870)	7,200 (15,870)
Engine nacelles, kg (lb)	8,000 (17,640)	8,000 (17,640)
Powerplant (total), kg (lb)	19,000 (41,890)	19,000 (41,890)
Engines, kg (lb)	16,500 (36,375)	16,500 (36,375)
Fuel system, kg (lb)	1,900 (4,190)	1,900 (4,190)
Other equipment, kg (lb)	600 (1,320)	600 (1,320)
Avionics and equipment (total), kg (lb)	10,400 (22,930)	11,800 (26,010)
Hydraulics and controls, kg (lb)	3,600 (7,940)	5,000 (11,020)
Electrics and avionics, kg (lb)	4,300 (9,480)	4,300 (9,480)
Air conditioning system, kg (lb)	1,800 (3,970)	1,800 (3,970)
Crew rescue system and brake parachutes, kg (lb)	700 (1,540)	700 (1,540)
Special equipment, kg (lb)*	4,500 (9,920)	4,500 (9,920)
Crew gear, kg (lb)	1,200 (2,645)	1,200 (2,645)
Crew, kg (lb)	400 (880)	400 (880)
Engine oil, fuel residue etc., kg (lb)	800 (1,760)	800 (1,760)
Empty operating weight, kg (lb)	83,300 (183,640)	106,000 (233,690)
Payload (total), kg (lb)	146,700 (323,410)	124,000 (273,370)
Fuel, kg (lb)	137,800 (303,790)	115,100 (253,750)
Weapons, kg (lb)	8,400 (18,520) †	8,400 (18,520) †
Cannon ammunition, kg (lb)	500 (1,102)	500 (1,102)
Take-off weight, kg (lb)	230,000 (507,050)	230,000 (507,050)

* associated with the weapons system † normal load

The new layout incurred a considerable weight penalty. Quite apart from the heavy-duty wing pivot box and the wing actuators, which added 4-4.5% of the overall empty weight as compared to the delta-wing version, the long slender fuselage was subjected to considerable bending loads. This required it to be reinforced – which increased weight by a further 1.5-2%.

On the other hand, the "swing-wing" version met the range requirements in subsonic flight profiles. On the delta-wing version this was true only for a combined subsonic/supersonic flight profile. This nameless alternative project version, combined with the materials on the Sukhoi and Myasishchev projects transferred to the Tupolev OKB (see below), evolved into the present-day Tu-160 *Blackjack*.

The Summing Up

Now, let's return to the contest arena, so to say. As you can see, the three competing projects by Sukhoi, Myasishchev and Tupolev were very different – the way a greyhound is different from a Great Dane or a German shepherd, though all of them are fast dogs. The different design practices and work styles of the three OKBs inevitably had their effect on the aircraft's design (after all, the Sukhoi OKB was primarily a "fighter maker" while the other two specialised in heavy aircraft from the outset). What they did have in common was the wish to use as many new design features as possible, providing they were technically viable; this was especially true for the Sukhoi and Myasishchev projects. Here it is worth quoting the memoirs of Air Marshal (Retired) Vasiliy V. Reshetnikov who was then in the rank of Colonel-General and commanded the Soviet Air Force's strategic bomber arm (DA – ***Dahl'****nyaya avi****ah****tsiya*, Long-Range Aviation) in the 1970s:

"Since the situation with Tupolev was clear, the commission first paid a visit to Pavel Osipovich (that is, to Pavel O. Sukhoi's OKB-51 – *Auth.*). *The aircraft he proposed overwhelmed you with its unconventional aerodynamic layout; it was almost a flying wing, with enough internal volume to accommodate both the engines, the weapons load and the fuel. What took me aback at first was the unusually thick airfoil of this giant wing with its hefty leading edge; this was not my idea of a supersonic aircraft. Feeling awkward, I asked Pavel Osipovich about it. However, he was prepared for this question; he showed me the design materials and demonstrated the test results obtained in TsAGI's supersonic wind tunnel. Gradually my doubts were dispelled and the project began to look quite realistic and appealing. The thick wing with the smoothly blended curves of its contours was probably Pavel Osipovich's brainchild, and he was eager to see it materialise on a large supersonic aircraft.*

Equally interesting – and equally well thought out – was the project offered by Vladimir Mikhaïlovich Myasishchev (the M-18 – *Auth.*). *It was an elegant aircraft with a slender fuselage and a sleek, barracuda-like appearance that made it look much lighter than it really was. Oh, I would that it would have a chance to fly! As was his wont, Vladimir Mikhaïlovich, a brilliant designer with a wealth of experience in developing heavy combat aircraft, introduced many novel features into the aircraft's systems, not repeating what he had done before. The combat capabilities of this of this aircraft looked set to be among the highest in the world."*

In the autumn of 1972 the MAP's scientific and technical council convened to hear reports on the projects described above. As mentioned earlier, Tupolev's Tu-160M had been developed in several versions differing in detail. The version eventually selected for participation in the tender featured double-delta wings with a sharply kinked leading edge, as on the production Tu-144 (*izdeliye* 004). This proved fatal; the MAP and Air Force top brass knew the Tu-144 well enough and the aircraft had quite a few opponents in high places. Thus, when the Tu-160M was unveiled the similarity was all too obvious. As a result, the Tupolev OKB project was rejected on the grounds that it "did not meet the specifications." Commenting on the Tu-160M at a session of the Air Force's Scientific & Technical Committee, Col.-Gen. Reshetnikov said that the Air Force was being offered a warmed-over airliner! The fact that an excessively high lift/drag ratio had been unintentionally quoted in the project documents certainly did not speak in the Tupolev bomber's favour either. Here's how Reshetnikov himself describes the episode in the aforementioned book: *"As we took our seats in a small conference room and examined the drawings and diagrams attached to a display stand, I was surprised to see the familiar lines of the Tu-144 supersonic airliner. Could it actually be the same aircraft? The Tu-144 fell short of its performance target, was beset by reliability problems, fuel-thirsty and difficult to operate. Moreover, there had been real disasters involving the type. The civil aviation would have no part of it..."*

(Note: While Reshetnikov correctly conveys the generally negative impression the Tu-160M project made on the military, he has mixed up the details a lot. The remark about "real disasters" must be a reference to the type's two fatal accidents (the crash of Tu-144 *sans suffixe* CCCP-77102 at Le Bourget during a demonstration flight at the 30th Paris Air Show on June 3, 1973 and the off-field crash landing of Tu-144D CCCP-77111 near Yegor'yevsk, Moscow Region, on May 25, 1978 after an in-flight fire); however, both of them occurred *after* the session where the Tu-160M was axed, which took place in 1972! Also, how would Reshetnikov know about operational difficulties with the Tu-144 when revenue services did not begin until 1975?):

"[...] Aleksey Andreyevich (Tupolev, the new General Designer – *Auth.*) *was not quite his usual self as he approached the stand, pointer in hand. His proposal boiled down to providing weapons bays for the bombs and missiles in the space between the engine packs occupying the fuselage undersurface. There is no need to relate Tupolev's discourse that followed; it was obvious that, weighed down by the offensive and defensive armament, this unsuccessful airliner-turned-bomber would be robbed of whatever structural strength reserves it had and all performance characteristics would drop.*

About five or ten minutes later I rose and, cutting the lecture short, stated that we were not going to consider the project any longer because, even in revamped condition, an aircraft originally designed for carrying passengers would still retain some inherent properties which were absolutely unnecessary for a combat aircraft while still not meeting the demands applying to a strategic bomber.

Apparently Aleksey Andreyevich was prepared for this outcome. Without saying a word he turned towards the largest dia-

gram pinned in the middle of the stand, grasped it and tore it down with a jerk. The sharp crack of heavy paper being rent asunder resounded in the complete silence. Then he faced me again and apologised, adding that he would invite us again when a new PD project would be ready."

Here it would be appropriate to quote another excerpt from Reshetnikov's book explaining who in reality was behind the Tupolev OKB's failed attempt to foist the unwanted airliner on the military (in their opinion):

"However, Aleksey Andreyevich was not to blame in this incident. The development and construction of the supersonic airliner, the future Tu-144, was included in the five-year economic development plan and was under the auspices of the influential D. F. Ustinov (Marshal Dmitriy F. Ustinov was then the Soviet Minister of Defence – *Auth.*) *who regarded this mission as a personal responsibility – not so much to his country and people but rather to 'dear Leonid Il'yich'* (Brezhnev, the head of state – *Auth.*) *whom he literally worshipped – sometimes to the point of adulation...*

Yet the supersonic passenger jet was apparently not making headway and, to the dismay of its curator, it looked like Brezhnev might be disappointed. It was then that Dmitriy Fyodorovich jumped at someone's bright idea to foist Aeroflot's 'bride in search of a wedding' on the military. After it had been rejected in bomber guise, Ustinov used the VPK to promote the aircraft to the Long-Range Aviation as a reconnaissance or ECM platform – or both. It was clear to me that these aircraft could not possibly work in concert with any bomber or missile carrier formations; neither could I imagine them operating solo as 'Flying Dutchmen' in a war scenario, therefore I resolutely turned down the offer.

Naval Aviation Commander Aleksandr Alekseyevich Mironenko, with whom I had always worked in close co-operation, followed suit.

Nothing doing! Ustinov would not be put off that easily. He managed to persuade the Navy C-in-C [Admiral] Sergey G. Gorshkov who agreed to accept the Tu-144 for Naval Aviation service as a long-range maritime reconnaissance aircraft without consulting anyone on the matter. Mironenko rebelled against this decision, but the Commander-in-Chief wouldn't hear or heed – the issue is decided, period. On learning of this I was extremely alarmed: if Mironenko had taken the Tu-144, this meant I was going to be next. I made a phone call to Aleksandr Alekseyevich, urging him to take radical measures; I needn't have called because even without my urging Mironenko was giving his C-in-C a hard time. Finally Ustinov got wind of the mutiny and summoned Mironenko to his office. They had a long and heated discussion but eventually Mironenko succeeded in proving that Ustinov's ideas were unfounded. That was the last we heard of the Tu-144."

Now we go back to the tender again. Sukhoi's T-4MS drew a very favourable reaction from the military and attracted a lot of attention. Myasishchev was less lucky; his M-18 project was highly commended (the commission stated it was carefully designed and met the Air Force's specifications) but nonetheless rejected because the recently reborn OKB lacked the necessary technological assets and manufacturing facilities for prototype construction. Plant No.23 (the OKB's former experimental production facility) in Fili, an area in the western part of Moscow, had been transferred to Vladimir N. Chelomey's OKB and was now busy producing missiles; at the Myasishchev OKB's new premises in Zhukovskiy south-east of Moscow there was little more than a flight test facility, which meant the M-18 prototypes could not be manufactured there.

Interestingly, in the numerous press articles and books on Myasishchev OKB history that have appeared in recent years Myasishchev spokesmen and executives invariably call the M-18 the official winner of the 1972 tender. In reality, the winner was apparently never announced officially but appropriate remarks on the projects and the advisability of further proceeding with them were made in the protocols of the tendering commission. These protocols were followed by Council of Ministers directives (backed up by appropriate MAP orders) which tasked the Tupolev OKB with the multi-mode strategic missile carrier programme. The minutes of the tendering commission and the final ruling of same are still classified, which puts both the Sukhoi and Myasishchev bureaux into a position to interpret the results of the tender as they see fit.

The long and short of it was that the Sukhoi OKB was declared the winner. This OKB had accumulated some experience of heavy aircraft construction and testing with the T-4 (*izdeliye* 100). Again, however, the Sukhoi OKB was not in a position to build even the T-4MS prototype at its experimental facility, MMZ No.51, which was overburdened with other work. To enable construction of the prototype (and subsequent production T-4MS aircraft) the Kazan' aircraft factory (MAP factory No.22, one of the Soviet Union's two principal factories producing heavy bombers) had to be assigned to the Sukhoi OKB. Nobody in the industry wanted to see it happen except Sukhoi themselves. Besides, the OKB had its hands full, being tasked with developing the new T-10 advanced multi-role tactical fighter (which emerged as the famous Su-27 *Flanker*) and creating new versions of the Su-17M *Fitter-C* fighter-bomber and Su-24 *Fencer* tactical bomber. An involvement with heavy bombers jeopardised all these important programmes.

The final session of the tendering commission was summed up by Soviet Air Force C-in-C Air Marshal Pavel S. Kutakhov: *"Look here* – he said, – *let's see it this way. Yes, the Sukhoi OKB's project is the best, we have given it due credit, but remember that the OKB is already heavily involved with the Su-27 fighter which we need badly. Therefore let's resolve the matter this way: we'll acknowledge that the Sukhoi OKB has won the tender and then order it to transfer all project materials to the Tupolev OKB so that the latter can proceed further with the project..."* It was similarly recommended that the Myasishchev OKB hand over the M-18 project materials to Tupolev – who, so to say, only had to wait until the fruit was ripe and then pick it.

There you are. To quote a famous phrase from Kurt Vonnegut's book *Slaughterhouse Five*, so it goes. "Frustrating" is too colourless a word to describe how it feels to win and then have your victory stolen in this fashion. And the more appropriate words are unprintable ones.

Later, however, the Tupolev OKB rejected the T-4MS project (but not the M-18 project!) and continued working on a VG-wing strategic strike aircraft of predominantly aluminium construction which ultimately became the Tu-160.

Chapter 2

The Bomber Takes Shape

After the final session of the tendering commission where the crucial decisions concerning the new-generation Soviet strategic bomber were taken the Tupolev OKB started designing a new version of the Tu-160 (the M suffix had been dropped by then) featuring variable geometry wings; fixed-sweep configurations were not considered anymore. The aircraft now bore the in-house designation *izdeliye* 70; there have been claims that the product code was purposely chosen to reflect the year when the Tu-160 programme started (1970).

In 1972, the Tupolev OKB launched a large-scale R&D programme aimed at optimising the aerodynamic layout, powerplant and various parameters of the future aircraft, selecting the proper structural materials and manufacturing technologies, and integrating the avionics and armament into a close-knit complex. The OKB's partners in this effort included TsAGI, the Flight Research Institute named after Mikhail M. Gromov (LII – ***Lyot**no-**issle**dovatel'skiy insti**toot***), the State Research Institute of Aircraft Systems (GosNII AS – *Gosu**dar**stvennyy na**ooch**no-**issle**dovatel'skiy insti**toot** aviatsi**on**nykh sis**tem***), the All-Union Research Institute of Aviation Materials (VIAM – *Vsesoy**ooz**nyy insti**toot** aviatsi**on**nykh materi**ah**lov*), the Research Institute of Aviation Hardware (NIAT – *Na**ooch**nyy insti**toot** aviatsi**on**noy **tekh**niki*), the Moscow Institute of Electrotechnics and Automatic Systems (MIEA – *Mos**kov**skiy insti**toot** elektro**tekh**niki i avto**mah**tiki*, formerly NII-923; not to be confused with MIREA – the Moscow Institute of Radio Equipment and Automatic Systems!), MKB Raduga, NPO Trood (*na**ooch**no-proiz**vod**stvennoye obye**din**eniye* – 'Labour' Scientific & Production Association), the Leningrad Electric Automatic Devices Design Bureau (LKBE – *Lenin**grah**dskoye kon**strook**torskoye by**uro** e**lek**troavto**mah**tiki*) and other

This wooden desktop model gives an idea of how the future Tu-160 was to look in its ultimate project form.

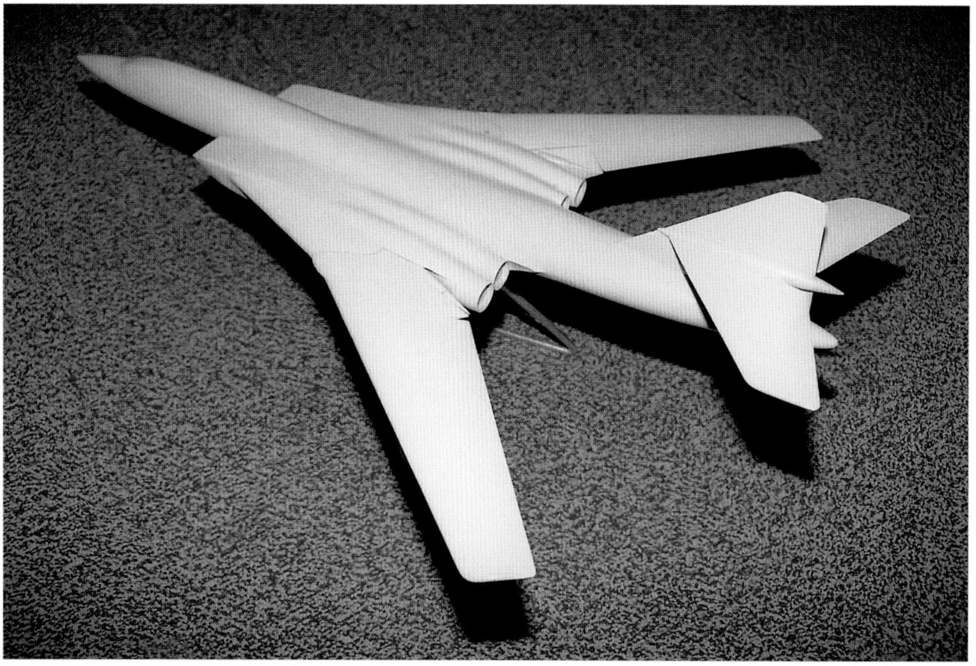

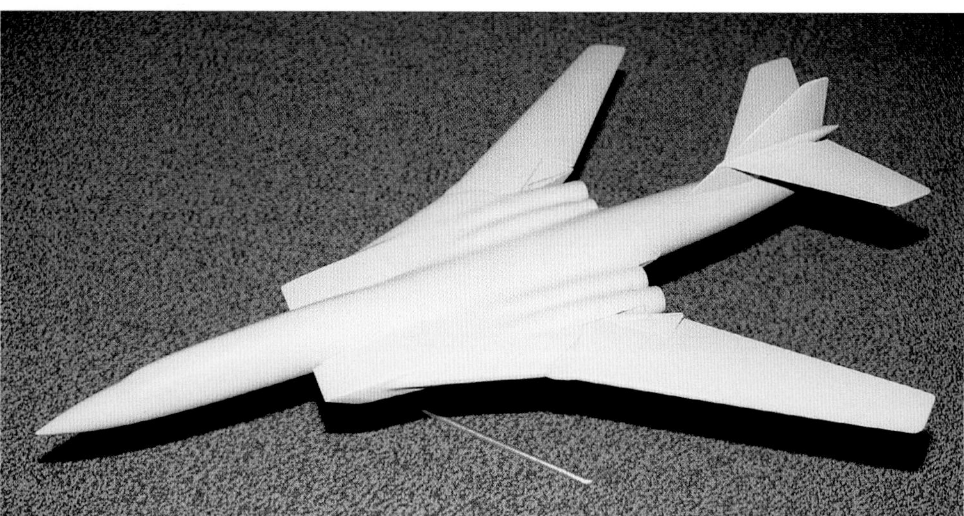

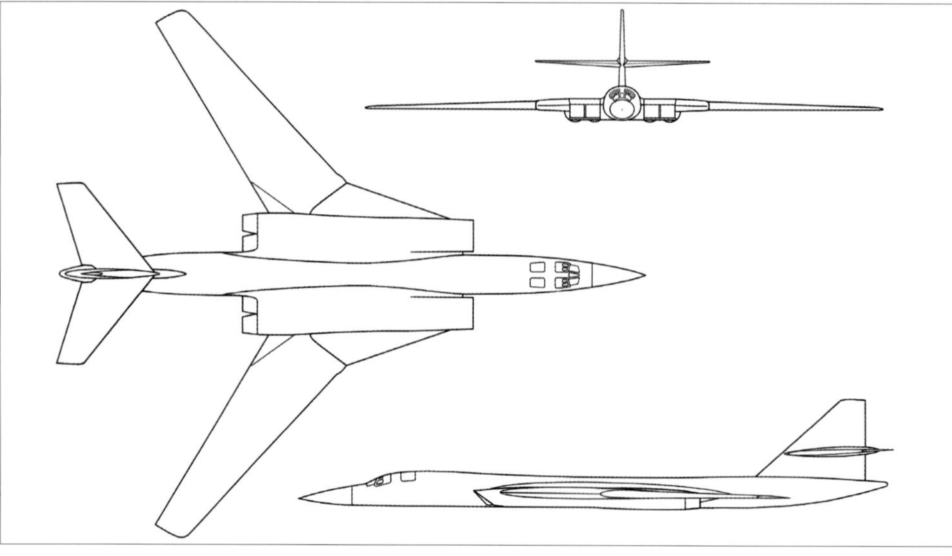

Soviet aircraft industry and defence industry enterprises. Assistance was also provided by the Soviet Air Force's own R&D organisations.

All in all, close to 800 enterprises and institutions working in various areas were involved in the Tu-160 programme which proceeded under the overall supervision of General Designer Aleksey A. Tupolev. The actual design effort and subsequent prototype construction were directly led by the Tu-160's project chief Valentin I. Bliznyuk and his aides Lev N. Bazenkov and Aleksandr L. Pookhov.

TsAGI, which traditionally maintained close ties with the Tupolev OKB, played a vital role at the initial stage of the 'swing-wing' bomber's development. The honour goes first and foremost to TsAGI's then-Director Gheorgiy P. Svishchev and the prominent aerodynamicist Gheorgiy S. Büschgens who were awarded the State Prize in 1975 in recognition of their contribution to the Tu-160 programme.

A special responsibility rested with GosNII AS, the main Soviet establishment which determined the general outlook of the new weapons system. Since 1969, the institute headed by Academician Yevgeniy A. Fedosov had been working on the technical concept of the new multimode strategic strike aircraft, analysing the main parameters and assessing the efficiency of the various project versions proposed by the competing design bureaux. Concurrently the subdivisions of GosNII AS substantiated the bomber's weapons fit and avionics/equipment complement. The work was done by B. P. Toporov, O. S. Korotin, G. K. Kolosov, A. M. Zherebin, Yu. A. Volkov and other employees of the institute.

After the tendering commission ruled that the Tupolev OKB should take over the new-generation strategic bomber programme, GosNII AS began developing the Tu-160's technical outlook and performing combat efficiency studies. As a result, the ultimate choice of the VG layout for

Left and below left: A desktop model of an interim project configuration of the Tu-160 (*izdeliye* 70) called Version 6B in the text. Note the engine nacelles flanking the fuselage, the Tu-144 style raked air intakes, the triangular root portions of the flaps which fold down to form wing fences at maximum sweep (here the wings are at an intermediate setting) and the pointed tailcone with no cannon installation.

Bottom left: A provisional three-view of Version 6B.

Right and above right: Two more views of the same model.

the Tu-160 was largely influenced by the expert opinion of GosNII AS founded mainly on calculations and analysis by the institute's Section 1.

From 1972 onwards, GosNII AS provided scientific and technical support of the Tu-160's PD project development. Anticipating the large amount of work to be done on heavy bombers, in August 1974, Yevgeniy A. Fedosov drew resources from several of the institute's departments and laboratories to create a new division, Section 14. Headed by Vladimir I. Chervin, this department was directly responsible for the development of airborne strategic strike systems. Due to the fact that this area of work was led by Fedosov himself, Section 14 quickly grew from a 60-man team to the largest research department within the GosNII AS structure, with a 290-strong staff and the best-equipped laboratories; the Tu-160 programme was its bread-and-butter project. By then Section 14 had moved into new premises specially built with the Tu-160 programme in mind. The staff started outfitting the new laboratory halls and mastering the new equipment; the work often proceeded in three shifts due to the pressure of time.

For the first time ever the staff of Section 14 had to deal with such challenges as exactly aligning the axes of a cruise missile's inertial navigation system (INS) with those of the carrier aircraft's INS, downloading a digital route map from the aircraft to the missile via data link, preparing the missile's automatic flight control system for launch and controlling the launch of missiles from internal bays and external hardpoints. Together with the institute's Section 5 headed by K. A. Sarychev, the algorithms of an autonomous correlation-extreme missile guidance system were developed, flight test results were analysed and so on.

In 1968–70, Section 5 – then under the direction of Vladimir I. Chervin – undertook the ***Ekho*** (Echo) R&D programme which culminated in a proposal to develop reasonably simple and affordable long-range cruise missiles with nuclear warheads. Given their small size and the ability to fly nap-of-the-earth at ultra-low levels

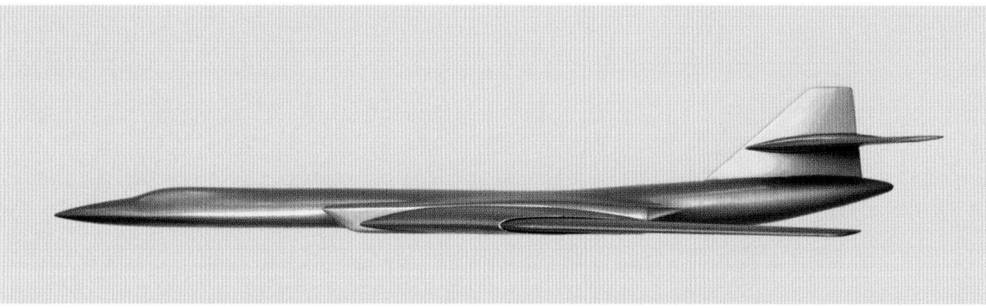

(making them hard to detect), such missiles could penetrate enemy air defences effectively and hit the targets with deadly accuracy. The idea crystallised long before the USA had begun developing strategic cruise missiles, but the Soviet military leaders were not interested at the time, citing the missiles' "low performance" as the reason. Serious research in this field at GosNII AS began only in 1975, when alarming news of ALCMs being fielded by the USA started coming in – and then, figuratively speaking, the Soviet researchers had to run hell-for-leather, working hard to complete development within the shortest possible time. This sure took a maximum of effort. Everyone in the industry was aware that the success (or failure) of the strategic weapons system built around the Tu-160 depended heavily on the work done by GosNII AS.

Gheorgiy P. Svishchev, Yevgeniy A. Fedosov, Konstantin K. Vasil'chenko at LII (he later became the institute's director in 1985), VIAM Director Radiy Ye. Shalin, MKB Raduga Chief Designer Igor' S. Seleznyov, MIEA Director Sergey P. Kryukov and other prominent Soviet researchers and designers did a lot to pinpoint the main problems associated with the Tu-160 programme and see them resolved.

Due to its importance and complexity the new multi-mode strategic

Top left, centre left, above left and left: Despite its obvious similarity to the model on pages 54-55, this is a different model (Version 6A). Note the different wing/nacelle junction, the wing gloves instead of wing fences and the slightly curved fuselage. Note also the low visual signature in a head-on view.

Top right: Rear view of the same model with the wings at maximum sweep.

Above right: Upper view of Version 6A with the wings at minimum sweep.

Right: A three-view of Version 6A.

strike aircraft programme enjoyed top priority with MAP. It was closely monitored by the Ministry's head – Pyotr V. Dement'yev (he remained in office until 1977), then his successor Vasiliy A. Kazakov (1977–81) and later still Ivan S. Silayev. Various aspects of the work were supervised by the Vice-Ministers of Aircraft Industry – Anoofriy V. Bolbot headed the Tu-160 programme co-ordination council, Yuriy A. Zateykin (Chief of MAP's 9th Main Directorate) and Yuriy A. Bardin co-ordinated the development of the bomber's avionics, and Vladimir T. Ivanov (Chief of MAP's 6th Main Directorate responsible for heavy aircraft) was also involved on a daily basis. Ghenrikh B. Stroganov at MATI headed the central board for technological support of the Tu-160's production entry.

Now let's get down to the meat and potatoes. What did the new version of the Tu-160 look like from a design standpoint? Basically it resembled a cross-breed between the Tu-160M's nameless "swing-wing" derivative of 1971, and the M-18's ultimate version with the addition of new features not present in either of the projects.

The choice of general arrangement and aerodynamic features was dictated by the GOR and the concept; it was also influenced a lot by structural design and manufacturing technology issues, the designers making use of their previous experience with heavy aircraft. According to the Tupolev OKB, from a design ideology standpoint the Tu-160 was the Tu-22M, Tu-95 *Bear* and Tu-144 all rolled into one; that is, it shared the *Backfire*'s VG wings giving the requisite multi-mode capability, the *Bear*'s high aspect ratio wings giving a high lift/drag ratio and hence long range in cruise mode, and elements of the *Charger*'s wing/fuselage integration with large LERXes. (Actually, the BWB design was not used on the Tu-144, which had a conventional circular-section fuselage mated to sharp-edged LERXes – rather different from the Tu-160 with its smoothly

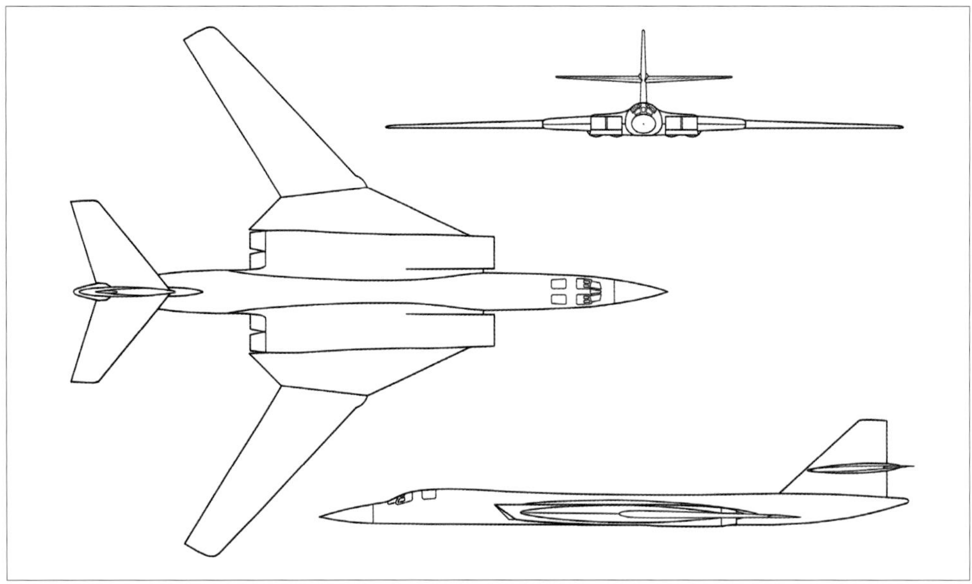

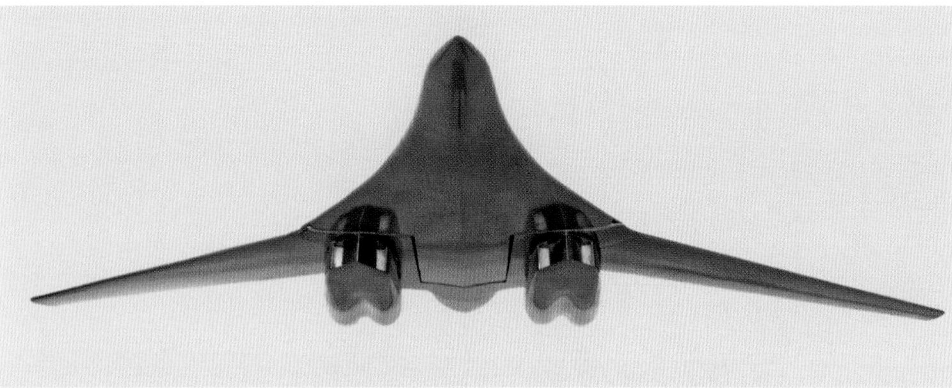

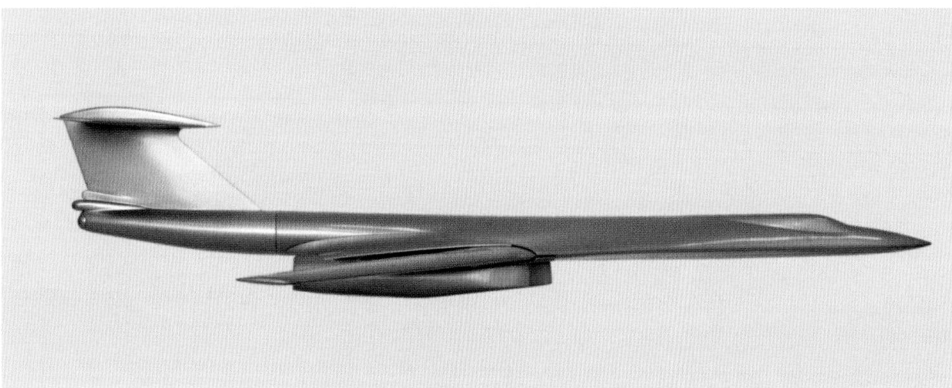

The model depicted on this page represents the T-tailed Version 3 with the wings at the intermediate setting. Note the bulged flight deck roof, the tail cannon installation and the modular design allowing different models to be assembled from interchangeable parts.

blended contours and rounded LERX leading edges.) This allowed the designers to kill three birds with one stone, making the structure very lightweight for its size while creating additional lift and providing large internal volumes for weapons and fuel. As a result, the Tu-160 was 50% heavier than the similarly sized Tu-95 thanks to a higher payload. Moreover, the avionics and equipment of the future Tu-160 were standardised to a considerable degree with those of the Tu-22M3 *Backfire-C* and Tu-95MS *Bear-H* when these aircraft made their appearance in the mid-/late 1970s.

The fuselage design was altered considerably as compared to the 1971 project. The shape and cross-sections were optimised to reduce drag; in particular, the banana-like curvature in side elevation was soon eliminated thanks to a redesign of the tail unit (see below) and the rear fuselage was made wider, with a quasi-elliptical section instead of a circular one. The forward fuselage was simplified – the designers rejected the Tu-144 style drooping nose visor tipped with a conical radome, settling for a conventional fixed nosecone and a stepped windshield giving the pilots a good field of view, in similar manner to the M-18 and the B-1. However, the shape of the nose in general, and the flight deck glazing in particular, differed from both of these aircraft – in fact, it was much closer to that of the Tu-22M: the sharply raked windshield consisted of an optically-flat trapezoidal centre panel tapering towards the bottom and two curved side quadrants. The entire lower half of the sharply pointed unpressurised nosecone was a large dielectric radome with a distinctive *Backfire*-style slightly bulged shape. On the other hand, access to the flight deck was from below (via a pressure door in the nosewheel well and a passage through an avionics bay), not via Tu-22M style individual upward-opening canopy doors. To minimise fuselage cross-section area the nosewheel well was placed aft of the flight deck, as in the original project (rather than below it, as on the B-1).

One fuselage-related issue which took quite a while to resolve was the location of the weapons bays. At first the designers wanted to place the two bays side by side in the centre fuselage, as on the Tu-160M; this minimised centre of gravity (CG) travel when bombs were dropped or missiles launched. However, this arrangement increased the fuselage cross-section area (and hence drag) too much and complicated engine nacelle design. Hence it was abandoned in favour of tandem bays located fore and aft of the wing pivot box. This, incidentally, was the main reason why the nacelles were placed under the outer extremities of the integral wing centre section – the designers needed to free the fuselage centreline for the weapons bays which had to be as close to the CG as possible. Unlike the nameless 1971 project version, the two bays were separate, each with its own pair of doors, and had identical dimensions.

The wing design of the Tu-160 (*izdeliye* 70) – specifically, the movable outer wings, their pivots and actuators – was generally similar to that of Tupolev's first "swing-wing" aircraft, the Tu-22M bomber. However, the new aircraft was a lot larger (the maximum all-up weight was more than twice as high!); this and the much higher aerodynamic loads required major structural changes and the provision of more powerful actuators. The outer wings were of five-spar construction (versus three-spar construction on the *Backfire*), each wing featuring seven chemically milled skin panels with integral stiffeners (three above and four below) and only six (!) ribs. They were hinged to a hefty wing pivot box carry-through unit – a hollow welded titanium structure which the entire airframe was effectively built around; the pivot box absorbed all the principal loads acting on the aircraft. Manufacturing such a large titanium structure was made possible by an unusual technology – electron beam

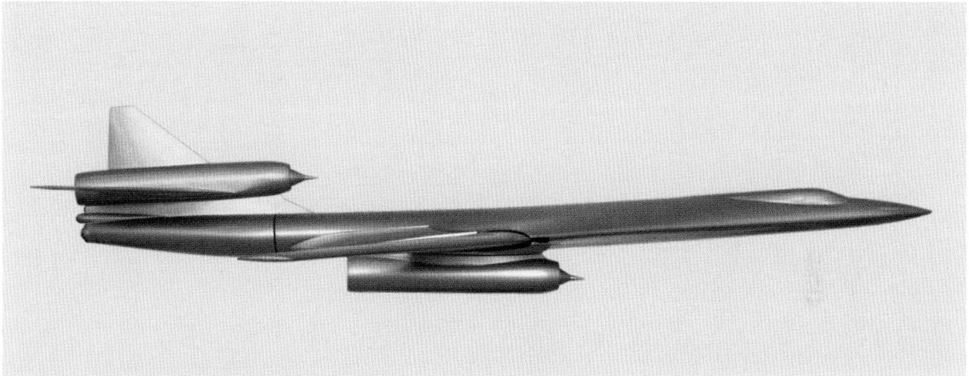

Four views of a model sharing the same forward/centre fuselage and wings which depicts Version 4 with three larger engines, a cruciform tail and a cannon barbette. The aircraft appears weighed down by the huge pylon-mounted engine pods. The rear fuselage has an elliptical cross-section.

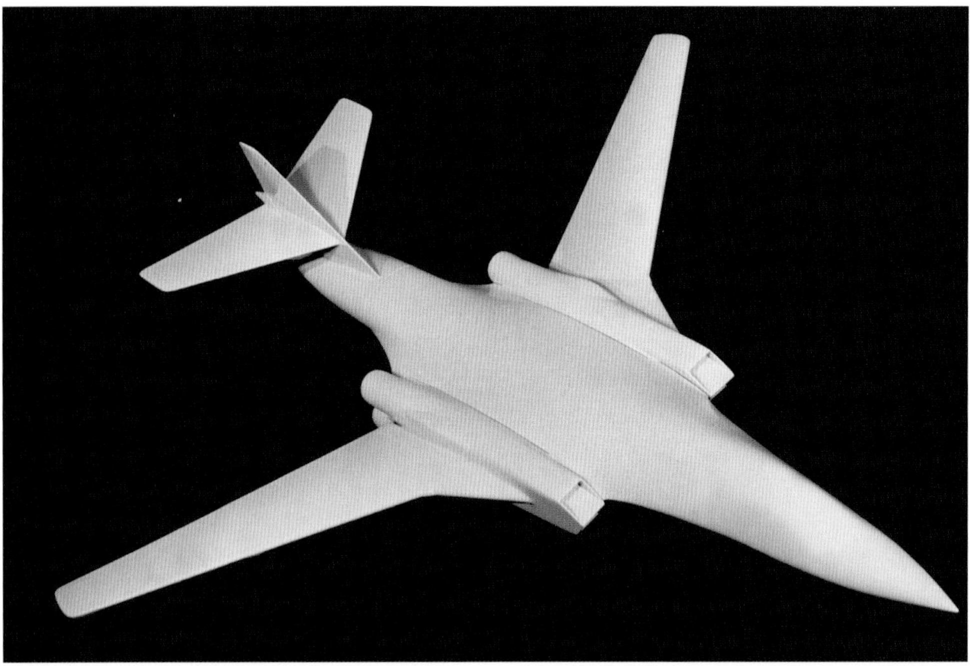

welding (EBW) in an inert gas environment; this technology, which was developed for the Tu-144, remains unique to this day and can be justly regarded as Russian know-how.

Still, designing variable geometry wings and wing pivots for such a heavy aircraft proved to be a major challenge. Using VG wings on a strategic bomber required a qualitatively new level of manufacturing technology. This brought into existence a special State Programme of New Metallurgy Technology Development co-ordinated by the then Minister of Aircraft Industry Pyotr V. Dement'yev.

The wing geometry changed at this point of the design process. The centre section built integrally with the fuselage received a curved leading edge with a sweepback reduced from 72° to 60° at the tips; this was different from the M-18, which had constant leading-edge sweep from root to tip when the wings were fully swept back. The outer wings' leading-edge sweep at minimum setting remained unchanged at 20° but the maximum setting was again reduced from 72° to 65° (as on the Tu-22M3), thus creating an odd-looking leading-edge kink "in the wrong direction" at maximum sweep. There was also a third setting for subsonic cruise flight – 35°, which just happened to be the traditional wing sweep angle of Tupolev aircraft. We will return to the subject of wing design shortly.

Another area where the engineers found themselves in a tight spot – quite literally – was the tail unit. The conventional tail unit of the 1971 project version, and the M-18 was soon rejected because of the low-set stabilisers' unfavourable interaction with the efflux of the engines, which were placed close to the fuselage. Also, in both of these projects the tail surfaces were excessively large and heavy. The first thing to do was to raise the horizontal tail so that it would be well clear of the jet exhaust. The big question was, how high? For a while the designers considered a T-tail which the OKB had used on the

Opposite page: Three views of a different (but likewise modular) model representing Version 7 with vertically paired engines whose inlet ducts passed above and below the wing pivot box; the front view shows the horizontal intake ramps. There is no defensive armament.

Here the same model has been reconfigured to show Version 5 with the wings at minimum sweep. It differs from Version 4 in having longer engine nacelles (those of the Nos. 1 and 3 engines passing through the wings rather than below them), a large fin root fillet under the No.2 engine nacelle and (though it is not obvious here) no cannon barbette.

Another model depicting Version 8A which combined the vertically paired engines of Version 7 with the intake design of Versions 1-3 and spiral inlet ducts. Note the scimitar-shaped LERXes (making an interesting comparison with Versions 1-3), the large fin fillet and the strongly tapered stabilators.

Tu-134 *Crusty* twin-turbofan short-haul airliner and the Tu-154; placing the stabilisers atop the fin would increase the rudder's efficiency while allowing the vertical tail to be downsized. However, the T-tail layout had its own problems, including higher structural weight and elevator authority issues at high angles of attack. Hence the designers settled for a cruciform tail unit with the stabilisers located at one-third of the fin's height. Then there was the problem of how to provide sufficient control authority while keeping the size and weight of the tail surfaces to a minimum. A vertical tail with a rudder divided into upper and lower sections (as on the B-1 – or some Soviet jet fighters, such as the Mikoyan/Gurevich MiG-15 *Fagot*) was considered at first. Soon, however, an unconventional arrangement was chosen – a cruciform tail unit with mid-set stabilators and a vertical tail having an all-movable upper half. This provided enough room for the hefty upper fin and stabilator pivots and the extremely powerful electrohydraulic actuators inside the fixed lower portion of the fin, despite the relatively thin airfoils (to work the large control surfaces the actuators were required to develop a force of around 7,000 kgf, or 15,430 lbf).

The landing gear was another design aspect where the M-18 project had an influence. As already mentioned, the definitive M-18 had four main gear units with four-wheel bogies, two of which retracted into the engine nacelles and the other two into the centre fuselage. However, this (and the very idea of stowing the main gear in the engine nacelles) was deemed excessively complicated and space-consuming. Therefore the Tupolev OKB designers limited

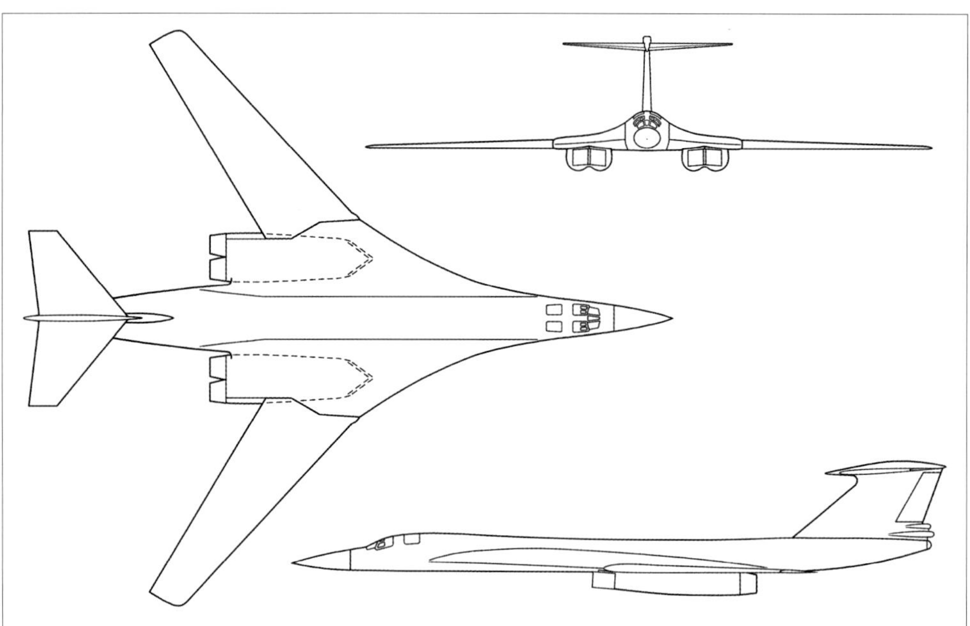

A provisional three-view drawing of the Tu-160's Version 3.

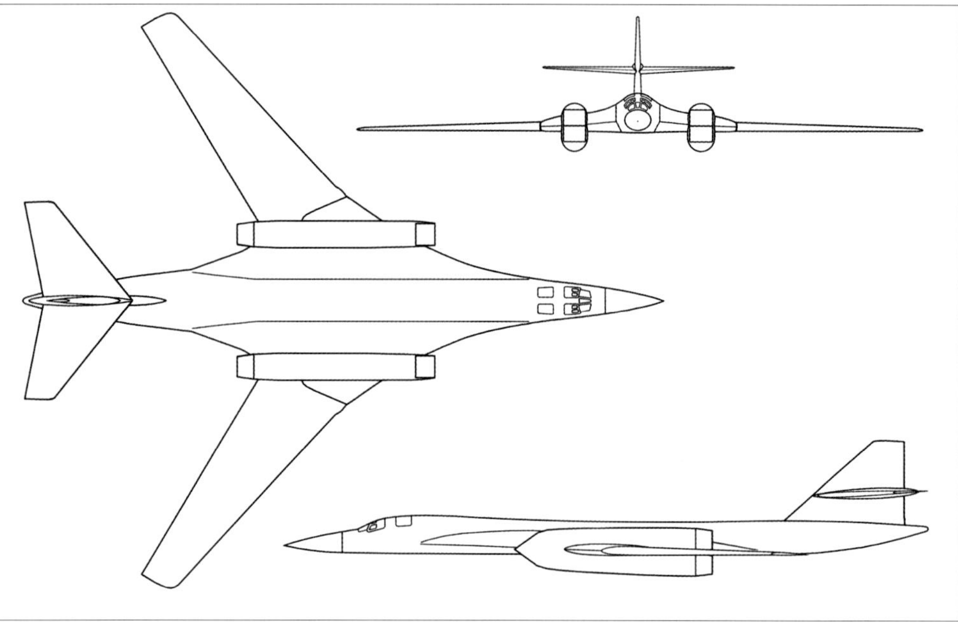

A provisional three-view drawing of Version 7.

the number of the Tu-160's main gear units to two, providing them with six-wheel bogies to ensure an adequately large footprint and cater for the aircraft's weight. The bogies had a simple design patterned on that of the Tu-154 (three pairs of wheels in tandem) – none of the Tu-22M's complexities where the bogie consisted of two articulated halves and had a telescopic centre axle increasing the track of the second pair of wheels. The project envisaged 1,350 x 440 mm (53.15 x 17.32 in) mainwheels; later the wheel size was slightly reduced on the actual aircraft. The main gear units were located immediately inboard of the engine nacelles, leaving the latter unencumbered with the landing gear. Typically of Tupolev's post-war aircraft, the main units retracted aft, the bogies somersaulting by means of mechanical linkages in so doing to lie inverted in the wheel wells. On the Tu-160, however, the oleo struts had a cunning design with double transverse hinges that allowed the bogies to move outward 0.6 m (1 ft 11⅝ in) during extension, maximising the rather narrow landing gear track. During retraction the main units contracted to fold into the smallest possible space.

The nose gear unit with twin 1,080 x 400 mm (42.5 x 15.7 in) wheels was redesigned to retract aft instead of forward and shortened (just like on the M-18), thereby eliminating the nose-up ground attitude. A retractable twin-wheel tail bumper similar to that found on most versions of the Tu-95 was envisaged to protect the rear fuselage in the event of overrotation; eventually, however, it was deemed unnecessary.

The powerplant was another important issue. Neither of the engines envisaged originally (the RD51-2 and the K-101) reached the hardware stage, and the Tupolev OKB had to look for other suitable engines. The Kuznetsov NK-25 three-spool afterburning turbofan (OKB-276 in-house designation *izdeliye* Ye), which

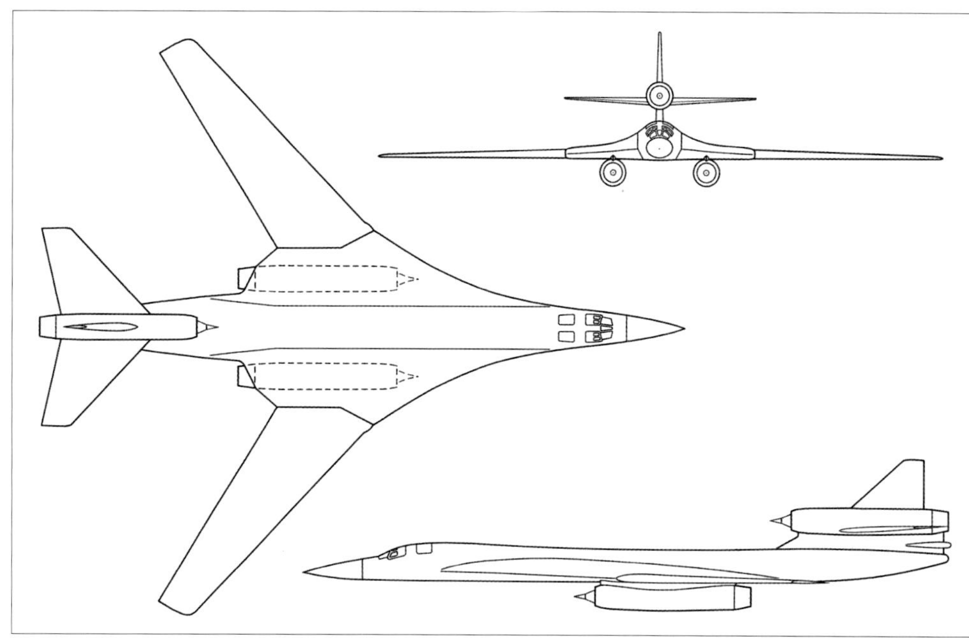

A provisional three-view drawing of Version 4.

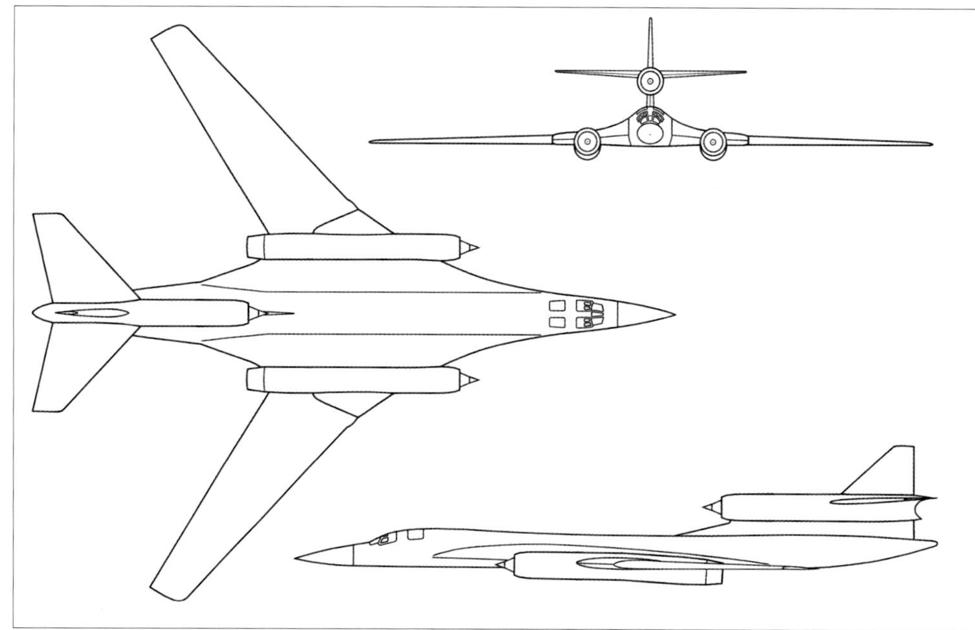

A provisional three-view drawing of Version 5. Note the high-set stabilators with respect to the No.2 engine nacelle (versus the low-set stabilators of Version 4) and the curious shape of the centre engine nozzle.

powered the Tu-22M3, came into consideration first; it met the thrust requirements, delivering 14,300 kgp (31,525 lbst) dry and 25,000 kgp (55,115 lbst) reheat, and four such engines would give the Tu-160 the required thrust/weight ratio. However, the NK-25's SFC was much too high (2.08 kg/kgp·hr at take-off power), making intercontinental range impossible even if the bomber had ideally refined aerodynamics. It was then that OKB-276 started work on a new three-spool afterburning turbofan, the NK-32 (*izdeliye* R). Possessing an identical thrust in full afterburner and a slightly lower dry thrust of 13,000 kgp (28,660 lbst), the new engine was expected to have an agreeable SFC of 0.72-0.73 kg/kgp·hr in subsonic cruise and 1.7 kg/kgp·hr in supersonic cruise. (Later the engine's dry thrust was increased to 14,000 kgp/30,860 lbst.) The NK-32 had considerable structural commonality with the production NK-25, which made it a realistic option.

Since the NK-32 had an air starter, a TA-6A auxiliary power unit (***too**rboagre**gaht*** – 'turbo unit') was provided for engine starting. This APU developed by the Stoopino Machinery Design Bureau (SKBM – ***S**toopinskoye **k**onstrooktorskoye **b**yuro **m**ashi-**n**ostroyeniya*), now called NPO *Aero**sila*** ('Aeropower' Research & Production Association), was a proven item that had already found use on many Soviet commercial and military aircraft, including the Tu-154 and the Tu-22M.

Earlier, when the Tu-144 (*izdeliye* 044) was being developed, the designers had run into problems with powerplant integration – the NK-144 engines 'didn't get along' with the air intakes designed by the Tupolev OKB, being prone to surging at take-off power. Now, learning from experience, the airframers and the engine makers worked in close co-operation from the start, developing the Tu-160's powerplant and everything that went with it – the

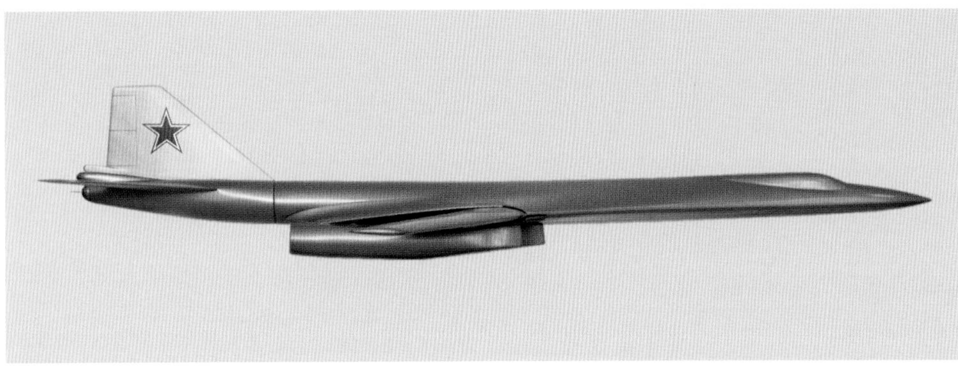

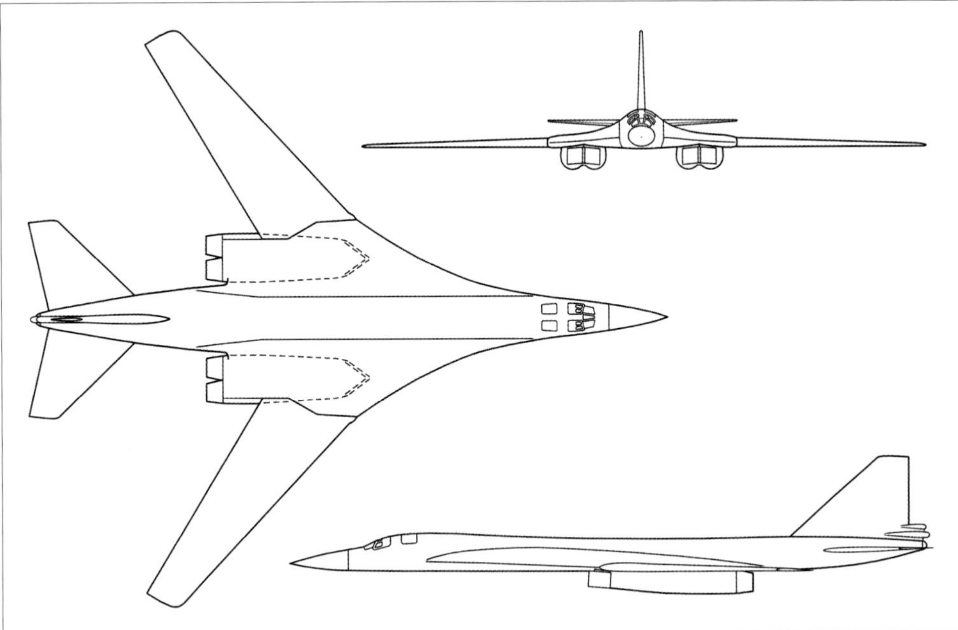

Top and centre: The modular model shown on pages 58-59 is seen here reconfigured to depict Version 1. Note the two-section rudder.

Above: A provisional three-view drawing of Version 1.

Top right: The same model configured as Version 2 with a cruciform tail and a cannon barbette.

Above right: A provisional three-view drawing of Version 2.

Right: A provisional three-view drawing of Version 8A.

engines proper, the engine nacelles, the variable supersonic air intakes and the placement of the engines – as an integrated system. This allowed many of the deficiencies that plagued the SST's powerplant to be designed out of the bomber at an early stage.

Speaking of engines and intakes, a lot of layouts was tried before the definitive one was selected. As mentioned in the previous chapter, on the M-18 the Myasishchev OKB had used the same arrangement as on the B-1 – the engines were housed in side-by-side pairs in conformal nacelles under the wing centre section close to the wing pivots, each nacelle having a V-shaped air intake in plan view and vertical airflow control ramps. Nevertheless, the Tupolev OKB decided to explore other options and see if something better could be devised. A major wind tunnel effort was undertaken jointly with TsAGI, involving no fewer than 14 models of various powerplant configurations. Again, the following numeration is purely for reference purposes, not reflecting the actual order in which the project versions appeared – although some details do give a hint.

One of the earliest project versions – we will call it **Version 1** – had conventional tail surfaces with a low-set horizontal tail, just like the nameless project version of 1971; the large size of the swept stabilisers suggested they were not necessarily all-movable. The four engines were housed in B-1/M-18 style nacelles as described above. In common with the 1971 version a cannon barbette and a ranging radar were still installed at the aft extremity of the fuselage, albeit the latter had an elliptical (not circular) cross-section.

Version 2 was almost identical, differing only in having a cruciform tail unit; the trapezoidal vertical tail had no trailing-edge sweep. There was no fairing at the fin/tailplane junction, suggesting this could be the abovementioned version with the two-section inset rudder. The rear fuselage and the defensive armament were the same. **Version 3** was also very similar but featured a swept T-tail vaguely reminiscent of the Tu-134's, which had comparable leading-edge (about 45°) and trailing-edge sweep, an inset rudder and a very similar pointed fairing at the top, albeit a rather lower aspect ratio. The unusual bit was that the moderately swept stabilisers were all-movable (that is, stabilators) – definitely not a normal feature on a T-tail aircraft!

Version 4 stood out among the rest, having three engines – obviously of a different and more powerful unspecified type. The engines were housed in massive cylindrical nacelles which had sharp-lipped axisymmetrical air intakes with adjustable conical centrebodies (shock cones) – rather like those of some supersonic fighters (such as the Mikoyan MiG-21 *Fishbed*). Two of them were carried on short pylons under the wings; at least three versions of the underwing nacelles were tried, including one with upward-angled front ends. The third engine was mounted smack in the middle of the cruciform tail unit, sitting directly above the lower fin/stabiliser junction, with the cropped-delta all-movable upper fin on top of the nacelle; it looked almost as if a jet-powered UAV with a tailless layout was perched on top of the rear fuselage! The horizontal tail of trapezoidal planform was quite large.

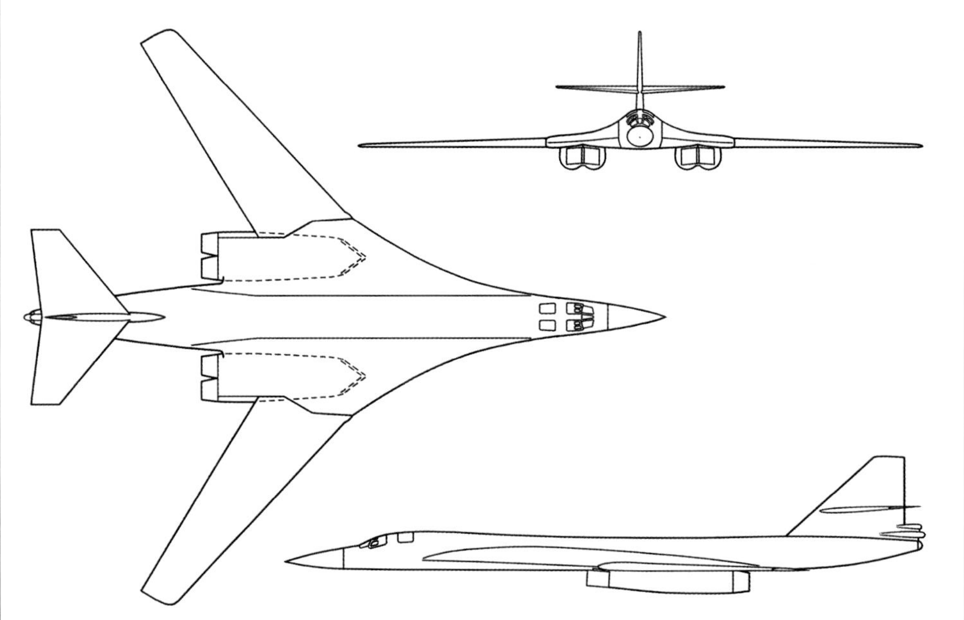

Version 5 was a very similar tri-jet but was even more unusual in that the nacelles of the Nos. 1 and 3 engines (with the same axisymmetrical intakes) were mounted laterally instead of ventrally, passing through the LERXes and the wing pivot box. All three nacelles were rather longer, the front end of the centre nacelle being supported by a long fin fillet. Also, the stabilators were set high on this nacelle (rather than low, as on Version 4) to reduce the influence of the outer engines' efflux because these were also set higher.

Now while Versions 1 through 4 had classic wing gloves with spring-loaded plates sealing the centre section/outer wing joint, in this case

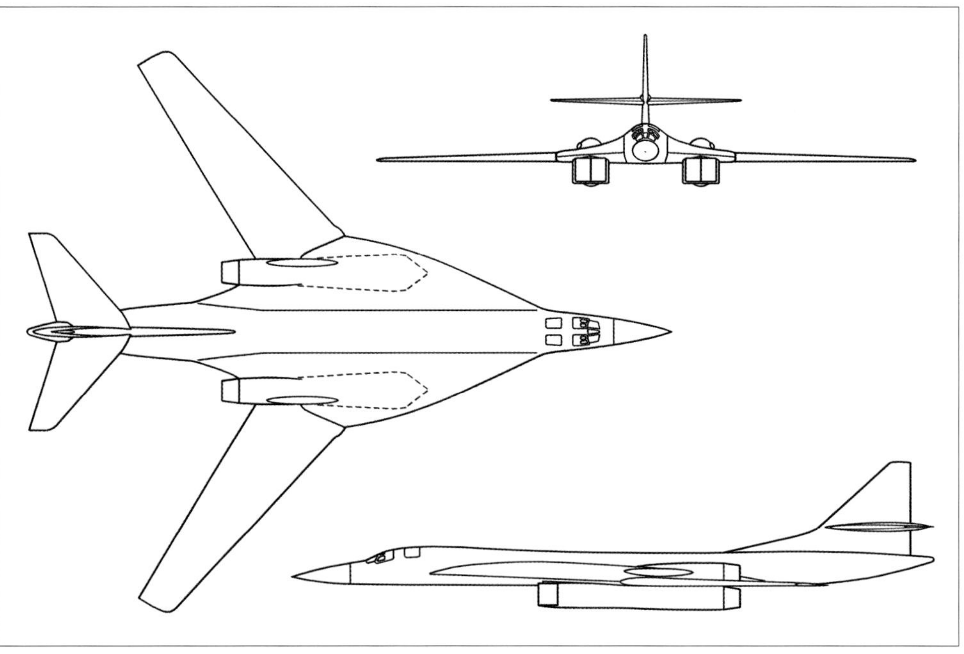

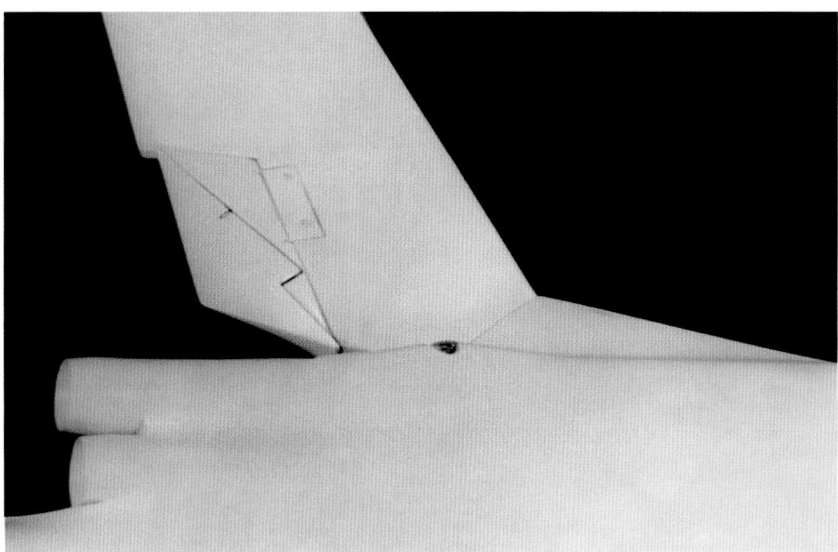

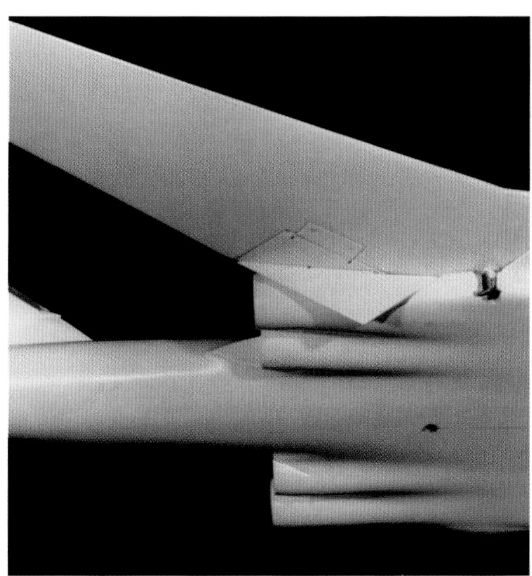

there was positively no room for the wing gloves because the engines were in the way. Hence the designers devised a feature unique among VG aircraft – large triangular segments of the inboard trailing-edge flaps folded downward as the wings pivoted, assuming a vertical position at 65° maximum sweep to form prominent boundary layer fences just outboard of the engine nacelles. In addition to optimising the airflow near the joint, these 'pop-up' fences obviated the need to seal the wing glove joint (which is always difficult).

Version 6A was a step or two towards the definitive Tu-160 thanks to a revised cruciform tail, which featured trapezoidal stabilators and an all-movable upper fin half, and the absence of

Above and above right: Close-up of Version 6B's starboard wing root showing how the triangular folding segment of the inboard flap section folds downward at maximum sweep to form a wing fence.

Below: Lower and upper views of a partial structural model of Version 9 showing the air intakes, wing gloves and weapons bays.

Opposite, above right: The rear ends of Versions 2 and 3.

Opposite, right: Structural models of the centre fuselage/starboard wing glove and the rear fuselage/tail unit of Version 3.

Opposite, below right: A structural model of Version 6A showing the main gear.

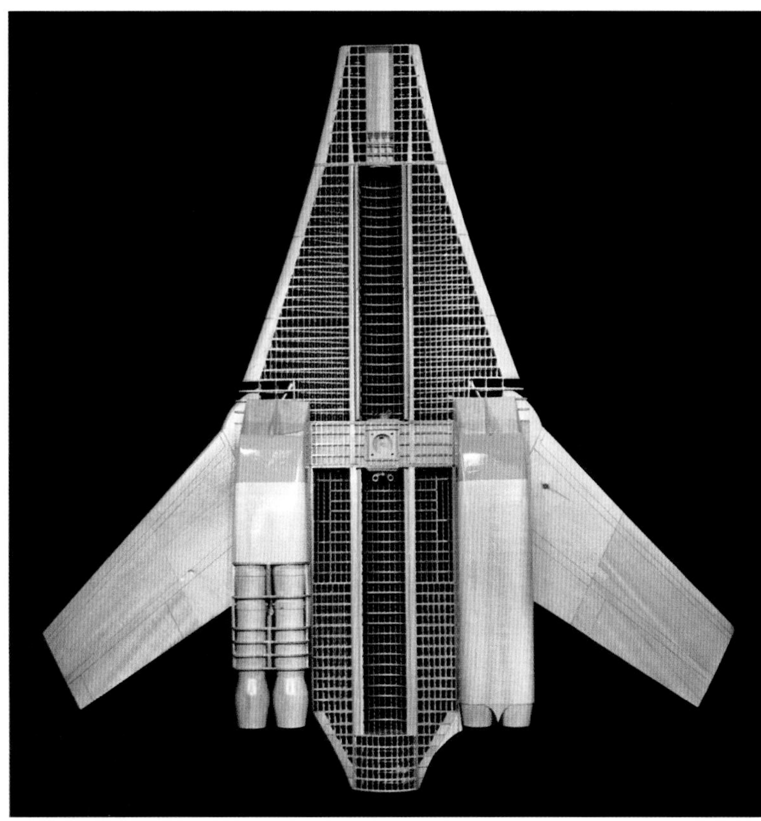

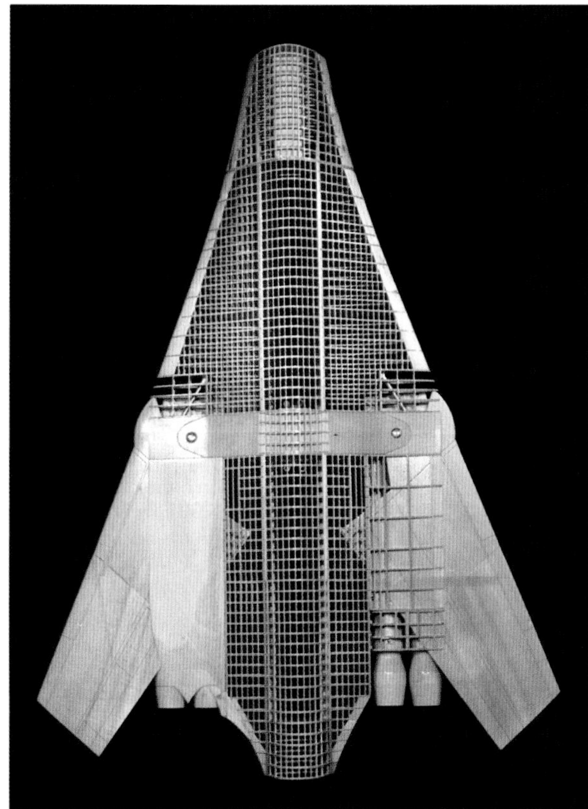

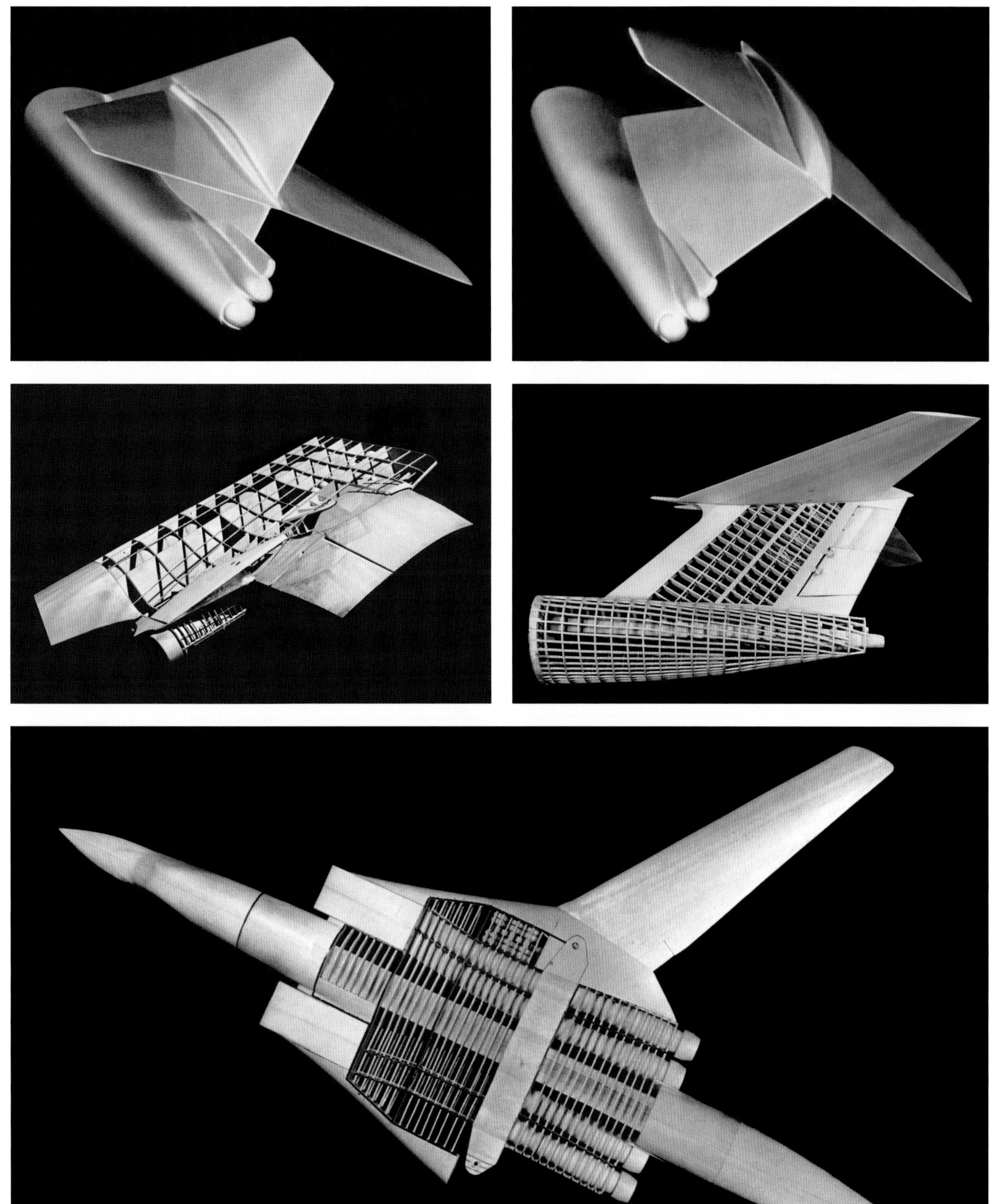

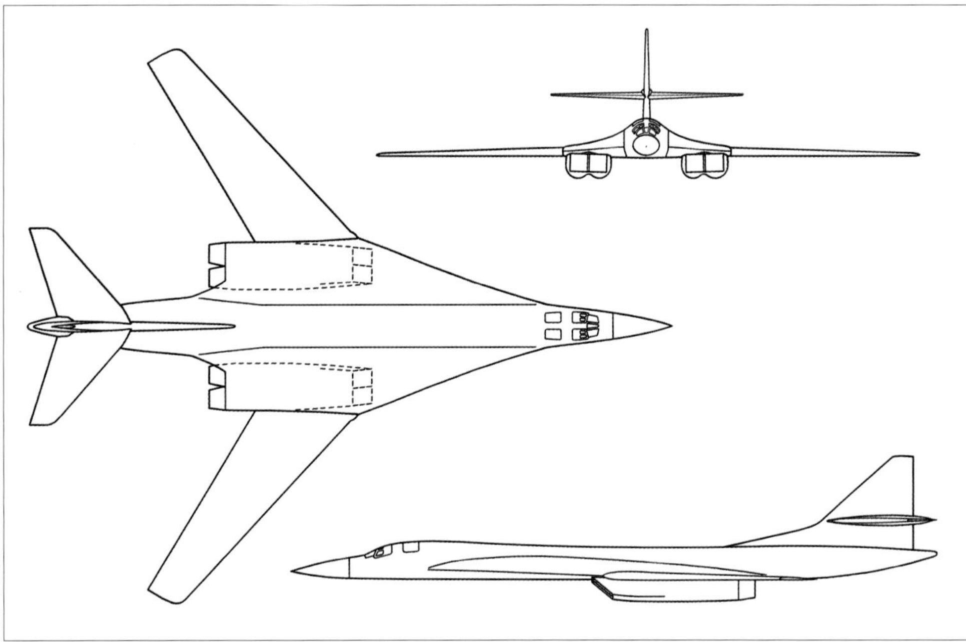

Left: A provisional three-view drawing of the penultimate Version 9 with the Tu-144 style air intakes.

Below: Two more views of the structural model seen on page 66, showing the wing gloves and the nosewheel well.

Opposite, top: A drawing from the PD project documents of the Tu-160 (*izdeliye* 70) showing the structural design of Version 9. The comments list the main structural materials and features used in the fuselage and wings, including areas where honeycomb structures are used.

Opposite, bottom: A similar drawing for the ultimate version with V-shaped air intakes (Version 10) which includes wing pivot and landing gear details.

defensive armament, which had been discarded in favour of a defensive avionics suite. The fin having constant 45° leading-edge sweep had a cigar-shaped fairing extending aft beyond the trailing edge at the fin/tailplane junction, indicating the presence of upper fin actuators, while the fuselage now terminated in a pointed tailcone. The engine placement, however, still had a long way to go. The four NK-32s were located in horizontal pairs just aft of the wing pivot box and higher than usual, flanking the fuselage and making the aircraft look flat as a flounder in head-on view. They breathed through Tu-144 style pairs of two-dimensional air intakes with horizontal airflow control ramps, the front ends of the intake trunks being squared off in plan view and sharply raked in side elevation; the inboard walls were set apart from the cylindrical forward fuselage to act as boundary layer splitter plates, so that very little was left of the BWB design. It was almost as if two engine nacelles from the Tu-144 had been grafted on to the fuselage sides. Thick LERXes/wing gloves were located outboard of the nacelles. Moreover, one model showed a nose shape oddly similar to that of the Tu-22K *Blinder-B* missile strike aircraft with its grossly bulged radome for the PN (NATO *Puff Ball*) radar.

The landing gear design was rather different and was a step backward, in a way. The chosen engine location left no room for the mainwheel wells at their previous position outboard of the rear weapons bay; therefore the main gear units were moved to the LERXes outboard of the inlet ducts (here the designers made a virtue out of necessity, increasing the gear track), and their design was borrowed wholesale from the Tu-144 prototype (*izdeliye* 044). In order to fit inside the thin wings each bogie had 12 small wheels (three rows of four); this gave the bonus of increasing the landing gear footprint and reducing the runway loading. The main units retracted forward instead of aft, the bogies likewise somersaulting forward during retraction instead of aft. In order to fit inside the very limited space available the oleo struts had a cunning "knee-action" design, the small upper segment swinging aft and the rest of the oleo forward (a similar solution had been used on the Fokker F-27 Friendship and several Soviet transport aircraft projects). The

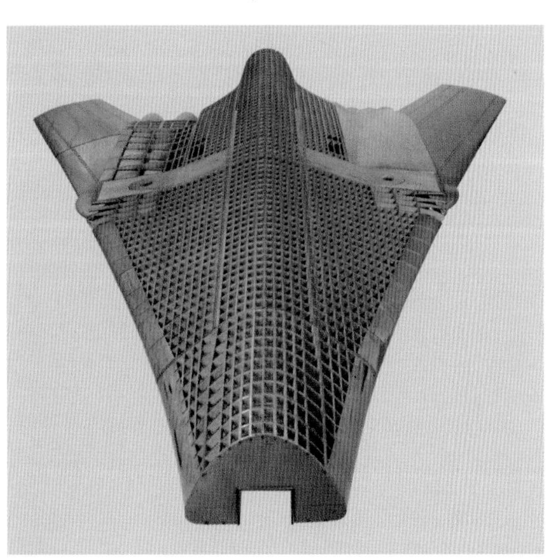

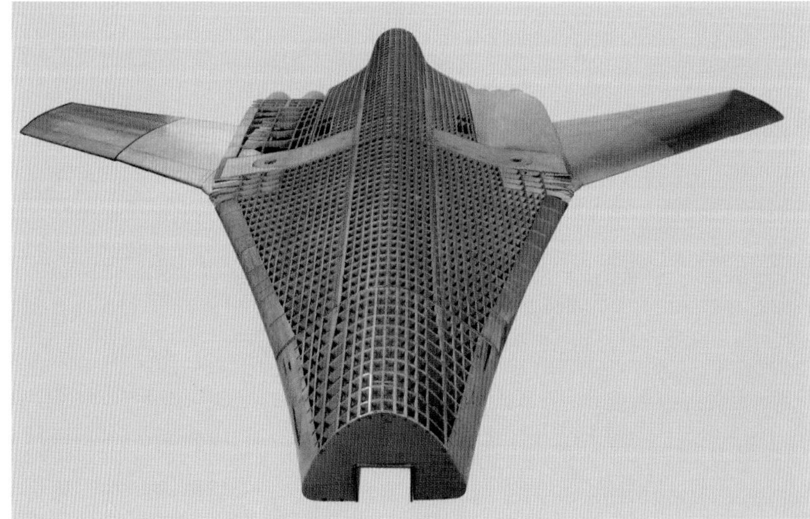

Конструктивно-силовая схема самолета Ту-160

Фюзеляж

Материалы АК4-1чТ1, В95пчАТ2

Конструкция фюзеляжа клепано-сборная, из набора шпангоутов, стрингеров и обшивки листов

Интегральная центральная часть самолета включает гермокабину, отсеки вооружения (с ПЧК и нишами шасси), центропланом, хвостовую часть фюзеляжа с килевой надстройкой и обтекателями. Стык фюзеляжа с центропланом технологический, неразъемный

Передняя часть крыла (ПЧК)

Конструкция клепаная, сборная из поперечных балок, стенок и панелей обшивки (химически фрезерованые листы с ребрами жестокости и стрингерами на ТЭС)

Материалы АК4-1чТ1, В95пчАТ2

Поворотные консоли (ПК)

Кессон консоли 5ти лонжеронный, собирается из монолитных панелей (плит 20000×1500×60) лонжеронов и нервюр-перегорродок

Механизация: предкрылки, однощелевые закрылки и интерцепторы — сотовой конструкции

Материалы АК4-1чТ1, В95пчАТ2

Вспомогательные („несиловые") элементы конструкции: предкрылки, закрылки, интерцепторы, законцовки, створки, крышки люков, панели воздухозаборников, обтекатели, рули, элементы стабилизатора и т.д.

Наиболее эффективно использована сварная и клепаная сотовая конструкция во вспомогательных элементах конструкции. Сотовые конструкции обеспечивают снижение веса до 20/25%, улучшение качества поверхности и увеличение ресурса.

Центроплан

Основные технологические процессы: механическая обработка, электронно-лучевая диффузионная сварка

Материалы плиты и поковки ВТ6ч

Конструктивно-силовая схема самолета Ту-160

Передняя часть крыла (ПЧК)

Конструкция клепаная, сборная из поперечных балок, стенок и панелей обшивки (химически фрезерованые листы с ребрами жесткости и стрингерами).

Интегральная часть самолета включает гермокабину, отсеки вооружения (с ПЧК и нишами шасси), центроплан, хвостовую часть фюзеляжа с килевой надстройкой и обтекателями. Стык фюзеляжа с центропланом технологический неразъемный.

Конструкция фюзеляжа клепано-сборная из набора шпангоутов, стрингеров и листов обшивки.

Алюминиевые сплавы (АК4-1чТ1, В95пчВТ2)	58%
Титановые сплавы (ВТ-6)	22%
Высокопрочные и жаропрочные стали	15%
Неметаллические и прочие материалы	5%

Вспомогательные (несиловые) элементы конструкции: предкрылки, закрылки, интерцепторы, законцовки, створки, крышки люков, панели воздухозаборников, обтекатели, рули, элементы стабилизатора и т.д.-клееные сотовые.

Узлы

Двухсрезные, сварные Э.Л.С. из титановых крупногабаритных штамповок и поковок.

О.Ч.К.

Кессон консоли 5ти лонжеронный собирается из монолитных панелей (плит 20000×1250×82), лонжеронов и нервюр-перегородок.

Механизация:-предкрылки, закрылки, интерцепторы - - сотовой конструкции.

Центроплан

Кессон собирается из титановых диффузионно-сварных панелей и стенок лонжеронов, сваренных ЭЛС. Внутренний набор из алюминиевых сплавов.

Шасси

Высота основной стойки шасси-3,5м

Габарит тележки - 4,1м

В конструкции широко применяются титановые сплавы.

bogies were hinged close to the rear axle so that most of the bogie lay against the oleo, reducing the overall length when stowed.

An obvious disadvantage of this version was that the engines' inlet ducts passed through the wing pivot box, weakening it where the loads were highest. To offset this, the pivot box would have to be reinforced, incurring a weight penalty.

Version 6B was near-identical, except that instead of wing gloves accommodating the inboard ends of the flaps it had the abovementioned downward-folding wing fences. Also, the LERXes were positioned slightly higher on the air intake trunks.

Version 7 was again a BWB design, but here the engines were located in vertical pairs (!) *à la* BAC Lightning just aft of the wing pivot box, so that the wings effectively passed through the boxy nacelles. The latter had V-shaped front ends in side elevation, the two-dimensional air intakes also being paired vertically and having horizontal airflow control ramps (located at the bottom in the upper pair and at the top in the lower pair); the inlet ducts did not encroach on the wing pivot box, passing above and below it. The main gear units reverted to the narrow-track aft-retracting version with six-wheel bogies.

This arrangement offered both the lowest possible drag and the lowest radar cross-section (RCS), that is, maximum "stealth" – an important quality for a strategic bomber. On the other hand, it made maintenance and removal/replacement of the upper engines more complicated. The "double-decker nacelle" version even reached the full-size mock-up stage.

Version 8A similarly had the engines arranged in Lightning-style vertical pairs but had a different air intake design. The front ends of the engine nacelles were placed below the LERXes and were similar to Version 1, being V-shaped, with side-by-side pairs of two-dimensional intakes having vertical airflow control ramps. Immediately downstream of the latter, however, the nacelles twisted through 90°, the inboard inlet ducts curving upward and outward to pass through the wing pivot box while the outboard ducts passed below it. The engines were installed at a small 'toe-in' angle, possibly to reduce the yaw in the event of asymmetric thrust. Eventually, however, technological problems (the complexity of integrating the "corkscrew" air ducts) and doubts as to the combat survivability of the vertically paired engines caused this arrangement to be abandoned.

That was not all. Version 8 featured wing LERXes with a convex leading edge in the manner of the Mikoyan MiG-29 *Fulcrum* tactical fighter instead of a concave one, as on the other versions (in other words, the leading-edge sweep gradually increased towards the wing pivots instead of decreasing). The tail unit was also revised – the vertical tail now had a large root fillet with 72° leading-edge sweep, while the stabilators' taper was increased by reducing the tip chord. The modified tail unit was adopted for the final version, while the modified LERXes were not.

Version 8B had the same 'twister' engine nacelles but the wing LERXes had a straight or concave leading edge. Also, the "pop-up" boundary layer fences – now consisting not only of the abovesaid triangular flap segments but also of the inboard trailing-edge portions that were not part of the flaps – were redesigned to fold upward instead of downward as wing sweep increased past 35°. This version of the wing fences was finalised. Oddly enough, a model of this version shows it had a conventional fixed fin with an inset rudder!

Version 9 reverted to engines mounted in side-by-side pairs under the wing centre section in conformal nacelles with short inlet ducts, but the two-dimensional air intakes had a Tu-144 style raked design with horizontal airflow control ramps. The nacelles were 12.56 m (41 ft 2$^{31}/_{64}$ in) long. Also, the model shows wing gloves, the outer wing trailing edges being accommodated above the engines at maximum sweep.

Eventually, however, the designers selected the nacelle layout featured in the M-18 project. Thus, the final configuration of the Tu-160 – that would be **Version 10** – looked as follows:

• fixed-geometry nose with a radome forming the lower half/front end of the nosecone;

• forward-facing four-man flight deck with central aisle, ventral access via the nosewheel well and upward ejection;

• BWB layout with LERXes beginning just aft of the flight deck section and having concave leading edges;

• outer wings with flaperons outboard of the flaps (terminating well short of the wingtips) and inboard flap/trailing edge segments folding upward to form wing fences;

• cruciform tail unit with a large fin fillet, no sweep on the fin trailing edge, an all-movable upper fin half and strongly tapered stabilators;

• long pointed tailcone with no defensive cannon barbette and associated radar;

• engines in side-by-side pairs in conformal nacelles under the wing centre section having V-shaped front ends, two-dimensional intakes with vertical ramps and short inlet ducts;

• narrow-track landing gear with aft-retracting main units having six-wheel bogies.

A large amount of wind tunnel research was undertaken at TsAGI to verify the chosen aerodynamic features, using 11 scale models. The tests showed that the engineers had succeeded in obtaining a maximum lift/drag ratio of 18.5-19 in subsonic cruise and more than 6.0 in supersonic cruise.

Generally speaking, the OKB succeeded in minimising the Tu-160's dimensions thanks to a well thought-out structural design. Drag reduction was also helped by the fuselage's high fineness ratio and carefully streamlined forward fuselage contours.

The bomber made large-scale use of state-of-the-art structural materials; titanium alloys accounted for 38% of the airframe weight, with aluminium alloys, high-strength steel and composites making up 58%, 15% and 3% respectively. Once the general arrangement had been frozen the OKB concentrated on detail design.

As already mentioned, the Tupolev OKB's armament section teamed up with GosNII AS and other establishments to develop the most effective armament for the Tu-160. Since the geopolitical and military situation in the years to come was unpredictable, the aircraft's weapons complement was to be determined by its multi-role status. The Tu-160 was intended to carry ultra-long-range, long-range and medium-range cruise missiles, guided and unguided short-range weapons (that is, "smart" and free-fall bombs); additionally, air-to-air missiles would be provided for self-defence. Priority was given to weapons which could destroy targets (including

Right: A structural model of the Tu-160 in Version 8B. Oddly, it features a conventional fixed fin with a three-section inset rudder (two sections above the stabilators and one below).

Below: A provisional four-view drawing of Version 8B (note the wing fences folding upward in the front view, not downward).

those with a small radar signature) without requiring the bomber to come within range of the enemy's air defences and were carried internally. The avionics suite was required to tackle navigation tasks and ensure accurate delivery of a wide range of weapons.

Originally the Tu-160's principal armament was to consist of either two Kh-45 long-range missiles (one in each weapons bay) or 24 Kh-15 short-range aeroballistic missiles. The Kh-45 programme was still alive then (a development batch of missiles was being manufactured), while the Kh-2000 was no longer under consideration. The size of the weapons bays – 11.28 m (37 ft $0\frac{3}{32}$ in) long, 1.92 m (6 ft $3\frac{19}{32}$ in) wide and 2.0 m (6 ft $6\frac{47}{64}$ in) deep – was therefore chosen to accommodate the Kh-45 missile which, as already mentioned, was 9.9-10.8 m (32 ft $5\frac{49}{64}$ in to 35 ft $5\frac{13}{64}$ in) long. Each of the two weapons bays was about equal in volume to the Tu-95 *Bear-A*'s bomb bay.

(Curiously, a Tupolev OKB drawing from the PD project documents of the Tu-160 [*izdeliye* 70] shows two missiles marked Kh-45MS side by side in the forward weapons bay. This seems odd, considering that getting the Kh-45 into the bay was a tight squeeze, the missile having a wing span of 2.0 m [6 ft $6\frac{47}{64}$ in] – from tip to tip, that is; with the wings at 45° to the horizontal plane, as suspended in the bay, it would be 1.414 m [4 ft $7\frac{43}{64}$ in] wide.

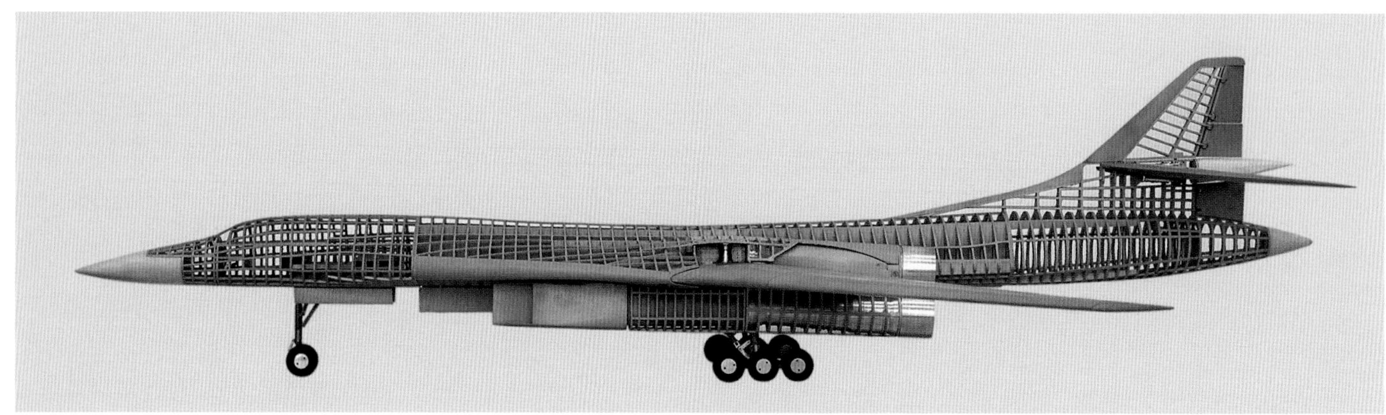

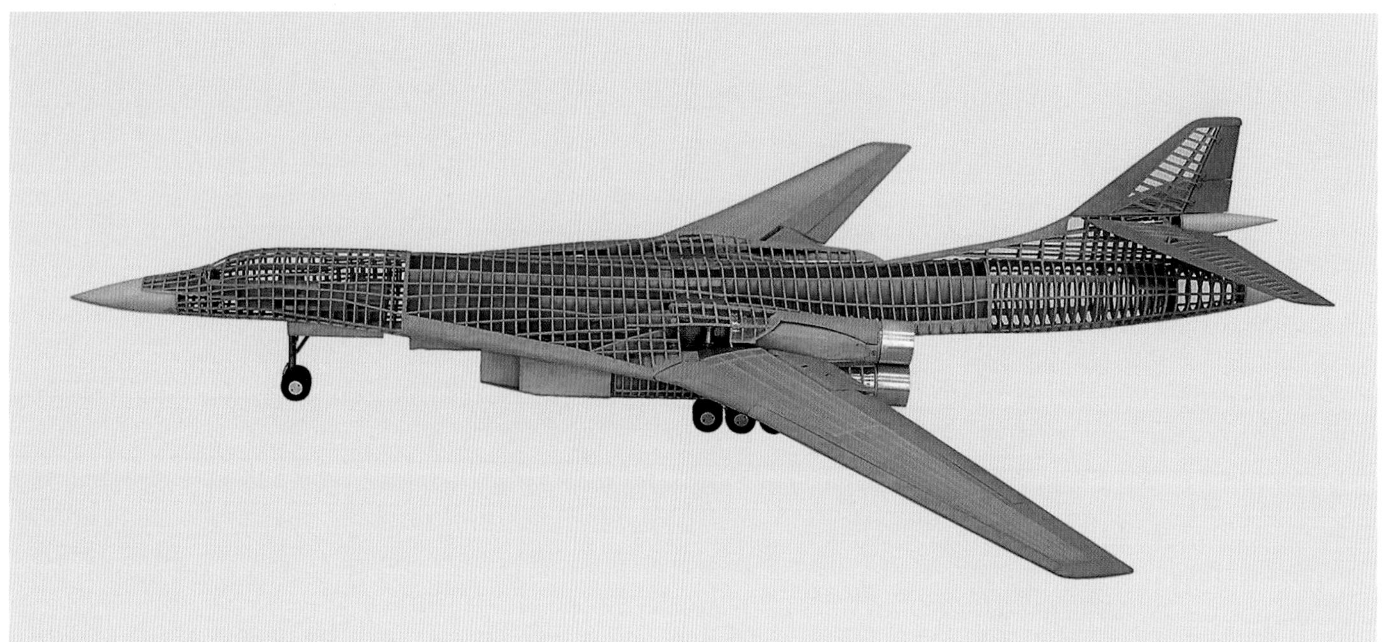

Left, below left and bottom left: Further views of the structural model of Version 8B with the wings at minimum sweep. The length and shape of the tailcone was yet to change. Note how the upper engines' inlet ducts pass through the wing pivot box.

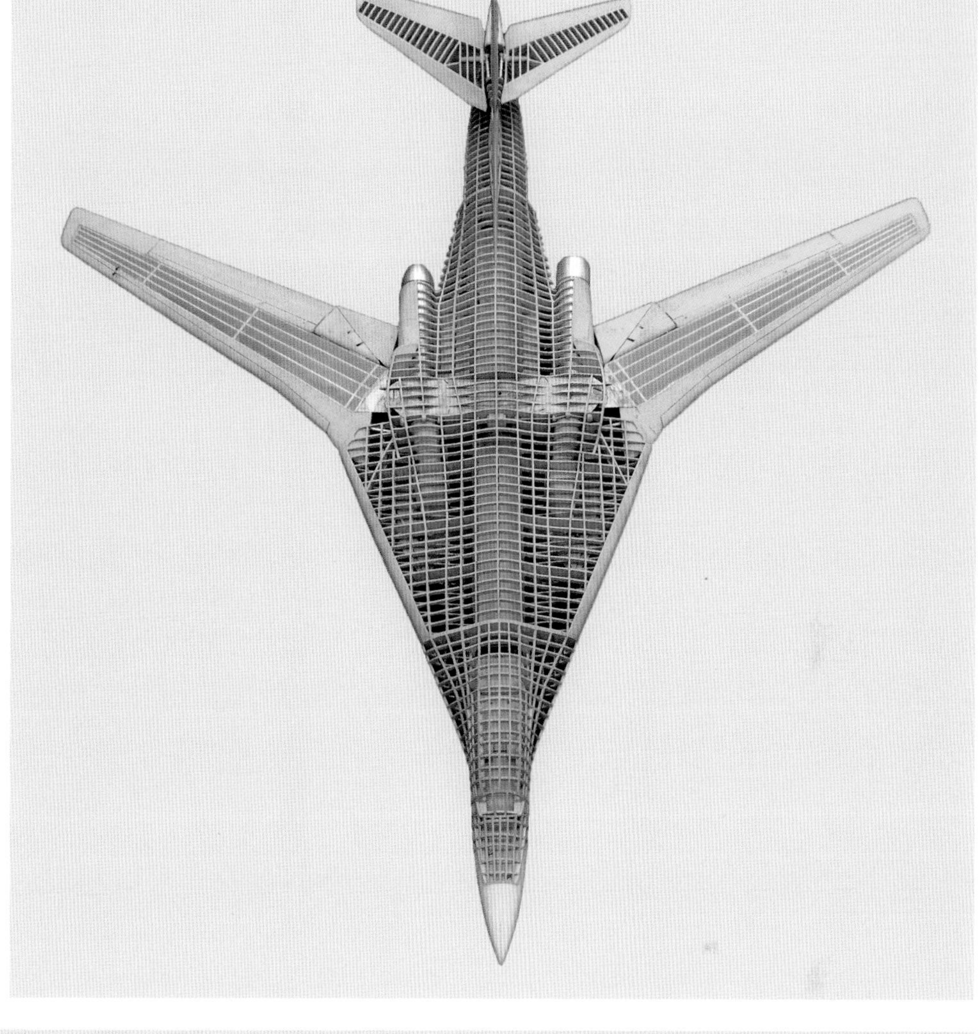

Right: An upper view of the same model showing the five-spar outer wings and the stabilator pivot axle (the latter would be replaced with a different hinge design on the actual aircraft).

Below: The same model with the wings fully swept and the wing fences raised. Note the shape of the nose-to-radome joint line.

Top and above: A scale model of the Tu-160's wing pivot box and outer wing torsion boxes on a test rig. The photo below gives a close-up of the pivots' design.

Above right/below right: Artist's impressions of the Tu-160 (Version 9) from the OKB materials. Right: A provisional three-view drawing of the Tu-160's ultimate configuration (Version 10).

However, the Kh-45MS depicted on the said drawing appears rather different from the Kh-45 *sans suffixe* described earlier, having very short strake-like wings and trapezoidal [not pentagonal] rudders. One may assume that the maximum number of Kh-45MSs carried by the Tu-160 would be four. Unfortunately no details are available of this version.)

The other missile – the Kh-15 (AS-16 *Kickback*) – was then under development at MKB Raduga as a successor to the obsolete Kh-22 Vikhr' (Whirlwind; AS-4 *Kitchen*) and KSR-5 (AS-6 *Kingfish*) missiles created by the same company. This was a hypersonic weapon capable of Mach 5 flight to be used against targets with pre-programmed co-ordinates. The Kh-15 was a wingless missile with a solid-propellant rocket motor and a nuclear warhead or a conventional shaped-charge/high-explosive warhead. It was 4.78 m (15 ft 8³⁄₁₆ in) long, with a body diameter of 0.455 m (1 ft 5²⁹⁄₃₂ in) and three fins set at 120° with respect to each other, two of them being all-movable; the tail surface span was 0.92 m (3 ft ⁷⁄₃₂ in). The missile had a launch weight of 1,200 kg (2,645 lb), including a 150-kg (330-lb) warhead. Its size and weight allowed the Tu-160 to carry up to 24 Kh-15s – two rows of six in each weapons bay on tandem rotary launchers. The latter were originally designated APU-15 (*aviatsi**on**noye pooskov**oye** oo**stroy**stvo* – aircraft-mounted launcher for Kh-15 missiles) but were later redesignated MKU-6-1 (***mno**gopozitsi**on**noye katapool'tnoye oostroystvo*** – "multi-position ejector device," that is, weapons rack, six-round, model 1).

After launch at a maximum range of 150 km (93 miles) the Kh-15 was to follow a ballistic trajectory as a means of extending range, accelerating to Mach 5 and entering the stratosphere with an apogee at up to 40 km (131,230 ft). The flight trajectory was formed by the aircraft's weapons control system (WCS) to suit the applicable launch range while the missile was still on the launcher. The missile featured an INS which guided it to the target, using pre-entered co-ordinates.

The *Obzor-K* (Field of view, or Perspective) WCS was built around the ***Poisk*** (Search, or Quest) multi-function navigation/attack radar whose large revolving antenna was housed in the pointed nose. To enable the use of bombs the Tu-160 was equipped with an OPB-15T electro-optical bomb sight (the T suffix denoted *televizionnyy*); the optical part of it was located in a small and neat centreline fairing ahead of the nosewheel well.

The sophisticated and highly complex weapons control system necessitated large-scale use of computers. In keeping with insistent recommendations from GosNII AS (voiced at an early stage), the WCS had provisions for using multiplex data exchange channels and included a dedicated missile control system (MCS) called SURO-70 (*sistema oopravleniya raketnym oroozhiyem* – MCS for *izdeliye* 70), which comprised 12 computers processing the data supplied by the navigation suite (current position, heading and speed) and fed them to the missiles. There was also a separate launch preparation subsystem called Sproot-SM (Octopus-SM) working with up to 12 missiles at once. The two subsystems owed their existence to the new generation of air-to-surface missiles whose guidance system plotted the course from the launch point, which would probably be over water or featureless terrain; this required a large amount of data to be prepared on board the aircraft and downloaded to the missile's computer prior to launch. The need was acknowledged to develop a flight data preparation system allowing the complete mission profile with digital maps to be prepared on the ground and uploaded to the aircraft's mainframe computer – a task which was solved in due course. Throughout the design effort GosNII AS worked in close co-operation with departments of the relevant organisations headed by Lev N.

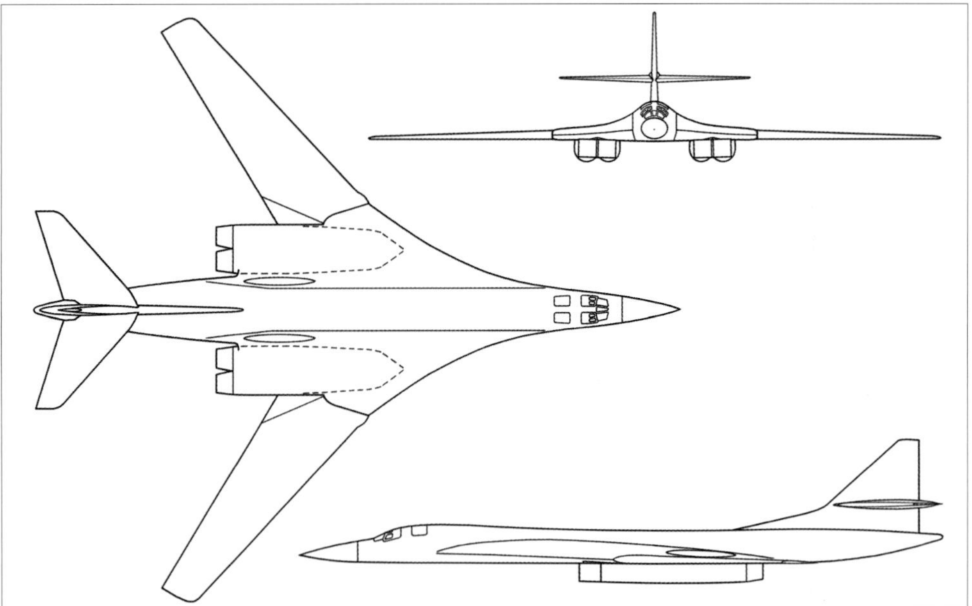

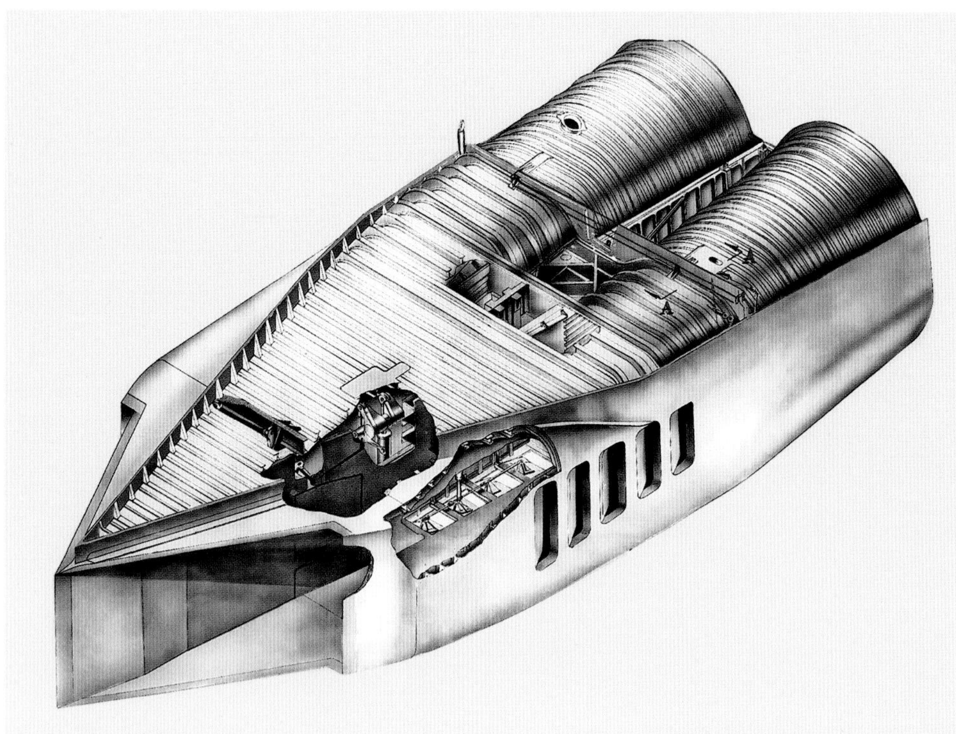

Left: A drawing from the Tupolev OKB materials showing the final design of the air intake assemblies. Initially there were five auxiliary blow-in doors per side as shown here.

Below: A cutaway drawing of an interim version from the project documents dated around 1976. It shows a fixed telescopic IFR probe at the tip of the nose (Tu-22M3 prototype style), two Kh-45MS missiles in the front weapons bay and 12 Kh-15 missiles in the rear weapons bay. Also shown are the Poisk multi-mode radar, the flight deck, the avionics bay aft of it, the slats, flaps and elevons with their travel limits, the outer wing torsion boxes (with the wing area), the minimum and maximum wing settings, the nosewheel and mainwheel sizes, the NK-32 engines, the Baikal active jammer, the Avtomat-F chaff dispenser, the Zarevo flare dispenser and the Ogonyok IR sensor.

Bazenkov (Tupolev OKB), O. N. Nekrasov and V. F. Khoodov (MIEA).

Initially the Air Force insisted that, in keeping with previous bomber design traditions, the Tu-160 be equipped with defensive armament – specifically, a remote-controlled tail barbette mounting a 30-mm (1.18 calibre) Gryazev/Shipunov GSh-6-30 six-barrel Gatling cannon. Pretty soon, however, the Tupolev OKB persuaded the military to dispense with cannon armament as an outdated concept – in a real-life war scenario a hostile fighter would most probably launch a missile attack without coming within

КОМПОНОВКА
САМОЛЕТА ТУ-160
ПРИЕМНИК ТОПЛИВА
МФРЛС „ПОИСК"
КАБИНА ЭКИПАЖА
ОТСЕКИ ВООРУЖЕНИЯ
(11,2м × 1,9м × 2 м)
ТЕХНИЧЕСКИЙ ОТСЕК
(РАДИОЭЛЕКТРОННОЕ ОБОРУДОВАНИЕ)
Х-45МС
Х-15
ПРЕДКРЫЛКИ $\delta_п = 20°$
ЭЛЕРОН ЗАКРЫЛОК
2х ЩЕЛЕВЫЕ ЗАКРЫЛКИ
$\delta_з = 25°$
2 кол. 1080 × 400
КЕССОН ОЧК
$S_{конс}$ - 86 м²
$\chi_{мин} = 20°$
2х СРЕЗНЫЙ
УЗЕЛ ПОВОРОТА
КОНСОЛЕЙ
6 КОЛЕСНАЯ ТЕЛЕЖКА
(1350 × 440)
ДВИГАТЕЛИ НК-32
$\chi_{макс} = 65°$
АППАРАТУРА РЭП
„БАЙКАЛ"
ЛТЦ „ЗАРЕВО"
АВТОМАТ-Ф
ТЕПЛОПЕЛЕНГАТОР „ОГОНЕК"

range of the bomber's cannon. Instead, the weight saved and the space freed by the deletion of the cannon barbette could be used for installing more capable ECM/ESM equipment. In addition, a specialised ECM/escort fighter (!) version of the Tu-160 was proposed; this aircraft would provide protection for large bomber formations (see Chapter 5).

Faced with the ever-growing lethality of the potential adversary's air defence systems, in the 1970s the aircraft designers had to focus on the combat survivability aspect of strike aircraft. Hence a special subdivision headed by O. S. Korotin was formed at GosNII AS to develop the structure and estimate the efficiency of defensive avionics systems; it was transformed into a laboratory in 1984. This team analysed the effectiveness of the Tu-160's ECM/ESM suite named *Baikal* (after the world's biggest freshwater lake in Eastern Siberia) and substantiated the choice of its components – the Baikal active jammer, the *Avtomaht-F* (Automatic device) chaff dispenser, the *Zarevo* (Glow) infrared countermeasures (IRCM) flare dispensers on the underside of the tailcone and the *Ogonyok* (Little light, or Little flame) infrared missile warning system (MWS) whose sensor was positioned at the tip of the tailcone to detect the heat signature of an incoming missile.

Another departure from previous design practices was the incorporation of stealth technology into the Tu-160's airframe and powerplant. The engineers took great pains to minimise the bomber's RCS and heat signature.

As befits a strategic bomber, the Tu-160 was to have in-flight refuelling capability – of course, using the probe-and-drogue IFR system which was standard for Soviet strategic aircraft by then. Originally the designers envisaged a fixed telescopic IFR probe located at the extremity of the pointed nose; therefore the radome terminated a little way short of the tip of the nose, the joint line going vertically down. The probe was to be "fired" pneumatically into the drogue when the bomber came close enough. In other words, the design of the Tu-160's extreme nose was virtually identical to that of the Tu-22M3 *Backfire-C* "swing-wing" heavy bomber which was under development at the same time; the first prototype Tu-22M3, which was rolled out in Kazan' in late 1976 and first flown on 20th June 1977, had this probe design. Shortly afterwards, however, the designers opted for a hydraulically retractable IFR probe which was placed higher and farther aft, stowing in the upper side of the nose; when retracted it was closed completely by flush-fitting doors. Hence the radome was revised, the joint line going vertically up a short way aft of the tip (in the manner of the Tu-22K).

On June 26, 1974, the Council of Ministers issued directive No.534-387 officially tasking the Tupolev OKB with developing the Tu-160 multi-role strategic bomber/missile strike aircraft powered by four NK-32 engines. Yet another CofM directive (No.1040-348) appeared on December 19, 1975; this was a "follow-up" document stipulating more accurate basic performance figures. In accordance with these documents the Tu-160's effective range in subsonic cruise mode with a 9,000-kg (19,840-lb) weapons load – that is, two Kh-45 missiles – was to be 14,000-16,000 km (8,695-9,940 miles); range over a 'hi-lo-hi' mission profile including a 2,000-km (1,240-mile) stretch of low/ultra-low-level flight at 50-200 m (165-6,560 ft) or in supersonic cruise

Valentin I. Bliznyuk, the Tu-160's project chief.

mode was specified as 12,000-13,000 km (7,450-8,075 miles). Maximum speed was required to be 2,300-2,500 km/h (1,430-1,550 mph) at high altitude and 1,000 km/h (620 mph) at low altitude. The service ceiling was stipulated as not less than 18,000-20,000 m (59,055-65,620 ft).

The aircraft was to have a normal weapons load of 9,000 kg and a 40,000-kg (88,180-lb) maximum weapons load. The following missile armament options were set forth: two Kh-45M missiles; 24 Kh-15 missiles or 10-12 Kh-15M missiles; and 10-12 Kh-55 subsonic cruise missiles. The aircraft was to be capable of delivering conventional and nuclear free-fall bombs, as well as laser-guided and TV-guided "smart bombs."

With the official state order for the development of the new bomber finally placed and the main general arrangement and systems issues resolved, the Tupolev OKB set to work on the advanced development project (ADP). A host of complex tasks was solved at this stage by the OKB's subdivisions headed by Gheorgiy A. Cheryomukhin (the OKB's chief aerodynamicist), V. I. Korneyev, Aleksandr L. Pookhov (he was later appointed Tu-22M3 project chief), V. I. Roodin, Ye. I. Schekhterman, Igor' S. Kalygin (he later became the Tu-334 short-haul airliner's project chief), V. T. Klimov (calculations group chief), Ye. I. Kholopov, V. V. Babakov, A. S. Semyonov and Z. A. Priorova. In the OKB's structural strength department, Vyacheslav V. Soolimenkov (static strength section) was responsible for ensuring the airframe's structural strength and optimising the structural design; he was one of

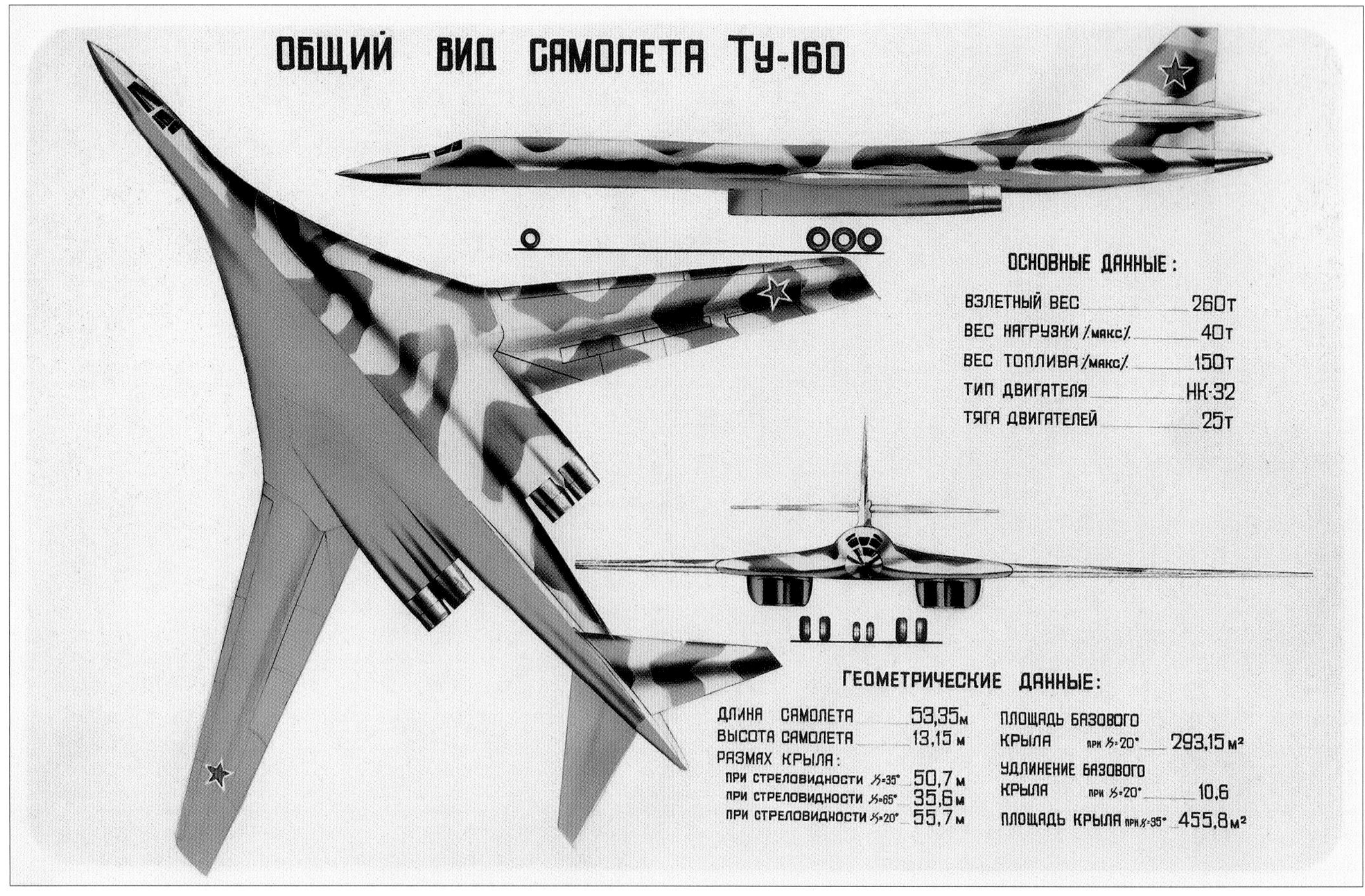

the first to get to grips with the variance of loads the airframe is subjected to at subsonic and supersonic speeds, which made it possible to increase the aircraft's designated service life. A major contribution was also made by structural strength department engineers Igor' B. Ginko, Valeriy P. Shoonayev, V. A. Ignatushkin, I. K. Kulikov and the work teams under their command; they determined the structural loads and developed structural strength calculation methods to be used by other departments. They worked in close co-operation with their colleagues at TsAGI in the town of Zhukovskiy (Moscow Region) and at SibNIA in Novosibirsk; together they performed a huge scope of static and fatigue testing on full-size components of the Tu-160's airframe. Also, considering the bomber's structural complexity and the OKB's lack of prior experience with the BWB layout, a scaled-strength model to one-third scale was built before testing the real thing; the model itself and the test rig for it were designed by Daniil I. Gapeyev.

The airframe structure was designed under the supervision of Iosif F. Nezval', a highly experienced designer who had worked at the Tupolev OKB since the day it was founded in 1922. At the time Nezval' headed the OKB's branch office in Kazan', Tatar ASSR – an important factor because MAP's aircraft factory No.22 in Kazan', which was long-time Tupolev "turf," had been earmarked to build the Tu-160. Thus any structural issues could be resolved by an authoritative designer on site without wasting time on shuttling paperwork back and forth between the plant and the head office in Moscow. The blueprints of the airframe were prepared by the teams headed by O. N. Golovin, Viktor M. Barinov, Nikolay T. Kozlov, Aleksandra S. Prytkova, S. I. Petrov, V. G. Rezvov, Ivan S. Lebedev, Daniil I. Gapeyev and Yu. L. Laponov.

The landing gear was developed by a special department of the Tupolev OKB headed by Yakov A. Livshitz, a top-notch "gear man" who had been responsible for the undercarriages of the Tu-16, Tu-95, Tu-22, Tu-144 and other heavy aircraft. The designers working under his command included M. T. Ivanov and V. N. Volkov.

Development of the Tu-160's flight control system proceeded under the guidance of Aleksandr S. Kochergin, head of the OKB's control system department; specific details of the design and manual/automatic control modes were developed by Vadim M. Razumikhin, V. I. Goniodskiy and M. I. Leytes. The Tu-160 was the first Soviet heavy aircraft to feature a fly-by-wire (FBW) control system with no mechanical connection between the controls and the control surfaces. This allowed the aircraft to be electronically stabilised in flight with the CG in neutral position. Another 'first' in Soviet bomber design practice was the provision of fighter-type sticks instead of the usual control columns. These measures increased the aircraft's range (due to lower drag at optimum flight attitudes), improved controllability and helped reduce crew fatigue in complex flight situations. It should be noted that many traditionalists in the Air Force were opposed to the stick, but the proponents got the upper hand – not least thanks to the support of Air Marshal Vasiliy A. Reshetnikov.

The pressurisation and air conditioning system was the responsibility of the section headed by S. V. Drozdov. Engineers

Left: A three-view of the Tu-160 from the project materials (with preliminary specifications, some of which were to change yet). In reality no Tu-160 was ever camouflaged.

This page: A desktop model of the Tu-160. The effect is spoiled by the rear fuselage being too thin and by the inaccurate engine nozzles.

L. D. Doobrovin, V. N. Fadeyev, A. V. Babochkin, G. A. Sterlin, V. S. Zonschain and V. G. Doodik. Relying on their considerable experience with similar systems developed for the Tu-22, Tu-22M and Tu-144, they succeeded in creating a highly effective environmental control system which catered both for the crew and for the avionics.

Speaking of environmental control, the design experience with the Tu-144 came in handy when calculating the thermal loads (primarily caused by the kinetic heating at supersonic speeds), which influence the choice of the structural materials and flight modes, and working out the parameters of the heat insulation/protection systems. This work was done by the section headed by Vladimir A. Andreyev (who later became the Tupolev PLC's Chief Designer for cryogenic-fuel aircraft) and Cand. Tech. Sc. Galina T. Koovshinova; it had been established as part of the Tu-144 programme.

Up-to-date methods of monitoring the Tu-160's assorted systems and equipment in flight and on the ground were devised, allowing health and usage monitoring systems (HUMS) to be developed. A large scope of work on data recording systems (including those documenting the strike results) was performed by a team under V. A. Sablev.

Powerplant integration was the domain of the OKB's propulsion department, which was headed by Vladimir M. Vool' since March 1972. Other Tupolev OKB employees who contributed a lot to the development of the Tu-160's powerplant included Valentin V. Malyshev, Yefim R. Goobar', Nina N. Foorayeva, V. A. Leonov and Valentin M. Dmitriyev. It deserves mention that Igor' S. Shevchuk, then a young engineer, took part in the development of the powerplant, he would eventually rise to President and General Designer of the present-day Tupolev PLC.

The avionics suite was composed under the guidance of Lev N. Bazenkov; the OKB's avionics section chief Yu. N. Kashtanov, I. A. Rapoport, V. A. Vishnevskiy and others were also involved. At General Designer Aleksey A. Tupolev's request prototype avionics integration took place at GosNII AS where a simulation complex utilising actual hardware components was specially built for the purpose. The high quality of the test and debugging work speeded up the commencement of flight tests a lot. It should be noted that later, in 1981, GosNII AS built the world's largest pressure chamber measuring 40.0 x 18.0 x 9.8 m (131 ft $2\frac{13}{16}$ in x 59 ft$\frac{21}{32}$ in x 32 ft $1\frac{13}{16}$ in) specifically for testing the bomber's avionics and equipment in simulated high-altitude conditions.

General Designer Aleksey A. Tupolev, head of the OKB at the time of the Tu-160 programme.

Vladimir M. Vool', head of the OKB's propulsion department.

Lev N. Bazenkov, who led the development of the Tu-160's avionics suite.

Iosif F. Nezval', head of the OKB's Kazan' branch, who led the structural design effort.

Gheorgiy A. Cheryomukhin, the OKB's chief aerodynamicist.

Vyacheslav V. Soolimenkov, head of the OKB's static strength section.

Aleksandr S. Kocherigin, head of the OKB's flight control system department.

Yakov A. Livshitz, head of the OKB's landing gear department.

Yevgeniy A. Fedosov, Director of GosNII AS.

Gheorgiy P. Svishchev, the then Director of TsAGI.

Radiy Ye. Shalin, Director of VIAM.

Igor' S. Seleznyov, Chief Designer of the MKB Raduga missile design bureau.

Right: Pyotr V. Dement'yev, who was Minister of Aircraft Industry at the time when the Tu-160 programme was launched.

Far right: His successor Vasiliy A. Kazakov, who became head of MAP in 1977.

In parallel with the design work the Tupolev OKB built extensive laboratory facilities at its experimental production facility, MMZ "Opyt" (formerly MMZ No.156), in order to conduct advance testing of the Tu-160's features and systems as they reached the hardware stage. (The word ***opyt*** translates as either "experiment" or "experience"; this was also the unclassified name of the Tupolev OKB.) This step saved precious time later, when the aircraft entered flight test. No fewer than 112 assorted test rigs were built under the Tu-160 programme, including an "iron bird" for the control system, rigs for the wing pivots and actuators, the crew rescue system (a flight deck section with ejection seats mounted on a rocket-propelled sled), the electric system, the fuel system, the air intakes, the landing gear, the weapons bays and so on, and the KPM-1600 integrated simulation rig (***kom****pleks* ***po****lunatoornovo* *mode****lee****rovaniya*). This direction of work was organised by the plant's chief engineer Aleksey V. Meshcheryakov and V. P. Voronkov. Much attention was also paid to developing and refining methods of computer-aided design. This was done under the guidance of Ivan L. Mindrul, Boris P. Beloglazov and A. S. Markov.

Speaking of ejection seats, the original KT-1 seats were by then replaced by K-36LM zero-zero ejection seats. Created by NPP *Zvez****da*** (*naoo****ch****no-proiz****vod****stvennoye predpri****yah****tiye* – 'Star' Scientific & Production Enterprise), a specialised enterprise under Chief Designer Guy I. Severin, the K-36 was by then the standard ejection seat of all new Soviet combat aircraft.

Serious research in the field of aircraft armament was conducted at the Tupolev OKB under the leadership of Dmitriy A Gorskiy with the participation of I. I. Tret'yakov, V. S. Demchenko, A. S. Smirnov and the personnel under their command. By then the Kh-45 was relegated to second place among the Tu-160's weapons options, if not yet eliminated from the list altogether (according to some sources, development this missile went on until the early 1980s). MKB Raduga and the Tupolev OKB submitted a joint technical proposal for a low-level subsonic cruise missile to be used against ground targets and surface ships with a low radar signature – the Kh-55. It was to have a nuclear warhead, a correlation navigation system and a terrain-following feature helping it to avoid detection and interception; the missile was to be developed in standard and strategic (extended-range) versions, the latter being designated Kh-55SM (*strate****gich****eskaya, modif****itsee****rovannaya* – strategic, modified). At first the MAP and Air Force top brass decided not to go ahead with the strategic version. However, they changed their minds in 1976 when it became clear that that the USA was speedily developing the Boeing AGM-86B (ALCM-B) strategic air-launched cruise missile and work on the Kh-55SM resumed.

Development of the Kh-55 was officially sanctioned by a Council of Ministers directive issued on December 8, 1976. By then, however, MKB Raduga had been working on the missile for nearly six months at its own initiative.

The missile changed appreciably in the course of the design work. The first project version of the Kh-55 had a fuselage with a long pointed nose, an untapered rear end (which gave no indication of the propulsion type – jet engine or rocket motor) and an almost full-length dorsal conduit; the fuselage cross-section was circular, except where the wings were attached at approximately one-third of the length. The missile had a low-wing layout with high aspect ratio constant-chord wings having about 35° leading-edge sweep and tips cropped parallel to the fuselage axis; the tail unit comprised a short fixed fin and much longer all-movable stabilisers in an inverted-V arrangement, all three having a trap-

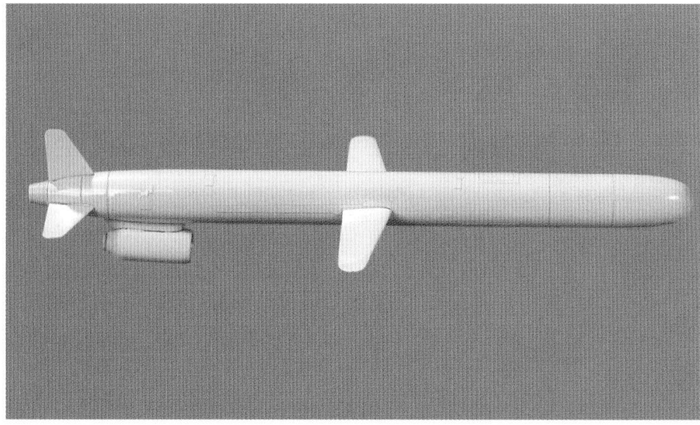

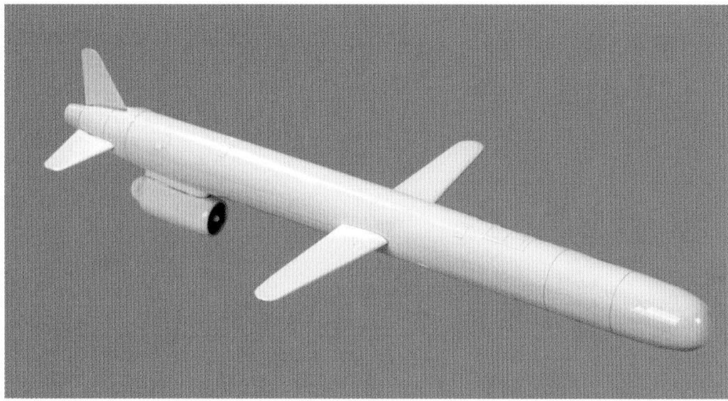

ezoidal shape with no trailing-edge sweep. In pre-launch configuration the wings and tail surfaces were folded, the wing panels being positioned above one another, to enable carriage on a rotary launcher.

The second version, known in house as *izdeliye* 120, still had the low-wing layout but the wings had a lower aspect ratio, less sweepback when deployed and rounded tips; they were repositioned aft, being located amidships. The fuselage nose had a blunter ogival shape and the conduit was gone. The powerplant was a small turbofan engine whose high fuel efficiency afforded the required range. The close-cowled engine was stowed in the rear fuselage when the missile was in pre-launch configuration, swinging down on a pantographic mechanism immediately after the missile was released; immediately aft of the engine bay the fuselage tapered to a cropped cone. For a while MKB Raduga contemplated a small propfan engine driving contra-rotating pusher propellers located aft of the tail surfaces. The tail unit was also revised, the sideways-folding fin being slightly larger and the stabilisers slightly smaller than before. The airframe was carefully shaped to minimise its RCS.

Three engine makers – MNPO *Soyooz* (*Mos**kov**skoye naoo**ch**no-proiz**vod**stvennoye obyedi**neni**ye* – 'Union' Moscow Scientific & Production Association), the Omsk Engine Design Bureau (OMKB – ***Om**skoye **mo**torno-kon**strook**torskoye **byu**ro*) and NPO Trood (the Kuznetsov OKB) – offered disposable turbofan designs for the Kh-55. MKB Raduga picked the R95-300 developed by MNPO Soyooz under the guidance of Oleg N. Favorskiy. Initially rated at 300-350 kgp (660-770 lbst), this engine with a bypass ratio of 2.0 had a two-stage fan (low-pressure compressor), a seven-stage high-pressure compressor, an annular combustion chamber, a two-stage turbine, an aft-mounted cartridge starter, a built-in generator and a self-contained lubrication system. The R95-300 had full authority digital engine controls (FADEC). The engine was 0.85 m (2 ft 9 15/32 in) long, with a diameter of 0.315 m (1 ft 13/32 in), and weighed 95 kg (209 lb). It ran on ordinary T-1 or TS-1 jet fuel or specially developed T-10 grade synthetic fuel (decilin), with an SFC of 0.785 kg/kgp·hr. The R95-300 entered production at the Zaporozhye engine factory in the Ukraine (now called Motor Sich). Some sources call this engine RDK-300 (*re'ak**tiv**nyy **dvig**atel' **ko**rotkore**soors**nyy* – short-life jet engine). (Note: The R95-300 turbofan is not to be confused with the Gavrilov R95Sh – a 4,100-kgp (9,040-lbst) non-afterburning turbojet developed for the Sukhoi Su-25 *Frogfoot* attack aircraft.)

The missile had an inertial navigation system with mid-course correction based on correlation with the digital map downloaded into the missile's computer. The digital map-making software was specially developed for the Kh-55.

Soon, however, MKB Raduga was asked to adapt the Kh-55 for naval use in addition to air launch because the KS-122 ground-launched/sea-launched cruise missile (GLCM/SLCM) under

Above left: A scale model of the standard Kh-55 air-launched cruise missile with the wings, tail surfaces and engine deployed.

Left: A Kh-55 missile in flight configuration.

development at the *Novator* (Innovationist) OKB was facing serious delays. (The KS-122 did eventually enter service as the RK-55 or *izdeliye* 3K12 *Rel'yef* [Terrain profile], receiving the NATO codename SSC-X-4 *Slingshot.*) Therefore the Kh-55's airframe was considerably redesigned. The definitive version, still known as *izdeliye* 120, had the fuselage diameter reduced from 0.77 to 0.514 m (from 2 ft 6 5/16 in to 1 ft 8 15/64 in) and the fuselage cross-section was made circular throughout in order to enable launch from a 533-mm (20 63/64 in) torpedo tube. Hence the missile now had a mid-wing layout; the wings, which had the same shape with rounded tips, were now unswept and folded aft into a recess in the fuselage. The nose had a parabolic shape, the rear fuselage was again gently tapered; the tail surfaces were now all of the same size and the stabiliser anhedral was reduced.

The fuselage was made mostly of aluminium/magnesium alloy and built in three sections. Section 1 featured a large dielectric radome enclosing the guidance system avionics. The front end of Section 2 (the centre fuselage) was a heat-insulated warhead bay, followed by a fuel tank incorporating the wing stowage bay. The wings, which were one-piece GRP structures lacking control surfaces, were stowed above one another to save space, making the missile look lop-sided when they were deployed by a pyrotechnical actuator with a synchronisation mechanism preventing asymmetrical deployment; the slits for the wings were closed by spring-loaded doors to ensure a smooth airflow. Further aft was the engine bay flanked by more fuel tanks; it featured ventral clamshell doors which closed around the engine pylon when the engine was lowered into position. Section 3 (the rear fuselage) accommodated the BSU-55 automated flight control system (*bortovaya sistema oopravleniya*) and the self-contained tail surface actuators. It terminated in a tailcone which consisted of a spring-loaded telescopic rod and a set of concentric rings held together by fabric strips; the tailcone was collapsed in pre-launch configuration to save space, extending at the moment of launch to reduce drag and improve control efficiency. The all-movable fin and stabilators made of GRP had a double-jointed "snap-action" design to make sure they were completely within the fuselage diameter when folded; they were similarly deployed by pyrotechnical actuators, the segments being held in position by locks.

Above right: A 1/17th scale model of the B-1 in the wind tunnel with the wings at minimum sweep. Note the small canard foreplanes giving the bomber a smoother ride in turbulence at low altitude. Soviet specialists kept track of all information on the B-1 published in the western press.

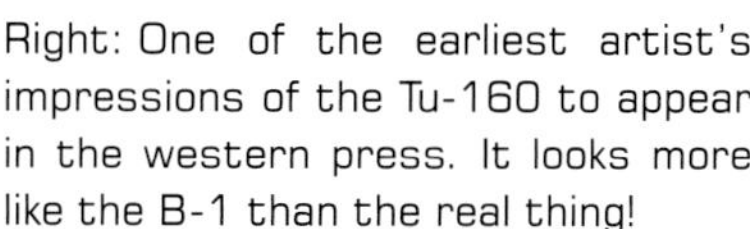

Right: One of the earliest artist's impressions of the Tu-160 to appear in the western press. It looks more like the B-1 than the real thing!

Apart from the fuselage diameter, the final version of the Kh-55 was dimensionally unchanged, with a length of 5.88 m (19 ft 3½ in) and a wing span of 3.1 m (10 ft 2 in). The missile had a launch weight of 1,185 kg (2,610 lb), including a 410-kg (904-lb) warhead; some sources state the launch weight as 1,300 kg (2,870 lb). After being launched by an aircraft flying at 200-10,000 m (660-32,810 ft) and 540-1,050 km/h (335-652 mph) the missile would descend to 40-110 m (130-360 ft) and follow the pre-programmed route to the target, making use of the terrain-following feature. Cruising speed was 720-830 km/h (447-515 mph) or Mach 0.8; maximum range was 2,500 km (1,552 miles).

The compact thermonuclear warhead with a yield of 200 kilotons was specially developed for the Kh-55 by the Moscow-based All-Union Automatic Systems Research Institute named after Nikolay L. Dookhov (VNIIA – *Vsesoyooznyy naoochno-issledovatel'skiy institoot avtomahtiki*) headed by Arkadiy A. Brish, a division of the Ministry of Medium Machinery (MSM – *Ministerstvo srednevo mashinostroyeniya*) responsible for the Soviet nuclear programme. Later this warhead found use on the Kh-15 missile as well.

The Kh-55SM strategic version differed from the baseline Kh-55 mainly in having a marginally greater length of 6.04 m (19 ft 9⁵¹⁄₆₄ in) and conformal tanks of complex shape mounted low on the forward fuselage sides to extend range, which increased maximum fuselage width to the original 0.77 m. The launch weight rose to 1,465 kg (3,230 lb), although some sources quote a figure of 1,700 kg (3,750 lb); maximum range was 3,000 km (1,863 miles). The baseline Kh-55 received the NATO codename AS-15A *Kent-A*, the Kh-55SM being the AS-15B *Kent-B*.

The new missile was longer than the Kh-15, necessitating development of a new rotary launcher. This was apparently initially designated MAPU-6-514 (*mnogopozitsionnoye aviatsionnoye pooskovoye oostroystvo* – multi-position aircraft-mounted launcher, six-round, model 514?); the designation was later changed to MKU-6-5.

Despite the complexity, the ADP was eventually completed in 1976 and the following year a full-size wooden mock-up was built at MMZ "Opyt." In 1977, the project and the mock-up were submitted to the so-called mock-up review commission (*maketnaya komissiya*), an expert panel composed of industry and Air Force representatives. This was an obligatory stage of the design process (similar to the so-called "gates" of today) ensuring that any obvious errors were detected and eliminated before the first metal was cut, thereby avoiding waste of time and resources.

The project and the mock-up were duly approved, albeit the military pointed out a few bugs which had to be eliminated. Here we will again quote the memoirs of Col.-Gen. Vasiliy V. Reshetnikov, who was on the commission. They bear testimony to the hard time the Tupolev OKB had when it came to defending the ADP of the Tu-160 (*izdeliye* 70).

"In the Oval Hall of the Tupolev OKB Aleksey Andreyevich, looking very composed and solemn, was presenting the preliminary design project (*sic – Auth.*) *of a new bomber called Tu-160.*

For a minute or two we were silent, taking in the estimated performance presented in the tables and graphs, studying the 'exploded view' of the airframe and mentally assembling it into a complete aircraft. The unfamiliar looks of the bomber were stern and forbidding, even though it bore a certain outward resemblance to the American B-1...

The reports delivered to us were so detailed as to seemingly preclude any ambiguity. Yet both the General Designer and his aides were literally swamped in questions. It was plain to see that in the estimates the engineers were taking the aircraft to the limit. (*Sic*; what Reshetnikov meant to say is that the estimated performance figures obviously looked over-optimistic – *Auth.*) *However, in real life all performance figures would inevitably slip dramatically. What then? Where would the real Mach limit be? What would the actual range be? What if the L/D ratio turned out to be lower than advertised? Would not the variable geometry wings make the aircraft overweight and sluggish? The questions kept coming, giving rise to new ones, and the answers were slow in coming.*

My work group, which was later transformed into the Tu-160's mock-up review commission and then into the State commission, spent a lot of time working at the OKB in frequent sessions. Weight figures were updated almost daily; the goddamn weight kept rising like a doomed patient's fever, a ton here and a ton there adding up to dozens, while the subcontractors responsible for the equipment and armament (or, at any rate, most of them) kept shamelessly cramming their obsolete, overweight goodies into the aircraft without a word of apology. And there was no stopping them because they had no competition. Balancing like a tightrope walker over an abyss, TsAGI worked hard to save the estimated performance, calculating the aerodynamics over and over again. Yet the recommendations they gave were to no avail because the weight kept rising still further."

As per ADP documents the Tu-160 had an estimated TOW of 260,000 kg (573,190 lb) and an operating empty weight of 103,000 kg (227,070 lb); the fuel load was 148,000 kg (326,280 lb) and the normal weapons load was 9,000 kg (19,840 lb). The aircraft was slightly larger than its American counterpart and look-alike, the B-1A.

Later the weapons range was somewhat narrowed; the OKB chose not to use the Kh-45 missile, leaving the Tu-160 with either air-launched versions of the Kh-55 on two six-round rotary launchers or Kh-15s on two or four rotary launchers (plus various bombs). Eventually, however, the missile armament was limited to a single type, the Kh-55 or Kh-55SM, of which twelve were carried.

In 1977, the Kuznetsov OKB started actual design work on the NK-32 afterburning turbofan. A flight-cleared engine entered flight test at LII in 1980 on the second of two Tu-142LL engine testbeds, a converted Tu-142M *Bear-F Mod 2* ASW aircraft (construction number 4243). The NK-32 was carried in a large semi-retractable nacelle under the former weapons bay.

Meanwhile the All-Union Radio Equipment Research Institute (VNIIRA – *Vsesoyooznyy naoochno-issledovatel'skiy institoot rahdioapparatoory*) in Leningrad, a.k.a. LNPO ***Leninets*** (*Leningrahdskoye naoochno-proizvodstvennoye obyedineniye* – 'Leninist' Leningrad Scientific & Production Association), proceeded with the development of the Tu-160's Poisk navigation/attack radar. VNIIRA, a division of the Ministry of Radio Industry (MRP – *Ministerstvo rahdiopromyshlennosti*), was one of the Soviet Union's leading avionics houses; it is now known as the

Above and below: A scaled-strength model of the Tu-160 to one-third scale at MMZ "Opyt"; the fork-lift truck provides a size reference.

Leninets Holding Company. In the late 1970s an Ilyushin Il-18V *Coot* four-turboprop medium-haul airliner registered CCCP-75786 was converted into the SL-18V avionics testbed (SL = *samo**lyot**-labora**tor**iya* – "laboratory aircraft," that is, testbed); the Poisk radar enclosed by a long conical radome was installed on a special adapter, supplanting the standard RPSN-3 *Em**ble**ma* weather radar in a parabolic radome. The SL-18V operated from VNIIRA's flight test centre in the town of Pushkin (Leningrad Region), sometimes venturing out over international waters where it was intercepted and photographed by NATO fighters.

Here it is worth quoting a report sent by the Tupolev OKB to MAP in order to sum up the work done so far:

"1. The Communist Party Central Committee/Council of Ministers directive dated 19.12.75 tasked the Ministry of Aircraft Industry and other militarily important ministries with creating the Tu-160 strategic multi-mode missile strike aircraft. The aircraft was to be capable of high supersonic speeds, of high subsonic speeds at low altitude and of prolonged flight (up to 20 hours) at high altitude.

Therefore we were forced (*sic – Auth.*) *to select variable geometry wings.*

2. In order to solve such a tremendous problem as the development of the Tu-160, a large scope of R&D work was performed jointly with TsAGI, TsIAM, NIAT and the research institutes of other ministries, which required completely new approaches [to design tasks] and new scopes of research. For example, 70 versions of wind tunnel models were tested, with a total wind tunnel time of 2,200 hours. The lift/drag ratio we have obtained is better than the B-1's at subsonic and supersonic speeds alike.

3. Regarding structural design and technology, in order to obtain the required payload/weight ratio, which is extremely difficult for such a huge aircraft with VG wings, we have opted for a blended wing/body design which combines the wing leading-edge root portions and the fuselage into a single whole – this reduces the wetted area and the drag, improves the lift/drag ratio and reduces the surface area of the structural components, thereby cutting structural weight.

As for the movable outer wings, in order to minimise weight and obtain good flutter resistance at high speeds we have used a new stringerless design and a new technology – [each outer wing has] six ribs and no stringers; sheets of extra pure aluminium 20 m [65 ft 7¹³/₃₂ in] long are used, the leading-edge and trailing-edge sections are made of composite materials with a honeycomb core, large titanium panels are used etc.

The wing centre section (the wing pivot box – *Auth.*), *which absorbs extremely high loads from the wing pivots reaching 3,000 tons [6,613,760 lb], is manufactured using electron beam welding, with a minimum of nut-and-bolt joints. A new method of structural design is used whereby the condition of the structural component under stress is determined and material (titanium) is accreted to suit that condition. To make this technology possible, MAP jointly with the [Kiev-based Electric Welding] Institute named after [Yevgeniy O.] Paton has developed automated welding chambers and vacuum annealing chambers.*

The design of the cargo doors (*sic* – that is, weapons bay doors – *Auth.*) *was a major design problem. In order to accommodate 12-24 items* (a euphemism for missiles – *Auth.*) *the cargo bays have a volume [...] three times larger than on the [Boeing] B-52 [Stratofortress] or the Tu-95MS. Consider that such a volume, such an 'apartment' has to be opened wide at supersonic speeds and [the structure] needs to be strong enough to withstand the fluctuating structural loads and thermal loads [arising in these conditions]. To cope with this problem we have developed a rigid structure made of composites with a honeycomb core.*

The tail surfaces utilise monolithic [skin] panels with a honeycomb filler. The aircraft will have honeycomb core composite structures with a total surface area of 500 m² [5,381.96 sq ft].

4. To make sure this radically new type of structure (by Soviet standards anyway – *Auth.*) *meets structural strength requirements we have undertaken a large scope of structural strength research and are planning to conduct more. 12,000 static test articles have been manufactured [under the Tu-160 programme], some of them weighing as much as 150 kg [330 lb]. A structurally similar model of the Tu-160 to 1:12.5th scale and a scaled-strength model to 1:3rd scale have been built; new methods of determining structural stress have been evolved; the second Tu-160 development airframe (the static test airframe) is currently under construction and there are plans to build a fatigue test airframe.*

5. A large scope of work has been undertaken to reduce the aircraft's radar signature.

6. V[asiliy] A. Kazakov (the then Minister of Aircraft Industry – *Auth.*) *has personally undertaken a large scope of work on integrating the avionics and the engines. This was aided by the MoD's special work group for scientific and technical support of the industry. A lot of work on the aircraft's equipment has been performed by MAP, MRP, MPSS* (*Mini**ster**stvo pro**mysh**lennosti sredstv **svyazi*** – Ministry of Communications Equipment Industry), *MOP* (*Mini**ster**stvo obo**ron**noy pro**mysh**lennosti* – Ministry of Defence Industry) and MEP (*Mini**ster**stvo elek**tron**noy pro**mysh**lennosti* – Ministry of Electronics Industry). *[...]*

In accordance with a Council of Ministers directive an engine with a take-off thrust of 25 tons [55,115 lbst], an SFC of 0.72-0.73 kg/kgp·hr, FADEC and very high performance, including thrust/weight ratio, is being developed for the Tu-160. The aggregate power of four such engines will be more than half a million horsepower (*sic – Auth.*). *[The] Kuznetsov [OKB] and other organisations have performed a large scope of work on the engines. Yet, a lot remains to be done in order to ensure the required engine life, SFC and stable engine operation in the conditions of real-life airflow fluctuations in the inlets. [...]*

8. Much attention has been paid to perfecting the design and the aircraft's equipment on test rigs. 60 ground rigs and seven testbed aircraft are being created to support the programme. [...]

9. New machine tools and [technological] equipment are necessary to support the new technology. MAP has developed a number of new machine tools, the Ministry of Machine Tool Industry is also working on it. [...]

10. At present the state of the Tu-160 programme in MAP is that we have a good grip on the problem, the aircraft looks set to meet the operational requirement and we have realised the actual scale and grandeur of the problem..." Well, this lofty style was occasionally encountered in official documents of the time.

Chapter 3

The Tu-160 Becomes Reality: The Trials Programme

The design of the Tu-160 (*izdeliye* 70) was finally frozen in 1977 and construction of the first prototype began at MMZ "Opyt" in Moscow that same year. Logically enough, this aircraft was known in house as *izdeliye* 70-01 (which may be regarded as its construction number) or "aircraft 01." However, it also had the slang appellation *noo**lyo**vka* (something like "Aircraft Zilch"). This derived from the Tupolev OKB's habit of designating the first airframe of a new type built by the prototype manufacturing facility as aircraft 00 (rather than 01) in its production batch (for example, the first prototype of the Tu-134 was c/n 00-00).

By the time the report quoted in the preceding chapter was filed to MAP, MMZ "Opyt" had set to work on the static test airframe, *izdeliye* 70-02 (or "aircraft 02"), and was preparing to build the second prototype, *izdeliye* 70-03 ("aircraft 03"). Alternatively, the latter may be regarded as the sole pre-production aircraft. Construction of the first three Tu-160 airframes proceeded in close co-operation with the Kazan' aircraft factory No.22 named after Sergey P. Gorbunov (the plant's director in 1930–33) which, as already mentioned, had been chosen to build the type in series.

A couple of comments need to be made here. Firstly, a peculiarity of the Soviet aircraft industry was that, unlike the western aircraft manufacturers, the OKBs had no aircraft factories of their own – only prototype manufacturing facilities which could build anything, but only in a few copies, being unsuited for mass production. The major aircraft factories were all controlled by MAP and built what the ministry told them to. On the other hand, most

The first prototype Tu-160 (*izdeliye* 70-01) at the LII airfield in Zhukovskiy in January 1981 upon completion of reassembly.

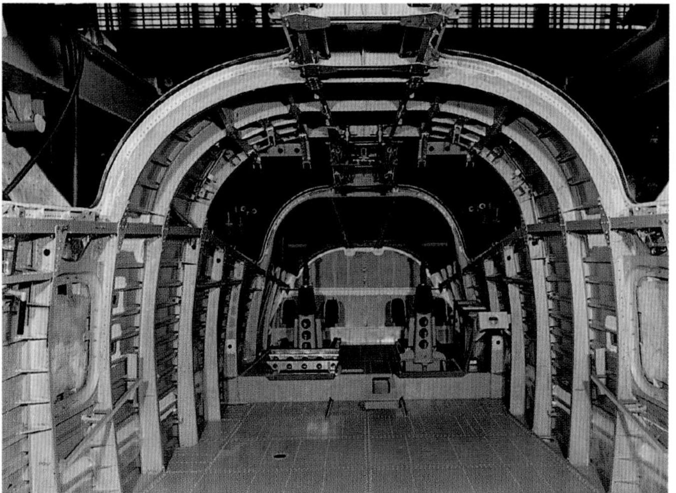

of these factories historically had strong ties with a particular design bureau, producing predominantly aircraft of the same make. This was because different aircraft from the same OKB usually had considerable technological commonality, meaning no complete change of the manufacturing process was required when a new type entered production. MAP plant No.22, which became known as KAPO (*Kazahnskoye aviatsionnoye proizvodstvennoye obyedineniye* – Kazan' Aircraft Production Association named after Sergey P. Gorbunov) in 1978, was a case in point. Its association with the Tupolev OKB had started back in the 1930s; such important aircraft types as the pre-war ANT-40 (SB) fast bomber, the wartime Tu-2 *Bat* medium bomber, the post-war Tu-4 *Bull* heavy bomber (a reverse-engineered Boeing B-29 Superfortress) and the Tu-22 supersonic heavy bomber had all been produced there. At the time plant No.22 was building the Tu-22M and thus was familiar with 'swing-wing' designs, which was also very probably a factor influencing the choice of the plant. At present the Kazan' aircraft factory is part of the Tupolev PLC.

Secondly, in the Soviet Union it was fairly common practice to launch series production of a new aircraft long before the trials programme had been completed – unless the aircraft was obviously a dead duck. In this case, however, full-scale preparations for series production began *before the Tu-160 had even flown*! Of course, this was a measure of the need to create and field a Soviet counterpart of the B-1 as soon as possible in response to the new threat from the United States. Still, this says a lot for the faith the leaders of the Soviet state, the Air Force and the aircraft industry had in the new Tupolev bomber.

In the course of the three airframes' construction the Tupolev OKB's experimental facility and the Kazan' plant did a lot of work

Far left: The NIAT ELU-24-8 electron beam welding machine at MMZ "Opyt" which was used for manufacturing the prototypes' titanium airframe parts.

Left: The outer half of a wing pivot, with a part of the wing pivot box in the background.

Below, far left: The first prototype's flight deck section in its assembly jig emblazoned "Socialist competition."

Below left: The wing pivot box in the course of assembly.

Bottom left: The as-yet bare interior of the first prototype's flight deck. Note the control stick podiums.

Right: The same machine's rear fuselage in the assembly jig at MMZ "Opyt."

Below: The forward fuselage takes shape. The slogan on the wall reads, "Implement the decisions of the 25th Communist Party Congress!"

Left: Another angle on the first prototype's forward/centre fuselage being assembled. The slogan on the back wall reads, "Assembly workers! The quality of your work is put to the test in flight." Note the absence of the IFR probe between the avionics bay access hatches in the extreme nose (fuselage section F-1). The captain's ejection hatch cover is in place for a trial fit; note that it appears to have four windows instead of the two seen on the project drawings.

Right and below right: More views of the same scene. Part of the skin on section F-4 is still missing, exposing the underlying structure (fuselage frames and front weapons bay walls); the front parts of the LERXes (section F-3) can be seen in the component build-up area in the lower photo, awaiting installation. The circular aperture is for the navigation system's star tracker. Note the varying skin colour; the golden-coloured panels are electrochemically coated.

to verify and master the manufacturing technologies developed for the Tu-160. The choice of the correct structural materials became crucial here; most of them had proved their worth on the Tu-144. The primary materials were much the same as in the preceding Tu-160M project – AK4-1Ch aluminium alloy (the Ch suffix denoted ***chistyy*** – pure, referring to the aluminium base) and OT-4 heat-resistant titanium alloy (*ogne**stoy**kiy ti**tahn*** – fireproof titanium). Additionally, V-95PCh-AT2 aluminium alloy (V = *vysoko**proch**nyy* – high-strength, 95 is the number of the foundry in the Urals producing the alloy, PCh = [*alyu**mi**niy*] ***povyshennoy chistoty*** – enhanced-purity aluminium, AT2 is a code for the thermal treatment mode) and VT-6Ch titanium alloy (*vysoko**proch**nyy ti**tahn*** – high-strength titanium), both of which had recently been put into production by the Soviet metallurgical industry, were used on a large scale. Much attention was paid to launching production of semi-manufactured articles made of these alloys, including large forged and rolled slabs, large stamped parts and extruded profiles, large skin panels made of 6-mm (15/64 in) sheet.

The manufacturing technology, which was put through its paces at MMZ "Opyt" before being introduced at plant No.22, included welding and machining of large titanium parts and structures, manufacturing bonded sandwich panels with a honeycomb core and so on. The fuselage was assembled from large stamped parts, profiles and skin panels, making use of a special riveting technique. The wings had monobloc torsion boxes assembled from chemically milled panels and profiles; the control surfaces (upper fin, stabilators, flaperons and spoilers) and high-lift devices made large-scale use of metal and GRP panels with a honeycomb core. The engine nacelles were constructed from thin-walled welded titanium elements and aluminium alloy sandwich panels, the air intake sections being made of AK4-1 and having a riveted design.

Implementing these manufacturing technologies called for a lot of specialised equipment to be developed, including large cutting and milling tools, extruding machines, welding equipment and thermal treatment (hardening and annealing) equipment. Many of these machines, such as the ELU-24 electron beam welding chamber (*elek**tron**no-loochevaya oostanovka*) and the UVN-4500M annealing oven (*oosta**nov**ka **va**kuumnovo nagre**va**niya* – vacuum heating installation), were unique. It proved possible to manufacture the welded titanium wing pivot carry-through structure as a single whole with the wing pivots, which were welded to it on the prototypes – albeit this was soon to change on production aircraft.

The manufacturing technologies devised for the Tu-160 that were successfully implemented at the Kazan' aircraft factory and

КАЧЕСТВО ВАШЕГО ТРУДА ПРОВЕРЯЕТСЯ В ПОЛЕТЕ
ПЯТИЛЕТКЕ КАЧЕСТВА-РАБОЧУЮ ГАРАНТИЮ!

other production plants participating in the programme were developed by the prototype manufacturing facility 's chief technologist Semyon A. Vigdorchik, engineers E. M. Rumyantsev and Vladimir V. Sadkov. A team under the direction of Boris A. Peshekhonov and V. P. Azhazha was responsible for the introduction of new non-metallic structural materials into production. The Tupolev OKB teams headed by Viktor I. Borod'ko (Director of MMZ 'Opyt'), Aleksey V. Meshcheryakov, Vladimir P. Nikolayev (armament section), G. F. Volkov, Mikhail A. Bormashenko (co-ordinator/procurement specialist), V. V. Antamokhin and V. P. Fadeyev also contributed much to the manufacturing of the three airframes at the experimental plant.

Construction of a first prototype is always a protracted affair, particularly in the case of an aircraft as large and complex as the Tu-160. *Izdeliye* 70-01 took nearly three years to build. In the summer of 1980 the partially assembled aircraft was trucked to the now-famous LII airfield in the town of Zhukovskiy south of Moscow where the Tupolev OKB, like most of the Soviet aircraft design bureaux, had its flight test facility. The latter was known as ZhLIiDB (*Zhoo**kov**skaya* ***lyot**no-ispy**tah**tel'naya i do**vod**ochnaya* ***bah**za* – the Zhukovskiy Flight Test & Refinement Base). Ground systems checks on the still-incomplete aircraft began on 22nd October 1980. In January 1981, the first prototype was finally completed and rolled out but still far from ready to fly. The aircraft had a mostly natural metal finish, with the exception of the radome, outer wings, upper fin section, stabilators, tailcone and weapons bay doors, which were painted white (it never did receive a full coat of paint). This, and the different shades of metal here and there, gave it a patchwork appearance. The radome had an ogival shape and featured an air data boom with pitch/yaw transducer vanes at the tip; this boom was part of the test equipment. The tactical code '18 Grey' was carried on the port nosewheel well door.

(Note: Unlike western military aircraft, which have *serial numbers* allowing positive identification, since 1955, Soviet Air Force aircraft had two-digit *tactical codes*, which were allocated within a particular unit and changed if the machine was transferred to a different unit; this system is still in use today. This resulted in lots of sister aircraft from different units having identical codes, making positive identification impossible [for security reasons]. Three- or four-digit codes are rare and are usually worn by development aircraft, in which case they tie in with the manufacturer's designation, c/n or fuselage number [line number], or by aircraft belonging to Air Force flying schools. On military transport aircraft, the occasionally encountered three-digit tactical codes are the last three of the former civil registration – most of the Soviet/Russian Air Force transports were, and still are, quasi-civil.)

Opposite page and below: The front and rear fuselage halves of *izdeliye* 70-01 are mated with the wing pivot box in 1980. The tail unit is in place, though the skin on the lower fin section is partly missing. The banner reads: "Comrades, workers and engineering staff! The successful completion of order No. 1918/1 is a worthy gift to the 26th Part Congress [in February-March 1981], socialist competition..."

Izdeliye 70-01 at Zhukovskiy in the spring of 1981. Note the pitot at the tip of the radome.

The ground test and systems refining stage continued until November, lasting nearly ten months. On November 14, 1981, the bomber moved under its own power for the first time, with Tupolev OKB project test pilot Boris I. Veremey in the captain's seat. Veremey was an old-timer, having worked at the OKB since 1965 (and before that at the Kazan' aircraft factory where he head check-flown production Tu-16 and Tu-22 bombers), and specialised in military aircraft. He had taken the Tu-22M0 *Backfire-A* up on its maiden flight as co-pilot on August 30, 1969, and tested other versions of the *Backfire* as captain; therefore his appointment as Tu-160 project test pilot was hardly a matter of chance.

There are varying accounts of how the crew for the Tu-160's first flight was picked. Well, test pilots are only human after all, and they have ambitions, friendships and animosities as much as anyone else. Tupolev OKB test pilot Sergey T. Agapov recounted the matter thus: *"Aleksey A. Tupolev [...] summoned me to his study in connection with the forthcoming flight tests of the Tu-160. Tupolev began coaxing me: 'Seryozha* (the pet form of the name Sergey – *Auth.*)*, why don't you fly [the Tu-160] as co-pilot? With Veremey. He has done a lot of training...'*

'Well, it's him who had to spend all that time practicing, not me; I don't need to' – I replied. – 'I won't fly as co-pilot! After all, who am I and who is Veremey?! He has got me into precarious situations more than once! Why me? There are good pilots who are younger than me – such as [Vladimir N.] Matveyev. Let him fly with Veremey! The aircraft will take ten years or so to get it up to scratch; this is why you need a young pilot.' (Agapov was then aged 49, Veremey was 46 and Matveyev was 35 – *Auth.*)

'No! Veremey won't fly without you!' – Tupolev pressed on.

I would not give in. 'Why does it have to be me? I'm recommending you a good young pilot with great potential.'

'No! I ask you kindly to take on this mission.'

'Aleksey Andreyevich, why on earth are you asking me when you're pinning your hopes on Veremey?'

'Seryozha, do fly! I'll get you the Hero of the Soviet Union title!' – Tupolev insisted.

'You have filed an official nomination for the HSU title twice, Aleksey Andreyevich; are you going to do it for the third time? That's all empty talk.'

'I promise you – you will get the HSU title when you fly! Can you do this for the common cause?'

'All right, all right – so be it' – I agreed."

(Jumping ahead of the story, we may add that Tupolev kept his promise; Sergey T. Agapov received the prestigious HSU title on August 12, 1982 – ahead of Veremey, who was awarded the HSU title on June 13, 1984. Both of them received it *"for mastering new combat hardware"* [a common phrase in official documents concerning awards in those days] – that is, the Tu-160.)

Agapov said in an interview for the press that there was a lot of underhand activity around the Tu-160 and the issue of who was to fly it. Due to his advanced age he genuinely felt no urge to fly the Tu-160 (no matter how prestigious it might be), considering it a 'not-in-my-lifetime' sort of aeroplane. Therefore he recommended first Viktor I. Shkatov and then Vladimir N. Matveyev as co-pilot. However, according to Agapov, the OKB's flight department chief Eduard V. Yelian (the test pilot who had taken the Tu-144 on its

Above and below: More views of the first prototype at Zhukovskiy, showing how the flaperons "bleed" down when the aircraft is parked. Note that the pilots' ejection hatches of *izdeliye* 70-01 had only two windows each (one lateral and one upper).

Left: This aspect of *izdeliye* 70-01 shows such details as the yaw sensor vanes of the air data system underneath the radome, the retracted landing lights between them closed by clamshell doors (the ones on the nose gear strut are the taxi lights), the wraparound nosewheel mudguard/ debris deflector and the differing leading edge treatment on the port and starboard LERXes.

Right: The same aircraft seen from a few feet farther off, showing an aerial or sensor on top of nose where the IFR probe should have been.

Below: This view of the first prototype accentuates its patchwork appearance. The aircraft was never fully painted during its flying career. The light grey panels on the nose and LERXes are detachable maintenance access panels.

Left and below left: These surreptitiously taken photos show the first prototype in an early test flight from Zhukovskiy with a bulged fairing (probably associated with test equipment) on top of the centre fuselage.

Right and below right: The first prototype Tu-160 on short finals to runway 30 at Zhukovskiy. The sharply pointed fairing at the fin/tailplane junction is clearly visible.

Bottom left: The notorious first photo of the Tu-160 circulated by the western media that was purportedly taken by a US surveillance satellite, showing *izdeliye* 70-01 in company with two Tu-144s on the Tupolev hardstand at Zhukovskiy. In reality it was taken by a passenger on an airliner passing over the LII airfield en route to Moscow-Domodedovo airport.

maiden flight in 1968) had a dislike for Matveyev – a claim that was strongly denied by Tu-160 project chief Valentin I. Bliznyuk. Furthermore, Agapov flatly refused to fly with Veremey, whom he considered a much less skilled pilot than himself. During the tests of the Tu-22M Veremey and Matveyev had almost crashed in one of the prototypes when Veremey retracted the flaps prematurely on take-off, and Agapov stated that Veremey had behaved dishonestly at the debriefing, laying the blame on Matveyev.

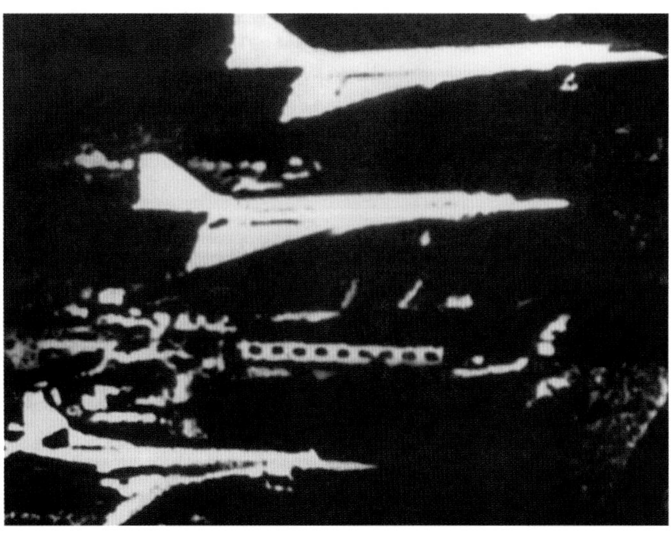

There is, however, an alternative account given by Vasiliy P. Borisov, the Tu-22M's original project test pilot. Borisov was involved at the early stage of the project, and it seemed logical that the pilot who had first flown the OKB's first "swing-wing" design should fly the second one as well because he had the experience. *"I was slated to be in the crew performing the Tu-160's first flight"* – Borisov recalled. – *"At the same time an official nomination was filed for my second HSU title. On learning of this Yelian, who was dead set against it, mustered his supporters who opposed the nomination; their reasoning was 'many of the OKB's test pilots don't even have one HSU title, how come you should have two?' The nomination foundered ...*

I participated in the Tu-160's mock-up review commission and spoke up fairly harshly at times. Now, Yelian would have gladly flown the Tu-160 on its first flight, but he was having heart trouble then; he had to take medical treatment for almost a year. Incidentally, this is the reason why I had to do a lot of test flying in the Tu-144 instead of him, as a stand-in. Then I received an offer to go to Europe for the purpose of training foreign pilots to fly the Tu-154 in poor visibility conditions. I jumped at the idea – I was eager to see the world, to visit other countries. Yelian, however,

Left and above left: *Izdeliye* 70-01 ("18 Grey") seen from a chase plane during its first flight on December 18, 1981. The landing gear remained down throughout the flight. The white-painted outer wings are visible here.

Above and below: The first prototype makes a high-speed flypast with the wings at maximum sweep at Zhukovskiy during one of the MAKS airshows. The lower photo shows the Tu-160's distinctive two-piece pop-up wing fences appearing at 65° wing sweep.

asked me: 'Who do you think is going to take the Tu-160 up on its first flight? Do you want them to write me off?' I said, 'Who? Your crony Veremey!' Veremey sided with Yelian, as did Vedernikov, Agapov and others as well."

Now that we mention Ivan K. Vedernikov, he put it plainly: *"Why did they pick Veremey as Tu-160 project test pilot? Quite simply, we chose the best men! When we selected him, Yelian was flight department chief and I was his deputy chief. Yelian insisted that pilots Veremey and Shkatov and navigators [Aleksandr S.] Shevtsov and [Anatoliy V.] Yeriomenko be assigned to the Tu-160. It was they who initially visited the full-size mock-up, and the number of airmen authorised to do it was initially limited to this foursome – allegedly because the aircraft was so top secret. Later, project chief Bliznyuk readily agreed to my suggestion that other pilots should be allowed to do it as well. Veremey was a brave and resolute man, which spoke in his favour [as a candidate to fly the Tu-160]. He had a lot of experience on the Tu-22 and the '45'*

Opposite top: The second prototype after overrunning the runway at Zhukovskiy and narrowly missing the approach lights; note the open IFR probe doors.

Opposite bottom: Seen through the lens of photo theodolite post 8, the second prototype Tu-160 (*izdeliye* 70-03, coded "29 Grey") takes off from runway 12 at Zhukovskiy past the Myasishchev EMZ compound. One of the engines appears to be belching huge flames.

Right: A lower view of *izdeliye* 70-03 with the wings at 65°. A segment of the front weapons bay doors is painted black, not missing. Note the absence of national insignia on the wings.

Below: The second prototype climbs away, showing its equally patchy appearance and traces of operational wear and tear.

Top and above: Seen here landing on runway 30 at Zhukovskiy, the second prototype had an incident at the MAKS-93 airshow, losing part of the fin fillet skin in a high-speed pass. Note the absence of the nose pitot.

Left: This fragment of a Tu-160 airframe dumped at the Tupolev PLC compound in Zhukovskiy is probably the remains of the static test airframe (*izdeliye* 70-02).

Above right: Here the second prototype is shown after repairs have been made to the damaged fin fillet.

Right: The same aircraft after landing (note the deployed spoilers).

The second prototype Tu-160 (*izdeliye* 70-03) in modified form

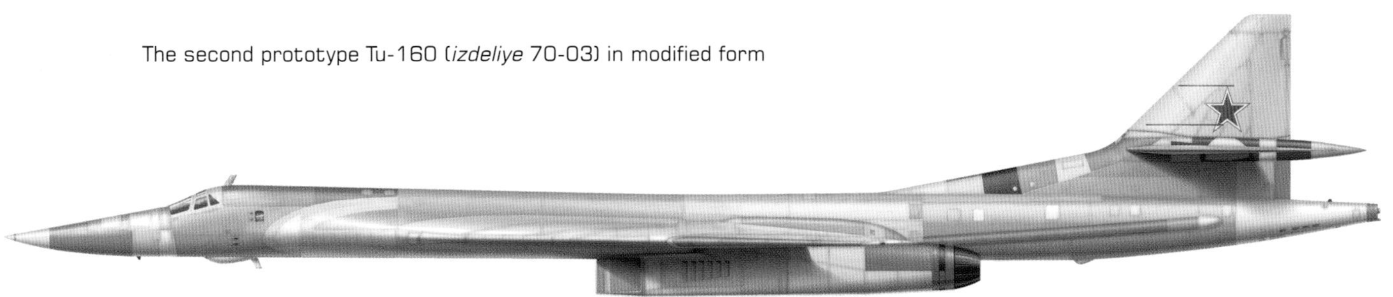

Left: Sitting outside the ZhLIiDB hangar in company with a Tu-22M3 and a Tu-95MS, *izdeliye* 70-01 was no longer airworthy by the mid-1990s.

Below: The second prototype makes a high-speed pass with the wings at maximum sweep during the MAKS-95 airshow.

Opposite page: *Izdeliye* 70-03 makes a climbing turn to starboard at the start of the same demo flight. Note the orange-coloured efflux with a high nitrous oxide content – after all, the NK-32 is a military engine and has manners to match.

(the Tu-22M whose versions have the product codes *izdeliye* 45-00 (Tu-22M0), *izdeliye* 45-01 (Tu-22M1 *Backfire-A*), *izdeliye* 45-02 (Tu-22M2 *Backfire-B*) and *izdeliye* 45-03 (Tu-22M3) – *Auth.). True, he made mistakes occasionally, but he never was at a loss what to do in a difficult situation. Incidentally, Ul'yanov, the engineer in charge of the flight tests, offered [Vasiliy P.] Borisov to take on the Tu-160. Borisov turned down the offer. Later, as the first flight date drew closer, Borisov was eager to fly the Tu-160 but it was too late ..."* Anyway, subsequent events showed that the choice of Boris I. Veremey and Sergey T. Agapov was a good one.

By the end of November, the first prototype had made three high-speed taxi runs. Finally, on December 18, 1981, Veremey took the Tu-160 aloft for its maiden flight. The crew also included co-pilot Sergey T. Agapov and, as the report goes, navigators Mikhail M. Kozel and Anatoliy V. Yeriomenko. The double number of navigators (***shtoorman*** in Russian) is explained by Russian

Top and above: The first production Tu-160 (f/n 1-01) shares the KAPO final assembly shop floor with a production Tu-22M3. Like the first prototype, it had a radome tipped with a long pitot. Note the protective covers on both bombers' windshields to prevent scratches.

Propped up on trestles, the fuselage of the second production Tu-160 (f/n 1-02) sits amidst a thicket of work platforms in one of KAPO's shops in 1984.

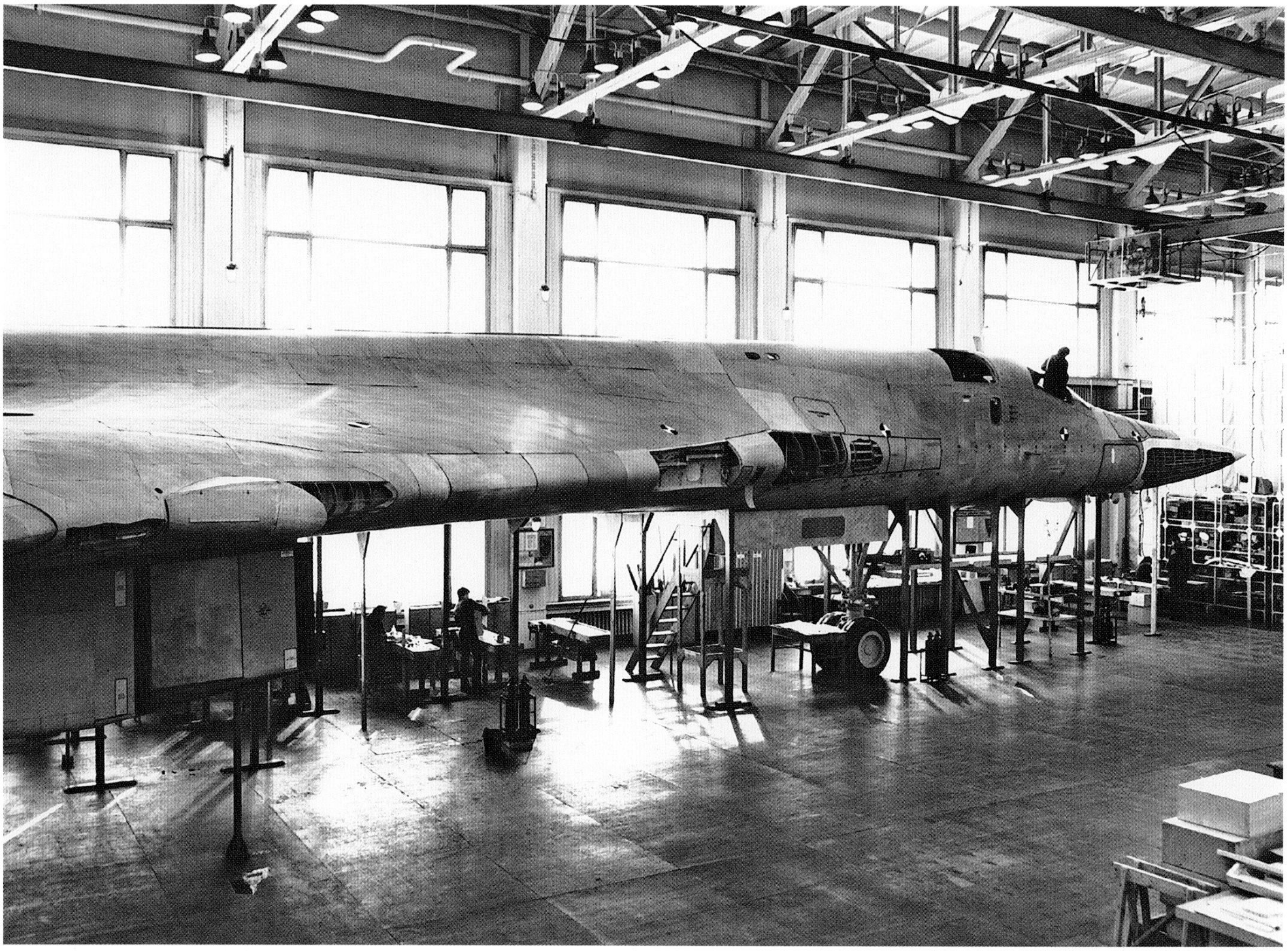

Left: A full-size wooden mock-up of the Tu-160 at MMZ "Opyt." This mock-up helped the specialists of KAPO to launch Tu-160 production.

Below left: The fuselage components of Tu-160 f/n 2-01. The forward fuselage build-up station is in the foreground; section F-1 has been mated to the bottom of section F-2 (note the crew entry hatch in the floor at the rear) but the roof of section F-2 is lying alongside and the side panels are missing. Sections F-4, F-5 and F-6 are arranged behind, waiting to be joined into a single whole.

Right: The first production Tu-160, "30 Grey." was the first Tu-160 to wear the customary all-white anti-flash colour scheme. It was delivered to the Tupolev OKB as a test aircraft.

terminological subtleties; one of the two was indeed the navigator (***shtoor**man-navi**gah**tor*) while the other was not a navigator at all but the weapons systems operator (***shtoor**man-ope**rah**tor*). He is thus called because the WSO has to know a lot about navigation to aim his weapons accurately; it is the same story on the Tu-22M, which also has a crew of four.

The maiden flight took place a day before the 75th birthday of Leonid I. Brezhnev, the then-current Communist Party Secretary General, and was therefore universally regarded as the Tupolev OKB's (and generally the Soviet aircraft industry's) "birthday present" to the Soviet leader. Well, as a matter of fact, so it was. However, before the reader denounces the Tupolev OKB for "toadying," it should be noted that timing major achievements to Communist Party congresses, major public holidays (especially those of ideological importance) and the like was the order of the day in Soviet times. Anyway, we'll let Boris I. Veremey tell the story:

"The bomber looked set to take to the air on 19th December. That was Leonid Il'yich Brezhnev's birthday. it is an established fact that the Secretary General paid much attention to the progress of the Armed Forces, which is why the original intention was to make him a gift in the form of a new bomber's first flight that same day. However, we had received no explicit instructions to make the Tu-160's maiden flight on 19th December, and the flight took place a day earlier. I still remember the 27-minute first flight of 'double zero' (that is, *noolyovka – Auth.*) *in the vicinity of the airfield; we took off, climbed to 2,000 m [6,560 ft], proceeded to the test flying area 150-220 km [93-136 miles] away, then came back and landed. The 'one sixty' had received its baptism.*

The flight was carefully analysed and our comments were checked against the results obtained on a ground test rig. For the first time in the OKB's history a hydromechanical test rig was used to check and refine the aircraft's systems, as is customary in the world's top aircraft manufacturing companies. A special test department headed by project engineer Anatoliy Yashukov had been formed (for the Tu-160 programme – *Auth.*). *We made about 20 flights. From the 13th flight onwards we switched places with Sergey Agapov – he flew the aircraft from the left-hand seat in order to get his own impression of the bomber's handling.*

The aircraft behaved predictably; the data obtained in the first flight matched the ground simulation results. Changes were introduced into the flight control system right away at the pilots' suggestion; the Tu-160 had a fly-by-wire control system which made such changes possible. [...] In addition to yours truly, test pilots Sergey Agapov, Vladimir Smirnov and Naïl' Sattarov took part in the trials." (Actually Lt.-Col. Vladimir S. Smirnov was an Air Force test pilot, and so was Col. Naïl' Sh. Sattarov before he joined the Tupolev OKB – but that was not until 1993! – *Auth.*)

Vadim M. Razumikhin, an engineer of the OKB's flight control system department who was responsible for the abovementioned 'iron bird' control system test rig-cum-flight simulator, recalled: *"All the experience we had accumulated with the '45s'* (Tu-22M versions – *Auth.*), *as well as with the Tu-22, the Tu-28* (the Tu-128 *Fiddler* heavy interceptor – *Auth.*), *all we had learned from many fatal and non-fatal accidents – all that experience went into the Tu-160. Once again we built an 'iron bird' and a processor [controlling the rig]... Boris Ivanovich [Veremey] was very fond of [test] pilot [Viktor I.] Shkatov; they were an incredibly well-matched pair who understood each other at a glance and acted with extreme co-ordination [in flight]. Boris Ivanovich became completely engrossed in the 'flight,' to the point that perspiration trickled from his brow – even though the rig was not very sophisticated: the 'flight deck' was fixed* (unlike a modern flight simulator with three degrees of freedom – *Auth.*) *and the visualisation was not particularly good. Shkatov was much the same in this respect. The short, terse commands they gave were enough to produce prompt and unerring actions at all stages of the 'flight.' Yet, life is life, and politics always have an influence* (or rather company policy, in this case – *Auth.*). *The situation at the [Zhukovskiy]*

flight test facility was very complicated. Shkatov was not assigned as [Tu-160] co-pilot; Agapov was assigned instead. Unfortunately, he had a dislike for the 'iron birds' and had no intimate understanding of them. Even before the maiden flight it was only Boris Ivanovich who practiced on the rig; Agapov did not, despite the fact that it was on the rig that we put the entire control system through its paces, verifying a lot of control laws and algorithms. We spent two years working with that rig..."

After the first flight, which went almost flawlessly, the OKB staff waited impatiently for the crew in a large hall at the ZhLIiDB. One of Veremey's first phrases during the ensuing discussion sounded like sweet music to the engineers' ears: *"The aircraft behaved just like on Razumikhin's rig!"*

Here we have to quote Razumikhin again. *"You can imagine how I felt – it isn't often you feel this way! I was as happy – I mean, as an engineer – as the first time, back when N. N. Kharitonov made the first flight in Tu-22 No.7* (the seventh Tu-22 off the Kazan' production line, c/n 3039022, f/n 3-02 – *Auth.*) *with freshly installed dampers designed by me. On that occasion Nikolay Nikolayevich [Kharitonov] jumped out of the aircraft after the flight and shouted to us, 'Boys, you have just saved this aircraft!' We had introduced dampers [in the control system] which radically improved the stability and handling of this temperamental machine..."* (As an aside, there are indications that the said dampers in the pitch and roll control circuits preventing pilot-induced oscillations which could overstress the Tu-22's airframe were first fitted to a different Tu-22.)

Thus began the manufacturer's flight test phase, which proceeded under the supervision of Valentin T. Klimov, the then Director of ZhLIiDB (he went on to become General Director of ANTK Tupolev, as the company was renamed in 1992) and his aide Vladimir G. Mikhailov. At various stages the complex flight test programme was supported by Mikhail V. Ul'yanov, engineers R. A. Yengoolatov, A. V. Goosev and V. A. Naoomov. A major contribution was made by Tupolev OKB engineers V. V. Babakov, Ye. L. Kornilov, V. V. Teryoshin, Ye. A. Alyoshin and many others who participated in the planning of the flight test missions and rectified the inevitable defects as they cropped up. OKB engineer Yuriy S. Gorbatenko did a lot to help refine the NK-32 engines and make the necessary modifications to the powerplant at short notice.

Of course, being project test pilot, Boris I. Veremey did more flying than anyone else; all in all he made more than 600 flights in the Tu-160, logging more than 2,000 hours. In so doing he formed a close affinity with the aircraft – a sort of kinship, as he put it.

Meanwhile, development of the bomber's principal weapon – the Kh-55 cruise missile – proceeded apace. In early 1978, the Doobna Machinery Plant (DMZ – ***Doob**nenskiy **mashino**stro**i**tel'nyy **z**a**vod***) began manufacturing a development batch of Kh-55s. However, the plant was overburdened with other work, and in March 1978 MAP ordered production of the missile transferred to aircraft factory No.135 in Khar'kov, the Ukraine, later known as KhAPO (***Khar'**kovskoye **a**viatsionnoye **p**roizvodstvennoye **o**byedineniye* – Khar'kov Aircraft Production Association named after the Lenin Young Communist League). Production of the missile in Khar'kov was launched under the direction of Anatoliy K. Myalitsa, who later became the plant's director. At first KhAPO supplied missile components to DMZ for final assembly there but soon started assembling the missiles on its own; the first fuselage was assembled in December 1979. The first Khar'kov-built production missile was delivered to the Air Force on December 14, 1980.

Joint trials of the Kh-55 were held by MKB Raduga together with the Red Banner State Research Institute of the Air Force named after Valeriy P. Chkalov (GNIKI VVS – *Gosudarstvennyy naoochno-issledovatel'skiy Krasnoznamyonnyy institoot Voyenno-vozdooshnykh sil*), a.k.a. 8th GNII VVS; the "Red Banner" bit means the institute was awarded the Order of the Red Banner of Combat. The first test launch took place on February 23, 1981, being timed to a date of great importance for the military – Soviet Army Day (it is now celebrated as Homeland Defenders' Day). The launch platform was the ill-fated Tu-95M-55 (*izdeliye* VM-021) weapons testbed – a one-off conversion of a Tu-142MK *Bear-F Mod 2* ASW aircraft which first flew on July 31, 1978; ten launches were made before the aircraft crashed fatally at Zhukovskiy on January 28, 1982. Before that, on September 3, 1981, the Kh-55 was launched from the first production example of the Tu-95MS *Bear-H*, it other intended missile platform. The missile completed its trials successfully in December 1982.

Left and above left: "30 Grey" (f/n 1-01) streams its triple brake parachutes as it completes the landing run at Zhukovskiy and vacates runway 30. Signs of weathering are very much in evidence.

Right: Tu-160 f/n 1-02 also became a Tupolev OKB test aircraft, receiving the tactical code "56 Grey."

Above and below: "56 Grey" also had the nose pitot. Note the unpainted fuel line conduits on the rear fuselage, the L-shaped aerials aft of them and the open APU exhaust door above the No.2 engine nozzle. The fin/tailplane fairing still has a conical shape.

Opposite page: Three more views of Tu-160 f/n 1-02. The rear fuselage underside is covered in dirt from the mainwheel tyres.

Above left: Tu-160 "86 Grey" (f/n 2-01) with the nozzles at minimum section. The undersides of the intake assemblies appear black but are unpainted. Left: "86 Grey" was the first Tu-160 with the new fat fin/tailplane fairing.

Above: Two versions of the nose gear mudguard tested on Tu-160 "86 Grey." Right: The same machine with FOD prevention screens on the air intakes for ground tests of the engines.

Opposite:
Top: Tu-160 "87 Grey" (f/n 2-02), another Tupolev OKB test aircraft, on the taxiway at Zhukovskiy. Note the extra pair of flight deck windows (in the pilots' ejection hatches).

Middle: The same aircraft parked in front of a concrete jet blast deflector, with ground support vehicles connected.

Bottom: "87 Grey" is prepared for towing by a BelAZ-7420 tug.

Above right: A landing gear test rig at the Tupolev OKB. The main gear bogie has had the real tyres substituted with wooden dummy versions incorporating metal weights.

Right: The nose gear unit on a test rig; the powered drum on the left spins up the nosewheels before retraction.

Below right: This rig was built for testing the weapons bay doors and their actuating mechanism.

Here's another excerpt from Boris I. Veremey's memoirs. *"Presently it was time to unveil the aircraft to the leaders of the nation. I remember the day in early 1983 when Marshal of the Soviet Union Dmitriy Fyodorovich Ustinov* (the then Minister of Defence – *Auth.*) *came to the airfield [in Zhukovskiy]. On seeing the Tu-160 he was overjoyed and started scurrying around the aircraft; as he told us later, he felt twenty years younger all at once. The Marshal postponed all his intended meetings at the OKB, spending all the time he had near the aircraft. He was very happy that we now had such a bomber."*

Yet long before the presentation for Ustinov news of the latest Soviet bomber had reached the West. Those who have attended the biennial MAKS airshows in Zhukovskiy have probably paid attention to the large wall-less sheds along the aircraft parking areas on both sides of the LII airfield's main runway 12-30, but not many know their true purpose. And the purpose of these shelters was to

The four pictures above are stills from a video showing the first IFR-capable Tu-160 (*izdeliye* 70-03) being refuelled by the prototype of the IL-78M non-convertible tanker, CCCP-76701, during IFR system tests. Note the blanked-off extra flight deck windows.
Below: Tu-160 "87 Grey" in landing configuration during tests.

Top and above: More in-flight refuelling – this time an early production Tu-160 topping up from IL-78M CCCP-76701.
Top right and above right: Tests at high speed with the jettisonable ejection hatches removed.
Below: Another view of "87 Grey" during tests with the wings at the 35° cruise setting; note the open spoilers on the starboard wing.

342

342

342

Opposite page: Three views of company-owned Tu-160 f/n 4-01 (with the Paris exhibit code "342") on the runway at Zhukovskiy. Above and below: The same aircraft in flight; note the nose pitot.

conceal sensitive new hardware from US surveillance satellites without occupying valuable hangar space which might be needed for maintenance or modification work. On November 25, 1981, one day before the second high-speed run, the prototype had been towed into the open from the shelter of such a shed and parked alongside two of the four Tu-144D SSTs operated by the Tupolev OKB. As luck would have it, that same day Ye Eville Spye Satellite passed over Zhukovskiy and photographed the scene – or so it was assumed.

Soon afterwards the first photo of the new Soviet bomber with two Tu-144s in the background (showing nothing but vague shapes) was circulated in the Western press. Some Western analysts went so far as to suggest that the bomber had been intentionally exposed for the US surveillance satellite for propaganda purposes – like, we got a new bomber! Hear ye! Fear ye! This explanation appears implausible because *perestroika* and the new Soviet policy of openness were still some years away. Also, the first available photo was of such appalling quality as to cast doubt on the satellite imagery theory, considering that US surveillance satellites of the early 1980s were reputed to be able to read the number plates of cars! Besides, the people in charge of the security measures at LII obviously knew the "schedule" of the surveillance satellite and were not so stupid as to expose the top-secret bomber exactly when the satellite was expected to pass over the airfield.

Only later was it revealed that in reality the picture had been taken with a hand-held camera by a quick-minded passenger on a scheduled Aeroflot flight "terminating at the nearby airport of Bykovo," as press reports claimed. The latter bit is dubious as well. The approach corridor to runway 28 of the now-defunct Moscow-Bykovo airport lies quite a long way north of the LII airfield; during Moscow airshows it was easy to see that aircraft on final approach to Bykovo from the east were passing low and far away. At this viewing angle the forest and the hangars would have obscured the Tupolev OKB hardstand completely from the eyes of passengers on flights inbound to Bykovo. On the other hand, aircraft bound for Moscow-Vnukovo and Moscow-Domodedovo airports often pass directly over the LII airfield at fairly high altitude, making such photos possible. Indeed, the angle from which the famous picture was taken indicates a high 'vantage point' – such as a high-flying aircraft, while the low resolution suggests the picture was an enlarged section of a negative.

Knowing the dimensions of the Tu-144 and using it as a reference point, American experts were able to calculate the dimensions of the new bomber fairly accurately. Not knowing the exact designation or even the manufacturer, NATO's Air Standards Co-ordinating Committee (ASCC) allocated the provisional reporting name *Ram-P* to the new bomber. 'Ram' stood for Ramenskoye, the name of the neighbouring town which for many years was erroneously believed to be the name of the flight test centre in Zhukovskiy (in fact, it *was* originally the nearest town to the LII airfield

Top left: A black and white striped dummy version of the Kh-55 cruise missile on its ground handling dolly.

Above left: Footage from the Tu-160's state acceptance trials showing two such dummy missiles being ejected from both weapons bays to simulate a dual missile launch.

Left: A red-painted inert Kh-55 missile on one of the Tu-160's MKU6-5U rotary launchers during trials.

Top right, above right and right: Tu-160 "342" launches an inert Kh-55 missile. The wings take a while to deploy.

Far right: A Kh-55SM cruises after being launched by a Tu-160 during trials. The conformal long-range tanks are evident.

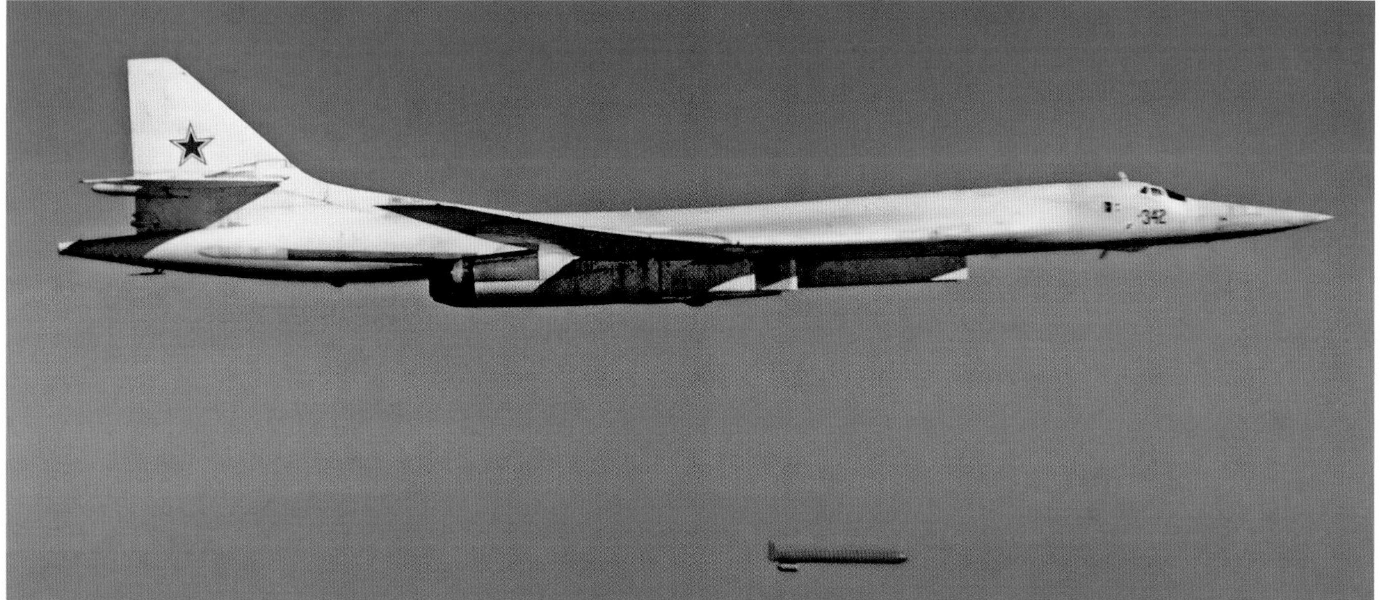

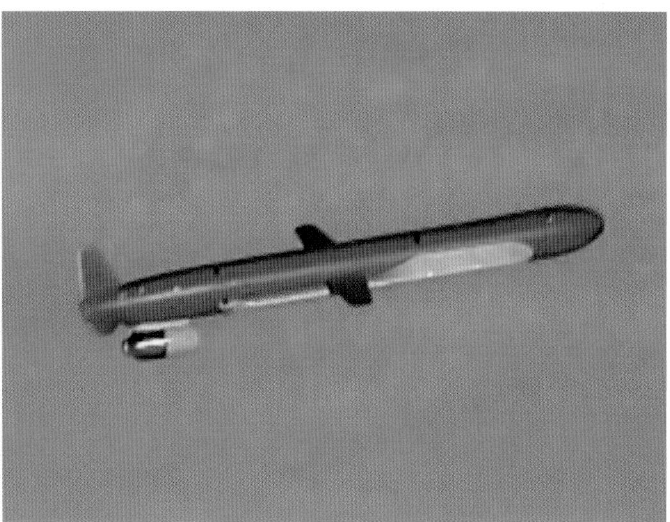

Left: Tu-160 (f/n 2-02) with the wings fully swept passes over Moscow-Tushino airfield on Aviation Day with a Sukhoi Su-27 fighter as an escort.

Below left: The same aircraft performs at Tushino during a different Aviation Day flypast – this time with the wings at minimum sweep. The single-seat Su-27 to port has to use the airbrake to keep formation; the two-seat Su-27UB may be a camera ship.

Below: Tu-160 f/n 4-01 in the static display at the MAKS-93 air-show with its original tactical code "63 Grey."

Right and below right: Two fine air-to-air studies of the same aircraft with the Le Bourget '95 exhibit code 342.

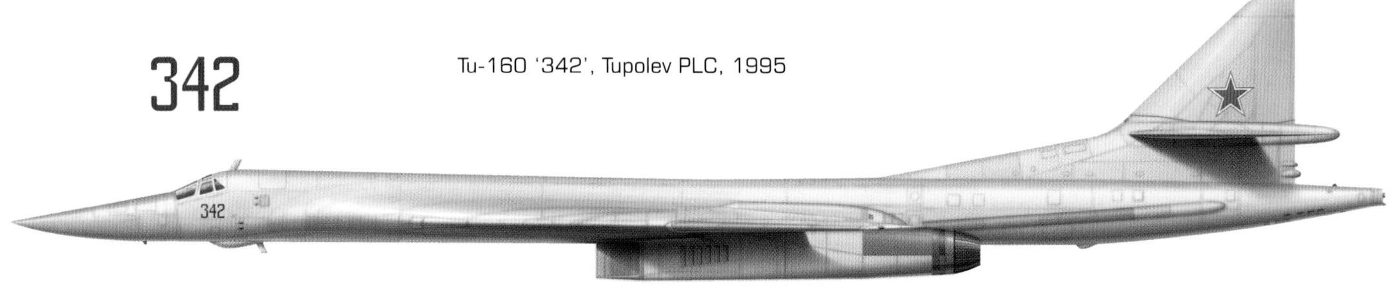

Tu-160 '342', Tupolev PLC, 1995

until the town of Zhukovskiy was built), while "P" denoted "16th unidentified type seen at Ramenskoye." By comparison, the Sukhoi Su-27 *Flanker* heavy fighter, the Mikoyan MiG-29 *Fulcrum* light fighter and the Myasishchev M-17 *Stratosfera* (Stratosphere/ *Mystic-A*) high-altitude aircraft were initially known to the West as *Ram-K*, *Ram-L* and *Ram-M* respectively – the 11th, 12th and 13th unidentified types.) Later the reporting name was changed to *Blackjack* in the "B for bomber" series. Oddly enough, this name caught on in the Tu-160's home country and was often mistakenly rendered as "Black Jack" in the Russian press – and sometimes

Tupolev OKB test pilot Boris I. Veremey – the Tu-160's project test pilot.

Tupolev OKB test pilot Sergey T. Agapov who was the co-pilot on the bomber's maiden flight.

Tupolev OKB test pilot Vladimir N. Matveyev.

Tupolev OKB test pilot Aleksey S. Meleshko who participated in the manufacturer's tests.

Tupolev OKB test pilot Valeriy V. Pavlov who captained the first production Tu-160.

Tupolev OKB test pilot Andrey I. Talalakin who participated in the manufacturer's tests.

Tupolev OKB test pilot Sergey G. Borisov who participated in the manufacturer's tests.

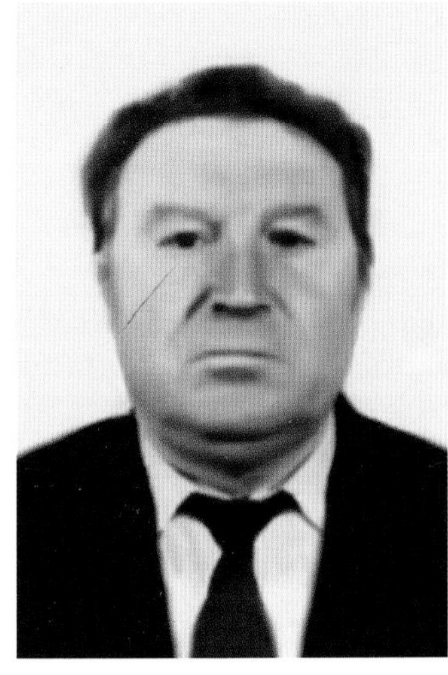

Tupolev OKB test pilot Grigoriy N. Shapoval who participated in the record-breaking flights.

even translated unthinkingly into Russian as such, which of course is stupidity. (Some people went so far as to mention a mythical "rowdy cowboy called Black Jack," which is even more stupid.) It's amazing that people never notice that the NATO codenames of Soviet aircraft are always *single* words (as distinct from the codenames of radar systems, which do consist of two words – such as *Flat Jack*!) and never take the trouble to look up the word 'blackjack' in the dictionary and see that it denotes a weapon!

From then on the CIA maintained a close watch on the Tu-160's development process. The advent of the Tu-160 led the US government to speed up the development and production entry of the Northrop B-2 Spirit stealth bomber.

The manufacturer's flight tests continued unabated, performed by OKB test pilots Boris I. Veremey, Sergey T. Agapov, Vladimir N. Matveyev, Valeriy V. Pavlov, Viktor A. Dralin and navigators Mikhail M. Kozel and Anatoliy V. Yeriomenko. A major contribution to the programme was made at this stage by the OKB's test engineer Anatoliy K. Yashukov, MMZ 'Opyt' Chief Engineer A. Mozheykov and KAPO Director Vitaliy Ye. Kopylov.

The static test airframe (*izdeliye* 70-02) was also delivered to Zhukovskiy, where it was tested to destruction in TsAGI's structural strength lab. In the 1990s, the remains of this aircraft – a good-sized chunk of the forward/centre fuselage – could be seen dumped at the Tupolev OKB's flight test facility.

The second prototype (*izdeliye* 70-03), likewise mostly unpainted, joined the test programme on October 6, 1984, making its first flight that day with OKB test pilot Sergey T. Agapov in the captain's seat. Coded "29 Grey," it differed outwardly from the first prototype in lacking the pitot at the tip of the radome and having extra flight deck windows in the pilots' ejection hatches (albeit these windows were obstructed on this machine and the first production examples).It was also the first Tu-160 with IFR capability (the first prototype lacked the retractable refuelling probe). The first version tested on *izdeliye* 70-03 was a straight and thick tele-

GNIKI VVS chief Col.-Gen. Leonid I. Agoorin who took part in the Tu-160's state trials.

Long-Range Aviation pilot Maj.-Gen. Lev V. Kozlov who also took part in the state trials.

GNIKI VVS test pilot Col. Mikhail I. Pozdnyakov.

GNIKI VVS test pilot Col. Sergey S. Popov.

scopic probe which was "fired" pneumatically into the tanker's drogue. Later this gave way to a curved fixed-geometry probe.

A major milestone was achieved in February 1985, when the first prototype went supersonic for the first time.

Yet, attaining high performance isn't all about aerodynamics. The Tu-160 had been designed in such a way as to achieve the maximum possible range not only in high-altitude supersonic cruise but also in ultra-low-level terrain-following flight. The bomber's crew were free to choose between these modes or use a combination of them to perform the mission with maximum efficiency.

To expand the scope of the test work it was decided to use the low-rate initial production (LRIP) Tu-160s manufactured in Kazan' along with the Moscow-built prototypes. The first Kazan'-built Tu-160 (c/n 83401517, fuselage number 1-01 – that is, Batch 1, 01st aircraft in the batch) took off from the factory's Borisoglebskoye airfield for its maiden flight on October 10, 1984, just four days after the second prototype's first flight; it was captained by Tupolev OKB test pilot Valeriy V. Pavlov. It was coded "30 Grey" and sported an overall white "anti-flash" colour scheme which became standard for production Tu-160s. Later, this colour scheme gave rise to the nickname ***Belyy lebed'*** (White swan) bestowed on the bomber in lieu of an "official" popular name. Thus the *Blackjack* is not black at all! Well, if production Tu-160s are White Swans, then the drab prototypes must be Ugly Ducklings, eh? (Interestingly, on the B-1 the situation was reversed: the B-1A prototypes were white overall, giving rise to sarcastic comments like "White hope or white elephant?," whereas production B-1Bs were invariably camouflaged.)

The second production *Blackjack* ("56 Grey," c/n 84401923, f/n 1-02) took to the air on March 16, 1985; the third ("86 Grey," c/n 82502618, f/n 2-01) on December 25, 1985, and the fourth ("87 Grey," c/n 84502324, f/n 2-02) on August 15, 1986. Thus, the first two Kazan'-built batches were almost entirely delivered to Zhukovskiy and assigned to the trials programme.

A note on the construction numbers should be made here. Production Tu-160s have eight-digit c/ns that basically follow the same system as on the Tu-22M2 (except the first production batches) and Tu-22M3. The first digit is always an 8 and may be an in-house designator to discern the Tu-160 from other types. The second and third digits denote the quarter and year of manufacture; the next two are the batch number. The sixth digit is allocated randomly, probably to confuse outsiders (the Kazan' factory had used this trick before on the Tu-16K-10 *Badger-D*, Tu-22 and Tu-22M, albeit usually with the first and last digits). The seventh digit is the aircraft's number in the batch (generally five to a batch, which is normal practice at KAPO), and the final one is the number of the work team assembling the specific aircraft. Thus, Tu-160 "87 Grey" (c/n 84502324) was built in the fourth quarter of 1985 (October-December) by Team 4 and is the second aircraft in Batch 02; however, the factory renders the fuselage number as 2-02 rather than 02-02). The c/n is embossed in the upper right-hand corner of two large metal plates found on the outer faces of the main gear oleos; these also carry the serial number of the oleo itself but the c/n is the same on both units.

GNIKI VVS test pilot Col. Naïl' Sh. Sattarov. He subsequently became a Tupolev PLC test pilot.

GNIKI VVS test pilot Col. Vladimir S. Smirnov.

Production bombers incorporated various refinements. For example, from Batch 2 onwards the extra flight deck windows became functional (not blocked), while the fairing at the fin/tailplane junction became shorter, with an ogival rear end instead of a conical one. This was meant to alleviate the vibrations which were ruining the avionics in the rear bay.

All six flyable aircraft listed above – the two prototypes and the four LRIP aircraft delivered to the OKB – participated in the Tu-160's joint state acceptance (that is, certification) trials programme. Like the manufacturer's flight tests, Stage A of the trials took place at Zhukovskiy. The trials programme included such "exercises" as a landing in supersonic cruise configuration (with the wings at 65° maximum sweep) to check if a safe landing was possible in the event the wing actuators failed and the wings would not move to minimum sweep; supersonic flight with the ejection hatch covers in the flight deck roof removed; flight with all electric power switched off, rendering the FBW control system inoperative (the back-up mechanical control system was used) and so on.

The manufacturer's flight tests and state acceptance trials were not altogether without incident. On one occasion Valeriy V. Pavlov was ferrying the brand-new second production Tu-160 from Kazan' to Zhukovskiy, with Sergey T. Agapov as co-pilot. En route the aircraft suffered a total electrics failure, all four engine-driven generators dying at once. The main electric circuits shut down spontaneously and the few that remained operational worked with excessively high voltage, creating a serious fire hazard. That was not the worst of it, though; the aircraft became almost uncontrollable, pitching and rolling like crazy. To top it all, the power failure rendered all flight instruments inoperative. Luckily the pilots quickly realised what had happened, managing to bring the seemingly hopeless situation under control and bring the bomber safely home in adverse weather.

Descending below cloud cover at 2,000 m (6,560 ft), the pilots got their bearings near the town of Shatoora (Moscow Region), some 85 km (52 miles) west of Zhukovskiy as the crow flies, spotting a familiar landmark – the Shatoora Power Station. From there they flew 60 km (37.2 miles) south-west to Voskresensk, then turned right onto a north-westerly course and flew the remaining 40 km (25 miles) to Zhukovskiy. The hardest part was the landing approach when the control authority at low speed could prove insufficient; still, the bomber landed safely.

Agapov recalled this dangerous incident as follows: *"When I made the first check flight in [this particular]* izdeliye *70 in Kazan', it was Pavlov's turn to be captain (he had been my co-pilot in that flight); we were to make the ferry flight together, so I let him take the left-hand seat then. There had been no problems when I check-flew the aircraft in Kazan', so I was confident. And then, as we came in to land at Zhukovskiy, he started rocking the aircraft. All four generators had failed, only one of the four providing a little bit of power. I was in the right-hand seat, but as soon as the oscillations began I grabbed the stick and told Valera firmly: 'Don't touch the stick, don't do anything, just keep the pedals steady!'*

'Shall we eject?,' he asked.

The altitude was 2,000 m and we were passing Voskresensk. I stopped him: 'Hang on there! Keep the pedals steady and don't fuss, the machine will stabilise itself in a moment!" The aircraft was oscillating because it had no dampers. Then the navigators (the navigator and WSO – *Auth.) joined in and started hollering: 'What do we do, captain?' 'Sit back,' I told them (although formally it was the guy in the left-hand seat who was in charge). 'Just sit back. We're working on it. We still have enough altitude.' I took over the controls. The aircraft was very sensitive to the rudder pedals, so we just held them steady, and I started working the stick – very gently. Making very flat turns, we came in and landed. We vacated the runway – and then the second navigator* (*sic* – the WSO – *Auth.*), *who was in charge of the electrics, let us down. As we rolled down the runway, he was so overjoyed that he ran [down the flight deck aisle] towards the pilots' seats, having switched off all the generators first. He was sure that all the generators were dead, but one generator must have been partially alive after all – otherwise we would have definitely ejected because the aircraft would have been uncontrollable. However, with all generators switched off the nosewheel steering went dead; the aircraft went off the taxiway, the port mainwheels resting on the earth verge, and stopped. We tried shutting down the engines – and found that we could not; it was impossible with no electric power. We had to summon a ground power unit to shut down the engines..."*

The air incident investigation panel established that the incident had been caused by an overload protection system failure, which had not even been considered possible. One of the generators went to maximum voltage mode, the power surge knocking out all the protection systems of the other circuits. Painstaking analysis of the fried electric circuits showed that the failure had occurred at the electronic component level and had never been encountered during bench testing. There was no way it could have been discovered, using test equipment and methods then in use. The incident gave rise to a term, "Pavlov's calculated failure," used for such unforeseeable breakdowns; accordingly the electric systems of all Tu-160s were checked and steps were taken to prevent this situation from happening again. (Speaking of which, on the Tu-22M a total electrics failure similarly rendered the aircraft completely uncontrollable within 10-15 minutes because hydraulic pressure dropped, and several *Backfires* were lost that way.)

During manufacturer's flight tests there had been other dangerous episodes, such as birdstrike, or a main gear bogie stuck in mid-extension due to a broken rocking damper. Fearing that the main gear unit would shear off, the crew was preparing to eject; luckily ground control set them straight, telling them to come in and land with a higher-than-usual angle of attack so that the bogie would assume its normal position on touchdown. It worked.

Still the aircraft usually landed in one piece. The only exception was the same second production Tu-160, "56 Grey" (f/n 1-02), that crashed on March 6, 1987, due to an in-flight engine failure and fire. The aircraft, again captained by Valeriy V. Pavlov, with Andrey I. Talalakin as co-pilot, had a light fuel load and was mak-

Right: An early-production Tu-160 seen a few seconds after take-off.

Below right: A Tu-160 displays its sleek lines, flying over a winter landscape with the wings set 35°.

ing a check flight with the gear and flaps down. Two circuits of the airfield were performed uneventfully but during the third circuit a warning light lit up as the aircraft was passing Bronnitsy (Moscow Region), indicating a fire in one of the port engines. Sergey T. Agapov recounted afterwards that the logical thing to do was to use the fire suppression system, shut down the affected engine – even both engines on the port side if necessary (with the light weight it would not have been a problem), and come in to land. However, again the navigator and WSO started hollering, and under pressure Pavlov initiated ejection, punching out the entire crew. Everyone survived, but Anatoliy V. Yeriomenko, for whom this was the third ejection in his flying career, suffered a spinal injury. Afterwards, the crew received a dressing-down from General Designer Andrey A. Tupolev because the aircraft worth 60 million roubles in the day's prices had been lost when it could have been saved.

One winter day a Tu-160 captained by Sergey T. Agapov was to make a long-range flight from Zhukovskiy. The aircraft was fully fuelled, the take-off weight reaching 275,000 kg (606,270 lb). As the bomber accelerated down runway 12, the afterburner on the No.2 (port inboard) engine popped a fuel nozzle and a fire ensued. As luck would have it, the crew was unaware of this at first. For one thing, the Tu-160 had no flame sensors in the afterburners, so there was no fire warning. For another, the control tower at Zhukovskiy is on the south side of the runway – that is, to the right of the aircraft taking off from runway 12; with the burning engine being obscured from view by the fuselage the fire was not observed until the aircraft had passed the tower. Actually, another Tu-160 captained by Boris I. Veremey was waiting its turn to take off next; Veremey noticed the engine fire on Agapov's aircraft but, being on intercom (as was Agapov at the same time), he was unable to warn Agapov immediately. Seeing the abnormal sheet of flame, the air traffic controller radioed to Agapov's navigator, *"You're on fire!"* The navigator immediately alerted the captain, who switched to radio and contacted the tower; the latter repeated: *"You have a fire in the port engine!"*

Agapov aborted the take-off almost at unstick speed – 290-300 km/h (180-183 mph), deciding that there was enough runway length left. However, when he told his co-pilot Aleksey S. Meleshko

Left: Tupolev OKB personnel pose with the second prototype Tu-160 after its record-breaking flight on November 3, 1989. Project chief Valentin I. Bliznyuk is sixth from left; flight test facility (ZhLIiDB) chief Valentin T. Klimov is eighth from left

Below left: The record-setting crew of *izdeliye* 70-03 (left to right: captain Boris I. Veremey, navigator Mikhail M. Kozel, navigator Anatoliy V. Yeriomenko and co-pilot Grigoriy N. Shapoval.).

Below: A GNIKI VVS test crew (left to right: captain Maj.-Gen. Lev V. Kozlov, co-pilot Col. MikhailI. Pozdnyakov, navigator Col. V. S. Neretin and WSO Lt.-Col. S. N. Mart'yanov) that set further records in an operational Tu-160.

Bird's eye views of Tu-160 "63 Grey" (f/n 4-01) in the static park at the MAKS-2003 airshow.

Above: The same aircraft (now as "342") breaks formation after a formation flypast with a Tu-204C freighter (RA-64021) at MAKS-2005.

Below: Tu-160 "342" in the static display at MAKS-2005 with the all-movable tail surfaces at maximum deflection.

Tu-160 *Boris Veremey*, Tupolev PLC, 2005

to deploy the brake parachutes, Meleshko did so immediately without waiting the required five or ten seconds for the engines to spool down to idle. As a result, one parachute was torn off and the other two did not open properly; even with emergency braking, the heavy aircraft overran and careered across some temporary ditches before coming to a halt 50 m (164 ft) beyond the runway. Luckily the landing gear stood up to the abuse; moreover, when afterburner thrust was cancelled the fire went out on its own. However, the aircraft suffered some fire damage to the port side of the fuselage, which was fortunately repairable.

Agapov reminisced: *"Later, at the debriefing, Aleksey Andreyevich Tupolev told me reproachfully: 'What do you think you're doing? You should have taken off and ejected! You were risking the crew's lives!' I replied, 'Aleksey Andreyevich, this beats me. Earlier, you were shouting at Pavlov for having ejected and wasted a 60 million rouble aircraft. Now the aircraft is OK, the crew is OK, and here you are, asking me why I haven't taken off and ejected.'*

'You could have blown up, with that kind of [take-off] weight!,' Tupolev chided.

'I guess I could, but it worked out. I was lucky.'"

Still, the Tu-160 did claim lives at this early stage. The abovementioned test engineer Yuriy S. Gorbatenko, who had contributed a lot to making the *Blackjack* fly, was tragically killed in an accident during ground tests.

As the trials progressed, GNIKI VVS joined in at Stage B and the action was transferred to the institute's main facility in Akhtoobinsk, Saratov Region (Vladimirovka airbase). This location near the Volga River estuary in southern Russia had been chosen with good reason: quite apart from the fact that the steppes of Kazakhstan (used as weapons practice ranges) were conveniently close at hand, the region had as many as 320 days of fair weather per year. Moreover, security was much easier to maintain in such outback areas.

In 2005 Tu-160 f/n 4-01 was named *Boris Veremey*, losing the exhibit code at the same time. Here it is seen returning from a test mission.

Starboard side view of the same aircraft

The team of military test pilots conducting the Tu-160's state acceptance trials was headed by Col.-Gen. Leonid I. Agoorin, the then head of GNIKI VVS. A number of test flights were performed by Maj.-Gen. Lev V. Kozlov, a Long-Range Aviation pilot, who subsequently succeeded Agoorin as the institute's director. Air Force test pilots and navigators Col. Mikhail I. Pozdnyakov, Col. Vladimir S. Smirnov, Col. Naïl' Sh. Sattarov, Col. Sergey S. Popov, Col. V. S. Neretin, Lt.-Col. P. Petrov and Lt.-Col. S. N. Mart'yanov contributed a lot to the *Blackjack*'s trials and eventual service entry.

The rolling steppes beyond the Volga were an ideal proving ground for the Tu-160's main weapon, the Kh-55SM cruise missile with its self-contained navigation system and 3,000-km (1,860-mile) maximum range. During live test launches the bombers were shadowed by an Ilyushin/Beriyev "Aircraft 976" *Mainstay-C* airborne measuring and control station (AMCS), a purpose-built derivative of the Il-76MD *Candid-B* military transport; five of these radar picket aircraft registered CCCP-76452 through CCCP-76456 were operated by LII. The AMCS monitored the trajectories of the Tu-160 and the missile, using its 360° search radar; it also received telemetry data from the bomber and the missile, recording it and transmitting it in real time to ground control and telemetry processing centres by radio or satellite link. On several occasions when the Kh-55 started 'acting up' and departed from the designated course, getting too close to the boundaries of the weapons range, a self-destruct command had to be transmitted.

Live weapons trials showed that in maximum range mode the Kh-55SM often pressed on towards the target after the aircraft had landed! In the course of the trials MKB Raduga brought the missile's accuracy margin to a commendable 18-26 m (59-85 ft).

The bomber's mission avionics – the Obzor-K navigation/attack suite and the Poisk radar it was built around, and especially the Baikal ECM/ESM suite – proved troublesome at first, and a lot of effort was required to bring them up to an acceptable reliability

Tu-160 *Boris Veremey* departs on yet another mission, showing the small 1950s/1960s-style Tupolev badge carried on the starboard side of the nose.

level. The Baikal suite was put through its paces at two instrumented test ranges near Orenburg, Russia, and in one of the Central Asian republics. According to press reports (though no documents have been found yet to substantiate this), by mid-1989 the Tu-160 test and development fleet had made a about 150 flights. Four of them involved missile launches; on one occasion two Kh-55SMs were launched in a salvo from both weapons bays.

In addition to long-range flights and live weapons trials, military test pilots practiced ultra-low-level/terrain-following flight and IFR techniques, working with Ilyushin Il-78 *Midas-A* convertible tanker/transports. As the trials progressed the initial-production bombers were prepared, step by step, for delivery to the Air Force for evaluation.

Changes were made to the design and to the flight manual proceeding from the trials results. As already mentioned, OKB test pilot Boris I. Veremey attained a top speed of 2,200 km/h (1,366 mph) in one of the test flights. In operational service, however, a speed limit of 2,000 km/h (1,240 mph) was imposed for structural integrity reasons and in order to conserve service life.

Incidents and accidents of varying seriousness continued as the trials progressed. On one occasion Veremey flying the first prototype, with a GNIKI VVS test pilot in the co-pilot's seat, found himself in a tight spot when the nose gear unit would not extend at the end of a test flight. He opted for a two-point emergency landing on the concrete runway at Zhukovskiy and executed it flawlessly, the aircraft suffering only minor damage and returning to active status a month later after repairs had been made.

In the course of the state acceptance trials the Tu-160 reaffirmed its promise by establishing world speed, altitude and payload-to-height records. In October–November 1989, and May 1990, GNIKI VVS and Tupolev OKB pilots flew the second prototype and a production machine from Batch 3 (f/n 3-04), setting a series of Class C-1r (landplanes with a gross weight of 200,000-250,000 kg/440,920-551,160 lb) and Class C-1s (ditto, with a gross weight of 250,000-300,000 kg/551,160-661,390 lb). In particular, the bomber reached a speed of 1,731.4 km/h 1,075.4 mph) and an altitude of 12,150 m (39,862 ft) in sustained level flight with no payload and 13,894 m (45,584 ft) with a 30,000-kg (66,130-lb) payload. These and other records are described in detail in Appendix 2.

In addition to the above machines, a Batch 4 production Tu-160 (c/n 84704217, f/n 4-01) built in late 1987, was delivered to the Tupolev OKB. This aircraft remains in use as a "dogship" to this day, having participated in various test programmes.

It may be mentioned here that the Tu-160s retained by the Tupolev OKB (and subsequently Tupolev PLC) have been regular participants at various air events both in the Soviet Union/Russia and abroad since the late 1980s. The first of these was August 20, 1989 during one of the annual flypasts which, for many years, had been held at the now-defunct Moscow–Tushino airfield on Aviation Day (or Air Fleet Day) celebrated on the third Sunday of August. The aircraft made a low pass, escorted by a pair of Sukhoi Su-27 *Flanker-B* fighters.

The first occasion when the aviation-minded public could view the *Blackjack* at Zhukovskiy was again Aviation Day – August 18, 1991, the day before the failed hard-line Communist coup d'état that brought an end to the Soviet Union's existence. One of the two prototypes was involved. The LII airfield was still off limits to the general public at the time (albeit a small selection of aircraft was on display in the town park and in the square in front of the TsAGI building), so the spectators had to watch the flypast from outside the fence. However, those who used the available vantage points were able to see the Tu-160 being towed to a taxiway at the end of runway 12, then starting up and taking off before making a high-speed run in a reciprocal direction.

Starting in 1992, when LII hosted the first fully-fledged Moscow international airshow (MosAeroShow-92, 11th-16th August 1992), the public was finally allowed onto the airfield and was able to examine the *Blackjack* at much closer quarters. The static display included Tu-160 c/n 84704217, then coded "63 Grey" (on the port nose gear door only), which was the youngest of the company-owned examples and was in the best show condition. The flying display included a flypast by the unpainted second prototype ('29 Grey') which took off and landed before the eyes of the public, making a spectacular steep climbing turn. The other Tu-160s were parked at the ZhLIiDB hardstand some 200 m (660 ft) from the static display, but these were in various states of disrepair.

"63 Grey" was again present in the static park of the MAKS-93 international airshow at Zhukovskiy (August 31 – September 5, 1993), while "29 Grey" again participated in the flying display. However, as the aircraft came back and landed it was seen to be missing a large chunk of the fin fillet which had come off in flight!

In 1995, Tu-160 c/n 84704217 made its only appearance abroad, being displayed at the 42nd Paris Air Show where it posed as the Tu-160SK suborbital launch platform with a mock-up of the Burlak space launch vehicle (see Chapter 5). Hence the aircraft lost its tactical code and gained the Le Bourget exhibit code 342 instead. Shortly afterwards, the same aircraft appeared in this guise (complete with the SLV mock-up) at the MAKS-95 (22nd-27th August 1995), while "29 Grey" again made a demonstration flight. Tu-160 "342 Blue" (this was now perceived as its tactical code) was shown again at MAKS-97 (August 19–24, 1997), MAKS-99 (August 17–22, 1999) and MAKS-2001 (August 14–19, 2001). On these occasions there was no more SLV mock-up. At subsequent MAKS airshows the Russian Air Force started putting up *Blackjacks* for the static display (more about this is said in Chapter 7). However, on the opening day of the MAKS-2005 (August 16–21), which was the official "Tupolev day" of the airshow with press conferences and such, the flying display was opened by an impressive flypast of five Tupolev machines – four company-owned aircraft (a Tu-160, a Tu-95MS, a Tu-204-100C freighter and the Tu-334 airliner prototype) and a Russian Air Force Tu-22M3. The five aircraft passed over the runway in V formation, fanning out spectacularly at the end.

Following the Air Force's example, the Tupolev JSC gave a name to Tu-160 "342." In 2005, this aircraft was christened *Boris Veremey* after the famous Tupolev OKB test pilot who had passed away in 2002. Later, in 2006, one of the company-owned aircraft ('87 Grey') was transferred to the Russian Air Force; after refurbishment the aircraft received a new code ("19 Red") and the name *Valentin Bliznyuk*. This was in contravention of all naming customs because, unlike Boris I. Veremey, Valentin I. Bliznyuk was alive and well then, and still is as of this writing (knock on wood).

Chapter 4

The Tu-160 in Production

As mentioned earlier, the Kazan' aircraft factory No.22 started gearing up for full-scale production of the Tu-160 not just before the new bomber had even flown but actually before the first metal for the first three airframes was cut at MMZ "Opyt" in 1977. There have been allegations that the original intention was to launch Tu-160 production at the new aircraft factory in Ul'yanovsk which was commissioned on June 10, 1976, and originally called UAPK (*Ool'**yan**ovskiy **a**viatsionnyy **p**roiz**vod**stvennyy **k**ompleks* – Ul'yanovsk Aircraft Production Complex). This is wrong because UAPK (known since the late 1980s as Aviastar-SP) had been designed specifically to produce the Antonov An-124 *Ruslan* (*Condor*) wide-body heavy transport aircraft. Besides, as early as 1975 – possibly even before the Council of Ministers issued the directive ordering the construction of the Ul'yanovsk plant in April – the construction of a new wide assembly shop capable of accommodating large one-piece airframe structures had begun at the Kazan' plant with the Tu-160 in mind.

Tooling up for production of the Tu-160 necessitated a far-reaching reconstruction of the Kazan' plant. New processing and assembly shops with a total floor area of more than 300,000 m^2 (3,229,170 sq ft) were built. These included shops for assembling titanium structures and machining long aluminium alloy panels on unique machine tools with computerised numerical control (CNC). The same building accommodated the aforementioned ELU-24 electron beam welding machine for manufacturing the wing pivot box carry-through structure, which was capable of

A substantially complete Tu-160 airframe in the final assembly shop at KAPO in company with two Tu-214 fuselages.

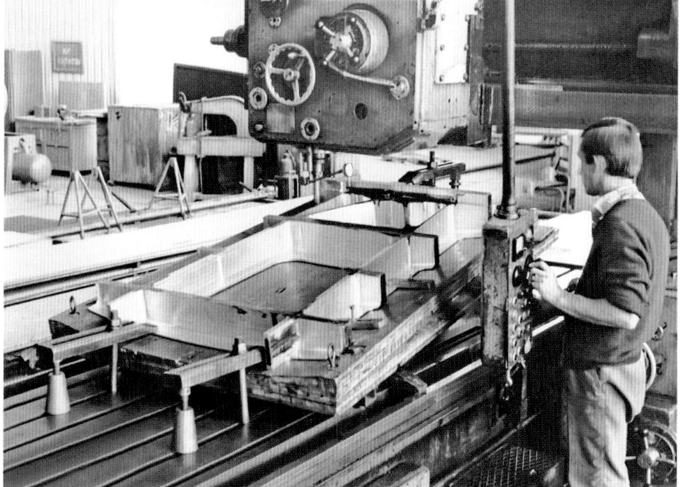

Top: A Tu-160 wing pivot being manufactured.

Above and top right: Titanium panels of the centre section's lower skin with integral stringers.

Above: The brake parachute attachment frame made of AK-4P aluminium alloy.

Below and right: An early production Tu-160 at Priluki AB.

Above: Tu-160 "11 Red" at Priluki AB. The flaperons and stabilators typically assume this position when the aircraft is parked. Note the matt finish on the nose aft of the radome which is a feature of the special paint.

Below: Brand-new and spotlessly clean Tu-160 "12 Red" shortly after arriving at its home base of Priluki.

Above: Another aspect of the same aircraft.

Below: A still-uncoded Tu-160 on the taxiway at Priluki.

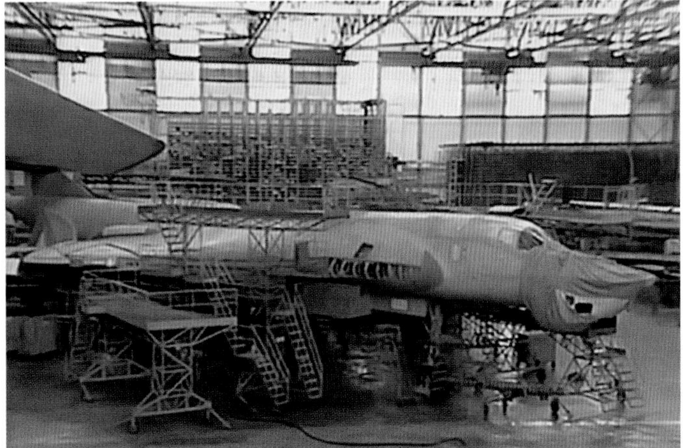

Top and right: Still minus landing gear and LERXes, a Tu-160 fuselage sits on trestles in KAPO's assembly shop. The forward pressure bulkhead is visible through the access hatches in the forward avionics bay. Note also the ejection hatches.

Above left: This *Blackjack* has reached a much greater degree of completion, sitting on its landing gear amidst a thicket of work platforms.

Above and left: Bombers and airliners share the floor in the final assembly shop. Note the red covers on the Tu-160s' windshields to prevent scratches.

Above right and top right: More scenes from the Tu-160's manufacturing process in Kazan'.

welding titanium parts up to 120 mm ($4\frac{23}{32}$ in) thick, the UVN-4500M annealing oven and an equally unique X-ray chamber for checking the quality of the welded joints.

The huge wing pivot box was 12.4 m (40 ft $8\frac{3}{16}$ in) long and 2.1 m (6 ft $10\frac{43}{64}$ in) wide. It was manufactured in upper and lower halves machined from titanium forgings which were then welded together in vacuum, using special additives and fluxes; this was the Kazan' aircraft factory's proprietary technology. This operation had to be performed strictly at night only, when the city's

Left: KAPO Director Vitaliy Ye. Kopylov who contributed a lot to the type's production entry.

Opposite top: Tupolev PLC and KAPO personnel (Valentin I. Bliznyuk is 12th from left) attend the roll-out of a new Tu-160.

Opposite bottom: A Tu-160 in primer finish on a pre-delivery test flight from Kazan'-Borisoglebskoye.

Below: Valentin I. Bliznyuk and KAPO Director Nail' G. Khairullin pose with Tu-160 f/n 8-02 after the rollout in 1999.

demand for electricity was lowest, otherwise the Peerless Welding Machine would knock out the electric power in half of the city.

Other new buildings accommodated the chemical milling shop with acid basins 20 m (65 ft $7^{13}/_{32}$ in) long, the electrochemical coating shop with basins 32 m (104 ft $11^{29}/_{32}$ in) long. Now the factory possessed unique technological equipment for manufacturing composite and honeycomb-core panels, forging and machining large structural components. The latter included variable-thickness panels with integral stiffeners made of titanium and high-strength aluminium alloys; the large size of these components allowed the number of manufacturing joints to be reduced, cutting structural weight and increasing airframe life. New buildings were built for the electric wiring assembly shop, the loft-floor and template department, warehousing facilities and so on. Last but not least, a new sewage facility was built for processing the toxic and corrosive waste of the chemical shops.

As already mentioned, the first production Tu-160 (f/n 1-01) made its first flight from Kazan'-Borisoglebskoye on October 10, 1984, followed by the second aircraft (f/n 1-02) on March 16, 1985; the third (f/n 2-01) on December 25, 1985, and the fourth (f/n 2-02) on August 15, 1986. All of them were delivered to the Tupolev OKB for participation in the manufacturer's flight tests and state acceptance trials. Deliveries to the Soviet Air Force began with Batch 3 – or f/n 2-03.

Apart from the Kazan' aircraft factory (KAPO), a lot of MAP enterprises were involved in the Tu-160 production programme as subcontractors. In particular, the outer wings and the rear sections of the engine nacelles were manufactured by the Voronezh aircraft factory No.64 which had built the Tu-144 in series (it is now called VASO, *Voronezhskoye aktsionernoye samolyotostroitel'noye obshchestvo* – Voronezh Joint-Stock Aircraft Manufacturing Co.). The tail surfaces and the air intake sections of the engine nacelles were subcontracted out to the Irkutsk aircraft factory No.39, or IAPO (*Irkootskoye aviatsionnoye proizvodstvennoye obyedineniye* – Irkutsk Aircraft Production Association; now part of the Irkut Corp.). Other plants supplied the engines, landing gear, avionics and equipment. The Kazan' factory manufactured the fuselage, wing centre section and wing pivots and was responsible for final assembly.

As had been the case at the development phase, the Tu-160's production entry was personally monitored and co-ordinated by Minister of Aircraft Industry Pyotr V. Dement'yev and his successors Vasiliy A. Kazakov and Ivan S. Silayev. A major contribution to launching Tu-160 production was made by Vice-Ministers of Aircraft Industry Anoofriy V. Bolbot (who had become Chief of MAP's 9th Main Directorate by then) and Vladimir T. Ivanov (Chief of MAP's 6th Main Directorate). An equally significant role was played by KAPO Director Vitaliy Ye. Kopylov, the factory's Chief Engineer Samat G. Khisamutdinov, his deputies N. R. Akhtyamov and G. Ya. Fomin and flight test facility Director A. A. Khabiboolin.

Even as production got under way, the Kazan' plant started seeking ways and means of refining the *Blackjack*'s design and manufacturing technologies. For example, at the insistence of Vitaliy Ye. Kopylov the wing pivots of production Tu-160s were manufactured as separate parts. They were not welded to the pivot box carry-through structure and to the outer wing torsion boxes, as on the prototype (that is, manufactured integrally) – instead, they were attached by shear bolts. This made it possible to check the massive pivots (each of them weighed 3,000 kg/6,610 lb) on a special bench before installation on the aircraft; as a result, the pivots' operational reliability was significantly enhanced.

One of the production airframes (f/n 3-03) was earmarked for repeat static/fatigue tests to check if production aircraft con-

Opposite: Tu-160 f/n 8-02 seen in primer finish at Kazan'-Borisoglebskoye.

Left: KAPO test pilot Mikhail L. Kovbasenko.

Right: Tu-160 f/n 8-02 during a pre-delivery test flight.

Below: A commemorative photograph with Tu-160 f/n 8-02 including Khairullin, Bliznyuk and the then DA Commander Mikhail M. Oparin (pictured fifth from left).

formed to the specifications. The tests were to take place at TsAGI in Zhukovskiy; therefore the airframe was loaded on a barge and taken up the Volga River to Gor'kiy (now Nizhniy Novgorod), then up the Oka River to Kolomna (Moscow Region) and thence up the Moskva River to Zhukovskiy. The horizontal tail, however, did not take the voyage with the rest of the airframe for some reason; instead, it was flown to Zhukovskiy as an external load attached under the fuselage of a modified Tu-95!

The NK-32 engine officially entered full-scale production in Kuibyshev in 1986. Previously, all Tu-160s had been powered by LRIP engines – actually development engines which had been used in the NK-32's trials programme. The APU was produced by the Ghidravlika plant in Ufa, the capital of the Bashkir ASSR.

The original production plans drawn up in Soviet days envisaged a production run of about 100 aircraft – roughly the same as for the B-1 whose eventual production run totalled four B-1As and 100 B-1Bs. As was normally the case at KAPO, Tu-160 batches mostly consisted of five aircraft each; this means the final production aircraft would be something like f/n 21-05. However, the *perestroika* policy initiated by the new Secretary General Mikhail S. Gorbachov (subsequently the first and only President of the Soviet Union) in 1985 led, among other things, to a reduction in the Soviet defence budget, which slowed the production rate down, and in 1991 the Tu-160 procurement plans were slashed to just 40 aircraft. Even these plans were not destined to materialise. In February 1992, shortly after the demise of the Soviet Union, Boris N.

A Kh-55 missile with the engine and tail surfaces deployed but the wings retracted in the assembly shop at the Khar'kov aircraft factory (KhAPO).

Yel'tsin, the first President of post-Soviet Russia, signed a decree which cancelled further production of the Tu-95MS at the Aviacor plant in Samara and envisaged the possibility of halting Tu-160 production (not an explicit cancellation), providing that the USA stopped production of the Northrop B-2 Spirit stealthy strategic bomber. The USA failed to reciprocate – the B-2 stayed in production until 2002. Nevertheless, Russia's economic hardships in the 1990s soon caused further production of the *Blackjack* to stop altogether – albeit this was not the end of the story yet.

Due to the type's strategic importance not much information on Tu-160 production statistics is released officially, and the figures that can be found in various sources are rather contradictory. However, it appears that the aircraft built and delivered in Soviet days were those up to and including Batch 6 – a total of 25 (or 27, if you include the static test airframes). Of these, the 18 in operational service were all outside Russia, having been taken over by the newly independent Ukraine; the rest were company-owned development aircraft, one of which was already dead (the crashed second production machine). Only six new-build aircraft were delivered to the Russian Air Force before production ground to a halt. The first aircraft of Batch 7 was delivered on February 16, 1992, the second and third in the spring of 1992, the fourth and fifth followed in 1993, and the first aircraft of Batch 8 (c/n 84308216, f/n 8-01) in 1994. Production of NK-32 engines had ended in 1993.

In 1995, at the end of his first term of office, President Boris N. Yel'tsin took the decision to resume Tu-160 production in order to give the Russian Air Force enough *Blackjacks* for a full bomber regiment. With funding again made available, Tu-160 c/n 82408427 (f/n 8-02) was ceremonially rolled out at Kazan'-Borisoglebskoye on December 23, 1997; some sources state this as the first flight date, which is improbable, as the aircraft had to undergo the obligatory ground checks first. Anyway, it was not until 2000 that this aircraft was taken on charge by the Russian Air Force. The final Tu-160 (f/n 8-03) was formally accepted in 2008. And that was it; the Tu-160's production run, including the Moscow-built examples, was a mere 34 aircraft.

Here is where the ambiguity lies: firstly, the number of Tu-160s delivered to the Air Force in Soviet times and taken over by the Ukraine is stated as 19, and indeed there are 19 known tactical codes for these aircraft, which means Tu-160 f/n 2-03 did exist after all. Secondly, it is not clear whether the final two airframes so far were already under construction in 1994 when f/n 8-01 was delivered and were mothballed when the funding dried up (to be completed later) or they were laid down in 1995 as some sources claim.

KAPO's most notable test pilot associated with the Tu-160 was Mikhail L. Kovbasenko. Other factory test pilots who flew the *Blackjack* include Sergey N. Zavalkin, Aleksey A. Booryachenko and navigator Vladimir I. Yas'ko.

In 1999–2000, the Ukraine transferred eight of its *Blackjacks* to Russia as foreign debt payments (this story is given in more detail in Chapter 7). Yet the Russian Air Force's fleet of 16 Tu-160s was not enough to meet the demands of Russia's strategic nuclear forces. Therefore in 2015, a decision was taken to relaunch production of the Tu-160; the decision was announced by Russian Air Force Commander-in-Chief Col.-Gen. Viktor N. Bondarev. The aircraft will be manufactured to Tu-160M2 standard (see Chapter 5 for details of this upgrade).

Furthermore, in 2010, a decision to relaunch production of the NK-32 engine had been taken at a session of the Russian government's Commission on Defence Industry Matters (the session was chaired by President Vladimir V. Putin). This is now one of the top priorities for the Kuznetsov Joint-Stock Co. Work in this direction began in 2011, more than RUR 8 billion being allocated for this under the Federal Programme of Russia's Defence Industry Development in 2011–2020. At the 12th international trade fair ***Dvigateli-2012*** (Engines-2012) in Moscow, the then Executive Director of the Kuznetsov JSC Yuriy S. Yeliseyev said that new production of the NK-32 would begin in 2014, adding that the new-build engines would be updated. *"When reinstating production of this engine it is inexpedient to repeat what was built 20 years ago in as-is condition. This is unacceptable for the nation and for the Ministry of Defence,"* said Yeliseyev. Later, Vladislav Ye. Masalov, General Director of the United Aero Engine Corporation (ODK – *Obyedi**nyon**naya **dvig**atelestro**it**el'naya korpo**raht**siya*) of which the Kuznetsov JSC is a member, voiced a more realistic date, saying that the first four or five engines will be manufactured in 2016. He added that several dozen NK-32 engines will be delivered to the military by 2020–30.

Chapter 5

Versions and Projects

Tu-160 (*izdeliye* 70) Production Bomber

The Kazan'-built production Tu-160s differed from the prototypes in several respects. The most obvious external difference was the shorter fairing at the fin/tailplane junction, whose rear end had a plumper ogival shape instead of the sharply pointed conical shape seen on the Moscow-built prototypes. Another difference concerned the air intake design but was not obvious unless the engines were running at full power: the number of auxiliary blow-in doors on each side of the engine nacelles was increased from five to six. Also, on production aircraft the insides of the air intakes were black, being coated with a graphite compound in order to reduce the RCS in the forward hemisphere.

Speaking of which, the air intakes were modified in the course of production – the forward sections of the inlet ducts were redesigned and the air intake leading edges reinforced to eliminate vibrations compromising the intakes' structural integrity. The latter were downright dangerous, as they caused rivets to pop and fatigue cracks to appear.

The design of the main landing gear units was simplified after 1988 for the sake of reliability. Changes were also made to the hydraulic system. The biggest change introduced in the course of production, however, concerned the stabilators whose bonded honeycomb-core panels failed at high speeds, causing severe vibration. The Tupolev OKB was forced to redesign the stabila-

Tu-160 "11 Red" *Vasiliy Sen'ko* with the IFR probe deployed and the probe doors open.

Left and above: Russian Air Force Tu-160 "17 Red" Valeriy Chkalov in pre-2009 markings with the tricolour fin flash.

Right: A three-view drawing of the Tu-160PP escort aircraft from the project documents. It shows well the longer and drooped nose (compare this to the photo above), as well as the sets of ECM blade aerials and aft antenna fairings.

tors, reducing the horizontal tail span from 17.6 to 13.26 m (from 57 ft $8\frac{29}{32}$ in to 43 ft 6 in).

Tu-160PP Ultra-Heavy Escort Fighter/Interceptor and ECM Aircraft (project)

As already mentioned, at the *izdeliye* 70's PD project stage in the mid-1970s the Tupolev OKB chose to dispense with defensive armament on the Tu-160 in favour of an ECM/ESM suite. However, a specialised version of the Tu-160 was also envisaged to provide protection for large bomber formations. Designated Tu-160PP (*posta**n**ov**sh**chik **p**o**mekh*** – ECM aircraft), it was actually more than simply an active ECM aircraft; it was to be an ultra-heavy escort fighter armed with long-range and medium-range air-to-air missiles for engaging hostile fighters scrambling to intercept the bombers. Thus it was a latter-day equivalent of the Boeing YB-40 Flying Fortress – a specialised gunship version of the B-17F built in small numbers by Lockheed-Vega in 1943 for escorting USAAF bomber formations making shuttle raids on Germany. Moreover, the aircraft was to operate as an interceptor in case of need, destroying oncoming enemy bombers with AAMs at long range!

Outwardly, the Tu-160PP differed from the standard bomber mainly in having a longer and visibly drooped nose which presumably housed part of the mission avionics. The lower half of the nose ahead of the flight deck was no longer dielectric; instead, the radome (which was still quite large) was located at the forward extremity, having a vertical joint line and an ogival shape reminiscent of the B-1. Three pairs of swept blade aerials were located high on the forward fuselage sides above the LERXes; an identical set of aerials was located low on the rear fuselage sides, while each engine nacelle carried four smaller blade aerials in tandem low on the outer side so that full 360° coverage was provided. Finally, large cigar-shaped antenna fairings pointing aft were located at the tip of the fin, below the fairing at the fin/tailplane junction and on top of the tailcone.

The active jammers and the powerful generators supplying electric power for the mission avionics, as well as the AAMs, were to be housed in the weapons bays. The "nose job" increased the aircraft's overall length from 54.095 to 55.1 m (from 177 ft 5²³⁄₃₂ in to 180 ft 9¹⁹⁄₆₄ in), while height on ground was surprisingly smaller than the bomber's – 13.35 m (43 ft 9¹⁹⁄₃₂ in) versus 13.6 m (44 ft 7⁷⁄₁₆ in), though some sources give the bomber's height on ground as 13.0 m (42 ft 7¹³⁄₁₆ in). The maximum take-off weight was the same as the bomber's at 275,000 kg (606,270 lb).

The premature termination of the basic bomber's production was the main reason why the Tu-160PP was never built.

Tu-160 with NK-74 Engines (project)

Among other things, in the 1980s, the Tupolev OKB proposed re-engining the Tu-160 with Kuznetsov NK-74 afterburning turbofans which were under development at the time – a derivative of the NK-32 uprated to 27,000 kgp (59,520 lbst) in full afterburner. The NK-74 was to be not only more powerful but also more fuel-efficient, giving the bomber a longer combat radius. Apparently the projected upgrade also included installing state-of-the-art mission avionics and integrating new precision-guided weapons. History records, however, that the NK-74 engine never materialised and the project died.

Tu-160M (project, second use of designation)

Also in the mid-1980s, the Tupolev OKB contemplated a version of the *Blackjack* armed with new Kh-32 missiles. The designation Tu-160M was revived for the occasion, the M suffix definitely standing for *modifi**tsee**rovannyy* (modified) in this case). The Kh-32 developed by MKB Raduga was nothing more than an upgraded version of the Kh-22M (AS-4B *Kitchen*) missile carried by the Tu-22M2/Tu-22M3. Basically it shared the predecessor's airframe (with mid-set cropped-delta wings and cruciform tail surfaces, the lower fin folding until the launch sequence) and powerplant (a twin-chamber liquid-propellant rocket motor running on TG-02 fuel and AK-27M oxidiser) but had a new guidance system utilising state-of-the-art electronics – supposedly with INS

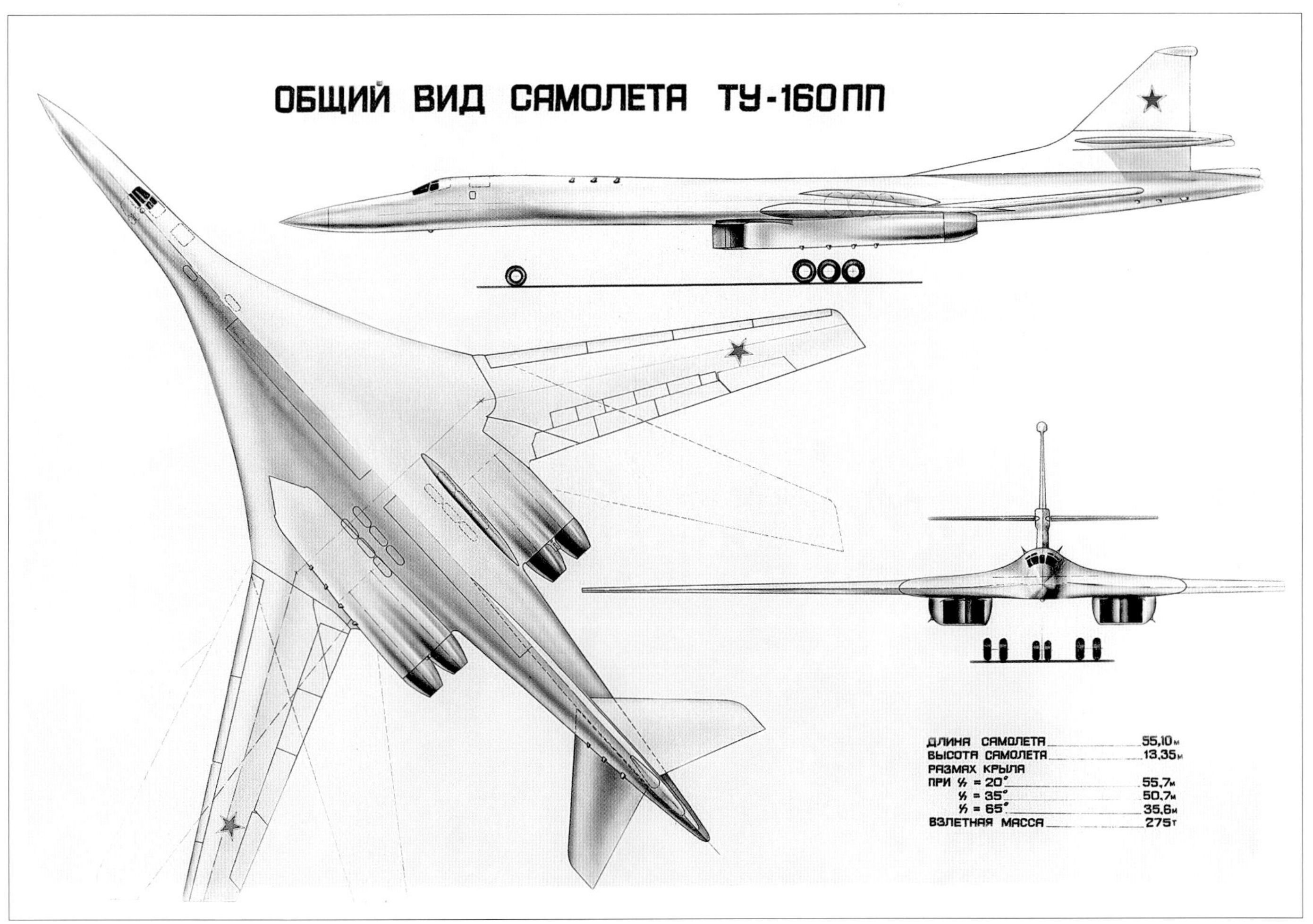

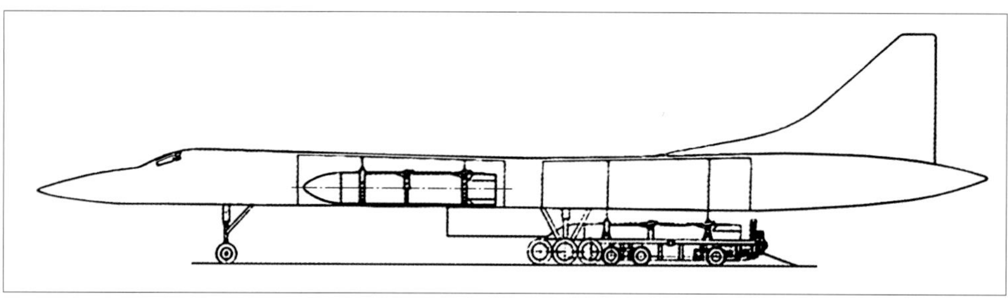

Left: A drawing showing the Krechet aeroballistic missiles being loaded into the Tu-160.

Below: A drawing from the project documents of the suborbital space launch system comprising the Tu-160SK and the Burlak SLV. The map shows possible flight routes to the SLV launch points.

АВИАЦИОННО-КОСМИЧЕСКИЙ КОМПЛЕКС

СОСТАВ КОМПЛЕКСА:

САМОЛЕТ-НОСИТЕЛЬ ТУ-160СК
РАКЕТА „БУРЛАК"

НАЗНАЧЕНИЕ

АВИАЦИОННО-КОСМИЧЕСКИЙ КОМПЛЕКС ОБЕСПЕЧИВАЕТ ЗАПУСК ИСЗ МАЛОЙ МАССЫ (ДО 700 КГ) НА ЛЮБУЮ ОКОЛОЗЕМНУЮ ОРБИТУ НЕЗАВИСИМО ОТ ВРЕМЕНИ СУТОК И ПОГОДНЫХ УСЛОВИЙ ИЗ ЛЮБОЙ ТОЧКИ ЗЕМЛИ.

ОСНОВНЫЕ ДАННЫЕ САМОЛЕТА

● МАССА:
- МАКСИМАЛЬНАЯ ЭКСПЛУАТАЦИОННАЯ ____ 275 т
- РАКЕТЫ ____ 25 т

● ДВИГАТЕЛИ:
4 ТВРД (Н Д КУЗНЕЦОВА) С МАКСИМАЛЬНОЙ СУММАРНОЙ ТЯГОЙ ____ 100 т

● ЭКИПАЖ ____ 4 ЧЕЛОВЕКА

● ПРАКТИЧЕСКАЯ ДАЛЬНОСТЬ:

	С ЗАПУСКОМ РАКЕТЫ (МАССА РАКЕТЫ 25т)	БЕЗ ЗАПУСКА РАКЕТЫ (ПЕРЕГОНОЧНЫЙ ВАР-Т)
- БЕЗ ДОЗАПРАВКИ	11260 км	10460 км
- С ОДНОЙ ПОПУТНОЙ ДОЗАПРАВКОЙ В ВОЗДУХЕ	14120 км	13150 км

● ДЛИНА РАЗБЕГА при m = 275 (СА) ____ 2120 м

● ДЛИНА ПРОБЕГА:
- БЕЗ РАКЕТЫ ____ 1300 м
- С РАКЕТОЙ ____ 1470 м

● ПОТРЕБНАЯ ДЛИНА ВПП (СА)
для m взл = 275 т ____ L впп = 3500 м
для m взл = 200 т ____ L впп = 3000 м

● РЕЖИМ ПУСКА РАКЕТЫ
χ = 32° m = 200-170 т M = 0.8 H = 9÷11 км
χ = 65° m = 200-170 т M = 1.6 H = 11÷12.5 км

МАРШРУТЫ ПОЛЕТОВ

guidance and mid-course correction from either a digital map or the missile's active radar homing seeker head.

The Kh-32 had a length of 11.65 m (38 ft 2 21/32 in), a wing span of 3.0 m (9 ft 10 1/8 in) and a launch weight of 5,780 kg (12,740 lb). Maximum launch range is estimated as 1,000 km (621 miles) and launch altitude as 1,000-13,000 m (3,280-42,650 ft). The Tu-160M project was not pursued further but development of the Kh-32 continued; the missile is now set to enter service on the upgraded Tu-22M3M.

Some sources claim that the Tu-160M – obviously the project version described above, not the real Tu-160M of today! – was also intended to carry two hypersonic cruise missiles provisionally designated Kh-90 (NATO AS-X-21). Developed by MKB Raduga, the Kh-90 was a huge and scary-looking missile having a tail-first layout and powered by a ramjet engine; the canards were carried on a distinctive "platypus nose" above the semi-circular air intake with a semi-cone centrebody. To fit into the Tu-160's weapons bay the trapezoidal wings had a cunning double-jointed "snap-action" design, the narrow root portions folding up and the remainder of the wing panels vertically down; the trapezoidal fin also had a double-folding design. Even so, the missile filled the entire weapons bay, being nearly 12 m (39 ft 4 in) long; the wing span was estimated as 6.8-7 m (22 ft 3 23/32 in to 22 ft 11 19/32 in). After the missile had been released and the wings and tail unfolded, a solid-propellant booster inside the ramjet nozzle fired and accelerated the missile until the ramjet sustainer could be ignited, allowing the missile to reach a cruising speed of Mach 4.5 at 8,000-27,000 m (26,250-88,580 ft).

The Kh-90 project was terminated in 1992. One of the missile's demonstrators was displayed at the MAKS-95 airshow in Zhukovskiy as the GELA (*ghiperzvookovoy eksperimentahl'nyy letahtel'nyy apparaht* – Hypersonic Experimental Aerial Vehicle).

Tu-160V Bomber (project)

By far the most radical modification of the *Blackjack* proposed in the 1980s would have resulted in what was, in effect, a completely new aeroplane. Much has been reported on airliner projects utilising cryogenic fuel – liquid hydrogen (LH_2) or liquefied natural gas (LNG); the feasibility of the concept has been proved by the Soviet Tu-155 research aircraft – a heavily modified Tu-154 airliner (CCCP-85035) which first flew on April 15, 1988. But have you ever heard of a cryoplane bomber? This is exactly what the projected Tu-160V would have been; the V stood for *vodorod* – hydrogen. Apart from the powerplant consisting of jet engines adapted for running on hydrogen, the Tu-160V featured a new fuselage which was of necessity much fatter in order to accommodate the heat-insulated LH_2 tanks and the inert gas pressurisation system.

Tu-160K 'Krechet' Air-Launched Ballistic Missile System (project)

The ***Krechet*** (Gerfalcon) air-launched ballistic missile system was under development between July 1983, and December 1984, reaching the PD project stage. It envisaged using the air launch technique as a means of enhancing the combat survivability of ballistic missiles in a retaliatory counter-strike scenario and increasing the payload carried by the missile. The system's main components were a specially equipped Tu-160 (this version was sometimes called Tu-160K, the suffix referring to the Krechet system) and a two-stage aeroballistic missile, two of which could be carried internally.

The Krechet missile was so bulky that it filled the entire weapons bay, being 10.7 m (35 ft 1 17/64 in) long, with a diameter of 1.6 m (5 ft 3 in), and had a launch weight of 24,400 kg (53,790 lb). Stage 1 had a solid-propellant rocket motor and jet rudders; stage 2 had a liquid-propellant rocket motor running on monofuel, which was less hazardous than hypergolic fuel, and was fitted with jettisonable ogival wings. The missile's 1,400-kg (3,090-lb) payload could be either a monobloc warhead, plus decoys for protection against interceptor missiles, or six multiple independently targeted re-entry vehicles (MIRVs). The estimated circular error probable (CEP) was 600 m (1,970 ft).

The Krechet system was to have a maximum operational range of 10,000 km (6,210 miles), including the Tu-160K's combat radius; the launch could take place at up to 7,500 km (4,660 miles) from the base. To enhance resistance to the effects of nuclear explosions the Tu-160Ks would be dispersed to reserve bases or take off and loiter once a nuclear alert had been declared (an attack was impending); this was expected to give the missiles a 89% survival rate. With the system on maximum alert (the crew in the flight deck), a take-off could be made within five minutes.

For the first time in Soviet practice the missile was to be launched at supersonic speed, although launch in subsonic mode was also possible. The first stage motor was to be ignited three seconds after release, whereupon the missile would make a programmed turn with 45° bank and 10° yaw in order to reduce the effect of the rocket motor efflux on the aircraft. The trajectory towards the target with pre-entered co-ordinates was computed by an on-board processor and a celestial tracker.

Tu-160SK (Tu-160 'Burlak') Suborbital Launch System (project)

Faced by the dwindling defence orders and decline in military hardware production in Russia as a result of political changes and economic problems, the Tupolev OKB attempted to find a niche for the Tu-160 on the civil market. In the early 1990s, the OKB teamed with MKB Raduga and the Moscow Energy Institute (MEI) to develop the *Burlak* suborbital launch system for putting small commercial satellites into orbit. (In 19th-century Russia, the *burlaki* (plural of "burlak"; pronounced *boorlakee*) were teams of strongmen whose job was to haul barges up rivers by means of ropes. Apparently someone perceived an analogy between this and "hauling" payloads into orbit.)

Suborbital launch offered many advantages as compared to ordinary space centres. The weather became less important – the aircraft could "chase the good weather" if necessary. The space launch vehicle (SLV) became lighter; the vertical part of its trajectory was eliminated, requiring less fuel for the launch. The latter could take place near the Equator where the launch conditions are more favourable for putting payloads into orbit – or from the territory of the customer nation. Last but not least, it was possible to do without extensive and costly ground infrastructure.

The Burlak system comprised a standard *Blackjack* suitably modified as a launch platform, the Burlak suborbital SLV and a

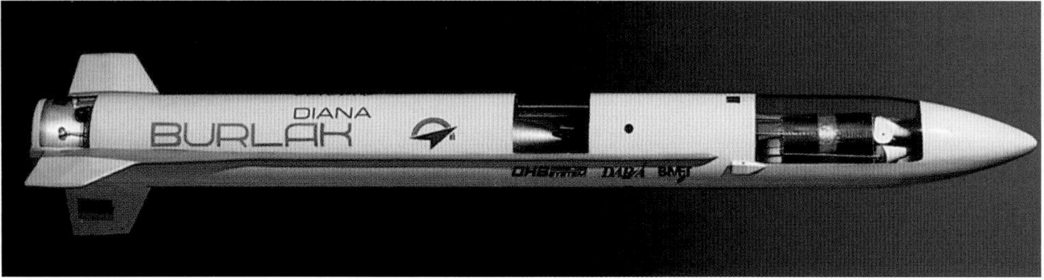

ground support complex, including a launch data preparation system. The modified aircraft was designated Tu-160SK (the suffix probably stood for *spetsi**ahl'**nyy kos**mich**eskiy* – Space Special). As originally envisaged, the Burlak was a three-stage liquid-propellant rocket; it had a cylindrical body with shoulder-mounted trapezoidal wings and a high-set twin-fin tail unit of equal span with the fins and rudders below the trapezoidal stabilisers to avoid fouling the Tu-160's fuselage. Being too large for internal carriage, the SLV was to be suspended under the centre fuselage on a special pylon. The maximum payload put into orbit was 800-850 kg (1,760-1,870 lb) and the estimated launch costs amounted to US$6,000-8,000 in the day's prices.

According to the project documents, the Tu-160SK with the SLV attached had a maximum TOW of 275,000 kg (606,270 lb) and the SLV had a launch weight of 25,000 kg (55,115 lb). Range on internal fuel was 11,260 km (7,000 miles) with the SLV launched in mid-mission or 10,460 km (6,500 miles) with no launch (in a positioning flight). Since the Tu-160SK retained the standard bomber's IFR system, with one fuel top-up on the outbound leg the range increased to 14,120 km (8,770 miles) or 13,150 km (8,170 miles) respectively. The take-off run was 2,120 m (6,960 ft); the landing run was 1,470 m (4,820 ft) with the SLV attached or 1,300 m (4,270 ft) with no SLV. The runway length requirement was 3,500 m (11,480 ft) with a maximum TOW or 3,000 m (9,840 ft) with a 200,000-kg (440,920-lb) TOW.

The Tu-160SK could launch the Burlak almost anywhere, depending on where the launch conditions were favourable at the moment. Typical flight routes with the aircraft departing from Moscow (to be precise, Zhukovskiy) were:

- due north with a launch over the Arctic Ocean between the Spitsbergen Archipelago and the North Pole;

Right and below right: The models of the Tu-160SK (in Tupolev corporate colours) and the Burlak SLV displayed at the 1995 Paris Air Show. Note that the Burlak is still in winged configuration with a twin-fin tail unit

Left: This model shows the Tu-160SK carrying the very different Burlak-Diana wingless SLV. Note the folded ventral rudder and the jettisonable fairing enclosing the rocket motor nozzle.

Below left: An artist's impression of the Tu-160SK launching the Burlak-Diana.

Bottom left: A cutaway model of the Burlak-Diana SLV, showing the deployed rudder and the long strakes ahead of the stabilisers. The logos are those of (left to right) MKB Raduga, OHB-System, DARA and MEI.

Below: Wearing the Le Bourget '95 exhibit code 342, Tu-160 f/n 4-01 is seen in the static display of the MAKS-95 airshow with a full-size mock-up of the Burlak-Diana SLV.

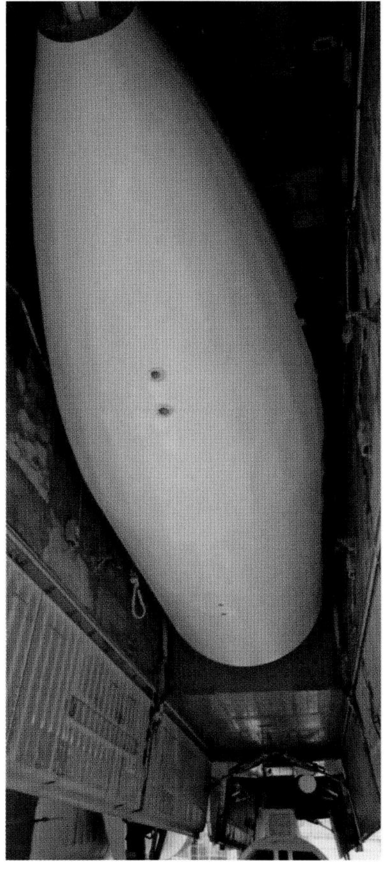

Opposite top: A rather crudely retouched photo dating back to the early days of the Burlak project, showing the SLV under the aircraft – in fact, the first production Tu-160.

Opposite, middle and bottom: The still-uncoded Tu-160SK demonstrator at Zhukovskiy shortly before departure to Le Bourget.

Above: The front half of the Burlak-Diana SLV mock-up in the forward weapons bay for the flight to Le Bourget; the rear half has been unloaded.

Top right and above right: "342" at the MAKS-95 and MAKS-97 airshows in company with Tupolev's reconnaissance UAVs.

Below and below right: The Burlak-Diana SLV under the Tu-160SK, showing the folded rudder and the jettisonable tail fairing.

• east/south-east with a launch over Western Siberia between Noril'sk and Novosibirsk;

• ditto, all the way to the Far East with a launch over the Pacific Ocean off the tip of the Kamchatka Peninsula;

• south-east across Uzbekistan, Iran and India and the Bay of Bengal with a launch over the Indian Ocean near the Equator;

• due south over the Black Sea, then turn south-east across Iraq, the Red Sea, the Arabian Peninsula and the Arabian Sea, with a launch near the Equator;

• south-west across the Balkans, the Mediterranean, Libya, Niger and Nigeria with a launch over the Gulf of Guinea near the Equator.

Launch was to take place at 9,000-11,000 m (29,530-36,090 ft) with the aircraft cruising at Mach 0.8 (wings swept back 35°) or at

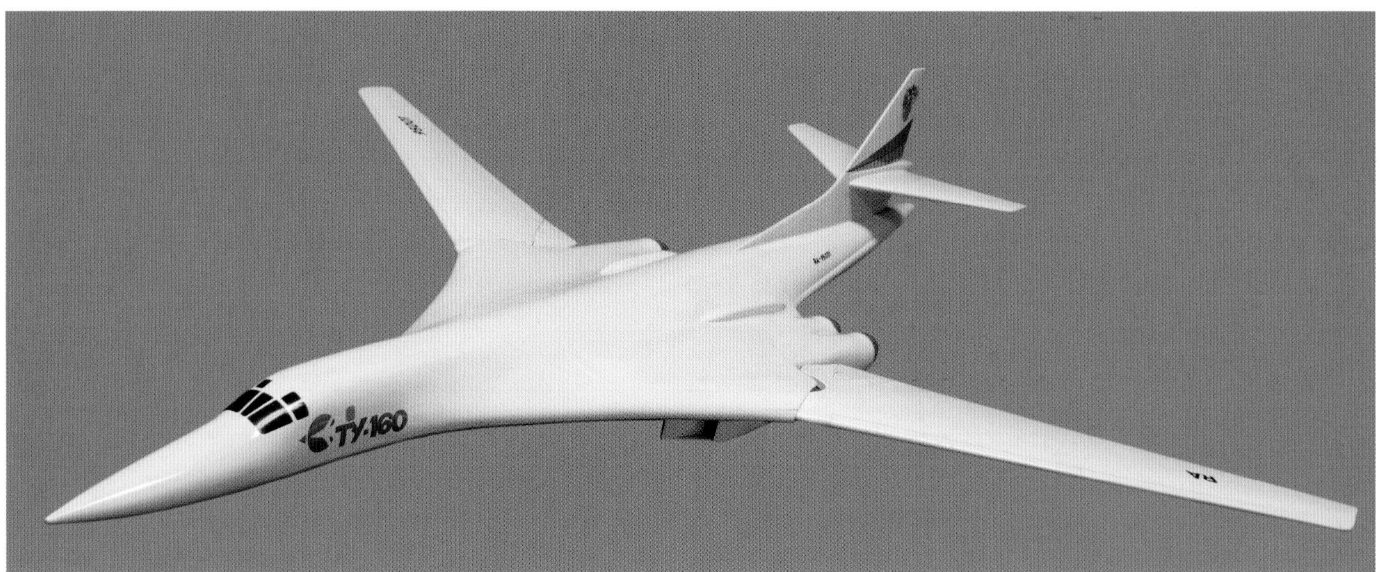

This model of the Tu-160 bearing the civil registration RA-95001 illustrates the Tupolev PLC's readiness to use the bomber for civilian needs, such as launching commercial satellites by means of the Burlak-Diana SLV.

11,000-12,500 m (36,090-41,010 ft) with the aircraft cruising at Mach 1.6 (wings swept back 65°). If necessary the Tu-160SK carrying a refuelled but unequipped Burlak could land at a predesignated military base in any country so that the satellite could be mated with the SLV. In so doing, due precautions would be taken to guarantee protection of the customer's technology against industrial espionage. All the satellite's manufacturer needed to do was to make sure that certain specifications (electric system parameters, dimensions, weight, operational temperature range and so on) met the requirements of MKB Raduga so that the satellite would be compatible with the rocket.

The Burlak system permitted the launch of several satellites at a time, providing their aggregate weight and dimensions were within the specified limits. Preliminary calculations showed that a high-speed, high-altitude suborbital launch required two to three times less energy to place an equivalent payload in orbit as compared to a conventional launch. Also, the costs would be cut by a factor of 2-2.5. The ability to launch the Burlak virtually anywhere over the World Ocean allowed satellites to be placed into any orbit while obviating the need to lease land for restricted areas where spent booster stages would fall after burnout – an issue which could lead to international disputes. The performance parameters of the Burlak system were far superior to those of its American counterpart – the Orbital Systems Corporation-Hercules Pegasus suborbital launcher rocket which was carried aloft by a subsonic Boeing B-52 Stratofortress bomber (to say nothing of the OSC-Hercules Stargazer launch platform based on the Lockheed L-1011-500 TriStar wide-body airliner). Thus, the Tu-160 strategic bomber offered unparalleled opportunities for commercial use.

Russia endeavoured to turn the Burlak programme into an international one, searching for foreign partners. Thus, on April 2, 1997, the Russian government issued directive No.428 ordering the Ministry of Economics, the Ministry of Foreign Trade (jointly with the Ministry of Defence and the Ministry of Foreign Affairs), MKB Raduga, ANTK Tupolev and the ***Rosvo'oruzheniye*** (= Russian Weapons) State Company, which was then the nation's main arms exporter, to hold negotiations on possible technical partnership in the programme with Deutsche Aerospace (DASA, the German space agency) and OHB System AG headquartered in Bremen which developed and manufactured space systems. However, no tangible results were forthcoming as of this writing.

MKB Raduga, the OKB of the Moscow Energy Institute, ANTK Tupolev and OHB-System GmbH unveiled the Tu-160SK and the very different Burlak-Diana SLV with a launch weight of 20,000 kg (44,090 lb) in model form at the Asian Aerospace '94 airshow which took place at Singapore–Changi airport. The Burlak-Diana was a two-stage rocket with no wings and a tail unit comprising high-set stabilators and a folding ventral rudder. In July 1995, one of ANTK Tupolev's Tu-160 "dogships" with no tactical code (ex-"63 Grey," c/n 84704217) was displayed at the 41st Paris Air Show with a full-size wooden mock-up of the Burlak-Diana rocket, bearing the exhibit code 342; this was the only occasion when the Tu-160 participated in a foreign airshow. A month later the same aircraft with the same mock-up attached was in the static park of the MAKS-95 airshow in Zhukovskiy (August 22–27); it was present again at the MAKS-97 airshow (August 1–24, 1997). Plans were in hand to build a heavier version of the SLV – the Burlak-M with a launch weight of 37,000 kg (81,570 lb). Yet, none of these plans bore fruit.

Interest in the Tu-160/suborbital launch idea was unexpectedly revived when the Ukraine started disposing of its *Blackjack* fleet in 1999. A US company called Platforms International Corporation (PIC) and based in Mojave, California, offered to buy three of the Ukrainian aircraft, plus spares, for US$20 million and transfer 20% of the shares of its division, Orbital Network Services Corporation (OrbNet for short), to the Russian Aerospace Consortium.

Right: Tupolev JSC test pilot Aleksandr I. Zhuravlyov who captained the upgraded Tu-160M on its first flight.

Below: The Tupolev test crew (left to right: navigator Viktor I. Pedos, WSO Yevgeniy A. Kudryavtsev, co-pilot Sergey G. Borisov and captain Aleksandr I. Zhuravlyov) pose with the Tu-160M prototype (f/n 2-02) during tests.

The Ukrainian Cabinet of Ministers approved the sale, and it seemed that OrbNet would be able to launch the first satellite in a year of two. Still, this project never materialised.

Tu-160M Mid-life Upgrade (third use of designation)

At the beginning of the 21st century the Tu-160, which had been in service for 15 years by then, was becoming obsolescent; this concerned first and foremost the avionics suite, which was based on 1970s technology. Therefore the Tupolev PLC, MKB Raduga, KAPO and other Russian defence industry enterprises began an

in-depth mid-life upgrade (MLU) programme for the *Blackjack*. For a while the subject of this programme had no separate designation, being referred to simply as the "upgraded Tu-160." Later the designation Tu-160M was applied semi-officially to the aircraft, the M now standing for *moderni**zee**rovannyy* (upgraded); it has now caught on.

The MLU focussed on two main areas: installation of up-to-date avionics and integration of new precision-guided munitions. As mentioned earlier, from the start of its career the Tu-160 had used almost exclusively Kh-55 and Kh-55SM cruise missiles; bombs had not been used, even though the *Blackjack* is provided with an electro-optical bomb sight. Therefore, at first the military toyed with the idea of "teaching the Tu-160 to drop bombs" – especially guided bombs. Here it should be noted that the Tu-160 has almost twice the warload of the Tu-22M3 – 45,000 kg (99,120 lb) versus 24,000 kg (52,910 lb). When writing on the subject, some journo waxed lyrical about the *"Tu-160 which can carry as many*

bombs as a squadron of Tu-22Ms" (*sic*), but that's clearly an exaggeration.

Yet, as the MLU programme progressed, the military had second thoughts and the "Bombin' *Blackjack*" issue was quickly removed from the agenda. Firstly, dropping bombs on a theatre target from the Tu-160 does not tie in with the aircraft's strategic role; this is a job for the Tu-22M3. Secondly, given the capabilities of current western air defence systems, even with the bombs being released from an altitude of 9,000-13,000 m (29,530-42,650 ft) at 5-8 km (3.1-4.96 miles) range, the Tu-160 will come under fire – and a lucrative and vulnerable target it will be. The risk of the already small Tu-160 fleet being depleted by theatre air defences was considered unacceptable.

Opposite page: Russian Air Force Tu-160s being refurbished/upgraded at KAPO. The slogan on the wall reads, "Thriftiness is the way to our wealth!"

Above: The stripped-out flight deck of a Tu-160 in the midst of an overhaul. The avionics suite was replaced completely in the process.

Right: Tu-160M "14 Red" *Andrey Tupolev* passes overhead, showing the blanked-off window where the OPB-15T EO bomb sight used to be.

Below: The same aircraft at Engels-2 AB after a sortie, showing the registration RF-94111. Note the western-made airport tug.

Therefore, the upgrade concentrated on new cruise missiles. The first of these was the Raduga Kh-555 (AS-15C *Kent-C*) – a thoroughly updated derivative of the Kh-55SM. Like the latter, the missile had conformal tanks to extend range but was equipped with a conventional high-explosive warhead. This resulted in a shift of the CG and hence a change of handling, so a pair of fixed canards was added to the Kh-555's forward fuselage to compensate for this. The missile has the same dimensions as the Kh-55SM, a launch weight of 1,500 kg (3,310 lb), a range of 2,000 km (1,242 miles) and a minimum flight altitude of 40 m (130 ft). The CEP is just 20 m (65 ft) – a fivefold improvement on the Kh-55. (Could this account for the "extra 5" in the designation?)

The other new missile– or rather missiles – developed by MKB Raduga were the Kh-101 equipped with a conventional warhead and its nuclear-tipped version, the Kh-102. Work on these missiles began back in 1995; the first test launches were made in 1999. Again, the Kh-101/Kh-102 shares the aerodynamic layout of the Kh-55SM and is powered by a very similar R95TM-300 turbofan stowed in the rear fuselage before launch. The dimensions, however, are somewhat different; the missile is 7.45 m (24 ft $5^{19}/_{64}$ in) long, with a wing span of 3.0 m (9 ft $10^{7}/_{64}$ in) and a maximum fuselage width of 0.742 m (2 ft $5^{7}/_{32}$ in). The missile has a launch weight of 2,200-2,400 kg (4,850-5,290 lb), including a 400-kg (880-lb) warhead, and a range of 4,500-5,500 km (2,800-3,420 miles). Minimum flight altitude in terrain following mode is 30 m (100 ft). The CEP is just 5-6 m (16-20 ft).

(That's where the Tu-160's long weapons bays designed around the stillborn Kh-45 missile came in handy. The Tu-95MS was likewise being upgraded to take the new missiles; it was immediately apparent that the *Blackjack* can carry the Kh-101/Kh-102 internally while the *Bear-H* cannot – the weapons bay is too short, having been tailored for the Kh-55. Hence the Tu-95MSM carries its eight Kh-101 missiles externally on underwing pylons.)

Apart from changes to the weapons control system, the new missiles necessitated installation of a new model of rotary launcher. This was designated *izdeliye* 9A-829K3 and was an improved derivative of the Tu-160's standard MKU-6-5U launcher (aka *izdeliye* 9A-829K2).

Little information is available as to the Tu-160M's avionics. However, it appears that the OPB-15T electro-optical bomb sight has been deleted as unnecessary, its sloping window being blanked off (this is the Tu-160M's chief recognition feature). Also, the upgrade concerns the navigation suite; in particular, the Russian avionics consortium KRET (*Kon**tsern** '**Rah**dio'elek**tron**nyye tekhno**lo**gii'* – Radio Electronic Technology Concern) has developed the new ANS-2009 celestial navigation system (***a**stronavigatsion**nay**a siste**ma*) for the Tu-160M to replace the existing AV-1SM (***a**strovi**zeer***).

The aircraft chosen to become the Tu-160M prototype was the company-owned '87 Grey' (c/n 84502324, f/n 2-02); the work began as early as 2000. Tupolev JSC test pilot Aleksandr I. Zhuravlyov was the Tu-160M's project test pilot. Upon completion of the trials the aircraft was transferred to the Air Force on July 5, 2006, as an attrition replacement, becoming the second example to be delivered.

In 2002, KAPO signed a RUR 3.75 billion contract with the Russian Ministry of Defence for the upgrade of the Russian Air Force's entire 15-strong Tu-160 fleet; the final aircraft was to be redelivered in 2015. The cost of refurbishing and upgrading each aircraft was RUR 250 million. It should be noted that KAPO, being the original equipment manufacturer, handles all heavy maintenance and refurbishment of the *Blackjack*, not trusting the regular aircraft repair plants to do it.

The first in-service aircraft to be brought up to the new standard was "07 Red" (c/n 82408427, f/n 8-02) built in 1999. After an overhaul combined with an upgrade Tu-160M "07 Red" was redelivered on May 5, 2002. The overhaul involved replacing 30-40% of the items in the aircraft.

Other *Blackjacks* were upgraded to Tu-160M standard in due course. For example, "16 Red" (c/n 82905836, f/n 5-03) was refurbished (and probably upgraded) in 2009. "15 Red" (c/n 83905953, f/n 5-03) followed in 2011. Tu-160M "18 Red" (c/n 82006458, f/n 6-05) made its first post-upgrade flight at Kazan'-Borisoglebskoye on November 16, 2014, and was redelivered on December 19. A total of six Tu-160Ms (the final six) are to be redelivered in 2015; one of them is "12 Red" (c/n 84906335, f/n 6-03).

Meanwhile, the Kh-555 missile was being put thorough its paces. One of the test flights involving a live launch of a Kh-555 took place at the Pemboy target range near Vorkuta (Komi Republic) on August 16, 2005; the aircraft in question was "03 Red" (f/n 7-03), and the flight was also notable because President of Russia Vladimir V. Putin was aboard, deciding to get a first-hand impression.

Additionally, as mentioned in the preceding chapter, the Russian Air Force plans to order new-build Tu-160s – possibly as many as 50. These aircraft will be built as Tu-160Ms from the start. Work is now under way on a new multi-function radar that will replace both the venerable Poisk radar on the Tu-160M and the even more venerable PNA-D radar on the Tu-22M3M. Also, the Tupolev PLC is working on integrating the Granit anti-shipping missile and the Oniks anti-radar missile on the Tu-160M, which will allow the revamped *Blackjack* to combat surface ships and AWACS aircraft.

Tu-160M2 (project)

In July 2015, Vladimir Mikhailov, an executive of the KRET consortium, stated in an interview to the Russian news agency ITAR-TASS that the consortium would submit proposals on a new integrated avionics suite for the new-build Tu-160. *"We are currently getting all design materials approved and the specifications and scope of work on this machine agreed upon. I believe that within a year we will float our proposals and have a clear idea of what will be installed on this aircraft,"* said Mikhailov. He said *"only the [avionics and weapons] platform will be left of the existing Tu-160, and the aircraft will have more capable equipment."* He mentioned that the aircraft will feature an all-new ECM system, which will incorporate elements of the *Ghima**lai*** (The Himalayas) suite and elements developed for the Tu-160's eventual successor provisionally designated PAK DA (*Perspek**tiv**nyy aviatsi**on**nyy **kom**pleks **Dahl'**ney avi**ah**tsii* – Future Long-Range Aviation Aircraft System), which is being developed by the Tupolev PLC.

Later, the Russian Ministry of Defence stated that the new-build aircraft will be designated Tu-160M2. The MoD source stated that production has been postponed until 2023; the Russian Air Force intends to take delivery of at least 50 Tu-160M2s.

Chapter 6

The Tu-160 in Detail

Type: Multi-mode strategic missile strike aircraft with a secondary bomber role designed to operate in daytime and night VMC and IMC, delivering weapons from both high and low altitude. The aircraft has a crew of four: captain, co-pilot, navigator and weapons systems operator.

The airframe utilises a blended wing/body (BWB) layout which maximises the use of internal space for fuel, weapons, avionics and equipment while reducing the number of manufacturing breaks, thereby cutting structural weight. It is of basically all-metal construction; the primary structural material is AK4-1ChT1 aluminium alloy. Additionally, V-95PCh-AT2 aluminium alloy, VT-6Ch titanium alloy, OT-4 heat-resistant titanium alloy and high-strength steel are used for critical components absorbing the main structural loads and subjected to high thermal loads. Some airframe components (mostly non-stressed items, such as wing/fuselage fairings, wheel well doors and weapons bay doors) and the trailing edge portions of the tail surfaces are made of glassfibre/Textolite composite with a honeycomb core. The share of structural materials by weight is 58% aluminium alloys, 20% titanium, 15% steel and 5% composites and other non-metallic materials. The airframe subassemblies are joined together by bolts and rivets.

Fuselage: Semi-monocoque stressed-skin structure with more than 100 frames and a set of stringers supporting the skin; the cutouts for the wheel wells and weapons bays are reinforced by longitudinal beams. The fuselage cross-section changes from quasi-circular at the front to rectangular with rounded corners in

A Tu-160 ("15 Red" *Vladimir Sudets*) with four Kh-55SM missiles on dollies; two of them are in flight configuration.

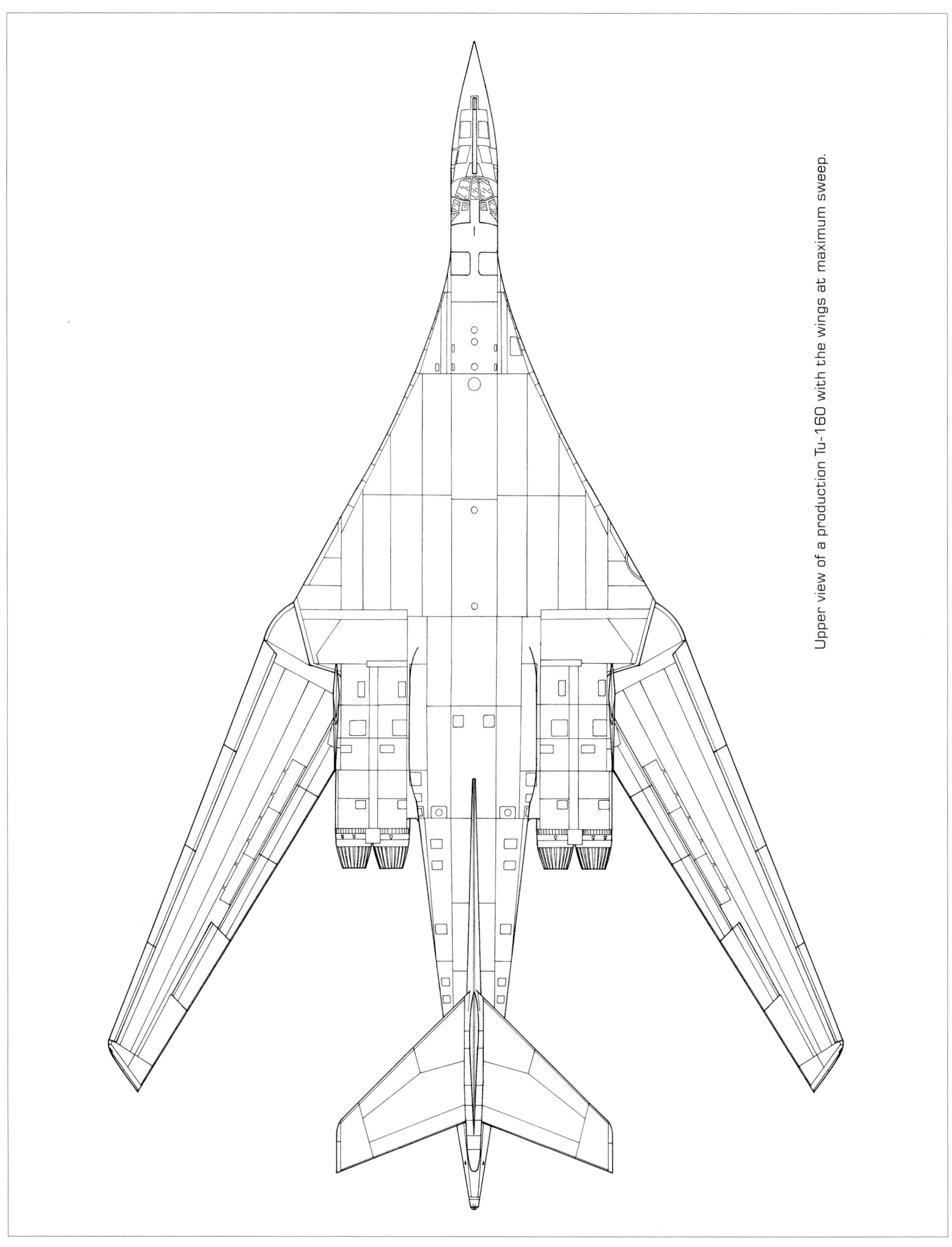

Upper view of a production Tu-160 with the wings at maximum sweep.

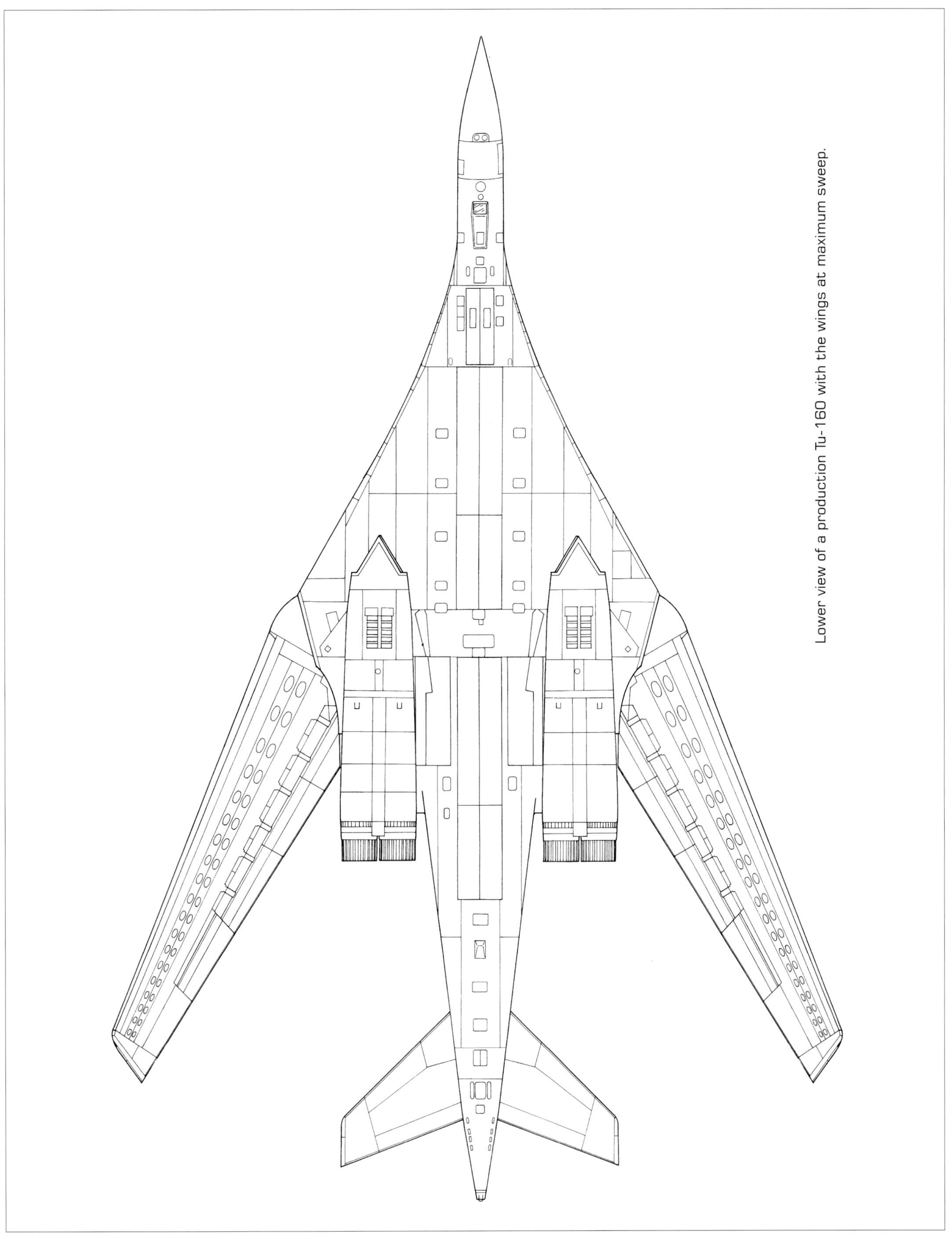

Lower view of a production Tu-160 with the wings at maximum sweep.

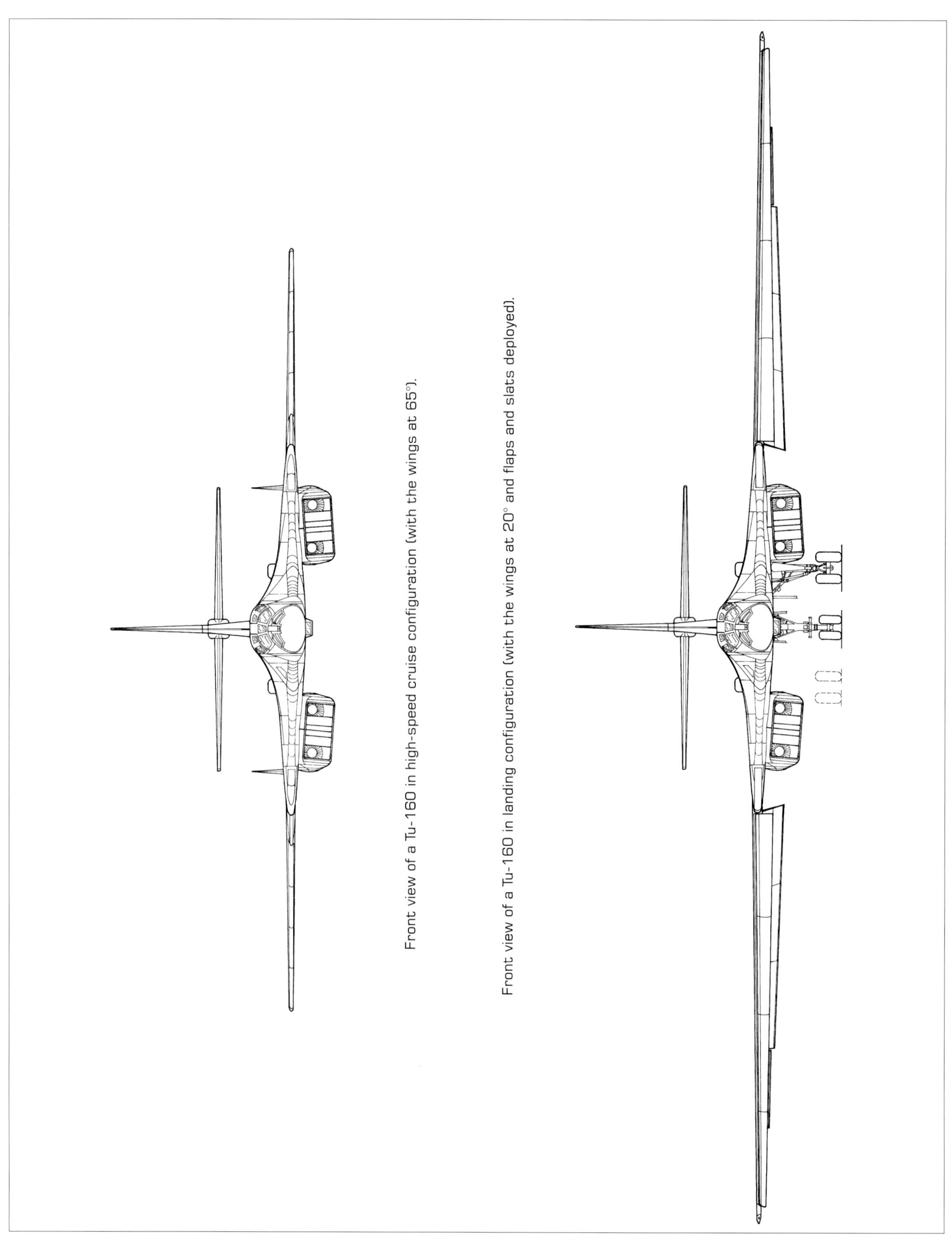

Front view of a Tu-160 in high-speed cruise configuration (with the wings at 65°).

Front view of a Tu-160 in landing configuration (with the wings at 20° and flaps and slats deployed).

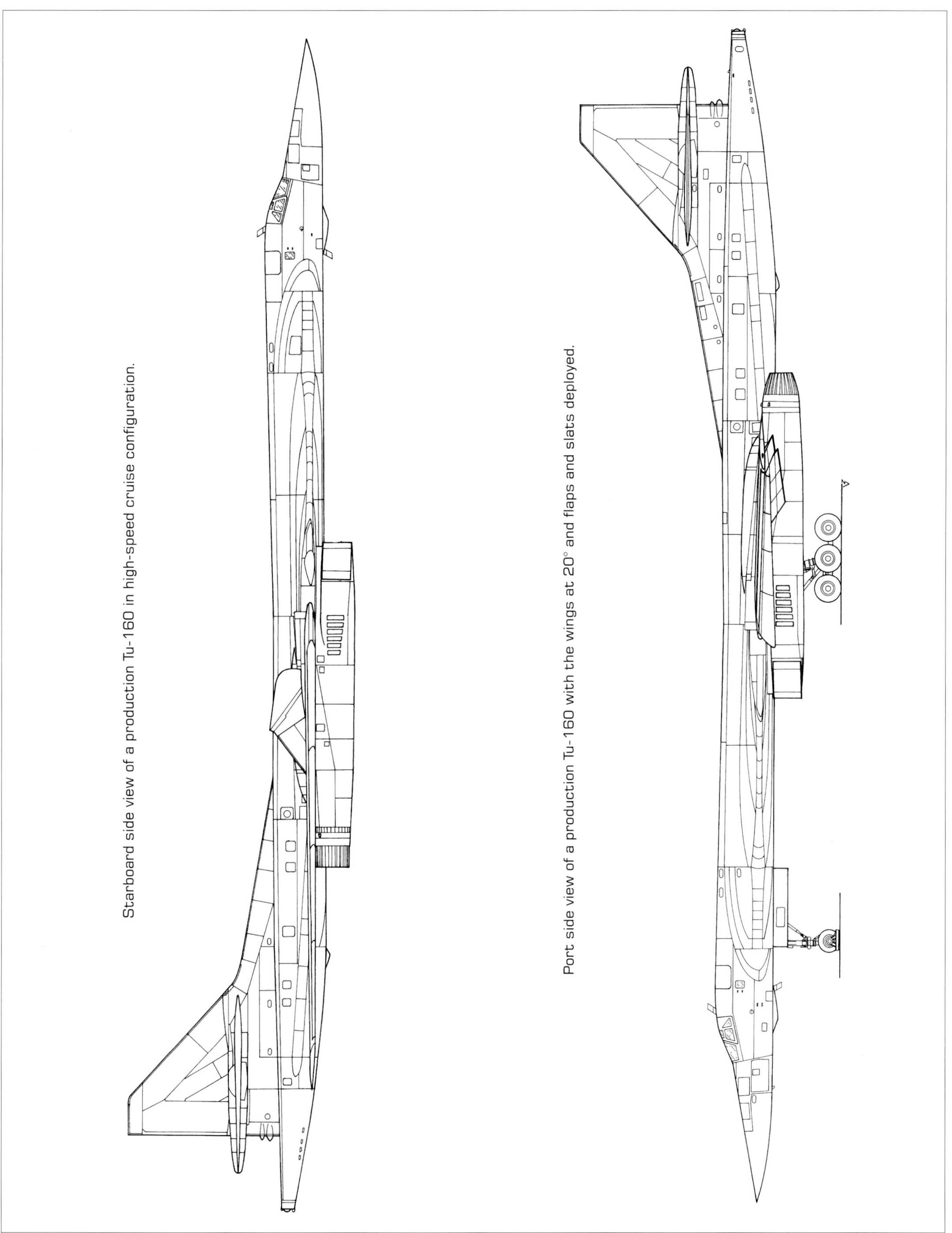

Starboard side view of a production Tu-160 in high-speed cruise configuration.

Port side view of a production Tu-160 with the wings at 20° and flaps and slats deployed.

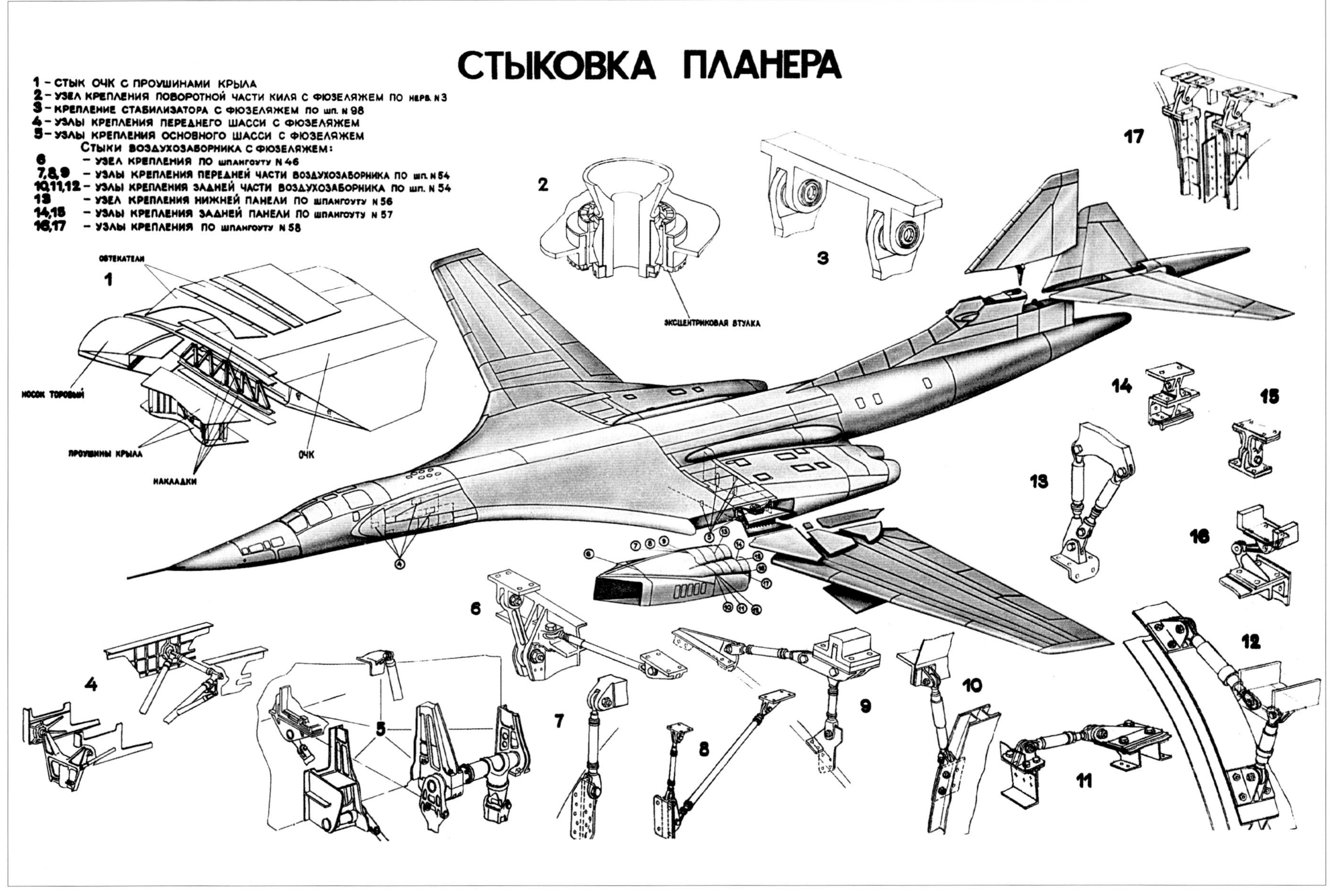

Some of the joints in the Tu-160's airframe. 1. The outer wing torsion box/pivot eye joint. 2. The movable upper fin section pivot at rib 3. 3. The stabilator hinge at fuselage frame 98. 4. Nose gear attachment points. 5. Main gear attachment points. // Air intake assembly to fuselage attachment points: 6. At frame 46; 7-9. Front section attachment fittings at frame 54; 10-12. Rear section attachment fittings at frame 54; 13. Lower panel attachment at frame 56; 14-15. Rear panel attachment at frame 57; 16-17. Attachment fittings at frame 58.

The joints in the fuselage. Sections F1/F2: the joints at frame 7N (bottom, 1 and top, 2). Sections F2/F3: the joints at stringers 12-13 (bottom, 3) and 8-10 (top, 4). Sections F2/F4: the joints at the LERXes and frame 25 (5), frame 25 (6), web (7), stringer 7 (8), beam (9) and upper skin (10). Section F4/wing pivot box/Section F5: the joints of the beam and web at frame 54 (11), the upper skin at frames 48-49 (12), the front weapons bay wall, beam, skin and pivot box rib 2 at frames 48-49 (13), the skin and pivot box rib 3 at frames 48-49 (14), the weapons bay wall and pivot box rib 4 at frames 48-49 (15), stringer 7 and the weapons bay wall at frames 48-49 (16). Sections F5/F6: the joints at the beam (17), upper skin (18), stringer 7 (19), stringer 7 and the rear weapons bay wall (20) and frame 71 (21).

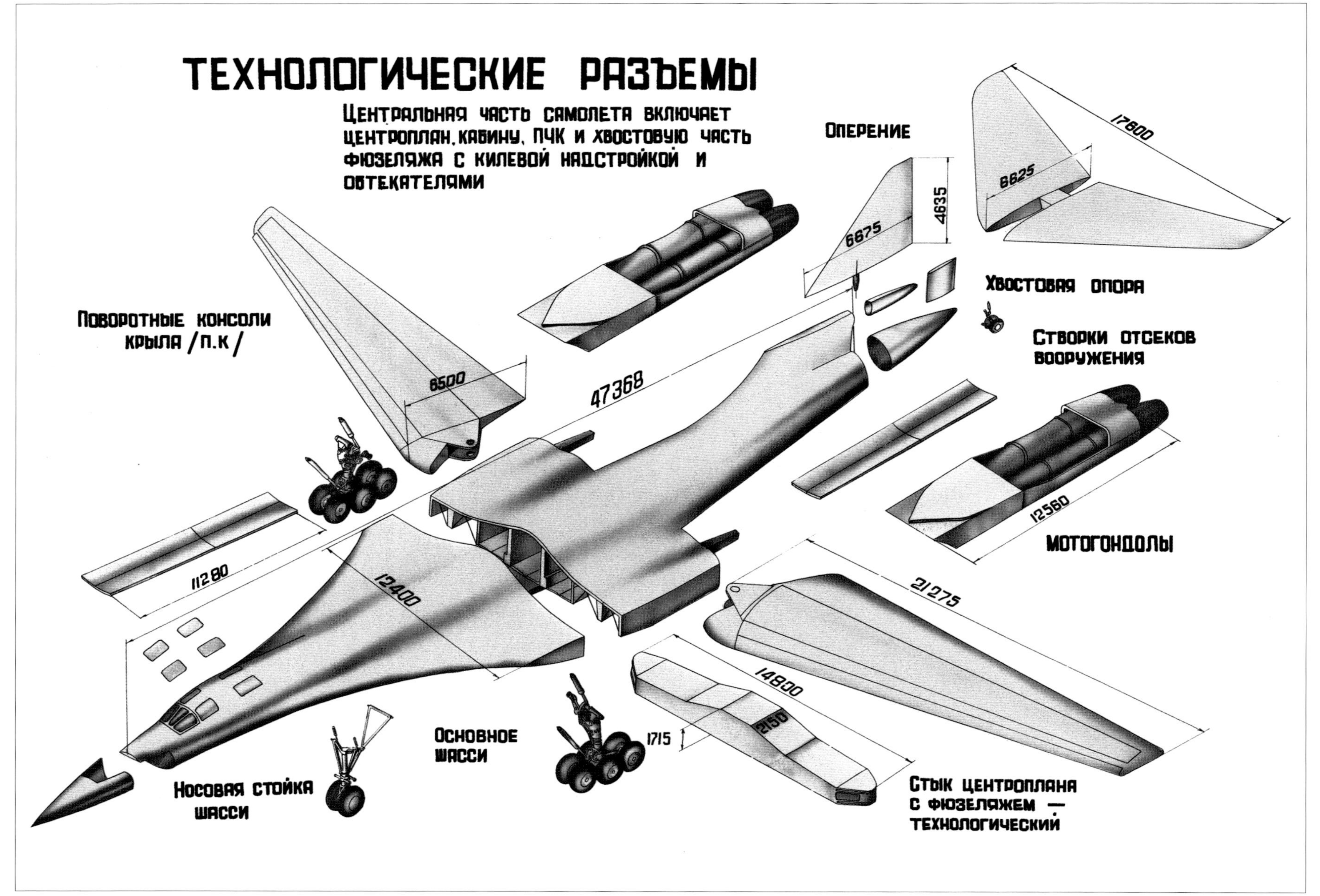

The manufacturing breaks in the Tu-160's airframe. As the legend reads, the centre portion comprises the wing pivot box, the flight deck, the LERXes and the rear fuselage with the fixed lower part of the fin and associated fairings. This is the penultimate configuration; note that the air intakes are still raked in side elevation (Tu-144 style), not V-shaped in plan view. Note also the retractable twin-wheel tail bumper, which was later deleted. The inscriptions read "Movable outer wings," "Tail surfaces," "Tail bumper," "Weapons bay doors," "Engine nacelles," "The wing pivot box is non-detachable (manufacturing break)," "Main gear," and "Nose gear strut."

Front and rear views of a Tu-160 from a high perspective. The bulges above the wing roots just inboard of the engine nacelles are fairings accommodating the main gear bogies' outer rows of wheels. Note the open spoiler section in the lower photo.

Above: The nose of a Tu-160 with the IFR probe deployed.

Front views of a Tu-160M (below) and a Tu-160 *sans suffixe* (bottom), showing the glazing shape and the many air data probes and pitch vanes (with ground covers in the former case).

the flight deck section to quasi-elliptical amidships to circular at the rear; the flattened centre fuselage underside contributes a measure of lift.

The fuselage is built in six sections. The *No.1 forward fuselage section* (Section F-1, frames 1N-7N) is the unpressurised ogival nosecone whose upper half is a riveted metal structure incorporating avionics bays with detachable lateral maintenance access panels secured by screws and a recess for a retractable IFR probe between them. The lower half and front end of the nosecone is a detachable dielectric radome made of glassfibre/Textolite composite enclosing the radar antenna.

The *No.2 forward fuselage section* (Section F-2, frames 1-25) assembled from upper, lower and lateral panels comprises the flight deck and the nosewheel well. The pressurised flight deck accommodates the captain (on the left) and co-pilot at the front with the WSO (on the left) and navigator sitting behind them; all crew members face forward. A crew rest area with a collapsible bunk is provided, as are a galley with electric food heaters and a lavatory. The flight deck is accessed via a pressure door in the nosewheel well roof by means of a telescopic boarding ladder which is part of the ground support equipment. The flight deck windscreen consists of a trapezoidal optically-flat centre panel made of triplex glass and two curved side quadrants made of birdproof Plexiglas. The flight deck roof features four jettisonable escape hatches over the crew seats to enable ejection in an emergency; they can be removed on the ground, allowing the seats to be removed for maintenance. The forward pair of hatches incorporates four small side windows for the pilots (the diamond-shaped forward ones are aft-sliding direct vision windows) and two eyebrow windows; a pair of rectangular side window is provided below the navigator's and WSO's hatches, which feature faired periscopic rear-view mirrors.

Further avionics bays are located in the pressurised area at the rear of Section F-2. An angular ventral fairing with a rectangular window for the optoelectronic sight is located in line with the pilots' seats; on the Tu-160M the window is blanked off.

Section F-3 consists of two halves attached to the sides of Section F-2 at the rear. These are the front ends of the wing leading-edge root extensions which house the pressurisation/air conditioning system bays.

The *No.1 centre fuselage section* (Section F-4, frames 25-49) is manufactured integrally with the fixed wing root sections; it is a riveted structure with transverse girder beams, longitudinal and diagonal webs, and chemically milled skins with integral stringers. The LERXes incorporate integral fuel tanks, while the fuselage proper accommodates the full-length forward weapons bay. The latter is 11.28 m (37 ft $0\tfrac{3}{32}$ in) long, 1.92 m (6 ft $3\tfrac{19}{32}$ in) wide and 2.0 m (6 ft $6\tfrac{47}{64}$ in) deep, with a volume of 43 m^3 (1,518.53 cu ft), and is closed by hydraulically actuated two-section clamshell doors whose rear sections are shorter than the front ones; the hydraulic actuation rams are located on the side walls between frames 39-40. The side walls feature 13 pairs of fittings for bomb cassettes; additionally, the walls and roof carry back-up mechanical control runs, wiring bundles, hydraulic system, fuel system and weapons control system components. Immediately behind the weapons bay is the wing centre section carry-through structure (pivot box, frames 49-54) forming the bay's rear wall (see Wings section).

Right: The port wing at 20° minimum sweep with the flaps up, showing the flaperon (typically drooped when the aircraft is parked), the fixed trailing-edge portion outboard of its (with static discharge wicks) and the twin navigation lights (in the wingtip fairing and in the LERX).

Below right: A similar view of the starboard wing.

Bottom and bottom right: The inboard sections of the double-slotted flaps, showing the fixed slot and the hinged triangular portions at the root which fold upwards as the wings move aft to form the wing fences.

The *No.2 centre fuselage section* (Section F-5, frames 49-71) incorporates the front half of the rear weapons bay (frames 54-71), which is dimensionally identical to the front one. This bay is flanked by the mainwheel wells (frames 54-65), avionics bays and the APU bay on the port side; the upper fuselage skin is bulged along the outer sides of the mainwheel wells to accommodate the outer rows of wheels. Section F-5 also carries the engine nacelles (see Powerplant).

The *rear fuselage* (Section F-6) incorporates the rear half of the rear weapons bay, three integral fuel tanks (with lateral conduits for the fuel lines from these tanks to the engines) and equipment bays. It also carries the fixed lower section of the vertical tail. The rearmost portion houses the brake parachute bay with ventral clamshell doors (frames 98-100) and the defensive avionics suite.

Wings: Cantilever low-wing monoplane with variable-geometry wings having three settings – 20° for take-off and landing, 35° for subsonic cruise flight and 65° for supersonic cruise. Wing aspect ratio at these settings is 6.78, 5.64 and 2.85 respectively. For structural integrity reasons the speed limit for wing transition from 20° to 35° or vice versa is 600 km/h (372 mph) IAS or Mach 0.6; the speed limit for wing transition from 35° to 65° or vice versa is 700 km/h (435 mph) IAS or Mach 0.83.

The *centre section* is integral with the fuselage; it is 12.4 m (40 ft 8$^{3}/_{16}$ in) wide and has a curved leading edge with a maximum sweep of 60°. Its key subassembly is the carry-through structure, or wing pivot box, conveying the loads from the wings to the fuselage – a large hollow welded titanium structure 14.8 m (48 ft 6$^{43}/_{64}$ in)

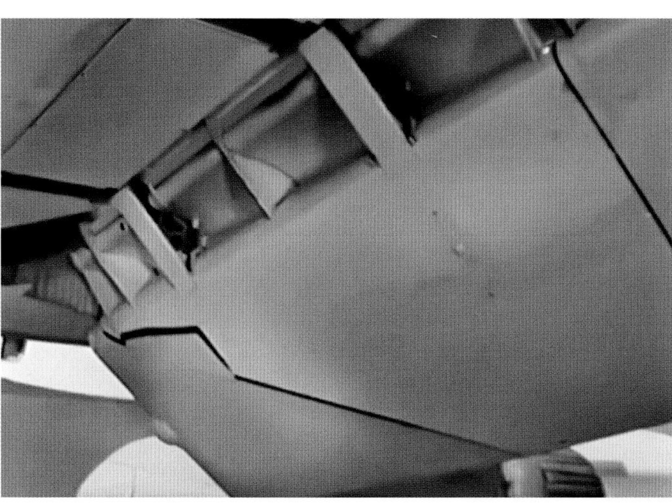

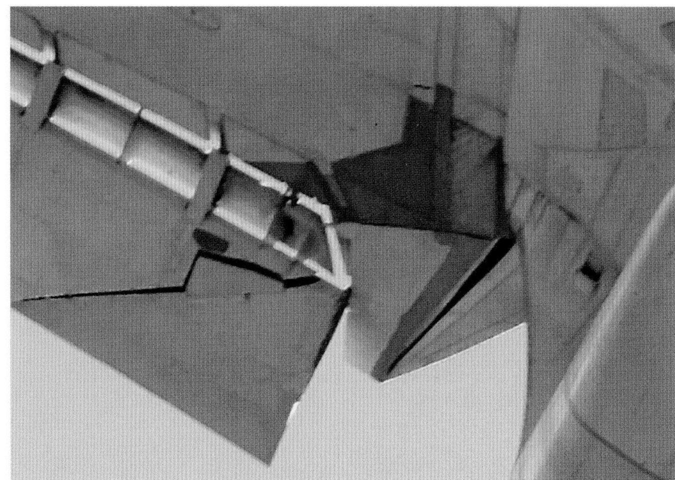

Top left, above left and left: This sequence starting with the wings at 35° intermediate setting and ending with the wings at 65° maximum sweep shows how the two-segment wing fences fold upwards into a vertical position as the wings move aft. A small gap remains between the fence and the engine nacelle.

Top: A gap is formed between the inboard end of the retracted flap and the fuselage at minimum sweep, allowing a glimpse of the fence actuation hydraulic ram.

Centre: Part of the outer wings' lower skin close to the pivots is protected by wear-resistant steel plates which are left unpainted.

Above: The starboard wing fence in fully erected position.

Opposite:
Top right, above right and right: The deployed port leading-edge slat.

Far right, top and centre: The four-section spoilers.

Far right: The port flaperon in fully drooped position.

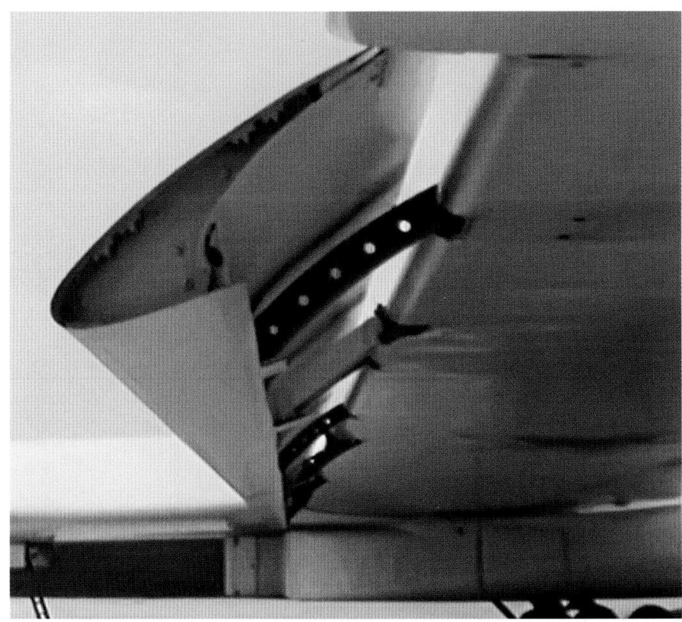

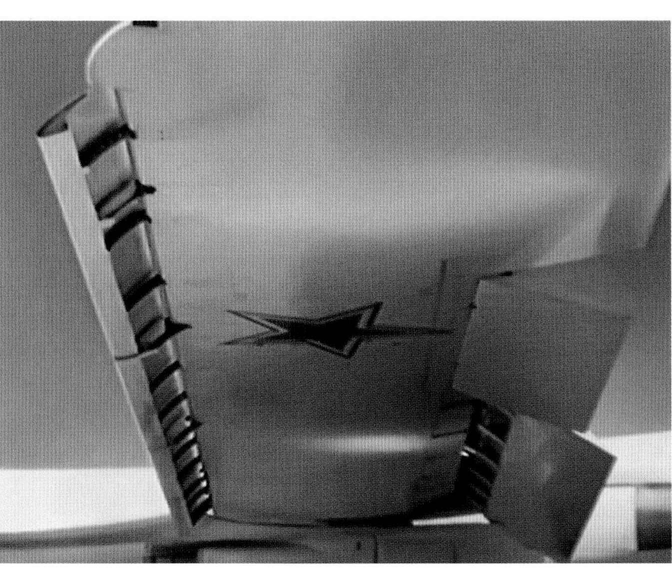

НИКОЛАЙ
КУЗНЕЦОВ

long, 2.15 m (7 ft $0^{41}/_{64}$ in) wide and 1.715 m (5 ft $7^{33}/_{64}$ in) high, with the pivots at the ends. The pivots, which are included in the length stated above, are one-piece forged and machined titanium parts whose halves are attached to the pivot box and to the outer wing torsion boxes by shear bolts. With the wings at minimum sweep,

Top left: The tail unit seen head on with the controls almost neutral.

Above left and left: The upper fin section at the limits of its travel. Note the buried light in the lower section's leading edge to show the tanker's refuelling systems operator that contact has been made.

Top: Here, all tail surfaces are at maximum deflection.

Above: The slightly deflected stabilators.

Opposite page: The tail unit of Tu-160 "19 Red"/RF-94113.

the pivots are at 25% of the wing span. The pivot box has solid internal webs made of aluminium alloy sheet and attachment fittings joining it to the fuselage structure; it also functions as an integral fuel tank.

The trapezoidal *outer wings* are five-spar structures made of aluminium and titanium alloys, with spars assembled from machined parts, only six ribs each and seven chemically milled skin panels 20 m (65 ft 7 13/32 in) long – three upper panels and four lower panels. The outer wings are attached to the wing pivot box via pivot bearings; each outer wing section is 21.275 m (69 ft 9 39/64 in) long, including the pivot. Wing sweep is changed by means of hydromechanical actuators with screw jacks attached to the front spar of the outer wing torsion boxes.

The wing torsion boxes serve as integral fuel tanks. The lower skins feature 19 pairs of detachable elliptical panels on each side for maintenance access to the tanks.

To improve field performance and low-speed handling the outer wings are equipped with full-span four-section leading-edge slats and three-section double-slotted trailing-edge flaps occupying approximately two-thirds of the span, with flaperons further outboard. The latter terminate well inboard of the wingtips (the outermost trailing-edge portions are fixed and carry six static discharge wicks each). The wings are also equipped with three-section spoilers/lift dumpers ahead of the flaps. The wing leading-edge and trailing-edge sections house control runs, control surface actuators, flap and slat drive shafts and electric cables.

Above left: This shot emphasises the narrow track of the main gear units, showing the complex hinges and actuation rams/drag struts.

Left: A slightly different version with additional hydraulic rams assisting contraction.

Below left: The mainwheels have built-in brake cooling fans.

Below and opposite: The nose gear unit has a mudguard and twin steering rams/dampers.

The LE slat deflection angle is 20° and maximum flap deflection for landing is 25°; the flaps feature movable curtains closing the gap between the rear spar and the foremost flap segment when the flaps are deployed. The flaperons have a travel limit of ±20° for roll control (acting as ailerons) and droop 30° concurrently with flap extension. The high-lift devices can only be deployed with the wings at 20° sweep. As wing sweep increases past 20° the innermost portions of the outer wing trailing edges, together with the triangular root portions of the inboard flap sections, fold upwards to form boundary layer fences outboard of the engine nacelles at maximum sweep.

Tail unit: Cantilever cruciform swept tail surfaces with the horizontal tail located at one-third of the vertical tail's height. The *vertical tail* consists of a fin built in two sections. The lower section (up to rib 3) is fixed, being manufactured integrally with the rear fuselage and extending forward into a large root fillet which curves sharply upward at the rear. The fillet's detachable leading-edge portion overlapping the joint of sections F-5/F-6 incorporates two large detachable dielectric panels, and the trailing edge of the lower fin section carries ESM antennas. The cropped-delta upper fin section is all-movable, serving for directional control, with a travel limit of ±20°; it accounts for just over 46% of the overall area. Leading-edge sweep 79° on the fin fillet and 47° on the upper section, aspect ratio 1.15. There is a large detachable bullet fairing extending beyond the trailing edge at the fin/stabiliser junction, enclosing the upper fin actuators and bellcranks. Five static discharge wicks are located on the trailing edge at the top.

The *horizontal tail* comprises all-movable stabilisers (stabilators) of trapezoidal planform rigidly connected by a centre section member into a single unit; it is attached to fuselage frame 98 via lugs and axles. Structural strength problems encountered soon after service entry necessitated a reduction of the horizontal tail span from 17.6 to 13.26 m (from 57 ft $8\frac{29}{32}$ in to 43 ft 6 in), the horizontal tail area being reduced from 60 to 55.6 m^2 (from 645.83 to 597.85 sq ft). Leading-edge sweep 44°, aspect ratio in modified form 3.16. The stabilator travel limits are 20° up/10° down. Each stabilator carries three static discharge wicks.

Landing gear: Hydraulically-retractable tricycle type; the design makes large-scale use of titanium. The steerable nose unit retracts aft and has an aft-mounted breaker strut; it is fitted with twin 1,080 x 400 mm (42.5 x 15.7 in) non-braking wheels. The nose gear strut has a twin-chamber oleo-pneumatic shock absorber and an aft-mounted torque link. The nosewheels are equipped with a mud/snow/slush guard consisting of left and right halves mounted directly on the nosewheel axle to prevent foreign object damage to the engines. The nose unit is equipped with an electrohydraulic steering actuator/shimmy damper; steering on the ground is by means of the rudder pedals.

The semi-levered suspension main units retract aft into the centre fuselage; they feature three-chamber oleo-pneumatic shock absorbers and forward-mounted torque links to which the telescopic retraction struts are attached. The main units are 3.5 m (11 ft $5\frac{51}{64}$ in) tall and have articulated six-wheel bogies 4.1 m (13 ft $5\frac{13}{32}$ in) long with three tandem pairs of 1,260 x 425 mm (49.6 x 16.7 in) wheels equipped with multi-disc hydraulic brakes; the wheels have built-in brake cooling fans. During retraction the bogies rotate 180° aft to lie inverted in the wheel wells. Additionally, the main gear struts feature double transverse hinges which allow them to shorten during retraction, reducing the landing gear track by 1.2 m (3 ft $11\frac{15}{64}$ in) at the same time. Soon after service entry the design of the main gear units was simplified to improve reliability, eliminating superfluous linkages.

The Kuznetsov NK-32 afterburning turbofan.

Landing gear transition is possible at up to 450 km/h (279 mph) IAS. Maximum flight speed with the gear down is 500 km/h (310 mph) IAS or Mach 0.5.

The nosewheel well is closed by a single pair of clamshell doors; each mainwheel well is closed by two large clamshell doors and a narrow door segment attached to the retraction strut. All doors remain open when the gear is down.

Three cruciform brake parachutes with an area of 35 m² (376.34 sq ft) each are housed in a container in the rear fuselage; they serve to shorten the landing run or decelerate the aircraft in the event of an aborted take-off. The brake parachutes are deployed electropneumatically and extracted by two 1-m² (10.75-sq ft) drogue parachutes; the parachutes can be deployed and released at the end of the landing run by either pilot.

Powerplant: Four Kuznetsov (SNTK Trood) NK-32 afterburning turbofans rated at 14,000 kgp (30,860 lbst) dry for cruise flight and 25,000 kgp (55,115 lbst) reheat for take-off. The NK-32 is a three-spool turbofan with a three-stage low-pressure (LP) compressor, a five-stage intermediate-pressure (IP) compressor, a seven-stage high-pressure (HP) compressor, a multi-burner annular combustion chamber, single-stage HP and IP turbines, a two-stage LP turbine, a core/bypass flow mixer, an afterburner and a convergent-divergent axisymmetrical nozzle with 18 petals.

The air intake assembly has a fixed spinner and 18 radial struts. The compressor blades have part-span snubbers and are made of titanium, steel and (in the HP cascade) nickel alloy. The HP compressor incorporates bleed valves supplying air for the de-icing system, pressurisation and air conditioning system and the like. Two of

Right: The V-shaped engine nacelle fronts. On most Tu-160s the insides of the air intakes are coated with a graphite-based RAM.

Below: The sharp intake lips require ground sheaths to prevent personnel injury.

Bottom: The rear ends of the nacelles have areas of unpainted titanium skin.

Below right: Here, only the engine nozzles appear to be fitted and the nacelles are empty.

Opposite page, below: The cowlings provide full access to the engines. Note the longitudinal firewall.

Left and below left: New Tu-160 air intake assemblies, showing the airflow control ramps and the auxiliary blow-in doors.

Centre left: The ventral air spill doors in fully open position.

Bottom left: This view shows the shape of the engine nacelles and the gap between the weapons bays where the wing pivot box is.

the combustion chamber's flame tubes feature igniters. The HP turbine has monocrystalline blades; the IP and LP turbines have blades manufactured using the directional crystallisation technology.

A ventral accessory gearbox is mounted near the front end of the engine casing; it features an integral constant-speed drive (CSD) for the AC and DC generators and hydraulic pump. The NK-32 has a self-contained lubrication system using IP-50 grade engine oil, a full authority digital engine control system (FADEC), with a conventional hydromechanical control system as a back-up, and built-in test equipment monitoring powerplant operation. The engine is started by an air turbine starter (ATS), using compressed air supplied by the APU or a ground source.

Bypass ratio 1.36, overall engine pressure ratio 28.2, turbine temperature 1,630° K (1,302°C/2,375°F). SFC 0.73-0.78 kg/kgp·hr (lb/lbst·hr) in subsonic cruise and 1.7-2.01 kg/kgp·hr in supersonic cruise. Length overall, including afterburner, 7.453 m (24 ft 5 $^{27}/_{64}$ in), inlet diameter 1.46 m (4 ft 9$^{31}/_{64}$ in), maximum diameter 1.7 m (5 ft 6$^{15}/_{16}$ in); dry weight 3,650 kg (8,050 lb).

The engines are housed in two paired nacelles 13.28 m (43 ft 6$^{53}/_{64}$ in) long adhering directly to the wing centre section underside; the nacelle cross-section changes from rectangular at the front to a figure-eight at the rear. Each engine is attached to the nacelle structure by struts via three mounting rings built into the engine casing. Each nacelle features a bifurcated supersonic intake (V-shaped in plan view) with a vertical splitter and multi-section vertical flow control ramps; the upper lip of the intake stands apart from the wing undersurface, acting as a fixed boundary layer splitter plate. The inlet duct cross-section changes gradually from rectangular at the intakes to circular at the compressor faces. The forward section of each inlet duct incorporates six spring-loaded auxiliary blow-in doors located on the outer and inner faces of the nacelle to supply additional air at high rpm, as well as five excess air spill doors on the underside. The air intake/inlet duct sections are attached to the fuselage/inner wing structure at frames 46, 54 and 56-58. The insides of the inlet ducts are coated with a graphite-based radar-absorbing material to reduce the aircraft's RCS in the forward hemisphere.

The throttles are positioned both on the captain's cockpit console and on the centre control pedestal. Thus they can be operated by either pilot.

An SKBM (Aerosila) TA-12 auxiliary power unit supplies compressed air for engine starting and air conditioning on the ground, as well as ground/emergency AC/DC power for systems and equipment. It is a single-spool gas turbine engine having a four-stage axial compressor with a diagonal-flow first stage, an annular reverse-flow combustion chamber and a three-stage axial turbine, driving a GS-12TO DC starter-generator and a GT40PCh8B AC generator via a forward-mounted gearbox.

Power 500 ehp, turbine temperature 550°C, mass flow 1.6 kg/sec (3.53 lb/sec; also stated in some sources as the bleed air supply rate!), maximum bleed air pressure 4.9 kg/cm^2 (70 psi), fuel burn 250-260 kg/hr (551-573 lb/hr). Length overall 1.588 m (5 ft $2\frac{33}{64}$ in), width 0.682 m (2 ft $2\frac{55}{64}$ in), height 0.721 m (2 ft $4\frac{25}{64}$ in), equipped weight 334 kg (736 lb). The TA-12 can be started at altitudes up to 4,500 m (14,760 ft) and run at altitudes up to 7,000 m (22,965 ft) and ambient temperatures of –60°/+60°C (–76°/+140°F); spool-up time 45 seconds, maximum continuous operating time 24 hours. The APU is housed in an unpressurised bay on the port side of the centre fuselage, just inboard of the port engine nacelle; the air intake and exhaust are located dorsally and closed flush by doors when the APU is not running.

Control system: Quadruplex analogue FBW control system enabling manual and automatic control. Should all four FBW control channels fail, there is an emergency mechanical flight control system in the pitch and roll channels as a last resort. Directional control is by means of the all-movable upper fin section; pitch control is by means of the stabilators, while roll control is by means of the flaperons at low speed and by means of spoilers at high speed when the wings are at 20° sweep and the flaperons are drooped.

The aircraft has full dual controls; unlike most heavy bombers, it features fighter-type control sticks instead of the usual control columns. All control surfaces are powered by irreversible hydraulic actuators; an artificial-feel mechanism is provided. The Tu-160 has an automatic angle of attack/G load limiter system preventing departure from controlled flight.

The control system includes various mechanical, hydromechanical, electromechanical, electrohydraulic, electric and electronic devices. It comprises the control surface actuators, the automatic flight control system (AFCS) – that is, autopilot and automatic approach/landing system – and the wing control system. The AFCS receives inputs from the sticks and rudder pedals, its own sensors and the sensors and computers of other systems. The wing control system optimises the wings' configuration to the respective flight modes. It comprises the high-lift device control system, the wing sweep control system and the boundary layer fence actuation system.

Fuel system: All fuel is carried in 13 integral tanks located in the wings and fuselage. The total fuel load is often quoted as 171,000 kg (376,980 lb); however, the maximum fuel load in operational conditions is 148,000 kg (326,280 lb).

The Nos. 1L/1R tanks located at the front of the wing LERXes (immediately aft of the equipment bays) are trim tanks holding 18,100 kg (39,900 lb) each; so are the Nos. 5 and 6 tanks in the rear fuselage (below the base of the fin), which hold 11,320 kg

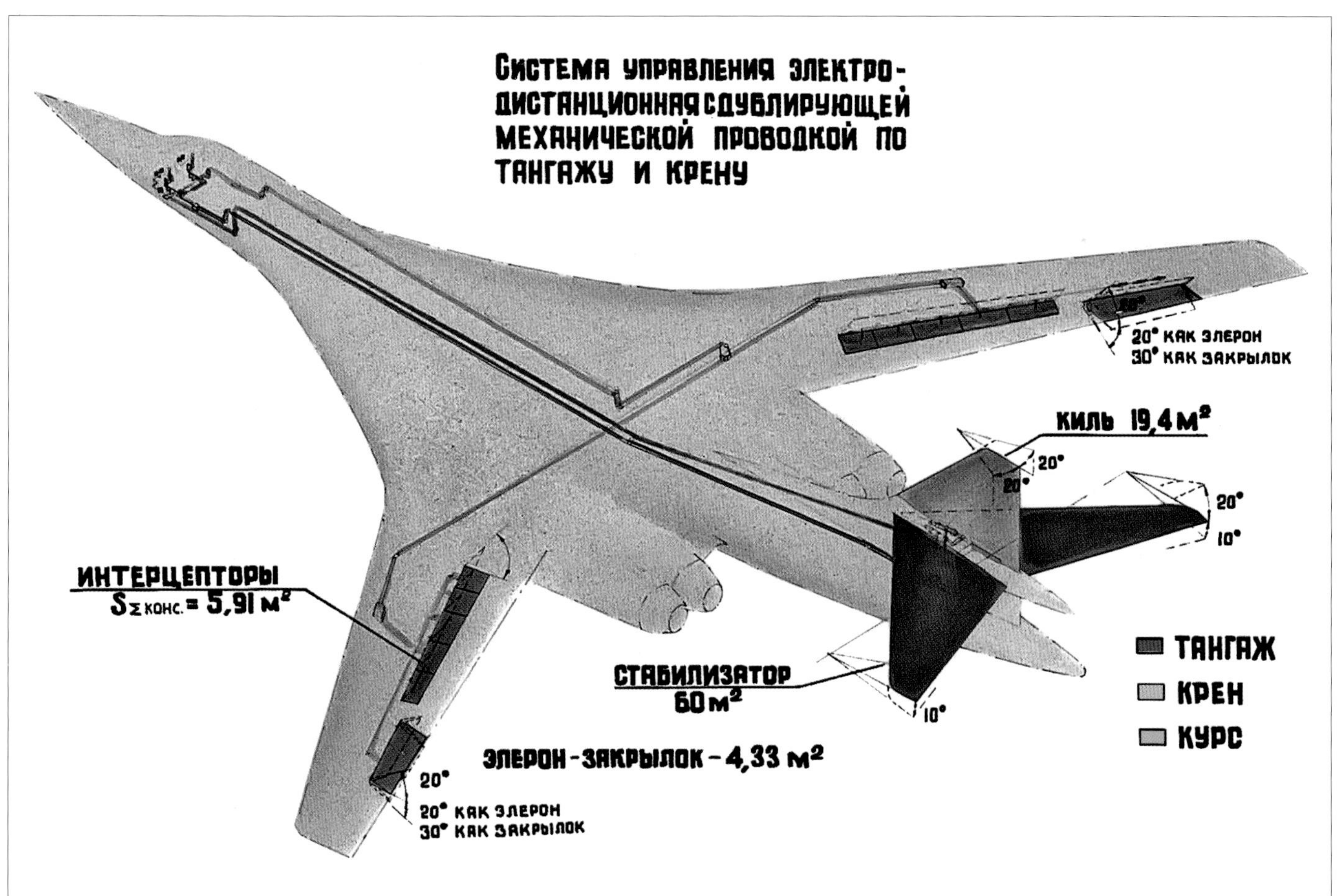

The layout of the Tu-160's FBW flight control system, with mechanical back-up in pitch and roll; the pitch, roll and yaw channels marked in red, grey and green respectively. The control surface travel limits and areas are shown.

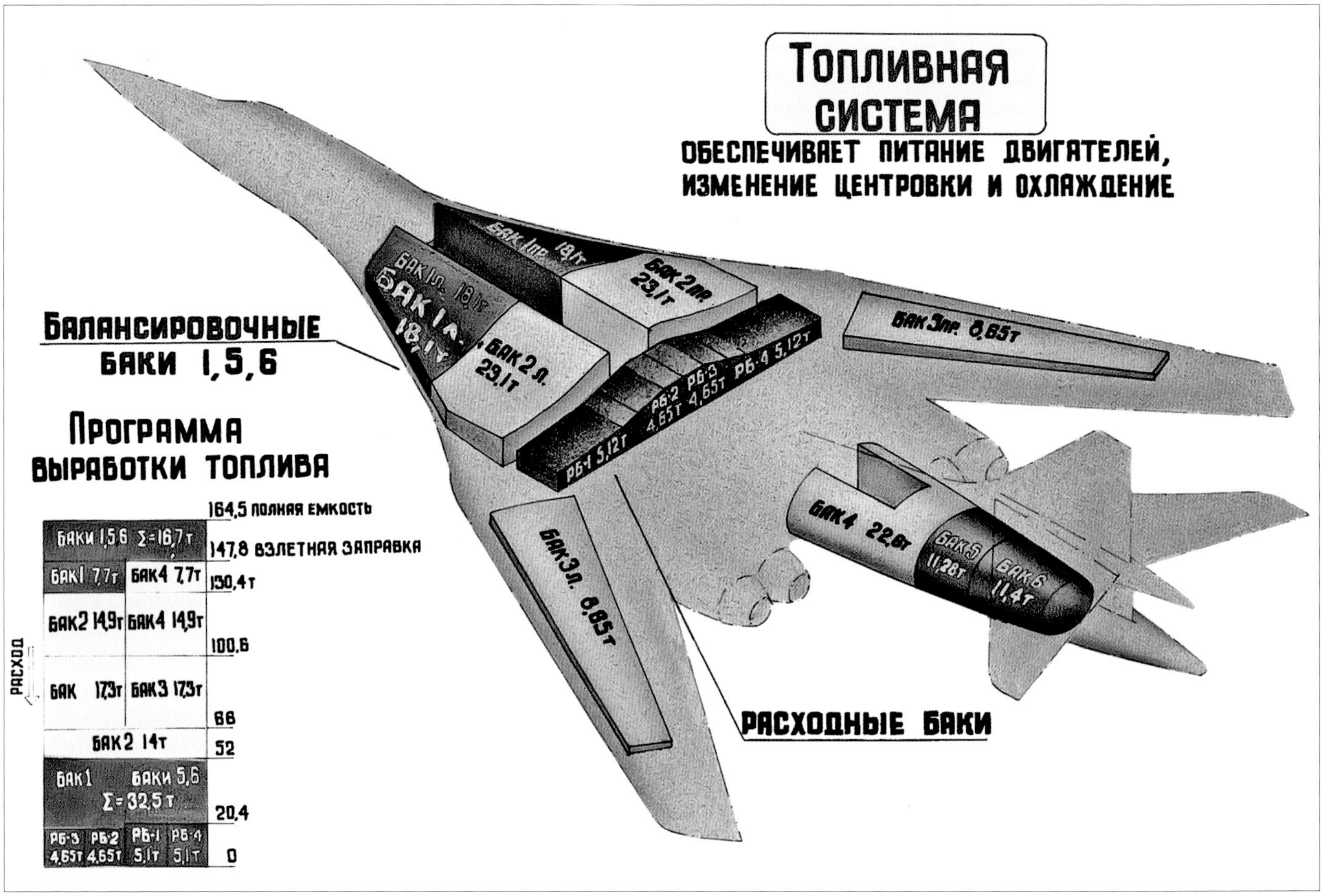

Above: The layout of the Tu-160's fuel system; the tanks shown in brown are the tim tanks (front and rear) and service tanks. The fuel loads in the individual tanks are shown. The diagram on the left shows the fuel usage sequence.

Below and below right: Close-up of the extended IFR probe with a GPT-2 connector. Note the clamshell doors at the front.

Opposite page: The second prototype and the first production Tu-160s had a thick, straight telescopic IFR probe. This was replaced by a thinner, curved non-telescopic version (bottom photo) on later production aircraft.

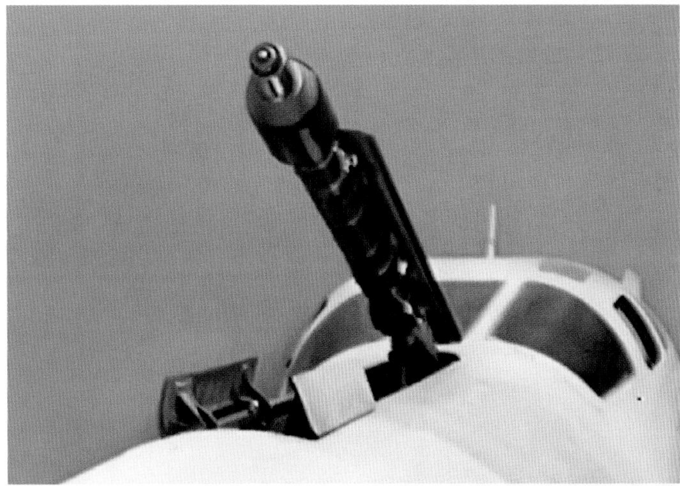

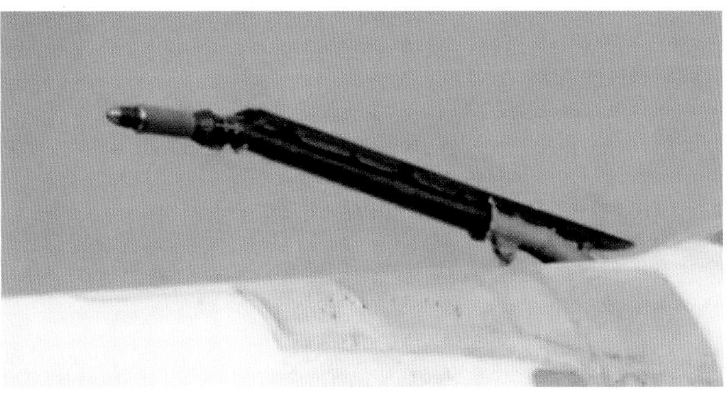

(24,960 lb) and 11,400 kg (25,130 lb) respectively. The main tanks are the Nos. 2L/2R tanks located further aft in the LERXes with a capacity of 23,100 kg (50,930 lb) each, the Nos. 3L/3R tanks in the outer wing torsion boxes holding 8,850 kg (19,510 lb) each and the No.4 tank (U-shaped in plan view) which is located around and aft of the rear weapons bay, holding 22,800 kg (50,270 lb). Finally, the wing pivot box houses four service tanks from which fuel is fed to the individual engines; the Nos. 1 and 4 service tanks hold 5,120 kg (11,290 lb) each while the Nos. 2 and 3 service tanks hold 4,650 kg (10,250 lb) each.

The fuel tanks are split into four groups, one for each engine, with a cross-feed system. Each group has a service tank to which the fuel is delivered by electric transfer pumps. Fuel is also transferred between the forward and aft trim tanks in flight to maintain CG position.

The Tu-160 has single-point pressure refuelling via a standard refuelling connector located under the port LERX. Fuel grades used are Russian T-1 or TS-1 kerosene and western equivalents (Jet A-1 and the like.)

A fully retractable in-flight refuelling probe with a GPT-2 connector (*golovka priyomnika topliva*) is installed ahead of the windshield, enabling the Tu-160 to receive fuel from IL-78/IL-78M *Midas-A/B* tankers. The recess for the IFR probe is closed by a long door attached to the probe itself and short clamshell doors at the front which open during extension/retraction. A fuel jettison system is provided to reduce the landing weight in the event of an emergency landing.

Hydraulics: Four separate hydraulic systems, each powered by a single engine-driven pump. The systems use 7-50S-3 grade hydraulic fluid; nominal pressure 280 kg/cm^2 (4,000 psi). Auxiliary turbo pumps are provided to supply hydraulic power on the ground or in an emergency (in the event of a quadruple engine failure).

The hydraulic systems power the control surface actuators, air intake ramps, high-lift devices, wing sweep change actuators, landing gear and the rotary launchers in the weapons bays. The systems and their units are remote-controlled ('power-by-wire').

Electrics: 208 V/400 Hz AC power supplied by four engine-driven alternators with integral CSDs and a 40-kVA GT40PCh8B generator (*ghene**rah**tor tryokh**fahz**nyy, postoy**an**noy chasto**ty*** – three-phase [AC] generator, stable frequency) driven by the APU. 27 V DC power supplied by four engine-driven brushless generators and a 12-kW GS-12TO starter-generator on the APU; backup DC power provided by batteries. The electric system includes power distribution panels and circuit breakers. A ground power receptacle is located under the starboard engine nacelle.

Exterior lighting equipment includes two pairs of port (red) and starboard (green) navigation lights under Plexiglas fairings in the wing centre section leading edge and at the wingtips and a white tail navigation light on top of the tailcone. Two retractable landing lights closed by clamshell doors are located just aft of the radome, augmented by two landing/taxi lights on the nose gear strut. Intermittently flashing white anti-collision strobe lights are located on top of the centre fuselage and under the starboard engine nacelle. A light buried in the lower fin portion leading edge

RF-94109
ОССИИ

informs the tanker's refuelling systems operator during IFR sessions that the Tu-160 has made contact with the drogue and fuel transfer is in progress. Strangely enough, however, the retractable FPSh-5 IFR probe illumination lights on the fuselage nose typical of other Soviet/Russian heavy aircraft with the probe-and-drogue IFR system are absent. Pilot lights on all three landing gear struts to show the ground personnel that the gear is down and locked during night approaches.

De-icing system: The engine inlet guide vanes are de-iced by engine bleed air. Electric de-icing on the engine air intake leading edges, windshield, pitot heads and static ports. There is a radioactive isotope icing sensor.

Air conditioning and pressurisation system: The ventilation-type flight deck and avionics bays are pressurised by engine bleed air to ensure comfortable working conditions for the crew and normal operating conditions for the avionics throughout the flight envelope. Pressurisation air is cooled by heat exchangers and filtered before being fed to the flight deck and avionics bays at reduced pressure.

Oxygen system and crew gear: All crew members are provided with oxygen masks, standard PPK G-suits (*protivoperegroozochnyy kostyum*) and ZSh-7B protective helmets (*zashchitnyy shlem*) with tinted visors. For extreme high-altitude missions the crew wears *Baklan* (Cormorant) pressure suits featuring full-face pressure helmets similar to those worn by astronauts.

Fire suppression system: A centralised fire suppression system with flame sensors is provided for extinguishing fires in the engine nacelles and the APU bay. Hand-held fire extinguishers are provided in the flight deck.

Avionics and equipment: The Tu-160 is equipped with state-of-the-art flight and mission avionics, including a specially-developed weapons control system. The avionics enable automatic flight along a predesignated route and accurate delivery of all weapons the aircraft is compatible with, day and night, in any weather. The avionics suite features more than 100 digital computers.

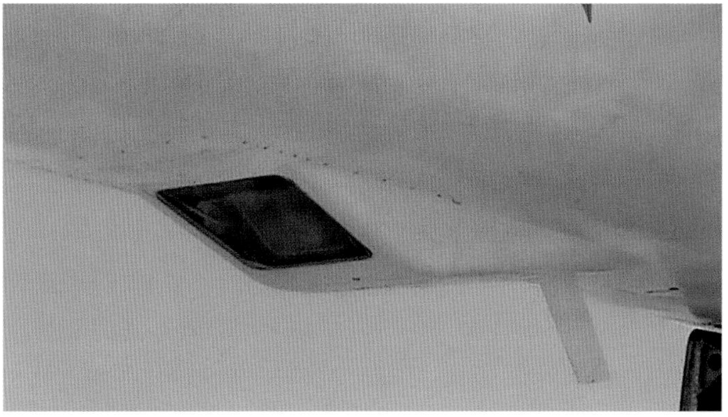

a) navigation and piloting equipment: Duplex K-042K astro-inertial navigation system and satellite navigation equipment.

The flight instrumentation consists largely of electromechanical instruments. The equipment on the pilots' instrument panels includes PKP-72-4 attitude director indicators (*pilotazhno-komahndnyy pribor* – ADI), PNP-72-3M horizontal situation indicators (*plahnovyy navigatsionnyy pribor* – HSI), the AGR-74-10S back-up artificial horizon (*aviagorizont rezervnyy*; captain's side only), KUS-3 or KUS-2500-2 airspeed indicators (*kombineerovannyy ookazahtel' skorosti* – combined ASI), ISP-1 speed parameter indicators (*indikahtor skorosnykh parahmetrov*), DA-200P combined vertical speed indicators/turn and bank indicators, IVP-1 vertical speed parameter indicators (*indikahtor vertikahl'nykh parahmetrov*), the VM-15MPB barometric altimeter (*vysotomer*; captain's side only), A-034-4 and UV-2Ts-1B or UVO-M1 radio altimeter displays (*ookazahtel' vysoty* – altitude indicator), the RMI-2B radio magnetic indicator showing the direction to VOR beacons during instrument landing approach (captain's side only), the IP-51 position indicator (*indikahtor polozheniya*; captain's side only), the NE-4B-4G RHAWS indicator with LEDs showing the direction of the threat (captain's side only) and master warning panels composed of TSK-2-1 red warning lights (*tablo svetosignahl'noye s kontrolem* – signal light with serviceability check function) and TSK-2-2 yellow caution lights. Pitot heads, static ports and pitch/yaw transducer vanes for the air data system are located on the forward fuselage.

b) communications equipment: Multi-channel digital communications suite, including an intercom for crew communication.

Top left: The modules of the Tu-160's communications suite.

Far left row: The tailcone carries the sensor of the Ogonyok missile warning system, with the tail navigation light above it and the rear IFF blade aerial further forward.

Above left: The rear fuselage underside features 24 APP-50 three-round flare dispensers. Note also the brake parachute bay doors.

Left: The ECM/ESM fairings on the fin trailing edge and at the tip of the fin/tailplane fairing.

Above right: The faired window of the OPB-15T optoelectronic sight.

Right: The "unblack unbox" – the MSRP-A-01 flight data recorder opened to show the tape reel and recording head.

Above: The flight deck of a fairly late production Tu-160. The red handles on the roof are for escape hatch jettisoning.

Below: The two banks of throttles are visible here. The faded pink handles on the centre pedestal are for emergency wheel braking.

Above: The flight deck of an older Tu-160 ("26 Red," f/n 4-02) now on display in the Ukrainian Air Force Museum in Poltava.

Below: The flight deck in power-on condition. The red figures on the display in the upper centre portion show engine parameters.

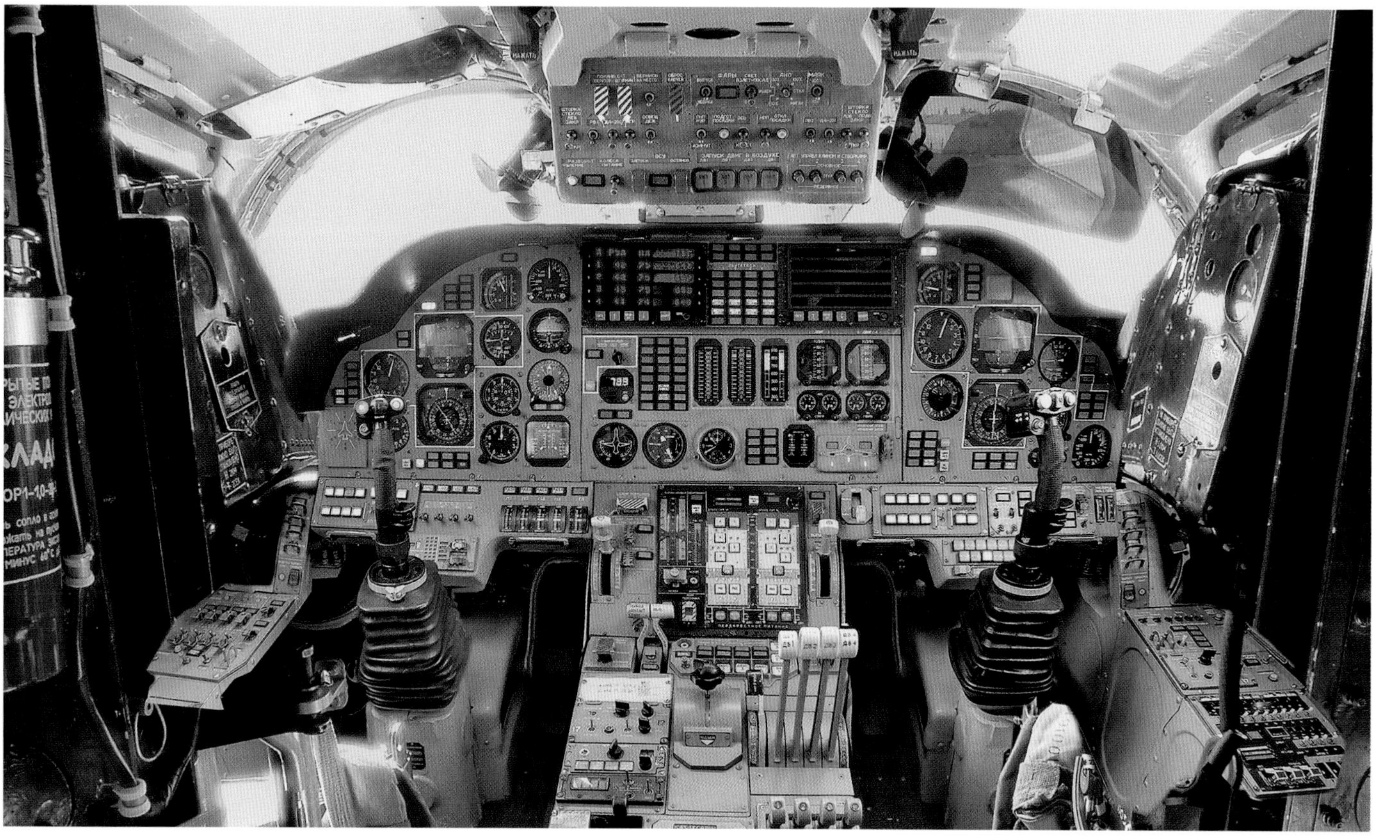

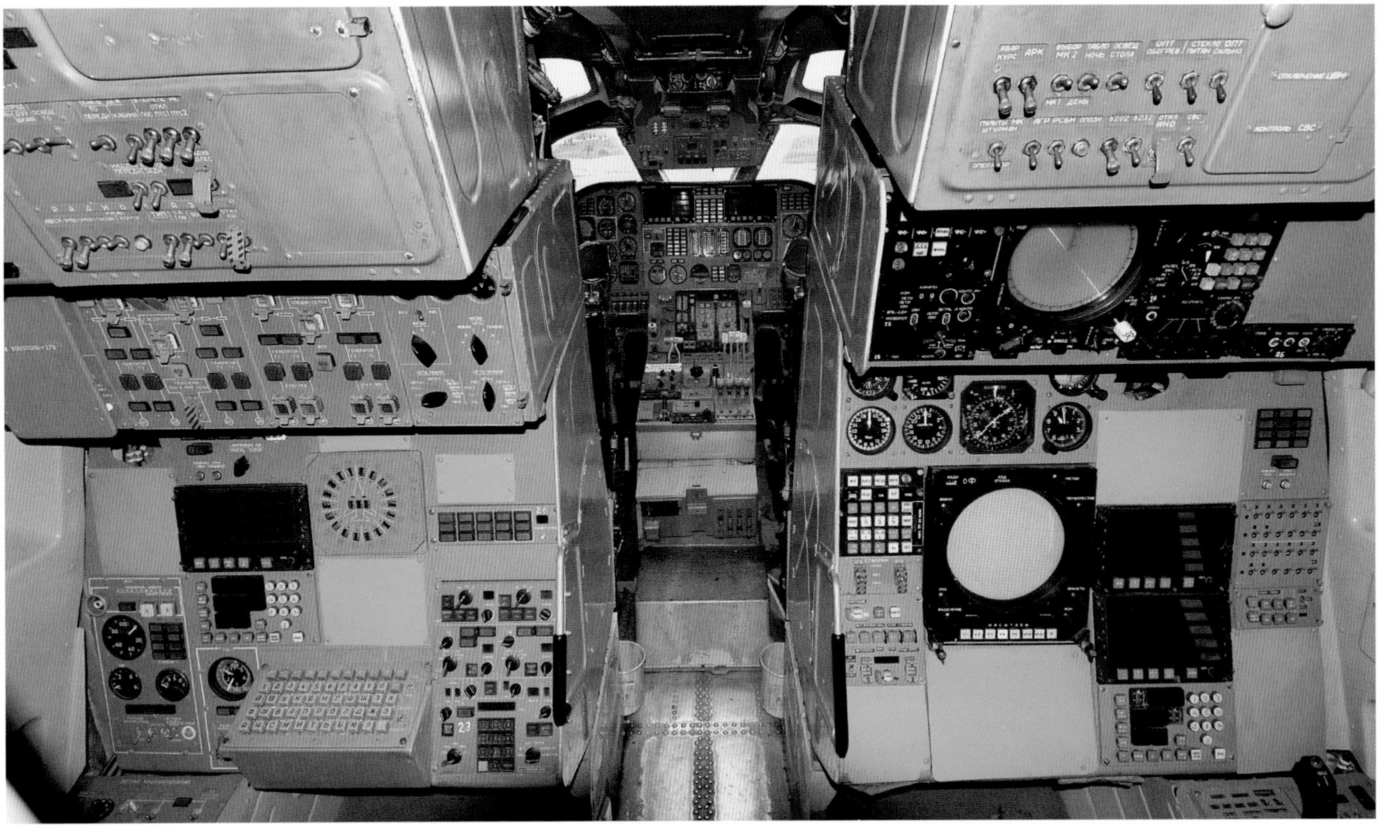

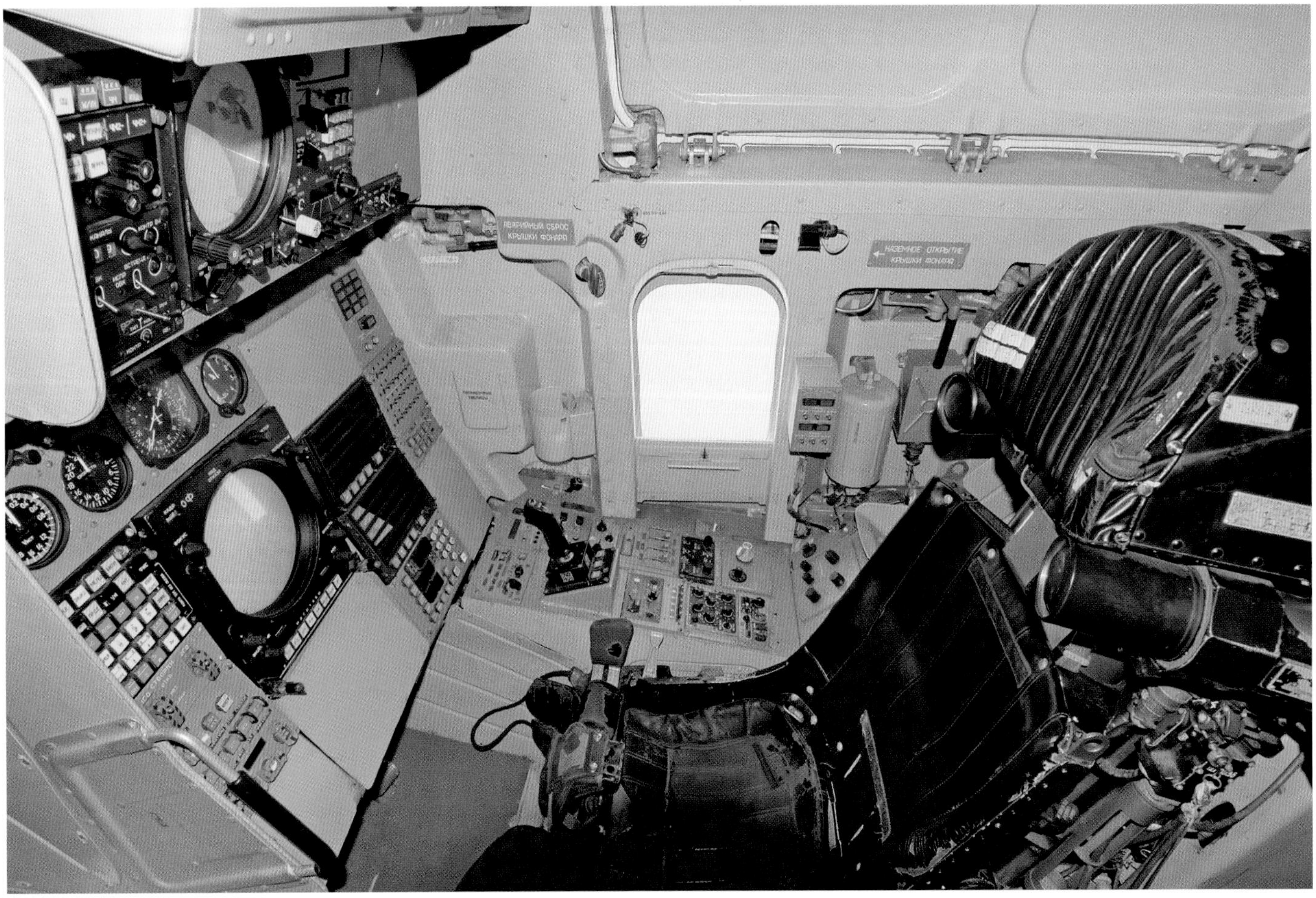

Left: The rear crew workstations of Tu-160 "26 Red" (f/n 4-02), with a narrow aisle in between. The instrumentation appears sparse because part of the equipment is missing on the preserved aircraft, being replaced by blanks whose colour differs from that of the instrument panels.

Below left: The navigator's workstation of '26 Red' with two radarscopes.

Right: The WSO's workstation of Tu-160 "26 Red."

Below: Here, for comparison, is the navigator's workstation of an operational Russian Air Force Tu-160, with all displays and control panels where they should be.

Below right: The WSO's workstation of the same aircraft.

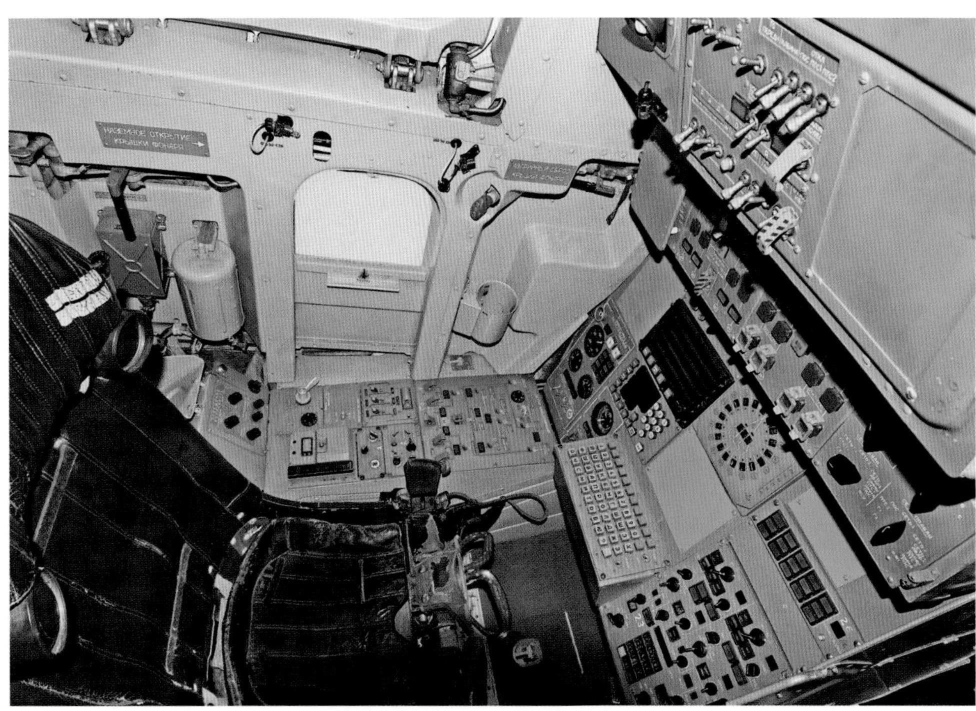

AShS-UD swept blade aerials (*an**ten**na shtyre**va**ya strelo**vid**naya*) for the communications and command radios are located above and below the flight deck. Further radio antennas closed by flush covers are built into the nosewheel well doors. An RI-65 audio warning system (*reche**voy** infor**mah**tor* – voice annunciator) is provided to alert the crew of critical failures or dangerous flight modes.

c) targeting equipment: Obzor-K navigation/attack suite with a Poisk multi-function radar in the nose radome for target illumination and ground mapping; it is capable of detecting ground and sea targets (surface ships) at long range. The radarscope is at the navigator's workstation. OPB-15T electro-optical bomb sight installed in a teardrop fairing with an optically-flat window under the flight deck for bomb-aiming in daylight/low light level conditions; the OPB-15T is deleted on the Tu-160M and the window blanked off. SURO-70 and Sproot-SM systems for preparing/downloading target data to the cruise missiles and controlling the missile launch.

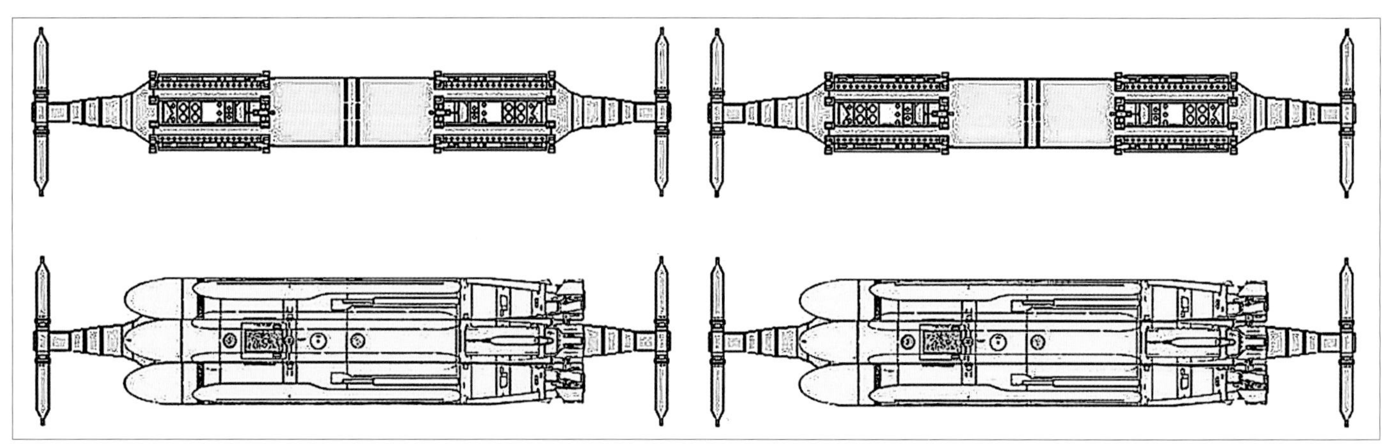

Opposite page, above: The front weapons bay with its MKU-6-5U rotary launcher, looking forward (far left) and aft (left). Note the extra actuators on the side walls at the front of the doors' rear segments.

Below left: The MKU-6-5U rotary launchers in empty condition and fully loaded with Kh-55SM missiles.

Above: The rear weapons bay, looking forward, with a single Kh-55SM on the rotary launcher.

Above right: The rear weapons bay, looking aft. Again, the extra actuators of the doors' rear segments are visible.

Right: An inert Kh-55SM marked ***oocheb**noye* [*iz**deli**ye*] (training article) on its ground handling dolly.

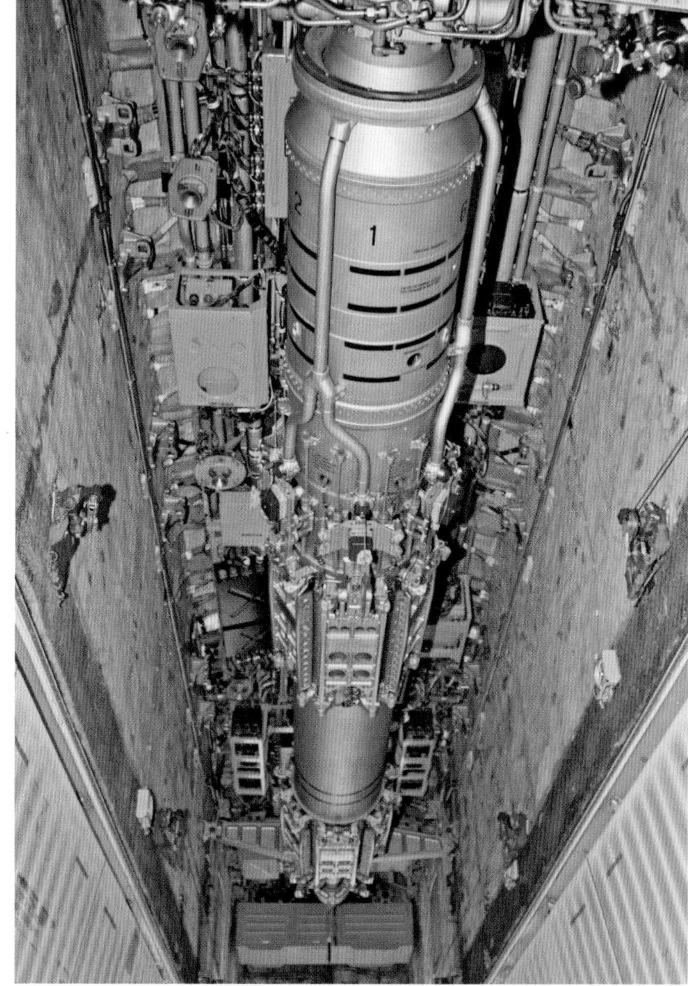
2
1

Opposite page, top row: The front weapons bay, looking forward (left) and aft (right); the MKU-6-5U rotary launcher is removed but the mounting beams are in place.

Bottom row: The rear weapons bay, looking forward (left) and aft (right); note the station numbers on the rotary launcher.

Top left and above left: A Kh-55 missile is loaded into the bay, using special fixtures and electric hoists.

Right, top and above: More Kh-55s on the rotary launcher.

d) identification friend-or-foe (IFF) system: SRO-1P ***Parol'*** (Password, a.k.a. *izdeliye* 62-01) IFF transponder (*samo**lyot**nyy **rah**diolokatsi**on**nyy ot**vet**chik* – aircraft-mounted radar responder). The triangular IFF blade aerials are located under the nose (aft of the radome) and on top of the tailcone.

e) ECM/ESM equipment: The Baikal ESM suite includes a radar homing and warning system (RHAWS) with aerials on the forward/aft fuselage sides and wingtips to give 360° coverage. Avtomat-F active jammer in the rear fuselage equipment bay, with antennas enclosed by flush dielectric panels in the LERXes and small rounded fairings on the lower fin section trailing edge. IRCM equipment consists of an Ogonyok missile warning system with a sensor at the tip of the tailcone to cover the rear hemisphere and 24 three-round APP-50 chaff/flare dispensers (*avto**maht*** [*posta**nov**ki*] *pas**siv**nykh po**mekh*** – automatic passive ECM/IRCM device; a.k.a. L-029) built into the rear fuselage underside to fire 50-mm (1.96-in) PPI-50 magnesium flares (*peeropa**tron** infra**kras**nyy* – infrared flare) or chaff bundles as a protection against air-to-air and surface-to-air missiles.

f) data recording equipment: MSRP-A-01 flight data recorder (*mag**nit**nyy samo**pis**ets re**zhim**ov pol**yo**ta* – magnetic flight mode recorder) and MS-61 cockpit voice recorder (*magnito**fon** samo**ly-ot**nyy* – aircraft tape recorder) for mission analysis or accident investigation.

Armament: The Tu-160's maximum weapons load is 45,000 kg (99,210 lb), although some sources quote a figure of 40,000 kg (88,180 lb). All armament is carried internally in two weapons bays.

a) missile armament: The principal armament consists of air-to-surface missiles for delivering nuclear or conventional strikes against targets with known co-ordinates. The missiles are carried on two MKU-6-5U (*izdeliye* 9A829K2) rotary launchers whose front and rear ends are supported by transverse beams attached to the weapons bay walls. The launchers are operated by hydraulic motors and the pantographic ejector mechanisms are operated pneumatically.

The primary missile type – one of the two original compatible types – is the Raduga Kh-55 (*izdeliye* 120; AS-15A *Kent*) strategic air-launched cruise missile and its extended-range Kh-55SM

Left: A Kh-55 marked KTS-120 on the nose radome, apparently to denote a practice version.

Below left: A Kh-55SM long-range cruise missile diplayed alongside Tu-160 "01 Red" *Mikhail Gromov*.

Right, below and bottom: Kh-55SMs in pre-launch and flight configurations. The conformal tanks are specially shaped to clear the wings as the latter deploy.

Tu-160 specifications	
Length overall	54.095 m (177 ft 5 23/32 in)
Wing span:	
at 20° sweep	55.7 m (182 ft 8 29/32 in)*
at 35° sweep	50.7 m (166 ft 4 in)
at 65° sweep	35.6 m (116 ft 9 37/64 in)
Stabilator span	17.6 m (57 ft 8 29/32 in)/ 13.26 m (43 ft 6 in) [1]
Stabilator root chord	6.625 m (21 ft 8 53/64 in)
Height on ground	13.6 m (44 ft 7 7/16 in)*
Vertical tail height:	
overall	6.95 m (22 ft 9 5/8 in)
movable upper section	4.635 m (15 ft 2 31/64 in)
Upper fin section root chord	6.675 m (21 ft 10 51/64 in)
Landing gear track	5.5 m (18 ft 17/32 in)
Landing gear wheelbase	17.88 m (58 ft 4 25/32 in) [2]
Maximum rotation angle	12°30'
Wing area:	
total, maximum sweep	293.15 m^2 (3,152.15 sq ft)
total, minimum sweep	455.8 m^2 (4,906.19 sq ft)
movable outer wings	189.83 m^2 (2,041.18 sq ft)
Leading-edge slat area	22.16 m^2 (238.28 sq ft)
Flap area	39.6 m^2 (425.8 sq ft)
Flaperon area	9.0 m^2 (96.77 sq ft) [3]
Spoiler area	11.76 m^2 (126.45 sq ft) [3]
Vertical tail area:	
total	42.025 m^2 (451.88 sq ft)
movable upper section	19.398 m^2 (208.58 sq ft)
Stabilator area	60 m^2 (645.83 sq ft)/ 55.6 m^2 (597.85 sq ft) [1]
Dry weight	110,000 kg (242,510 lb)
Operating empty weight	117,000 kg (257,940 lb)
Maximum take-off weight	275,000 kg (606,260 lb)
Maximum landing weight:	
normal	140,000 kg (308,650 lb)
maximum	155,000 kg (341,710 lb) [4]
Maximum ordnance load	45,000 kg (99,210 lb)*
Maximum operational speed	2,000 km/h (1,240 mph) [5]
Landing speed at 140,000-150,000 kg (308,640-330,690 lb) LW	260-280 km/h (161-174 mph)
Maximum rate of climb, m/sec (ft/min)	60-70 (11,800-17,710)
Service ceiling	15,000 m (49,210 ft)
Maximum technical range on internal fuel	13,950 km (8,670 miles)
Effective range in subsonic (Mach 0.77) cruise on internal fuel, with 5% fuel reserves and six missiles launched in mid-mission	12,300 km (7,640 miles)
Range with maximum payload	10,500 km (6,520 miles)
Range at Mach 1.5	2,000 km (1,242 miles)
Combat radius with normal payload	6,000 km (3,730 miles)
Maximum endurance on internal fuel	15 hours
Take-off run:	
at 150,000-kg (330,690-lb) take-off weight	900 m (2,950 ft)
at 275,000-kg (606,260-lb) take-off weight	2,200 m (7,220 ft)
Landing run:	
at 140,000-kg (308,640-lb) landing weight	1,200 m (3,940 ft)
at 155,000-kg (341,710-lb) landing weight	1,600 m (5,250 ft)
G limit	+2.5 Gs

version (*izdeliye* 125; AS-15B *Kent*); 12 of these weapons can be carried with wings and tail surfaces folded and the engine stowed (six in each weapons bay). The Kh-55SM has a launch weight of 1,700 kg (3,750 lb) and a maximum range of 3,000 km (1,860 miles). Before launch a digital map of the route to the target is downloaded to the missile's computer by the SURO-70 MCS. Then the missile is ejected downward from the launcher; a second later the turbofan engine is deployed and started up, the tail surfaces and wings unfold (in that order), and the missile commences cruise flight.

The other missile type originally envisaged is the Raduga Kh-15S aeroballistic missile (*izdeliye* 115; AS-16 *Kickback*) designed for use against enemy air defence systems or surface ships. 24 of these short-range ASMs were to be carried (12 on each rotary launcher in two rows); in this case the Tu-160 was to operate in low-level mode. However, the Kh-15S is no longer used.

The upgraded Tu-160M will be armed with Raduga Kh-555 and Raduga Kh-101 (conventional) and Kh-102 (nuclear) long-range cruise missiles. These will be carried on revised MKU-6-5U rotary launchers designated *izdeliye* 9A829K3 to suit the missile's greater length.

b) bomb armament: From the outset the Tu-160 had provisions for carrying conventional or nuclear free-fall bombs, hence the OPB-15T precision electro-optical bomb sight and the provisions for installing bomb cassettes. Plans were in hand to adapt the aircraft for carrying "smart bombs," including KAB-1500 TV-guided or laser-guided bombs (*korrek**teer**uyemaya **a**via**bom**ba*).

c) defensive armament: The Tu-160 lacks defensive armament, relying on the ESM suite for self-protection.

Crew rescue system: The crew rescue system comprises four Zvezda K-36LM zero-zero ejection seats, the escape hatch jettison system and an ejection sequencing system making sure the seats will not collide during ejection. Each seat is provided with a built-in rescue parachute stowed in the headrest and an NAZ-7 survival kit (*nosimyy avareeynyy zapahs* – portable emergency supply) attached to the parachute harness. An LAS-5M inflatable rescue dinghy (***lod**ka avareeyno-spasahtel'naya*) is provided in case of ditching or an overwater ejection.

The crew members may eject individually, or any crew member may initiate ejection, punching everybody out if any of the crew are disabled.

Notes:

1. Pre-modification/post-modification
2. Measured at the middle of the main gear bogies
3. One Tupolev OKB drawing gives the flaperon area per wing as 4.33 m^2 (46.61 sq ft) and the spoiler area per wing as 5.91 m2 (63.61 sq ft), which adds up to 8.66 m^2 (93.22 sq ft) and 11.82 m^2 (127.23 sq ft) respectively
4. Also reported as 165,000 kg (363,760 lb)
5. The never-exceed speed attained in full afterburner at 13,000 m (42,650 ft) is 2,200 km/h (1,366 mph)

* Previously certain official documents gave different figures. Thus, the wing span at 20° sweep was stated as 57.7 m (189 ft 3 21/32 in), the height on ground as 13.0 m (42 ft 7 13/16 in) and the maximum ordnance load as 40,000 kg (88,180 lb)

Chapter 7

The Tu-160 in Service

As mentioned in Chapter 3, Merited Military Pilot Maj.-Gen. Lev V. Kozlov – the then Deputy Commander of the DA (Chief of Combat Training) – was the first service pilot to fly the Tu-160. (Merited Military Pilot is an official grade reflecting experience and expertise.) His next-in-command Lt.-Gen. Pyotr S. Deynekin – then CO of the Long-Range Aviation's 37th VA (*vozdooshnaya armiya* – air army, roughly equivalent to a numbered air force in USAF terms) – was just as quick to master the new type. Tu-160 project test pilot Boris I. Veremey recounted the story as follows:

"Lev Vasil'yevich Kozlov would come from the Long-Range Aviation headquarters in his car to pick me up and we would go to Zhukovskiy to perform a standard [familiarisation training] programme which included between seven and 14 flights. I was also the instructor pilot when Pyotr Stepanovich Deynekin took his training [on the Tu-160]. He made seven flights with high class, flying the aircraft smoothly and beautifully. Marshal [Aleksandr N.] Yefimov, the then Commander-in-Chief of the Air Force, had banned the Long-Range Aviation Commander from flying, citing safety concerns as the reason. Thus Deynekin had to make his flights clandestinely while the C-in-C was on vacation."

In 1987, the Tu-160 achieved initial operational capability (IOC) with the 184th *Poltavsko-Berlinskiy* Red Banner GvTBAP (*Gvardeyskiy tyazholyy bombardirovochnyy aviapolk* – Guards Heavy Bomber Regiment, roughly equivalent to a Bomb Squadron in USAF terms). It was based in the Ukrainian town of Priluki (Chernigov Region), which was in the Carpathian Military District (MD), but reported to the 201st TBAD (*tyazholaya bombardirovochnaya aviadiveeziya* – Heavy Bomber Division, ≈ Bomb Wing (Heavy)), which was headquartered at Engels-2 AB near the city of Engels (Saratov Region) on the Volga River in

Seen from an IL-78, Tu-160 '10 Red' *Nikolay Kuznetsov* escorted by two MiG-31 interceptors approaches Moscow en route to an air parade.

southern central Russia, in the Volga MD. The regiment had fought with distinction during the Great Patriotic War of 1941–45, thus earning the prestigious Guards status for gallantry above and beyond the call of duty. It was awarded the Order of the Red Banner of Combat (one of the highest military decorations in the Soviet Union) and earned the honorary titles for its part in the liberation of the Ukrainian city of Poltava and in taking Berlin.

After the war the 184th GvTBAP remained one of the Soviet Air Force's top-notch units. It had been the first to re-equip with the Tu-4 long-range bomber; later the regiment operated various versions of the Tu-16 medium bomber, and in 1984, it transitioned from the Tu-16A *Badger-A* nuclear-capable bomber and the Tu-16K-26 *Badger-G Mod*

Above left, left and below: Tu-160 "21 Red" is pushed back onto its parking spot on the flight line at Priluki AB by a BelAZ-7420 tug in 1987. The number of auxiliary blow-in doors increased from five to six on each side of each engine nacelle from Batch 3 onwards. Note the grid-type jet-blast deflector behind the aircraft.

Below right: Resplendent in its all-white finish, "21 Red" prepares to taxi at Priluki AB on a sunny day.

missile strike aircraft to the then-latest Tu-22M3, retaining a handful of Tu-16P *Badger-J* ECM aircraft. That said, it was no coincidence that the unit was chosen to introduce the *Blackjack* into service. The advent of the Tu-160 brought about a major reconstruction of Priluki airbase; among other things the runway was reinforced and extended to 3,000 m (9,840 ft).

Teething Troubles – and Full Capability

The aircrews and ground crews of the 184th GvTBAP had to master the Tu-160 while the state acceptance trials were still in progress. This was because the trials looked certain to be a protracted affair due to the large

Above right: An early-production Tu-160 in an earthen revetment at Priluki AB, which has both concrete and metal jet blast deflectors. A technician is using an adjustable stepladder to remove the ground covers from the air data system pitch vane and pitot heads. A shorter stepladder used for flight deck access via the nosewheel well is just visible.

Right: Tu-160s of the 184th GvTBAP in the dispersal area at Priluki AB; this one's engines are being worked on. The ZiL-131 6x6 army lorry with a K-131 van body under the port wing is probably a test equipment van, while the other one is a UPG-300 hydraulics test vehicle.

Above: "22 Red," another 184th GvTBAP Tu-160, with the landing gear in mid-retraction.
Below: "21 Red" shows some strange soot deposits on the underside of the wingtips as it makes a low pass with the wings at maximum sweep.

scope of work necessitating a large number of test flights. The decision to start Tu-160 operations (or, to be precise, evaluation of the new bomber) made it possible to assess the *Blackjack*'s strengths and weaknesses, ironing out bugs and accumulating first-hand experience which other units slated to re-equip with the type would find invaluable.

Operating such a complex aircraft, especially during the induction phase, demanded higher-than-average skill and responsibility on the part of the flight and ground crews. Usually Long-Range Aviation personnel took conversion training on new types at the DA's 43rd TsBP i PLS (*Tsentr boye**voy** podgo**tov**ki i pere**oo**chivaniya **lyot**novo sos**tah**va* – Combat Training & Aircrew Conversion Centre) at Dyagilevo AB near Ryazan' in central Russia. This time, however, the training took place right at the factories; the flight crews were trained at KAPO in Kazan', while the technicians studied the NK-32 at engine factory No.24 in Kuibyshev. A priority task for Tupolev OKB test pilot Boris I. Veremey and the factory test pilots in Kazan' was to train qualified flying instructors (QFIs) for the 37th VA which the 184th GvTBAP was part of; the QFIs would then pass on their skills to service pilots transitioning to the *Blackjack*.

Conversion training of the flight crews was done using Tu-134UBL *Crusty-B* twinjets. The Tu-134UBL (*oo**cheb**no-boye**voy** [samo**lyot**] dlya **lyot**chikov* – combat trainer for pilots) is a purpose-built derivative of the Tu-134B 80-seat short-haul airliner designed for training heavy bomber crews. Its *raison d'être* was that, unlike the earlier Tu-22, the Tu-22M and Tu-160 did not have specialised trainer versions, and using the bombers for conversion/proficiency training would be a waste of their service life. Also, the Tu-134 is similar to the *Backfire* and *Blackjack* in thrust/weight ratio and low-speed handling.

The first two *Blackjacks* destined for the 184th GvTBAP arrived at Priluki AB at noon on April 17, 1987, although some sources quote the date as April 23rd or 25th. These were apparently f/ns 2-03 (although some sources call the existence of this fuselage number into question, stating Batch 2 consisted of two aircraft) and 3-01; one of the bombers was captained by DA Deputy Commander Lev V. Kozlov, by then promoted to Lieutenant-General. The ferry flight went uneventfully; in addition to the usual welcoming committee and brass band attending the arrival of a new type, at Priluki the airmen were "welcomed" by a host of counter-intelligence corps officers whose job was to keep any information about the Tu-160 from leaking out.

On May 12, Kozlov made the first flight of a Tu-160 from Priluki; on 1st July this was followed by the first sortie of a 184th GvTBAP crew captained by the regiment's CO

Above: A production Tu-160 breaks formation with a 409th APSZ IL-78 tanker (CCCP-76675). Below and bottom: The same pair seen during the same sortie over the High North.

Lt.-Col. Vladimir D. Grebennikov. That same day Maj. Aleksandr S. Medvedev, the first commander of the first operational *Blackjack* squadron, flew the type solo for the first time. (Incidentally, in the 184th GvTBAP he was jokingly called *"ahs Med**ved**ev"* (Ace Medvedev) – a pun on his initials, A. S.) By the end of the month Maj. Nikolay Stooditskiy, Maj. Valeriy Shcherbak and Maj. Vladimir Lezhayev got their taste of flying the Tu-160. Interestingly, the same aircraft was used initially by all crews; it did not even taxi in to the flight line and the preparations for the next flight (refuelling and the like.) took place directly on the runway.

A year earlier, in 1986, the Kh-55SM cruise missile was formally included into the DA's inventory. In arms reduction talks with the West

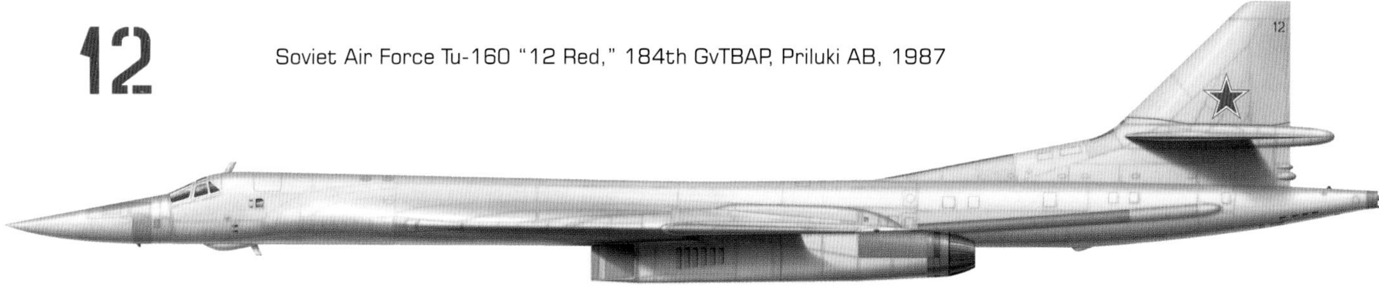

Soviet Air Force Tu-160 "12 Red," 184th GvTBAP, Priluki AB, 1987

the baseline Kh-55 and the Kh-55SM were referred to as the RKV-500A and RKV-500B respectively (*raketa krylahtaya, vozdooshnovo bazeerovaniya* – cruise missile, air-launched). In late July 1987, a Tu-160 crew captained by Lt.-Col. Vladimir Grebennikov performed the unit's first Kh-55SM launch with excellent results. The crew also included WSO Maj. Igor' Anikin and inspector pilot Lt.-Gen. Lev V. Kozlov. (Some sources give the date as August 1, 1987, or mention a different crew – see page 218.)

To speed up conversion training and conserve the bombers' service life a flight simulator was commissioned at Priluki AB. In order to make maximum use of the two aircraft delivered initially and train as many pilots as possible, it was standard operational procedure (SOP) at first to have the crews literally queueing beside the runway, waiting for their turn to fly!

The airmen liked the Tu-160. The bomber was very much a "pilot's aeroplane," possessing excellent acceleration and rate of climb (pilots said of the Tu-160 that it "climbed by itself"). The aircraft also possessed good low-speed handling, which facilitated the landing procedure; at 260 km/h (161.5 mph) the minimum control speed was even lower than the Tu-22M3's. The engines' aggregate thrust was tremendous. On one occasion a Tu-160 even managed to become airborne and climb with the spoilers deployed by mistake; of course the climb was very slow at first but when the pilots realised what was wrong and retracted the spoilers the aircraft "shot up with such force that the crew almost punched through the seats with their backsides," as one of the crewmembers put it! The *Blackjack* featured an audio warning system and a stick-pusher which prevented grave piloting errors.

Above: Tu-160 "12 Red" lands at Kubinka AB to take part in a new military aircraft display for high-ranking statesmen.

Right: A Kh-55SM long-range cruise missile is prepared for loading into the rear weapons bay of a Tu-160 at Priluki. The dark ring aft of the radome is a protective canvas wrap.

Top left: "18 Red" parked at Priluki with the telescopic boarding ladder in place.

Left: "10 Red," another 184th GvTBAP Tu-160, touches down at Priluki, showing the double-slotted flaps and flaperons.

Russian Air Force Tu-160 "01 Red," 1096th TBAP, Engels-2 AB, 1992; the mission markers denote test launches of Kh-55SM missiles

Top and above: A red-painted inert Kh-55 cruise missile falls clear of the aircraft with the engine and tail unit already deployed and then trails smoke from the cartridge starter as the engine fires up.
Above right: A Kh-55SM has just assumed cruise configuration after being released by Tu-160 "01 Red" during trials.

Dubbed 'The Pride of the Nation' by newspaper reporters, the Tu-160 commanded respect from everyone who had to deal with it. Hence every due care was taken to ensure trouble-free operation. For instance, in the first months of service the crews were expressly forbidden from taxying to the holding point under the aircraft's own power in order to prevent foreign object damage (FOD) to the engines. The *modus operandi* was this: the engines were started on a special hardstand which had been painstakingly swept clean of all loose objects; then the bomber was towed to the runway with the engines running at ground idle, preceded by a string of soldiers picking up loose stones and twigs. As for the runway, the ground personnel did everything to keep it clean short of washing it with soap!

Speaking of nicknames, as already mentioned, the Tu-160 was also dubbed ***Belyy lebed'*** (White Swan) because of its overall white finish and sleek lines. This is not an "official" popular name, however, and the author of an article in *Nezavisimoye voyennoye obozreniye* (Independent Military Review), a weekly supplement to the *Nezavisimaya gazeta* daily (Independent Newspaper), proposed officially naming the bomber "***Il'ya Muromets*** II." The original "Il'ya Muromets," named after a Russian epic hero of great strength, was the Sikorsky S-22 – a four-engined bomber biplane of pre-World War One vintage (the world's first four-engined bomber, in fact) which was designed in Russia by Igor' I. Sikorsky. Thus, the author of the idea alluded both to the S-22 and to the US practice of reusing popular names (McDonnell FH-1 Phantom/McDonnell F4H-1 (F-4) Phantom II, Douglas C-74 Globemaster/Douglas C-124 Globemaster II/McDonnell Douglas C-17A Globemaster III, Republic P-47 Thunderbolt/Republic A-10 Thunderbolt II and so on).

Combining the final stage of the *Blackjack*'s state acceptance trials with the service tests saved the Soviet state a lot of money. Still, the Tupolev

Top: Lit by the bright sun, a Tu-160 shows off its sleek lines.

Above: A pair of *Blackjacks* in echelon port formation. The aircraft have a well-worn appearance.

Below: For extreme high-altitude missions Tu-160 crews wear Baklan pressure suits with full-face pressure helmets similar to an astronaut's attire.

Opposite bottom: A Tu-160 with the wings at minimum sweep is pictured over the Russian coastline. Note the window of the navigation suite's AV-1SM star tracker amidships.

Opposite top: The ill-fated Tu-160 "01 Red" about to be demonstrated to the military top brass at Engels-2 AB, with stored Tu-22s in the background. Note the two Kh-55SM missiles (the red one is an instrumented test round) and the data placards beside the port wing. The flight crew are wearing their 'bone dome' helmets, which indicates that the day's programme included a demonstration flight.

Bottom: A Russian Air Force Tu-160 displays its underside as it rolls to starboard, breaking formation with the camera ship.

OKB and the Air Force had to wrestle with the bomber's design flaws and operational problems for many years yet. At the evaluation stage malfunctions occurred in virtually every single sortie – primarily in the avionics which were a royal pain in the neck. Luckily there were no serious accidents, mainly thanks to the multiple redundancy of the vital systems. The teething troubles and the generally hasty approach to the development of the Tu-160 caused the evaluation period to drag on for several years. However, it should be remembered that the nation's leaders kept urging the Tupolev OKB and the Air Force to field the new bomber as soon as possible, which is why the Tu-160 entered service with lots of bugs still to be ironed out.

Problems with the powerplant were encountered regularly; engine starting was especially troublesome and the full authority digital engine control system could not cope with it. FADEC failures occurred in flight as well. On one occasion, a Tu-160 captained by Maj. Vasin lost two engines at once. The petals of the NK-32's variable nozzles often failed. On the other hand, the *Blackjack* had adequate power reserves to maintain level flight and even take off with one engine inoperative (which saved the day on an important occasion, as described later in this chapter).

One particular problem area was the air intakes whose aerodynamic imperfections created an annoying rasping noise and vibrations. The latter were downright dangerous, as they caused rivets to pop and fatigue cracks to appear. This defect was eradicated in due course by redesigning the forward sections of the inlet ducts and reinforcing the intakes' leading edges.

The original design of the main landing gear units proved excessively complicated, leading to malfunctions (the bogies would get stuck halfway through rotation and so on). Reliability problems even caused 184th GvTBAP crews to refrain from retracting the gear for several months in 1988. This led the OKB to develop a simpler version which was introduced on the production line in Kazan' and retrofitted to some of the existing aircraft. Changes were also made to the hydraulic system.

As mentioned earlier, structural strength problems were encountered with the bonded honeycomb-core panels utilised in the Tu-160's tail unit which cracked open at high speeds, causing severe vibration. One of the 184th GvTBAP aircraft captained by "Ace Medvedev" lost a good-sized fragment of the horizontal tail – an uncanny repetition of an incident which had occurred on one of the prototypes during a test flight. On another occasion, a glassfibre section of the fin fillet broke away during a demonstration flight from Dyagilevo AB. Eventually, the Tupolev OKB was forced to suspend Tu-160 operations and redesign the horizontal tail. New sets of shorter-span stabilators were manufactured by KAPO for the entire Tu-160 fleet. Now the aircraft had to be modified, and an immediate problem arose: flying the bombers to Kazan' for a refit was ruled out for safety reasons, and the all-movable horizontal tail was a one-piece structure too large to be carried internally by any transport aircraft in Soviet Air Force service. The solution was to carry the stabilators externally. An Ilyushin Il-76 *sans suffixe* (*Candid-B*) transport owned by KAPO (CCCP-76496, c/n 073410301, f/n 0806) was modified to carry Tu-160 horizontal tail assemblies atop the fuselage immediately aft of the wings on special struts; hence the aircraft was unofficially known as the ***triplahn*** (triplane). CCCP-76496 made several flights with its unusual cargo from Kazan'-Borisoglebskoye to Priluki AB where the bombers were modified *in situ*. When the job had been completed the IL-76 was reconverted to standard configuration.

One more problem (which, incidentally, affected the B-1 as well) quickly surfaced in service. Generally it is standard operational procedure for 'swing-wing' aircraft to keep the wings fully swept back on the ground in order to minimise the required parking space. However, with the wings at maximum sweep (65°) the Tu-160's CG shifted aft so much that the bomber could easily tip over on its tail, and getting it back into normal position without inflicting damage wasn't easy at all. Hence the wings had to be left at minimum sweep (20°) on the ground, even though the Tu-160 required a lot more apron space in this configuration.

True, some of the incidents were caused by pilot error. For instance, there were several cases when the aircraft overran the runway on landing because the brake parachutes were deployed too late. Slowing the *Blackjack* down was not easy due to the aircraft's high landing weight and hence inertia, and the pilots were unwilling to deploy the parachutes too early for fear of losing face. Yet most problems were of a technical nature; for instance, the wheel brakes sometimes locked uncommandedly on take-off.

Much aggravation was caused by the state-of-the-art avionics, notably the Baikal ESM suite, 80% of which was housed in the rear fuselage. This area was subjected to serious vibration when the engines were running (particularly in full afterburner) and the vibrations shook the delicate electronics to bits. Tu-160 pilots caustically commented that they were carting two tons of ballast around for no practical purpose. By the spring of 1990 the ESM suite had worked up an acceptable reliability level, but still malfunctions did occur from time to time.

Another thing which caused a lot of problems for the ground personnel was the lack of manuals for the Tu-160. Sure, the Tupolev OKB had a full set of manuals but no one had given a thought to making and disseminating copies of these for the units operating the bomber!

Despite being easy to fly and stable in all flight modes, the Tu-160 gave the aircrews many causes for criticism. For instance, the pilots were unhappy with the Zvezda K-36LM zero-zero ejection seat. Though a magnificent piece of engineering in itself (a fact proved by the many lives it saved), the K-36 was basically a fighter seat which turned out to be totally unsuited for the long missions of a strategic bomber. The same applied to the standard-issue flying suits designed for fighter pilots. The special protective helmets were in short supply for a long time, forcing several crews to take turns using the same set of helmets; as often as not the helmet was not the right size, creating an additional inconvenience for the crewman. Special heat-insulated rescue suits for overwater flights which made it possible to survive an ejection into ice-cold water were not available either (see below).

That was not the worst of it, however. The K-36LM seats could be adjusted lengthwise, and it turned out that ejection was impossible with the seat in certain positions. This was an extremely dangerous defect, and strictly speaking, an aircraft with such a defect should not be allowed to fly at all. For a long time NPP Zvezda tried to persuade the airmen not to slide the seats into the controversial position but eventually admitted that the situation was insupportable and set about modifying the seat.

The flight deck ergonomics also gave cause for complaint. For instance, originally the main and back-up flight instruments were of different types, which was inconvenient; later the instrument panels were modified as recommended by service pilots to feature standardised main/back-up instruments.

To give credit where credit is due, the Tu-160's flight deck had a number of features enhancing crew comfort which had been unheard-of on Soviet bombers until then. These were a small electric heater for the crewmen's food rations and a toilet bowl – both very useful features on a long sortie. By comparison, on other bombers the crews had to chew cold meals and make do with a tin bucket, should they feel the urge to relieve themselves. There have been claims in the press that the Air Force refused to accept the new Tupolev bomber for several months because it was not satisfied with the design of the toilet!

It should also be noted that at an early stage the Tupolev OKB had taken steps to facilitate the Tu-160's maintenance procedures as much as possible. Hydraulic systems components were arranged on the walls of the weapons bays for easy access, while the electric power distribution panels and fuse boxes were located in the wheel wells. Access to the engines was also reasonably good, and the avionics racks at the rear of the flight deck and in the avionics bays were well designed. Still, the *Blackjack* turned out to be extremely 'labour-intensive', so to say, setting an unofficial Soviet Air Force record (of the unwanted kind) – it required 64 man-hours of maintenance per flight hour.

Preparing the Tu-160 for a sortie required between 15 and 20 ground support vehicles. These included the huge TZ-30 and TZ-60 articulated fuel bowsers (***toplivozaprahvshchik*** – refueller or, in this case, refuelling truck) consisting of a semitrailer with a 30,000- or 60,000-litre (6,600 or 13,200 Imp gal) tank respectively towed by a MAZ-537 or MAZ-7410 *Ooragahn* (Hurricane) 8x8 tractor unit; three TZ-60s were required to refuel the Tu-160 fully. Moreover, the Tu-160 used so-called nitrogenated (or nitrogen-enriched) fuel; this called for a special fuel nitrogenation unit in which nitrogen under pressure would be forced through the fuel to substitute the oxygen dissolved in it. During the climb and in cruise flight this "sparkling drink" would give off gaseous nitrogen, automatically filling the empty space in the fuel tanks with inert gas as the fuel was used up. Other support vehicles were an AK-1.6-9A heavy-duty air handling unit (*aerodromnyy konditsioner* – airfield air conditioner) mounted on a semitrailer with a KamAZ-5410 6x4 tractor unit for cooling the avionics, a minibus for the crew equipped with an air conditioner for the pressure suits and the like.

Incidentally, the NK-32 had a high nitrous monoxide content in its exhaust due to running on nitrogenated fuel – after all, it was a military engine and had manners to match. Hence at full power the Tu-160 emitted a distinctively orange-coloured efflux aptly dubbed *lisiy khvost* (fox tail).

The "black men," as Soviet Air Force technicians were nicknamed because of their black fatigues, were confronted with other problems which were just as serious. When the engines were started the noise and vibration were horrendous, the volume reaching 130 dB, which is 45 dB over safe limit determined by the medics; the TA-12 APU was not quiet either, to say the least. To make matters worse there was an acute shortage of ear protectors, special vibration-damping boots and vibration protection belts. Instead of the usual AMG-10 or AMG-16 oil-based hydraulic fluid (*aviatsionnoye mahslo ghidravlicheskoye*) the Tu-160 used a special

Above left: Tu-160 "18 Red" parked in a revetment at Priluki AB.

Left: A Tu-160 in high-speed cruise with the wings at maximum sweep. The erected wing fences are clearly visible.

Opposite top: Escorted by four Su-27s in the striking livery of the Russian Air Force's Roosskiye Vityazi aerobatic team, Tu-160 "24 Red" is pictured during a practice flight for the 1995 VE-Day parade in Moscow.

Opposite bottom: Seen from an IL-78 tanker, a Tu-160 moves into position for refuelling.

7-50S-3 grade hydraulic fluid (originally created for the Tu-144) which had a high resistance to heating in supersonic flight but had the disadvantage of being highly corrosive. The lack of proper protective gear meant that the ground personnel could not do their job properly. Finally, some of the bomber's structural components and equipment items were difficult to repair and maintain.

Here it is worth quoting an article published in ***Krasnaya zvezda*** (Red Star), the Soviet MoD daily, on July 23, 1989. After describing the "acute problems" experienced with the Tu-160, something they could do without, the pilots who had tested the bomber confided to the newspaper reporter, *"The aircraft won our hearts with its impressive capabilities. Still, you can tell that nobody was, so to say, snapping at the Tupolev OKB's heels. They hold a monopoly in this field!"* Guards Col. Ye. Ignatov, the 184th GvTBAP's Chief of Maintenance, had a similar opinion: *"Eliminating the Myasishchev OKB was a mistake. We need competition!"* Despite all these initial problems, the 184th GvTBAP's Squadron 1 was fully combat-ready with the Tu-160 after an eight-month period. The unit did its best to overcome the learning curve; the average Tu-160 utilisation rose steadily, reaching 100 flight hours per annum. Six-, ten- and twelve-hour missions were flown on a regular basis. Many pilots who transitioned to the *Blackjack* from the Tu-16 or Tu-22M3 said this was the best aircraft they had ever flown.

A weapons system of this complexity demanded a completely new approach to ground crew training. Suffice it to say that in the first days of Tu-160 operations in the 184th GvTBAP it took up to 36 hours (!) to prepare the aircraft for a mission. Gradually mission preparation times were reduced to an acceptable level thanks to the persistent work of the unit's tech staff and the immense help of the OKB's operations department.

The bomber's inevitable teething troubles were the subject of close attention from the aircraft industry. Up to 300 MAP representatives were on temporary detachment to Priluki AB at any one time to resolve any problems on site; the defects discovered were quickly eliminated on both operational aircraft and the Kazan' production line. For instance, the NK-32's service life, which initially was a mere 250 hours, was tripled in due course. The number of auxiliary blow-in doors in the engines' inlet ducts was increased from five to six in order to prevent compressor stalls and their control system was simplified. Some honeycomb-core metal panels were replaced by composite panels of a similar design, saving weight and improving fatigue life.

At high speed the pointed fairing at the fin/tailplane junction created vortices which caused vibrations ruining the ESM equipment in the rear fuselage. The problem was cured by shortening this fairing 50% and giving it a more bulbous ogival shape from Batch 2 onwards. Late-production aircraft introduced rear vision periscopes for the navigator and WSO. These upgrades were made on operational Tu-160s at Priluki AB by KAPO specialists.

Some time after service entry the *Blackjack* received an avionics upgrade. Improvements were made to the long-range radio navigation (LORAN) system working with ground beacons. The navigation system was augmented by a self-contained celestial corrector which accurately determined the aircraft's position with the help of the sun and the stars; this was a real asset when flying over the ocean and in extreme northern latitudes. The navigators were pleased with the new PA-3 moving map display (MMD) showing the aircraft's current position. A satellite navigation system with an accuracy margin of 10-20 m (33-66 ft) was also due for introduction on the Tu-160; it worked with several MoD satellites placed into geostationary orbit under a special government programme. The engineers also succeeded in debugging the software of the targeting/navigation avionics suite.

The Tupolev OKB devised and implemented a multi-stage programme aimed at making the *Blackjack* more stealthy. The air intakes and inlet ducts were coated with black graphite-based radar-absorbing material (RAM). The forward fuselage received a coat of special organic-based paint which reduced the radar signature; on the minus side, it attracted dust and dirt, resulting in a rather untidy appearance. Some engine components were provided with special screens minimising radar returns, and a wire mesh filter was incorporated into the flight deck glazing to reduce electromagnetic pulse (EMP) emissions which could give the bomber away. This filter also helped to protect the crew from the flash of a nuclear explosion.

The persistent and concerted efforts of the Air Force and the aircraft industry soon bore fruit; little by little the Tu-160 turned into a fully capable weapons system. The reliability of the aircraft in first-line service was improved no end. Still, many of the planned improvements never materialised, including the intended upgrade of the navigation/targeting suite. Unlike their American colleagues flying the B-1B, Tu-160 pilots never mastered ultra-low-level terrain-following flight, and far from all *Blackjack* crews were trained in IFR procedures which gave the aircraft its intended intercontinental range. The Kh-15S short-range ASM was never integrated, leaving the Tu-160 with the Kh-55 cruise missile as its only weapon.

Gradually, as the Soviet Air Force built up operational experience with the type, the range of the Tu-160's missions expanded. The bombers went as far up north as the North Pole, sometimes even venturing across the Pole. The longest sortie – flown by a crew under Col. Valeriy Gorgol' who succeeded Vladimir Grebennikov as 184th GvTBAP CO in 1989 – lasted 12 hours 50 minutes; the bomber got within 450 km (279.5 miles) of the Canadian coast. NATO fighters often scrambled to intercept the Tu-160s over international waters; the first such occasion was apparently in May 1991 when a pair of Royal Norwegian Air Force/331st Sqn Lockheed Martin F-16A Fighting Falcons from Bodø AB intercepted Tu-160 "17 Red" over the Norwegian Sea.

This is how Merited Military Pilot Aleksandr S. Medvedev ("Ace Medvedev"), who gained Russian citizenship after the break-up of the Soviet Union and subsequently became a Senior Inspector Pilot with the Combat Training Department of the 37th VA of the Russian Armed Forces' Supreme Command (the former Long-Range Aviation), describes the *Blackjack*'s service entry period:

Above right: A Tu-160 flies high over a winter landscape. Note the greyish areas on the nose and the LERXes where a special paint reducing the RCS is applied.

Right: Another aspect of the same aircraft.

Opposite, top left: On most missions Tu-160 crewmen wear ordinary flying suits and ZSh-7B "bone dome" helmets.

Top right: The crew of a 1096th TBAP Tu-160 coded "05 Red" discusses the forthcoming flight while the aircraft is refuelled by a TZ-22 articulated fuel bowser.

Below left: The same crew pose for a photo. The captain (rightmost) is Lt.-Col. Anatoliy M. Zhikharev, who was then the 1096th TBAP's CO; he is now Commander of the DA. Note the hose from the fuel bowser attached to a pressure refuelling connector under the port LERX.

Right: Unlike the photo on the left, this is an obvious publicity shot, with a Tu-160 crew acting out a "find this place on the map" scene in front of their aircraft. A huge TZ-60 fuel bowser is just visible on the right.

"We first got acquainted with the Tu-160 about a year before the first bombers arrived at Priluki. We visited the factories where the aircraft proper, its engines and avionics were manufactured to study the hardware firsthand. Once we had received the Tu-160s, flight and combat training got under way. The Cold War was far from over then, and we were tasked with mastering the new aircraft as quickly as possible. Note that we had to do this in the course of service tests, which we had to perform instead of the factory pilots. This is why we got up to 100 systems malfunctions per flight in the early sorties. As we grew familiar with the machine the number of failures decreased, and in due time we came to trust the aircraft.

Where did we fly, you may ask? We departed Priluki in the direction of Lake Onega (near Petrozavodsk in Karelia, north-western Russia – *Auth.*), *thence we flew to Novaya Zemlya Island* ('New Land' – *Auth.*), *the Franz-Joseph Land archipelago and onwards, heading towards the North Pole. The guys back at home used to joke that 'the Cowboy* (the individual nickname of one 184th GvTBAP Tu-160 – *Auth.*) *is studying the States'; indeed, the 'potential adversary' was within easy reach for us. However, over the Pole we would turn and head towards Tiksi* (on the Laptev Sea coast – *Auth.*); *all the more reason to do so because the terrain there was similar to the coasts of northern Canada. Next we would overfly Chelyabinsk* (in the southern part of the Urals mountain range – *Auth.*), *Lake Balkhash and the Caspian Sea, heading across the North Caucasus back towards Priluki. There was also a route from Priluki to Lake Baikal and back again; I used to fly it with Vladimir Grebennikov. Missiles were launched against targets on a range in Kazakhstan* (the Sary-Shagan test range, a.k.a. 10th Research & Test Range, located west of Lake Balkhash in the Betpak-Dala Desert – *Auth.*); *we would enter the designated launch zone and say goodbye to our missiles. Later we also practiced missile attacks at target ranges in other parts of the USSR."*

On some occasions the Tu-160s were escorted by Sukhoi Su-27P *Flanker-B* interceptors of the Air Defence Force's 10th Army operating from bases near Murmansk and on Novaya Zemlya Island. Overwater missions were flown in pairs because the presence of a wingman (or flight leader, depending on what aircraft in the pair you flew) added psychological comfort; if one of the crews ran into trouble and had to ditch or eject over water, the other crew could radio for help, indicating the co-ordinates of the crash site. This was important because Tu-160 crews had nothing except ASP-74 aviation-specific life jackets (*aviatsi**on**nyy spa**sah**tel'nyy **po**yas*) for such an emergency; the VMSK-4 heat-insulated waterproof rescue suit (***vo**donepronit**sa**yemyy mor**skoy** spa**sah**tel'nyy kos**tyum***) was a privilege of Naval Aviation pilots. This situation was caused by the lumbering bureaucratic machine responsible for materiel supplies in the Armed Forces.

One of the reasons why the new strategic bomber became operational very quickly was the targeting and navigation system's high degree of automation which reduced the WSO's workload. The WSO was the key member of the crew during missile launch. As already noted, the Kh-55SM cruise missile was guided to the target by a pre-entered programme featuring a digital route map; therefore the WSO's duties basically boiled down to accurately guiding the aircraft to the launch point, monitoring the missiles' systems status and pushing the release button at the right time. The missile was then ejected pneumatically from the rotary launcher; at a safe distance from the aircraft its wings and tail surfaces unfolded, the engine was deployed and fired up, and the missile followed its intended course. Meanwhile the launcher rotated, bringing the next missile into position for release.

All practice launches of the Kh-55SM took place at the GNIKI VVS target range in Kazakhstan and were supported by the "aircraft 976" airborne measuring and control stations. Live weapons training with the new cruise missile proceeded on a much wider scale than even with the Tu-22M3 armed with the proven Kh-22N

Left: Armourers at Engels-2 AB unstrap an inert Kh-55 training round (duly marked as such) from the dolly before loading it into the weapons bay of a Tu-160.

Right: The 184th GvTBAP crew that made the first Kh-55 launch from the Tu-160 in Soviet Air Force service on August 1, 1987. Left to right: captain Guards Lt.-Col. A. S. Malyshev, navigator Guards Maj. A. Vishnyakov, WSO Guards Maj. M. Krasnov and co-pilot Guards Maj. S. Kolesnikov.

(AS-4C *Kitchen*) ASMs. One of the Tu-160s – the one known in the regiment as "the Cowboy" (presumably because the aircraft had two "six-shooters" inside! – *Auth.*) launched no fewer than 14 missiles. Maj. I. N. Anisin, the 184th GvTBAP's Chief of Intelligence, was one of the top-scoring WSOs – which was understandable enough, as he had to know all about the unit's potential targets.

Towards the end of 1987, the 184th GvTBAP had increased its Tu-160 complement to ten aircraft; nevertheless, the regiment stuck to its Tu-22M3s and Tu-16Ps in order to maintain combat readiness during the transition period. Later, as the number of *Blackjacks* grew, the *Backfire-Cs* were progressively transferred to other units, while the Tu-16s were scrapped on site to comply with the Conventional Forces in Europe (CFE) treaty limiting the number of combat aircraft a unit was authorised to have. The strategic bombers themselves were governed by a different treaty, the Strategic Arms Reduction Talks (START); a group of US inspectors was to arrive at Priluki AB in order to monitor the number of strategic aircraft, and a bungalow was specially built for them near the runway and aircraft hardstands.

As the economic downturn caused by Mikhail S. Gorbachov's *perestroika* got worse, Tu-160 production and delivery rates slowed down somewhat; by late 1991 the 184th GvTBAP had 21 *Blackjacks* in Squadrons 1 and 2. At the beginning of that year the unit's Squadron 3 had received a small number of Tu-134UBLs; until then the type had been operated solely by the military flying schools in Orenburg and Tambov. The *Crusty-Bs* were used for lead-in and proficiency training, saving the bombers' service life and helping to avoid unnecessary breakdowns and costly repairs.

A Kh-55SM in flight configuration is displayed beside Tu-160 "01 Red" at Engels-2 AB.

Right: An uncoded *Blackjack* escorted by two Su-27s makes a flypast at Moscow-Tushino during the 1998 Aviation Day air fest.

The Western intelligence community maintained a close interest in the Tu-160, and especially its mission equipment, long before the aircraft entered service. The Soviet counter-intelligence service (the notorious KGB) was extremely alarmed to discover a self-contained SIGINT module near Priluki AB in the spring of 1988. Disguised as a tree stump, this unit monitored and recorded air-to-ground radio exchanges and other signals emitted by the aircraft operating from the base. It was never ascertained who had planted the module there, but countermeasures were not slow in coming: operational Tu-160s were provided with "nightcaps" made of metal-coated cloth which were placed over the nose on the ground to contain electromagnetic pulses. As a bonus, these covers protected the ground personnel from harmful high-frequency radiation when the avionics were tested on the ground.

On the other hand, Gorbachov's new domestic and foreign policies of *perestroika* and *glasnost'* (openness) removed the pall of secrecy (sometimes exaggerated secrecy) from the Soviet Armed Forces and defence industry, making a lot of previously classified information available via the mass media. Also, in addition to military delegations from allied nations the Soviet Union began inviting high-ranking military officials from countries previously regarded as 'potential adversaries'. New Soviet military hardware was demonstrated to Western experts both at home and abroad during major international airshows and defence trade fairs.

The West got its first close look at the *Blackjack* on August 12, 1988, when Frank C. Carlucci, the then US Secretary of Defense, visited Kubinka AB near Moscow during his Soviet trip. Kubinka had a long history as a display centre where the latest military aircraft were demonstrated to Soviet and foreign military top brass. The aircraft shown to Mr. Carlucci included a Mikoyan MiG-29 *Fulcrum-A* tactical fighter, a Mil' Mi-26 *Halo* heavy-lift helicopter, an Il-78 *sans suffixe* (*Midas-A*) tanker/transport – and a 184th GvTBAP Tu-160 coded "12 Red." In an unprecedented show of openness, the Secretary of Defense was allowed to examine the weapons bays, the flight deck and other details of the *Blackjack*. The US delegation was accompanied by TV crews and press photographers, and soon the first reasonably good pictures of the Tu-160 were circulated in the world media; the event also made the evening news on Soviet TV. Also, some performance figures were disclosed for the first time, including a range of 14,000 km (8,695 miles) on internal fuel.

As is usually the case on such occasions, a flying display was staged; it included two more Tu-160s which were parked elsewhere on the base. When the bombers (captained by Vladimir D. Grebennikov and Aleksandr S. Medvedev) were due to taxi out for their demonstration flight, a single engine would not start on each of the two aircraft (!). Realising the embarrassment that would result if the demonstration flight was cancelled for this reason, the VVS top command authorised the crews to take off on three engines – which they did. The flights went well, thanks as much to excellent airmanship as to the *Blackjack*'s good flying qualities.

Nevertheless, the fact that only three of each bomber's engines were emitting the characteristic orange efflux did not escape the attention of the US Air Force representatives who demanded an explanation. Worried though he was about the situation, DA Commander Col.-Gen. Pyotr S. Deynekin answered with a straight face that the Tu-160's engines had several operational modes, not all of which were characterised by a smoke trail.

It is not known whether the Americans believed him; indeed, it would appear improbable that ordinary service pilots would run the risk of taking off with one engine dead. However, even if they had guessed the truth and had the grace to say nothing, they surely acknowledged that the Soviet pilots were real pros.

Another embarrassing situation arose when Frank Carlucci climbed into the Tu-160's flight deck. As he moved about in the confined space he bumped his head painfully on a carelessly positioned circuit breaker panel (which the witty airmen promptly dubbed "the Carlucci panel"). Indeed, almost every person making his first visit inside the *Blackjack* bumps his head on it!

After this event the bomber became a familiar feature both of such shows for foreign military delegations at Kubinka and of the air events at Moscow-Tushino and Zhukovskiy for the benefit of the general public (more will be said about these later). For instance, the French Defence Minister Jean-Pierre Chevènement examined a 184th GvTBAP Tu-160 coded "16 Red" at Kubinka AB in March 1989. Three months later, on June 13, another 184th GvTBAP *Blackjack* ("21 Red") was shown to Adm. William Crowe, the then Chairman of the US Joint Chiefs of Staff, at the same location. Climbing down the steep ladder from the flight deck (and presumably having avoided the famous panel), Crowe described the Tu-160 as *"a world class aircraft."*

On February 13, 1992, Tu-160 "16 Red" was demonstrated to the political leaders and top-ranking military officials of the Com-

monwealth of Independent States (CIS) republics at Machoolishchi AB on the southern outskirts of Minsk along with other advanced military aircraft. Curiously, the data plates for the exhibits were carefully draped with black cloth to hide the "top secret" figures from prying journalists (who arrived in force) and unveiled only for the visiting VIPs. Obviously *glasnost'* still had a long way to go in 1992! Yet, this was not the Soviet era any longer – see next section.

Post-Soviet Operations

With the collapse of the Soviet Union in 1991, when it came to dividing the assets of the former superpower between the CIS republics, it became clear that it was utterly impossible to

Top left: This 184th GvTBAP Tu-160 ("18 Red") was among the latest combat aircraft demonstrated to the political and military leaders of the newly-formed Commonwealth of Independent States at Machoolishchi AB near Minsk, Belorussia, on February 13, 1992. Here the show has yet to begin and flight deck is still under wraps, looking like a babushka.

Above left: The day before the morning after. Technicians clear the upper surfaces of "18 Red" of snow at Machoolischchi on February 12th prior to the following day's demonstration.

Left: "Fill her up, and clean the windshield, please!" A technician swings himself half-way out of the captain's sliding window to wipe the glazing of a Russian Air Force Tu-160 while another prepares to connect the refuelling hose.

Above right and top right: Early morning scene at Engels-2 AB as 1096th TBAP Tu-160 "03 Red" is readied for a practice sortie. The vehicle is a TZ-30 fuel bowser (pulled by a MAZ-537 tractor unit in this case).

Top row, far right: The rear end of the same aircraft. This view shows well the rear ESM antennas and APP-50 flare dispensers. Note the Tu-22KD and Tu-22KPD missile carriers of the 121st GvTBAP in the background.

assess each republic's contribution to the creation of the Soviet industrial and military power. Therefore all members of the Commonwealth agreed that each of the new states would manage whatever assets were on its territory.

The demise of the Soviet Union had a detrimental effect on one of the world's most potent offensive weapons systems – the Tu-160. On August 24, 1991, the Ukrainian Cabinet of Ministers issued a decree placing all military units and installations on the territory of the former Ukrainian Soviet Socialist Republic under Ukrainian control. The Ukrainian Ministry of Defence was formed that same day. The fledgling Ukrainian Air Force (*Viys'**kovo**-povi**tr**yany* ***see**ly Ook**ray**iny*) took over the 19 Tu-160s operated by the 184th GvTBAP (more about this later). Moreover, it also appropriated the 409th APSZ (***avia**polk* *samo**lyo**tov-zap**rahv**shchikov* – Aerial Refuelling Regiment) at Uzin AB south of Kiev which operated nearly all of the Soviet Air Force's Il-78 tanker/transports.

As already mentioned, in February 1992, Russian President Boris N. Yel'tsin signed a directive which contained a clause about the possible end of Tu-160 production if the USA stopped building the B-2 bomber. However, this initiative did not find support in Washington. Moreover, since the only operational Tu-160 unit was stationed outside the Russian Federation, the break-up of the Soviet Union left the new Russian Air Force without up-to-date strategic aircraft. Thus, costly though the bomber was, the *Blackjack* production line remained open for the time being.

New-build Tu-160s were now delivered to the 1096th TBAP stationed at Engels-2 AB. This unit was part of the 37th VA's 22nd *Don**bass**kaya* GvTBAD (*Gvar**dey**skaya tya**zho**laya bombardi**ro**vochnaya **a**viadi**vee**ziya* – Guards Heavy Bomber Division, formerly the aforementioned 201st TBAD), which had received its title for the liberation of the Donetsk Coal Mining Basin (Donbass, short for ***Do**netskiy bas**seyn*) in the war. Before re-equipping with the Tu-160 the 1096th TBAP had operated Myasishchev 3MS/3MN *Bison-B* and 3MD *Bison-C* four-turbojet subsonic bombers; these were supported by the co-located 1230th APSZ operating 3MS-2 tankers converted from bombers. It

03

05

Left: 1096th TBAP Tu-160s on the flight line at Engels in 1994, still in standard all-white colours without any "embellishments." Most of the aircraft have the flight deck under wraps to save the glazing from being damaged by the ultraviolet radiation of the sun (this is standard operational procedure). Note the open cowlings and the support placed under the tail of the nearest aircraft ("04 Red").

Below left: "03 Red," the third *Blackjack* delivered new to the Russian Air Force, taxies at Engels

Right: Another view of the same aircraft, showing the natural metal upper portions of the engine nacelles and the heat shields over the fuel transfer conduits from the rear fuselage fuel tank.

Below and below right: Tu-160 pilots go through the checklist before taxying out for take-off. Note the aircraft's tactical code, "01," painted on the captain's seat harness.

Bottom left and bottom: Tu-160 "05 Red" taxies out at Engels, with 1230th APSZ 3MS-2 and IL-78M tankers (the latter both in quasi-civil and overtly military guise) parked in the background.

Overleaf: A dramatic view of a high-flying Tu-160 over the Volga River and one of its tributaries.

deserves mention that the original plans (drawn as far back as the Tu-160's design stage) had envisaged delivery of the first production bombers to Engels, while the regiment in Priluki was then regarded as a reserve unit.

The 1096th TBAP took delivery of its first brand-new Tu-160 on February 14, 1992 (some sources say February 16); by May this number had increased to three aircraft. A large proportion of the 184th GvTBAP's flight and ground crews gave up their positions at Priluki and arranged a transfer to Engels in order to serve in the

Above: Tu-160 "03 Red" makes a banked turn in the fading afternoon light.
Below: The sun filtering through the clouds makes a pretty dramatic backdrop for this *Blackjack*.

The day's flying is done ... ready for tomorrow's flight shift.

Russian Armed Forces, refusing to swear allegiance to the Ukraine which was at odds with Russia over a number of issues. The first Tu-160 squadron was formed at Engels-2 AB. At the same time major reconstruction and upgrade work began at the base; all ground support equipment associated with Tu-160 operations, the flight simulator and a lot of other materiel had been left behind in Priluki, and the 1096th TBAP had to start from scratch. About the same time the 1230th APSZ re-equipped with Il-78/Il-78M *Midas-A/B* tankers, retiring the last 3MS-2s in 1994.

Even though three Tu-160s were available, it was not until July 29, 1992, that the *Blackjack* made its first flight in Russian service. The aircraft was captained by Lt.-Col. Aleksandr S. Medvedev, one of the former 184th GvTBAP airmen who had moved to Russia; the crew also included co-pilot Maj. S. Kolesnikov (another ex-184th GvTBAP pilot), navigator Lt.-Col. Vladimir Adamov and WSO Maj. V. Karpov. On October 22, 1992, a 1096th TBAP Tu-160 successfully performed the Russian Air Force's first launch of a Kh-55SM cruise missile against a practice target; it was flown by the unit's CO Lt.-Col. Anatoliy M. Zhikharev as captain, co-pilot Lt.-Col. N. Moiseyenko, navigator Lt.-Col. A. Gavrilov and WSO Lt.-Col. A. Pakulev. An identical mission was flown the following day by a crew under Lt.-Col. A. V. Malyshev. Thus Russia demonstrated *urbi et orbi* that it was still a strong aviation power to be reckoned with.

In early 1993, the unit received its fourth new-build Tu-160. This was clearly insufficient to maintain full combat capability. To bolster Russia's operational *Blackjack* force it was suggested that the six Tu-160s owned by ANTK Tupolev should be transferred to the 1096th TBAP, even though they were high-time airframes. However, only one was ever transferred (see below).

Thus, defying all difficulties caused by the chaos of the early post-Soviet years (fuel and spares shortages were the worst problems), the Russian Air Force's 37th VA managed to keep at least a degree of combat readiness. Even in 1992, which was the hardest year, Long-Range Aviation pilots tried to maintain their class ratings by flying 80-90 hours each, which was twice the number of hours per annum flown by Tactical Aviation (fighter and fighter-bomber) pilots!

In May 1993, Russian Air Force Tu-160s participated in Exercise ***Voskhod-93*** (Sunrise-93) – their first combined-arms exercise which involved a rapid reaction scenario in the event of a sudden threat to Russia's national security. The bombers' long range enabled them to deploy rapidly to the Far East, covering one of the key defence areas where they bolstered a group of Sukhoi Su-24M *Fencer-D* tactical bombers and Su-27 fighters deployed to the

Another fine air-to-air look of a Russian Air Force Tu-160.

area. This time the *Blackjack* crews had to make do with simulated missile launches because there were no suitable target ranges in the Transbaikalian MD.

A live launch of a Kh-55SM missile was performed in the course of a strategic nuclear forces exercise which took place on June 21–22, 1994; the exercise was inspected by President Boris N. Yel'tsin himself. The missile destroyed a practice target at the Koora target range on the Kamchatka Peninsula, Far Eastern MD; other targets at the same range were destroyed by RS-12 *Topol'* (Poplar; NATO SS-20 *Sickle*) ICBMs and missiles launched by a North Fleet Type 941 *Akoola* class (Shark/NATO *Typhoon* class) nuclear submarine. Of course, all the missiles were equipped with conventional warheads for practice purposes.

It took the Russian government several years to realise the full magnitude of the losses inflicted on the DA by the break-up of the Soviet Union and try to make them good by forming the Long-Range Aviation anew from the remaining assets. In the mid-1990s, the government took the decision to "optimise" the armed forces (and when the government starts talking of optimisation, this usually means cuts and closures).

This is where a controversy lies. Some sources claim that in 1994, the 1096th TBAP was disbanded, ceding its six Tu-160s to the 121st *Sevastopol'skiy* Red Banner GvTBAP which redeployed to Engels after its pullout from Belorussia (it was previously based at Machoolishchi AB, operating Tu-22KD/Tu-22KPD *Blinder-B* missile carriers and Tu-22UD *Blinder-D* trainers). This unit, which was part of the original 22nd GvTBAD, had received its honorary appellation and Guards title for the liberation of Sevastopol' on the Crimea Peninsula in 1944 during the Great Patriotic War. Other sources state just about the opposite – it was the 121st GvTBAP that was disbanded after moving to Engels, but to ensure continuity of combat traditions its number and regalia were transferred to the 1096th TBAP (which simply changed its identity on 1st December 1994 while keeping its then-current hardware and remaining within the 22nd GvTBAD). The latter appears more plausible because this did not entail conversion training of the Tu-22 crews.

On October 24, 1995, the 121st GvTBAP received ten Tu-134UBL trainers from the Tambov Military Pilot College named after Marina M. Raskova (TVVAUL – *Tam**bov**skoye **vy**ssheye vo**yen**noye aviatsi**on**noye oo**chil**ishche **lyot**chikov*) and the Orenburg Military Pilot College. These aircraft were operated by the newly formed Squadron 3.

Pursuant to the Russian Armed Forces' General Staff directive No.314/4/0714 dated November 1, 1997, the DA Commander's command structure was transformed into the 37th VA VGK (SN), that is, *voz**doosh**naya **ar**miya **V**erkhovnovo **glav**noko**mahn**dovaniya (strate**gich**eskovo nazna**ch**eniya)* – 37th (Strategic) Air Army of the Supreme High Command. Thus, all Long-Range Aviation assets were concentrated within a single air army. The latter comprised two divisions – the 22nd *Donbasskaya* Red Banner GvTBAD and the 326th *Ter**nopol'**skaya* TBAD, plus the 43rd TsBP i PLS, an independent aerial refuelling regiment, aviation commandant's offices at auxiliary airfields, and various logistics and support units. In turn, the 22nd GvTBAD comprised four regiments, including the 121st GvTBAP operating the *Blackjack*.

The Ukrainian Affair

In the Ukraine, the collapse of the Soviet Union had no dramatic effect on the daily activities of the 184th GvTBAP at first. However, in the spring of 1992, the Ukrainian government began administering the oath of allegiance to the military units stationed in the republic, and an exodus of personnel ensued. The 184th GvTBAP's turn was on May 8, 1992, but only about 25% of the flight crews and 60% of the ground personnel chose to take the oath; the regiment's then-current CO Col. Valeriy I. Gorgol' was the first to do so. As already mentioned, the Ukraine also appropriated the 409th APSZ at Uzin AB which supported the Tu-160s' operations. Most of the Ukrainian Air Force aircraft received the new national insignia in the form of blue/yellow roundels on the wings and a blue shield with a yellow trident on the tail (the Il-76MD transports and Il-78s were an exception, remaining civil-registered). On the Tu-160s at Priluki, however, in most cases the Soviet star insignia were simply painted out (rather untidily) and the UAF insignia never applied.

At first the Ukraine even took pride in possessing strategic aircraft. However, it soon became clear that the bombers were in reality a white elephant. For a maximum-range sortie each aircraft required 170 tons (374,780 lb) of kerosene, and 40 tons (88,180 lb) of fuel were needed for a training flight over home ground. According to the Ukrainian Air Force command, the maintenance costs of the strategic bomber fleet amounted to US$1.4 million per year.

Dire as the situation in the Russian Air Force was in the early 1990s, the Ukrainian military airmen were even worse off. The units operating heavy aircraft – the ones most difficult and expensive to maintain – were the hardest hit. Combat training had to be curtailed at once; the Ukraine had no target ranges of its own, and plans to establish a combat and conversion training centre for the Ukrainian heavy bomber crews never materialised. Furthermore, ANTK Tupolev and the Kazan' aircraft factory (which had delivered the bombers with a ten-year warranty) were no longer providing product support. Fuel and spares shortages, coupled with the exodus of qualified cadre, quickly grounded part of the bomber fleet. The severance of traditional ties within the former Soviet Union was a prime cause; for instance, the special IP-50 engine oil for the NK-32 turbofans was produced only in Azerbaijan, the landing gear wheels were manufactured in Yaroslavl' (Russia) and the engines in Samara (formerly Kuibyshev). As systems components ran out of service life and no replacements were forthcoming, the maintenance department of the 184th GvTBAP was forced to cannibalise some of the aircraft for spares to keep the others flyable.

Still, by mid-1994, these unpopular measures could no longer save the day – the unit was left with only a handful of pilots qualified to fly the Tu-160 and they had the opportunity to fly only four or five times a year due to the constant shortage of fuel. Occasionally a single Tu-160 would take off from Priluki to participate in an airshow or a military parade. The drop in flying hours per annum and the resulting lack of proficiency led to a higher number of malfunctions; the unit's CO Valeriy Gorgol' had to cope with the worst one on May 7, 1993, when one of the main gear units jammed halfway through extension. The bottom line is that the Russian Air Force's small fleet of *Blackjacks* (numbering five at the time) was more potent than the 19 Ukrainian examples!

18

Even more to the point, the strategic bombers absolutely did not fit into the Ukrainian defensive doctrine, since the Ukraine had declared a non-nuclear status. In March 1993, V. Zakharchenko, the advisor of the Ukrainian military attaché in Moscow, stated that, *"the Ukrainian Armed Forces have no missions which these aircraft could fulfil."* Even keeping the Tu-160s in storage was both too expensive and pointless. Therefore, soon enough Kiev began to reflect on how to get rid of them. There wasn't much of a choice: the bombers could be either transferred to Russia (following the example of Kazakhstan, which had exchanged its unwanted Tu-95MS bombers for fighters) or scrapped. In an interview at Priluki on February 15, 1995, Col.-Gen. Vladimir M. Antonets, the then Commander-in-Chief of the Ukrainian Air Force, said that the crisis affecting the Ukrainian economy made it impossible to adequately maintain the Tu-160s and therefore the Ukraine was interested in selling them to Russia.

Of course, Russia tried to recover the *Blackjacks*; almost immediately the Russian government started negotiating the purchase of the Tu-160s at Priluki AB and the Tu-95MSs operated by the 1006th TBAP at Uzin AB. The first negotiations about the fate of the strategic aircraft and air-launched cruise missiles remaining in the Ukraine began in 1993. These failed to yield any results: the price of US$25 million apiece offered by Russia was regarded as ridiculous by Kiev, which demanded US$75 million for each aircraft. Then Russia proposed exchanging the bombers for tactical aircraft and spares for same, but the Ukraine was not interested.

The negotiations on the purchase by Russia of ten fully serviceable Ukrainian Tu-160s continued in 1995. While Russia needed these aircraft badly, having only six Tu-160s at Engels, the prospect of Russia bolstering its strategic aviation absolutely did not suit Russia's arch-opponent, the USA, which would much rather see the bombers destroyed than have them fall into Russian hands. Hence, riding hard upon the anti-Russian sentiment that existed in certain Ukrainian circles, the US State Department started putting pressure on Kiev, demanding that the Ukraine comply with the START-2 treaty which required the Soviet Union to dismantle its strategic bombers not later than December 4, 2001. Starting in 1993, the possible sale of the Tu-160s was brought into discussion more than 20 times but the parties could not agree on the price. Meanwhile, the condition of the bombers slowly deteriorated. (Given the tensions between Moscow and Kiev, many people in Russia believed that the Ukraine was intentionally dragging out the deal and would sooner let the bombers rot away than let the Russians have them!)

After the first round of negotiations the Ukrainian National Security and Defence Council took the decision to dispose of the Tu-95MS and Tu-160 strategic aviation/missile systems. The

Top left: Many Ukrainian Tu-160s, including these two pictured on the flight line at Priluki AB, had the Soviet stars painted out but never gained Ukrainian insignia.

Left and above left: Nine Tu-160s in storage at the dispersal area in Priluki, including "18 Red" and "22 Red," both of which went to Russia. "22 Red" was the only one to change its identity, becoming Russian Air Force "14 Red."

Above right: A different angle on the taxiway in the same dispersal area.

Right: Two more Tu-160s, "30 Red" and "31 Red," stored at the base.

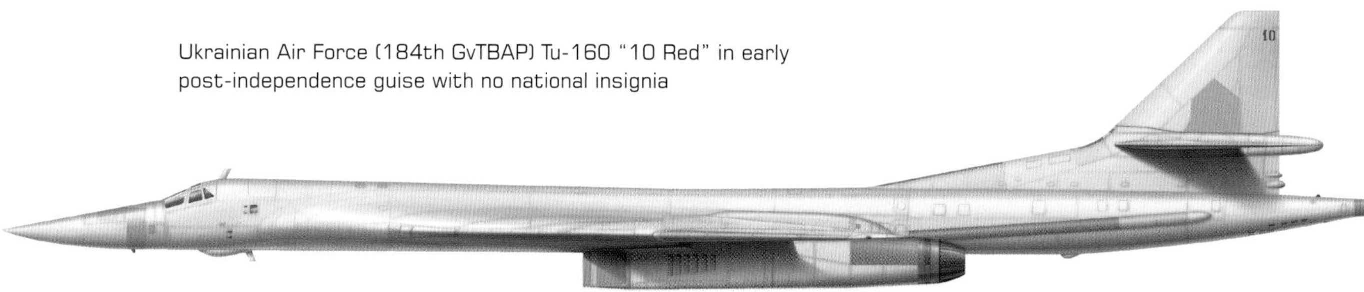

Ukrainian Air Force (184th GvTBAP) Tu-160 "10 Red" in early post-independence guise with no national insignia

Above: "25 Red" and "26 Red" with grey pentagons instead of insignia sit on the taxiway of the dispersal area at Priluki AB; two further *Blackjacks* are visible inside the revetments. Most of these aircraft were destined for the breakers (although "15 Red" wearing Ukrainian insignia likewise found its way to Russia).

Left: A different perspective of "26 Red," with six more Tu-160s behind it. This aircraft is now preserved in the UAF Museum in Poltava.

Below and below left: "33 Red," one of the oldest Tu-160s in the 184th GvTBAP, was one of those that did not survive.

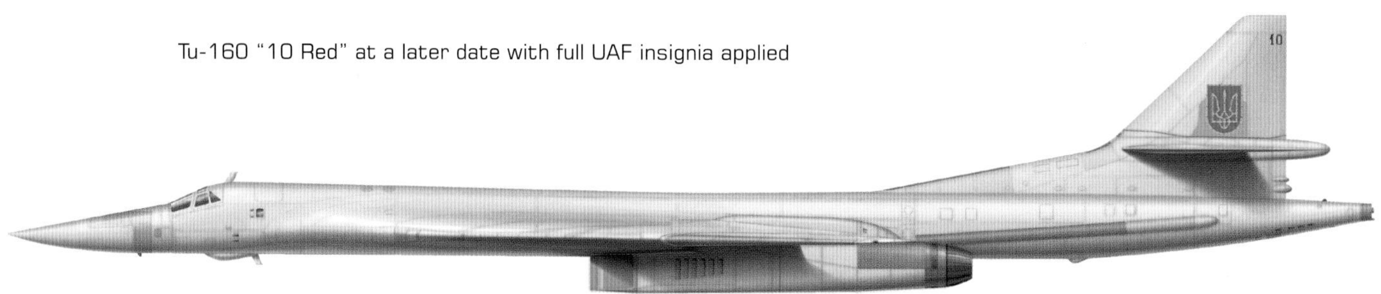

Tu-160 "10 Red" at a later date with full UAF insignia applied

carnage was funded by the USA under the Co-operative Threat Reduction Program (also called the Nunn-Lugar Program after Senators Samuel Nunn and Richard Lugar who got it through Congress). The US Congress officially allocated funds – variously reported as US$8 million or US$13 million – for the destruction of the heavy bombers and cruise missiles remaining on Ukrainian soil; appropriate deals were signed with specialised contractors. After the completion of the scrapping operation Ukraine would have the right to sell the metal.

In 1998, the Ukraine began scrapping its Tu-160s which the US military were so worried about. On November 16, 1998, the first victim – a Tu-160 coded "24 Red" (f/n 5-02) – was ceremonially broken up at Priluki AB in the presence of Senators Richard Lugar and Charles Levin; the aircraft, which was manufactured in 1989, had logged 466 hours total time since new (TTSN), which is next to nothing for a strategic bomber. The work was supervised by the American aerospace company Raytheon.

The second *Blackjack* to be disposed of was "14 Red" (f/n 6-04), one of the few that did receive Ukrainian Air Force markings; it had gained fame in the aviation community after being displayed at Poltava in late September 1994, during the celebrations marking the 50th anniversary of the American shuttle raids over Germany with a staging point in Poltava. This aircraft, which was built in 1991, had less than 100 hours TTSN! Its scrapping was completed in November 1999. The American experts worked in Priluki day and night.

Vadim Antakov, an officer of the 1006th TBAP who refused to swear allegiance to the Ukraine, recalled: *"The Americans had supplied all the equipment free of charge, although word was around that they would take the equipment back after the scrapping had been completed. However, when I was there, there was no end in sight to the work. What I saw was the actual guillotine for severing the rear fuselages almost immediately aft of the wings, hydraulic scissors for cutting up smaller pieces of the airframe, such as wings, then there was a special vehicle like a fire engine – an unforgettable sight and sound, especially at night, – and a compactor pressing the metal into cubes measuring about 1x1 m [3x3 ft]. Besides, the personnel working the equipment had been trained in America, the USA accepting the training costs. The scrap area was big enough to accommodate three or four Tu-95s, or four or five Tu-22s/Tu-22Ms. They were lined up put along a fence running along the perimeter road and the tails were chopped off, whereupon the actual dismantling began ..."*

On December 5, 1998, the Ukrainian Ministry of Defence and the US Department of Defence formally signed an agreement on the destruction of 44 Ukrainian heavy bombers and 1,068 Kh-55 cruise missiles. Under a supplementary agreement the deal was amended: 16 Tu-160 bombers would be scrapped, and three would be spared from the guillotine and modified for use as the first stage of a suborbital launch space system. In March 1999, the Ukrainian MoD was authorised by the government to sell the three *Blackjacks*, plus spares, to the American company Platforms International Corp., which was to convert the bombers into launch platforms for Pegasus SLVs placing satellites into low-Earth orbit. The price was to be just US$20 million for the lot (!). The organisation of the launches was assigned to the American company Orbital Network Services Corporation.

The Russians, however, blew the whistle, pointing out to the Ukrainian and US governments that the deal would be a breach of the START-2 treaty. Understandably enough, Russia would do everything to stop its most modern bomber from falling into American hands. Somewhat surprisingly, Russia's position found support in Washington, which also spoke up against any infringement of the treaty's basic stipulations by the Ukraine; therefore Kiev had to abandon the plan.

In April–May 1999, Moscow and Kiev discussed the possibility of exchanging eight Tu-160s and three Tu-95MSs for Antonov An-22 ***Antey*** (Antheus/*Cock*) and An-124 Ruslan heavy transports from Russian Air Force stocks. The Ukrainians were in a hurry to strike a deal on favourable terms because of the abovementioned December 4, 2001 deadline. The USA attempted to throw a spanner in the works, trying by all means to prevent Russia from bol-

stering its strategic power, and insistently urged the Ukraine to scrap the bombers, promising to finance the disposal.

Nevertheless, the American plans were foiled. In early August 1999, Russia and the Ukraine finally drafted an intergovernmental agreement on the transfer of eight fully serviceable Tu-160s, three Tu-95MSs and 575 Kh-55, Kh-55SM and Kh-22NA cruise missiles (the latter type was carried by the Tu-22M3), plus ground support equipment, to Russia. This was to offset the Ukraine's US$275 million outstanding debt for Russian natural gas deliveries. Having no money to settle the debt, the Ukraine had to agree. The total worth of the bombers was approximately US$285 million.

On September 6, 1999, Vladimir V. Putin, the then Prime Minister of Russia, signed a directive in Yalta formally approving this draft agreement. The same directive ordered the creation of a Russian interdepartmental work group which would work out the actual agreement between the governments of the Russian Federation and the Ukraine on the transfer of strategic aviation systems and associated equipment. The group was headed by Aleksey L. Koodrin, Russia's first deputy Minister of Finance. The Russian MoD was represented in the work group by first Vice-Minister of Defence Nikolay V. Mikhailov (deputy head and permanent secretary), the Air Force C-in-C Army General Anatoliy M. Kornukov and Maj.-Gen. Pyotr D. Kazazayev; the latter was then Deputy Commander of the 37th VA (Engineering Aviation Service), but since a certain government official level was required for executing government directives, he was listed as the C-in-C's reviewer. Besides, the structure of work group included representatives from the Foreign Ministry, the Ministry of Taxes and Duties, the Minis-

Above: A better view of "15 Red" as it rolls past the camera, displaying its Ukrainian Air Force insignia – a bit grimy but very much alive. Note the extended landing lights under the nose.

Left: "14 Red" was one more of the few Tu-160s to wear full UAF insignia.

Right: Here the same bomber is pictured at Poltava AB in late September 1994 during the Shuttle Raid 50th anniversary celebrations. Note the visiting B-52 (a 2nd Bomb Wing aircraft) and B-1B and their supporting McDonnell Douglas KC-10A Extender tanker.

550

Left: "16 Red" wearing no insignia was one of the eight Tu-160s transferred to Russia in 1999–2000.

Below left: Tu-160 "26 Red" without insignia takes off from Priluki on its way to Poltava for preservation at the Ukrainian Air Force Museum.

Bottom left: Some of the *Blackjacks* were transferred in full UAF insignia, such as "12 Red" shown here with the landing gear in mid-retraction. The roundels on the wings are evident.

Right: "15 Red" leaves Ukrainian soil, heading for its new home in Engels.

try of State Property, the Ministry of Economics, the Gazprom natural gas company, the Russian Aerospace Agency and the governmental body of the Russian Federation. The group was to define the nomenclature, quantity and cost of the property to be transferred from Ukraine to Russia and the transfer procedures.

The Ukrainian delegation was headed by Vice-Minister of Economics V. A. Choomakov (the head of the work group). The work groups held two sessions, and the joint draft agreement was approved on September 30, 1999.

On October 8, 1999, at a meeting of the governmental delegations in Yalta the Agreement between the government of the Russian Federation and the Ukrainian Cabinet of Ministers on the transfer of the strategic missile carriers, cruise missiles and support equipment was finally signed.

On October 20, 1999, a group of 37th VA specialists numbering 65 men led by Maj.-Gen. Pyotr D. Kazazayev flew to the Ukraine aboard a Russian Air Force Il-78 tanker to take charge of the newly-acquired bombers. Having landed at Uzin AB, the *Midas* disgorged part of the group tasked with accepting and ferrying the three Tu-95MSs, while the greater part of the group headed by Kazazayev departed for Priluki in the same Il-78 the following morning.

At Priluki, right after the Russian personnel had been assigned their temporary accommodation, a briefing took place with the participation of the Ukrainian military led by S. A. Osipov, the CO of the resident bomber regiment. At the briefing it was decided to tow the Tu-160s across the hardstand of the maintenance base, two at a time, and move them to the flight line. At the maintenance base the bombers were guarded by Ukrainian servicemen; on the flight line this responsibility would pass to the Russians. The management of the Ukrainian base declared immediately that no jet fuel or automotive fuel (petrol and diesel fuel) was available and the tech staff would have to be transported jointly by the Russians and the Ukrainians. The vehicle assigned for carting the tech staff around the base was dubbed "Santa Maria" (after Christopher Columbus' caravel) by the local wits.

Originally the Russians intended to fill the *Blackjacks'* tanks from the Il-78, but the bomber needed to be towed up to tanker first. A serviceable tug was available in the base's motor vehicle pool, but there was no driver to drive it! The regiment's Deputy CO (Armament) V. M. Makagon gave orders to allocate two empty TZ-22 refuelling bowsers (KrAZ-258B1 6x4 conventional tractor units with 22,000-litre/4,840 Imp gal tanker semitrailers); these were filled up from the Il-78 and then transferred the fuel to the bomber. As the saying goes, if the mountain won't come to Prophet Muhammed, then Prophet Muhammed goes to the mountain.

Tu-160 "10 Red" (c/n 84906217, f/n 6-01) was the first machine selected for handover and preparation for the flight to Engels. Most of the Ukrainian *Blackjacks* had not flown for three or four years but this aircraft was a notable exception, having participated in the parade in Kreshchatik (Kiev's main street) on August 24, 1998, on occasion of the Ukraine's Independence Day. The jets sat with empty tanks. Even to start up the APU it was necessary to fill two tons (4,410 lb) of kerosene in each aircraft's tanks. It has to be said that, despite sitting idle for a long time, the general condition of the bombers was not too bad. The aircraft had 90% of the designated service life remaining on them. All the aircraft were fully equipped and came complete with a full set of manuals and 'ship's papers'. They had been diligently prepared for storage – it was obvious that the local tech staff took their job seriously.

The acceptance of the bombers by the Russian party began on October 22. By then the first of the Tu-160s selected by the Russians was ready for engine running. This warrants a more detailed description, since the aircraft had not even been towed at all for the past eight years, never mind flying!

The tanks of "10 Red" were filled with the required two tons of fuel which the Russians managed to wheedle out of the Ukrainians. The electrics engineers started up the APU, using a ground power unit (GPU), and then began warming up the avionics bays and flight deck by means of the onboard air conditioning system (ACS). Each and every avionics module was carefully examined, removed from its rack and dried to remove condensation before it could be switched on. The drying was done right in the flight deck, using the ACS; the flight deck was filled with such dense steam it looked like a darn steam bath! Majors V. M. Toptygin, A. A. Kurkanin, Ye. V. Sofiï, V. N. Aleksandrov and V. A. Moskalyov, Captains V. I. Stolerov, S. V. Balabonin, G. S. Fedorenko and V. V. Lichman worked with the onboard equipment. Defying the

Left and below left: "24 Red," one of the Tu-160s with no insignia, was the first to be broken up on 16th November 1998. Here a heavy-duty mobile crane lifts the severed tail section.

Bottom left: A special demolition machine (known in Russian slang as *koo***sa***chiyekska***vah***tor* – "biting excavator") chews off the flight deck section of a Ukrainian Tu-160.

cold and biting wind, Majors V. I. Doodin and S. A. Kalinin, Captains N. A. Bederov, A. A. Dobryukha, D. V. Bobyr' and A. P. Russkikh examined the airframe and engines, eliminating the defects that came to light. Maj. Yu. S. Kalinin supervised the work of the ground personnel.

On October 23, the second Tu-160, "16 Red" (c/n 82905836, f/n 5-03), was towed to the maintenance base from the storage area. The next day it was jacked up for landing gear checks, which turned into a real can of worms. First, the electric pump on the right-hand hydraulic jack failed; undeterred, the technicians began to work the manually driven back-up pump. Then the hydraulic fluid in the jacks ran out. The ground crew replenished the fluid and eventually managed to lift the aircraft. It seemed that the gear checks could finally begin. Then, however, it turned out that no UPG-300 hydraulics test vehicle (*oostanovka dlya proverki ghidravliki*) was available to build up the pressure in the bomber's hydraulic system! The APU had to be started up to create the necessary pressure.

On October 25, Tu-160 "15 Red" (c/n 83905953, f/n 5-05) was towed to the maintenance base hardstand.

The Russian delegation ran into daily problems with ground support equipment availability. For several days the situation with fuel, oil and lubricants remained dire. The reply of Deputy CO Makagon was always the same: *"There's no kerosene, no petrol, and no diesel fuel either."* Still, a solution was always found in the end. Hydraulic fluid was only delivered by 2000 hours local time on October 27, and then only enough for one aircraft ("10 Red"). According to plans, five Tu-160s should have been at the maintenance base by October 27; in reality there were only three because the airfield tug had broken down.

Preparation for ferrying "10 Red" to Engels began on October 28. That day there had been delay upon delay since the early morning – first it turned out that "Santa Maria" had not been refuelled in time, then the GPU and the UGZS.M-AR nitrogen charging vehicle (*oonifitseerovannaya gazozaryadnaya stahntsiya* – standardised gas charger unit; A = *azot* – nitrogen) were not allowed to leave the motor vehicle pool.

All the same it was necessary to tow the bomber to the runway for engine checks at all power settings; should the engines be run on the maintenance base hardstand, the jet blast would simply blow away all structures located behind the plane. A KrAZ-255B1 6x6 conventional prime mover was on site and would do for the purpose, but its tyres were totally worn out and could not provide the necessary traction! Besides, regiment CO Osipov had forbidden the use of the runway until a Ukrainian Air Force Il-78 tanker had landed at Uzin AB; Priluki was its designated alternate airfield, and the weather service had given a storm warning, which meant a diversion was probable. Once a representative of the local motor depot had been summoned airside, the tug availability problem was resolved, and the fuel transfer from the TZ-22 to the bomber's tanks could begin. The refuelling took nearly two hours, but when it was finished the tug still was not there! Lt.-Col. Osadchiy, the commander of the local aircraft maintenance base, clarified the situation: *"There will be no tug – the driver is nowhere to be found, but we keep looking"* (again!). After standing speechless for ten seconds or so, the Russian ground crew took the decision to tow the Tu-160 with the KrAZ-255B1, augmenting it with an APA-5 (a GPU on an Ural-375D 6x6 conventional army lorry chassis) connected by a rigid towbar. This, too, was easier said than done – the "sacred hour" (lunch time) had come, and after lunch the local drivers needed a siesta. Towage was postponed once again.

In the afternoon "10 Red" was at length towed to the runway. The engine running procedure was performed by Col. Aleksey R. Serebryakov, the CO of the 1096th TBAP based in Engels and operating six Tu-160s. No sooner had the first engine begun spooling up than some sort of liquid started dripping and pouring from everywhere on the aircraft. The start-up was aborted and the entire Russian ground personnel on site rushed to the machine; fortunately, however, the liquid turned out to be plain water, not fuel. Serebryakov ran the engines in all modes, cycled the wings and checked the operation of the control system. All systems functioned normally. After starting all four engines the crew was even authorised to taxi down the runway a little bit. When the work was done the commander reported that virtually no faults had been discovered; this again bore testimony to the reliability of the strategic aircraft created in Soviet days.

Right: Maj.-Gen. Pyotr D. Kazazayev, Deputy Commander of the 37th VA, played a key role in the transfer deal.

Having eliminated some minor faults in the aircraft's systems, the personnel started preparing for working on the second bomber, while Gen. Pyotr D. Kazazayev reported to the Russian Air Force C-in-C that the first *Blackjack* was ready for the positioning flight to Engels. Here is how Kazazayev describes the first days of team's sojourn at Priluki:

"On arrival at Priluki I went immediately to the airfield, to the part of it where the Tu-160s were parked. The area was surrounded by a barbed wire fence, and inside it was a Ukrainian guard post. As I was in military uniform, I went through this post unhindered and went immediately to the aircraft which had been half reduced to scrap metal. What struck me at once was that the Americans and Ukrainians had seemingly made a lot of effort to cut up the wing centre section (the wing pivot box – *Auth.*) *– and failed. It lay*

Below: Russian (right) and Ukrainian Air Force officers discuss matters associated with the transfer of the bombers.

Tu-160 "17 Red" with the name *Priluki* applied in stylised Old Slavic script and the city crest

there, still in one piece, and did not succumb to these efforts; apparently the Americans were having trouble with the scrapping of these aeroplanes, which says a lot about the power of Tupolev OKB design school (sic – Auth.).

One thing that hurt me personally, as an aviation engineer, very much was that the scrapped aircraft included a machine with only 44 hours TTSN. It seems that the best machine in the unit had purposely been chosen for scrapping. This fact testifies that our aircraft were, are and will be the best in the world and, as such, are certainly the bane of our competitors' existence.

However, it was time to get down to work. That same day our technicians and engineers towed the first aircraft to the territory of the regiment's maintenance facility and started assessing its condition and preparing the machine for ferrying. I have to point out at once that the men set to work with a will, being aware that they were, in effect, saving these unique flying machines. I can give you such a comparison: when we first saw all the aircraft standing in the so-called 'reservation' they were a sorry sight – they reminded us of plucked chickens. And when we prepared the first machine and performed full power-on checks, it began to look like a white swan."

The first Tu-160 was ready to depart on the eleventh day after the Russian delegation's arrival at Priluki. As early as November 1, the Russian military had filed a request via the command posts of the Russian and Ukrainian Air Forces, requesting permission to fly two aircraft to the Russian Federation – one Tu-160 from Priluki and one Tu-95MS from Uzin which had also been prepared by the Russian tech staff.

Yet, this was exactly when the problems began in earnest – the Ukrainian party, seemingly regretting the deal, denied permission to fly for three days, demanding some fictitious 'documents giving export clearance'. Maj.-Gen. Kazazayev addressed the

Opposite bottom: Although it did not wear UAF insignia, Tu-160 "17 Red" (seen here at Priluki AB in the winter of 1999-2000) was named *Priluki* and bore the city crest.

Top: The personnel at Engels lines up to greet Tu-160 "17 Red" as it taxies in after landing.

Above: The captain of "17 Red" flies the Russian flag from the flight deck window on arrival.

Above right: The Russian flag is hoisted on the first aircraft ("10 Red") during the welcoming ceremony. This became standard procedure for the transferred bombers

Right: Col. Aleksey R. Serebryakov has the honour of hoisting the flag after ferrying another *Blackjack* to Engels.

Far left: Col. Aleksey R. Serebryakov, one of the pilots who flew the ex-Ukrainian Tu-160s to Russia.

Centre left: Maj. Yuriy G. Paltusov in the WSO's seat of a Tu-160.

Left: Lt.-Col. Igor' V. Skitskiy, another Russian pilot involved in the ferrying operation.

Ukrainian Air Force Commander-in-Chief Col.-Gen. Viktor I. Strel'nikov with this problem; thanks to his help, he was able to address the Ukrainian Minister of Defence, who in turn reported the issue to the then Prime Minister of the Ukraine Valeriy P. Pustovoytenko, requesting that the go-ahead to ferry the two bombers to Russia be given ahead of the official Ukrainian Cabinet of Ministers directive concerning the intergovernmental agreement. After much bureaucratic wrangling (including a special official telegram from the State Customs Committee of Russia) the clearance was finally given on November 4.

The Russian maintenance specialists started preparing the bombers for departure. After noon the Ukrainian Border Guards personnel arrived at the base, examined the aeroplane, looked inside the flight deck and gave the crew permission to take their seats. However, the Ukrainian customs officials (whose clearance was required) were still absent. The crew of Col. Aleksey R. Serebryakov stayed in the aircraft for about an hour but the border guards did not allow anybody else to approach the aircraft. Maj.-Gen. Kazazayev recalls this episode as follows:

"All of a sudden I heard the APU cranking up, followed in short order by the first engine. Totally bewildered, as the customs officials were not there [to give authorisation], I drove to the control tower and, on entering the driveway to it, saw a car with the customs officers. I stopped my car and climbed out. Noticing the [Russian] general, they accosted me and asked why the aircraft was starting up without customs inspection. Being in no amiable mood, I retorted: 'What took you so long? You might as well have come at midnight.' Whereupon they cancelled the take-off without giving any plausible explanation.

We had no choice but to re-submit the request for the next day. Having had a talk with the Ukrainian Air Force command and reported the scandalous actions of the customs officials, I received assurance that next day (that is, 5th November) the chief of the Customs Service would arrive from Chernigov to attend the take-off.

Next day we began preparing the aircraft for take-off first thing in the morning. Around 10 AM the 'big brass,' as we call it, did indeed arrive from Chernigov. We were introduced to each other; what struck me was that the man was wearing a very handsome uniform and general's epaulets, and his peak-cap featured very expensive gold embroidery. I have to say that the customs chief turned out to be a fairly decent man; in my presence he gave the customs officers I spoke to yesterday a dressing-down for negligence and ordered them to complete the formalities within 30 minutes – and so they did, by the way.

Right: Russian Air Force Tu-160 "03 Red" flies over the Russian countryside with the wings at maximum sweep.

Left: 121st GvTBAP officers and their wives welcome an arriving Tu-160 captained by Igor' V. Skitskiy at Engels AB with flowers in early 2000. Sister ship "11 Red" one of the ex-Ukrainian machines, can be seen in the background.

Two versions of the Russian Air Force's Long-Range Aviation badge featuring the Tu-160 as the DA's most advanced aircraft and the motto *Ot**va**ga, master**stvo**, do**sto**instvo, chest'* (Courage, skill, dignity, honour).

When the crew started the engines and the bomber started taxying out to the runway, the customs general asked me if he could videotape the take-off. I gave my consent, asking what he wanted it for – especially considering that there was a thick fog on the field [and the video would be of poor quality]. He told me that he had orders to deliver video proof of the bomber's take-off to the Ukraine's Security Council.

Finally, at 1530 hours on 5th November 1999, Col. Aleksey R. Serebryakov took up the Tu-160 from Priluki and set course for Russia, having first made a low farewell pass over the garrison and the airfield. I was contacted on the phone by the Ukrainian Air Force Commander-in-Chief Viktor I. Strel'nikov, who told me that a group of media correspondents from Kiev would shortly arrive at the airfield and asked me if I would kindly give an interview for the local TV channels. I told him that I would have to report to my superiors first and ask for permission, and if it was granted I would be glad to oblige.

Having reported to the Air Force C-in-C Army General Anatoliy M. Kornukov, I obtained permission. In the interview I said many a word of praise for the technical staff of the Ukrainian Air Force who had maintained the bombers as best they could and assisted us in preparing them for the flight; the first plane departed, many of the local servicemen came to see it off in full parade dress. And not to the grave, mind you, but to a place where, I hope, it will

Russian Air Force Tu-160 "04 Red" *Ivan Yarygin*, 121st GvTBAP

Above: 121st GvTBAP Tu-160 "04 Red" seen in 1999 with the name *Ivan Yarygin* applied in stylised Old Slavic script. The blue/yellow nose "feathers" and the fin flash are not yet applied.
Below: 121st GvTBAP Tu-160 "02 Red" was named *Vasiliy Reshetnikov* in December 1999.

Russian Air Force Tu-160 "02 Red" *Vasiliy Reshetnikov*, 1096th TBAP

find a long and happy life – to spite those who had been destroying these aeroplanes."

The departure of the first "White Swan" from the Ukraine to Russia was also closely watched by the Americans from the scrap yard; they must have been disappointed to watch their 'prey' get away. Once the first two aircraft had returned to Russia, the next group of technical staff led by the DA's Deputy Chief Engineer Col. V. V. Ghermanovich was formed in December of the same year, departing to the Ukraine; in 2000, this team finished the preparation and ferrying of the remaining aircraft. Among the Tu-160s transferred to Russia were "12 Red" – the very aircraft Frank C. Carlucci had hit his head on in 1988 – and "18 Red," which had been displayed at Machoolishchi AB in 1992. Most of them kept their original tactical codes; "22 Red" was the only exception, being recoded "14 Red" (almost *in memoriam* of the original "14 Red" that, as already mentioned, had been destroyed).

Overcoming the considerable difficulties associated with the shortage of ground support equipment, social problems in day-by-day life, problems with spares deliveries (all damaged and time-expired items were replaced with new ones delivered from Russia by an Il-78), the engineers and technicians of the Russian Air Force nevertheless coped with their task. By the end of January 2000, all 11 bombers covered by the agreement had been flown to their new home in Engels. The last of the transferees to land at Engels-2 AB were the *Blackjacks* coded "11 Red" and "18 Red." The latter aircraft had not flown for nearly nine years and was in pretty bad shape; it took a maximum of effort from the Russian tech staff on temporary duty at Priluki AB to return the bomber to airworthy status. The transfer was completed on February 21, 2000. Five of the Tu-160s were ferried by a crew comprising captain Lt.-Col. Aleksey R. Serebryakov, co-pilot Maj. Aleksey V. Kalinin, navigator Lt.-Col. Igor' A. Sazonov and WSO Maj. Yuriy G. Paltusov; the other three were ferried by captain Lt.-Col. Igor' V. Skitskiy, co-pilot Lt.-Col. Vladimir Adamov, navigator Lt.-Col. N. M. Barsukov and WSO Maj. S. P. Alyoshin. The cruise missiles were delivered to Russia by rail.

As one might imagine, in Engels the aircraft and their crews were given a grand reception. After the bombers wearing Ukrainian insignia (or grey pentagons where the red stars had been painted out) had taxied in to the hardstand, the Russian national flag rose over them. The then DA Commander Lt. Gen. Mikhail M. Oparin and the Air Force's Chief of Combat Training Arkadiy Barsukov presented the crews which had ferried the bombers with valuable gifts. A new page in the history of the ex-Ukrainian, and now Russian, Tu-160s had begun. The bombers appeared to be in pretty good condition; nevertheless, all of them were given an overhaul by the manufacturer, the KAPO plant in Kazan', after arrival in Russia.

According to Oparin, all the aircraft transferred from the Ukraine were in good condition (presumably this means after all defective or missing units had been replaced – Auth.). The engines had used up only about 10% of their service life and would not need to be replaced for more than twenty years.

Thus the 121st GvTBAP, which until then had operated six Tu-160s, now had 15 Tu-160s – enough to equip two full squadrons (a second *Blackjack* squadron was indeed formed in due course). All the other Tu-160s in the Ukraine were destroyed – except one,

The 121st GvTBAP unit crest. with a front view of the Tu-160.

A pennant marking the 121st *Sevastopol'skiy* Red Banner GvTBAP's 60th birthday which was celebrated at Engels-2 AB on 27th June 2000. Note the blue and yellow "sunburst" colours and "star, wings and propeller" emblem of the Soviet Air Force flag which were inherited by the Russian Air Force.

The badge of the 22nd *Donbasskaya* GvTBAD, also with the Tu-160 and the Air Force flag motif.

Heave-ho! 121st GvTBAP armourers roll an inert Kh-55 practice round on a dolly past Tu-160 "04 Red."

Here the same aircraft takes off at Engels past the Tu-134UBLs of the unit's Sqn 3 with their trademark pointed noses and full-length "lightning bolts" (interspersed with a few Tu-134Sh-2 *Crusty-A* navigator trainers in an equally distinctive red/white TWA-style livery). The Tu-22s of the former 121st and 203rd GvTBAPs at the co-located 6213th Aircraft Storage and Disposal Centre can be seen further down the line.

which has been preserved for posterity at the Ukrainian Air Force Museum in Poltava.

The irritation of the USA caused by the transfer of eight *Blackjacks* and three *Bear-Hs* to Russia passed largely unnoticed for the outside world. However, people who were directly engaged in the negotiations recall that Washington had expressed its displeasure to Kiev at the MoD delegation level in connection with the transfer of the 11 aircraft to Moscow. The formal pretext was that the Raytheon company tasked with the scrapping had been deprived of a part of the planned work (and hence money), but the real reason was that the transfer had given Washington some food for thought. The Russian Air Force was then due to field two brand-new air-launched cruise missile types (the conventional Kh-101 and the nuclear-tipped Kh-102) capable of striking at targets within 5,000 km (3,105 miles) from the launch point with a circular error probable of just a few metres. Together with the strategic bombers available to Russia it would appreciably reinforce the airborne component of the "former" potential adversary's nuclear triad (and the "former" bit was open to doubt); the Russian Air Force could strike at targets on the territory of any state without coming within range of its air defences.

Operations Continue

Even before the second Tu-160 squadron was established, the 37th VA resumed intensive combat training in keeping with personal instructions from the President – a decision further confirmed, no doubt, by NATO's intervention in ex-Yugoslavia in 1999 (Operation *Allied Force*). The war in ex-Yugoslavia was primarily an air war – something the decision makers in Russia could not miss.

Thus, April 1998, saw yet another command and staff exercise of the Russian Armed Forces. In the course of the exercise two *Blackjacks* from Engels flew an ultra-long-range sortie to the

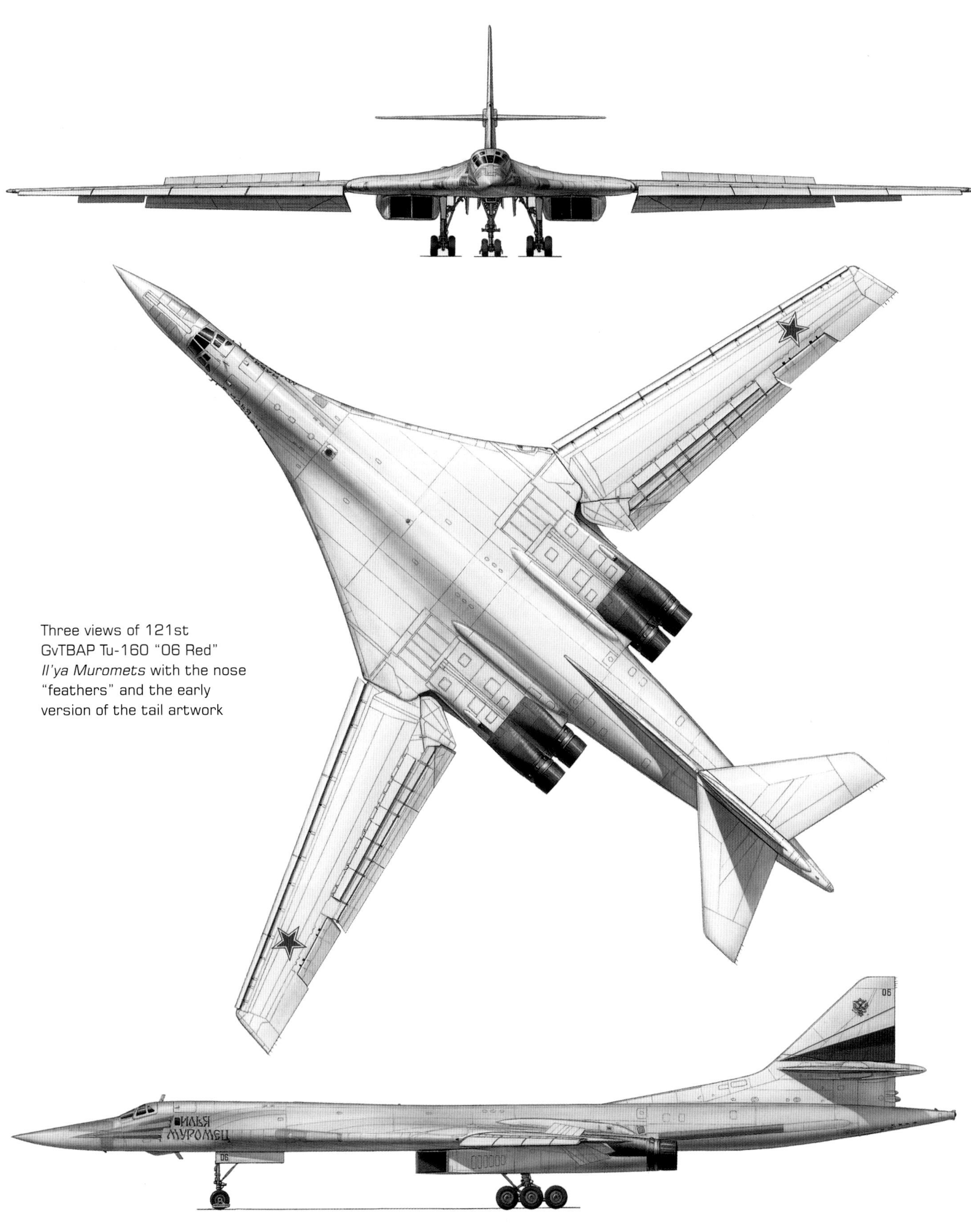

Three views of 121st GvTBAP Tu-160 "06 Red" *Il'ya Muromets* with the nose "feathers" and the early version of the tail artwork

Left: "06 Red" *Il'ya Muromets* No.2, one of the first two *Blackjacks* to be christened.

Below: Tu-160s "15 Red," "02 Red" *Vasiliy Reshetnikov* and "03 Red" *Pavel Taran* on a winter morning in the early 2000s. The latter aircraft is due to be refuelled by a TZ-22.

Right: Now wearing the nose "feathers" and the fin flash, "04 Red" is readied for a sortie in the 2000s.

Below right: Another view of "06 Red" – the one which retained the name *Il'ya Muromets* (the other one, "05 Red," was later renamed). Note the new style of the tail flash which became the fleetwide standard on the Russian Tu-160s until the 2010s.

Tu-160 "06 Red" *Il'ya Muromets*, 121st GvTBAP, mid-2000s

Starboard side view of Tu-160 "06 Red"

Here Tu-160 "04 Red" is shown as it looked in the 2000s

Tu-160 "01 Red" *Mikhail Gromov* with early-style fin flash and missile launch markings

Above: By 2003 Tu-160 "01 Red" *Mikhail Gromov* had exchanged the early low-set fin flash and the Russian "double eagle" (as worn by "05 Red" and "06 Red") for a high-set fin flash with the red star below it.

Right and above right: Spotlessly clean Tu-160 "11 Red" *Vasiliy Sen'ko* is resplendent in its white finish with nose and tail colours. Note the Gold Star Medals marking the Twice HSU status of the person after whom the bomber is named.

Left: A red-painted Kh-55SM instrumented test round coded "649 Black" on a ground handling dolly. Note Russian coat-of-arms on the fuselage aft of the the conformal tanks. The rear ends of the latter are specially shaped to clear the wings as they deploy.

Starboard side view of Tu-160 "04 Red"

Starboard side view of Tu-160 "01 Red" in early colours

Tu-160 "11 Red" *Vasiliy Sen'ko*, 121st GvTBAP, mid-2000s

North Pole. A third Tu-160 captained by Guards Lt. Col. Aleksey R. Serebryakov launched a Kh-55SM cruise missile which scored a hit on the designated practice target.

Since the late 1990s, the resumption of missions flown outside Russia's borders and demonstrative exercises involving the use 'of all kinds of weapons' became a routine in the life of Long-Range Aviation crews. Another major exercise called ***Zapad-99*** (West-99) took place on June 21–25, 1999. On the closing day, a pair of Tu-160s and a pair of Tu-95MSs departed from Engels-2 AB, heading north. The *Blackjacks* were captained by Guards Lt.-Col. Igor' V. Skitskiy and Guards Lt.-Col. Vladimir A. Popov. After reaching a predesignated point over the North Sea they turned south-west, parting company near the Norwegian coast. The aircraft passed along the entire Norwegian coastline, making so-called "tactical" (that is, simulated) missile launches. Then one of the crews proceeded to the Ashuluk test range in southern Russia in southern Russia where a Kh-55SM missile was launched for real. The Tu-160s stayed airborne for 12 hours on that occasion – without IFR.

The Western media immediately raised Cain, claiming that "Russia was planning a nuclear attack on the USA" or that "Moscow had intruded into Icelandic airspace." Both claims were in fact false – the Russian Air Force's 37th Air Army had simply given another effective demonstration of its capabilities.

In the autumn of 1999, the Tu-160s taking part in a series of exercises performed flights towards the North American continent, demonstrating "Russia's response" to Operation *Allied Force* and to the eastward expansion of NATO. Part of the scenario involved flights to within a short distance of the North American continent. These exercises aroused special interest – not least due the fact that Long-Range Aviation activities were unmistakably linked to the hard-line military and political course pursued by the new Russian President Vladimir V. Putin and his team. In particular, as early as the mid-1990s, the 37th Air Army's missile carriers had practiced for the first time simulated 'nuclear strikes' against unpopulated regions of the country and over international waters as the strategy of an all-out nuclear war was revisited.

Yet another show of force in which the Tu-160 was involved took place on April 18–21, 2000, when the Russian Air Force held what was officially called a "flight and tactical exercise." As the Russian military put it, *"you have to show force at the right time*

Note that "11 Red" carried the two Gold Star medals on the starboard side only

Right: Here "11 Red" is seen taxying out onto the runway.

Below left: Lit by the low sun, Tu-160 "03 Red" *Pavel Taran* makes a splendid picture as it makes a low pass with the high-lift devices at the take-off setting.

Below: Still nameless, "17 Red" is caught by the camera a second before touchdown (note the fully deployed flaps). The aircraft could use a fresh coat of paint – the red stripe of the fin flash has faded to pink.

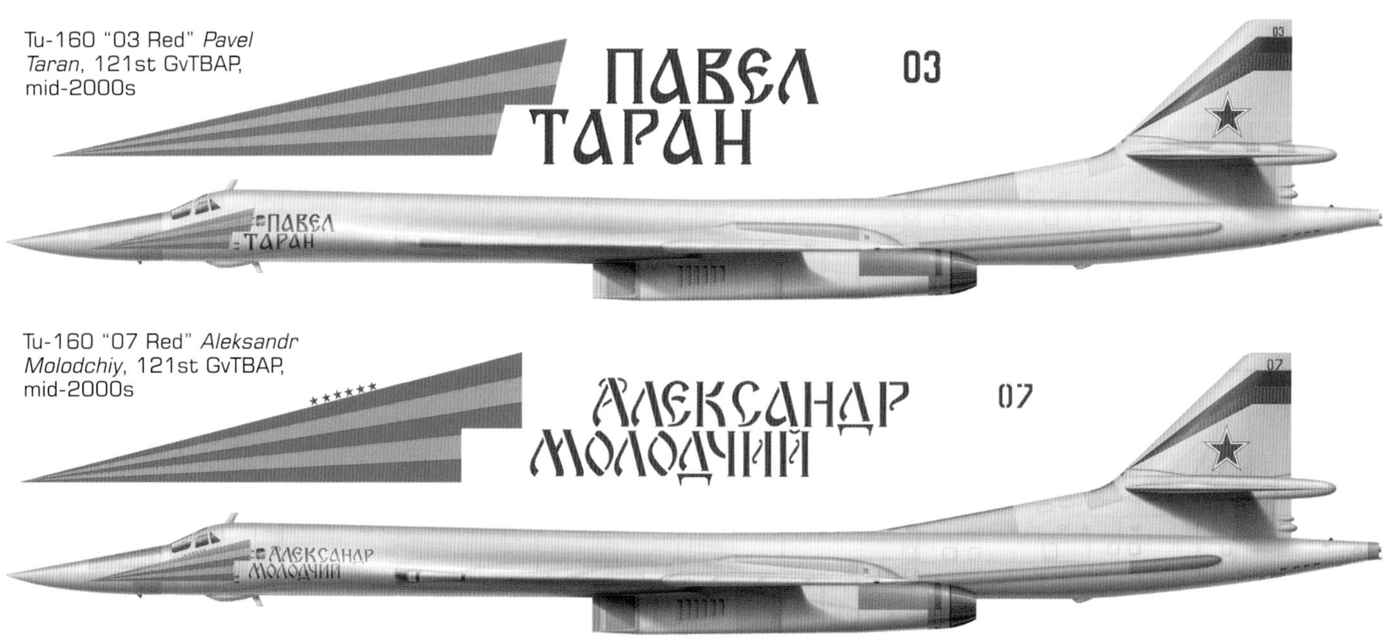

Tu-160 "03 Red" *Pavel Taran*, 121st GvTBAP, mid-2000s

Tu-160 "07 Red" *Aleksandr Molodchiy*, 121st GvTBAP, mid-2000s

Left and above left: Here "03 Red" *Pavel Taran* and "07 Red" *Aleksandr Molodchiy* are seen at Minsk-Machoolishchi AB during the joint Russian-Belorussian exercise *Shchit Soyooza-2006*.

Above: *Pavel Taran* streams its brake parachutes when landing at Machoolishchi for the exercise on June 21, 2006.

in order to avoid actually using force later." Si vis pacem, para bellum. The main purpose of the exercise was to "check the combat readiness of the aviation hardware after a prolonged grounding and improve the participants' proficiency." This time the ex-Ukrainian Tu-160s joined the fun, launching cruise missiles together with *Bear-Hs*, while Tu-22M3 bombers attacked their targets with free-fall bombs. Interaction with ground command, control and communications (C^3) centres, as well as targeting with the help of Ilyushin/Beriyev A-50 *Mainstay-A/B* airborne warning and control system (AWACS) aircraft during air defence penetration in an ECM environment, were also practiced.

The 2000 exercise featured an important "first" – for the first time the Russian Air Force practiced using precision-guided cruise missiles with conventional warheads. This again was a result of analysing the course of the First Gulf War (Operation *Desert Storm*) and the war in the former Yugoslavia where the USA had used Boeing AGM-109A Tomahawk cruise missiles extensively.

In 2003, for the first time in Russia's modern history, Tu-160 and Tu-95MS strategic missile carriers performed an ultra-long-range flight involving simulated launches of cruise missiles over the Indian Ocean. Moreover, in the course of Exercise *Zapad-2003* –

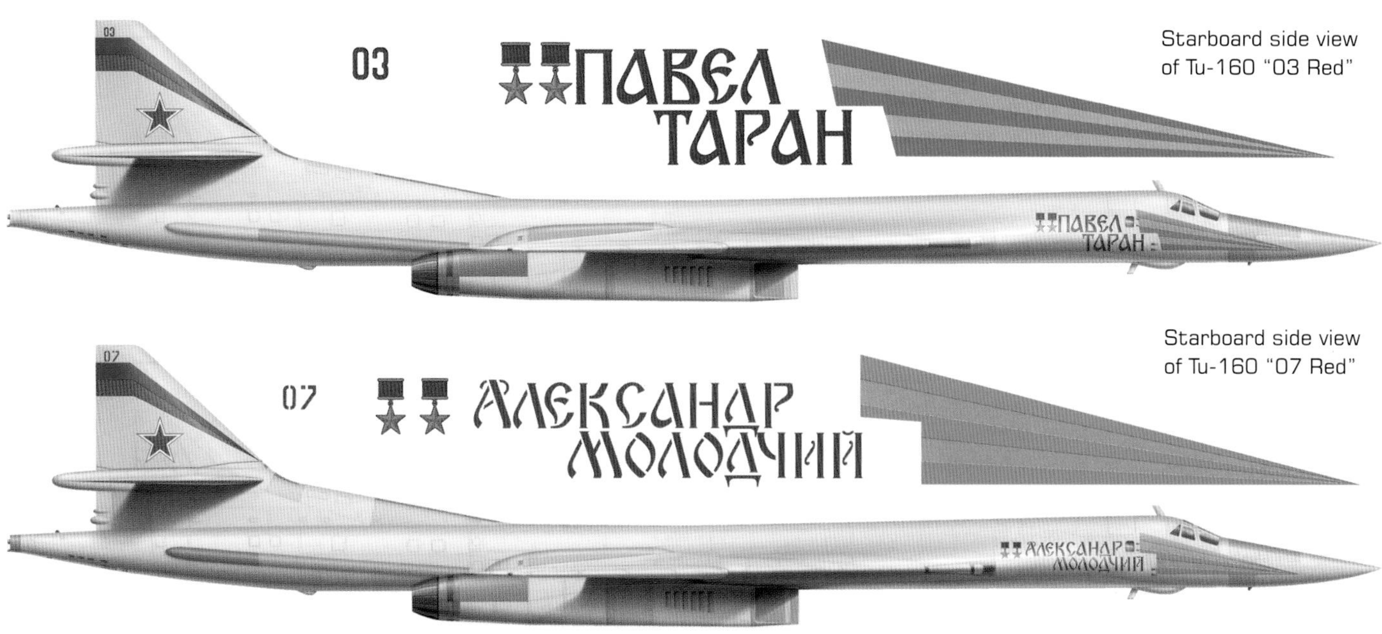

Starboard side view of Tu-160 "03 Red"

Starboard side view of Tu-160 "07 Red"

Above: The crew killed in the crash of Tu-160 "01 Red" on September 18, 2003. Left to right: Lt.-Col. Yuriy M. Deyneko (captain), Maj. Grigoriy A. Kolchin (navigator), Maj. Oleg N. Fedusenko (co-pilot) and Maj. Sergey M. Sukhorookov (WSO).

Below: Wreckage of "01 Red" at the crash site near Sovetskoye.

Opposite top: Crewmen in discussion beside Tu-160 "07 Red."

Bottom: The southeastern apron at Engels-2 AB with Tu-160s (top to bottom) "07 Red," "06 Red," "04 Red," and "03 Red."

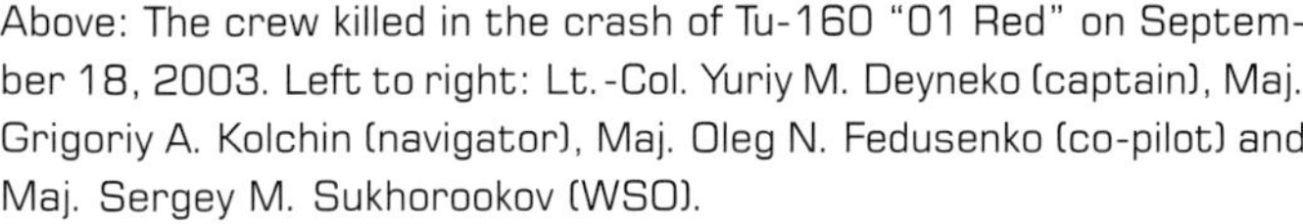

again for the first time in the post-Soviet period – Tu-160, Tu-95MS and Tu-22M3 bombers of the DA took off almost simultaneously from several bases across Russia and set off to carry out the assigned combat training tasks simultaneously in their designated areas, some of which lay far beyond the Russian borders. After a flight of many hours' duration along the designated routes the bombers performed live and simulated missile launches and dropped bombs on target ranges in northern and southern Russia. On May 11–16, more than 30 Long-Range Aviation aircraft were involved in the exercise, and its key episode, in the light of the war in Iraq, had a clearly anti-Western flavour – in particular, Tu-160s simulated a launch of Kh-55SMs against the atoll of Diego Garcia from a distance of 2,500 km (1,554 miles).

In August 2003, a pair of *Blackjacks* took part in Exercise *Vostok-2003* (East-2003) – a major command and staff conducted by the Pacific Fleet. In accordance with the exercise's scenario, the Tu-160s escorted by Su-27 fighters headed for a distant oceanic area (several thousand kilometres from the coast of Russia) where, acting on information from satellite-based intelligence and target designation assets, they detected and identified a notional enemy surface target and performed a simulated attack.

The Crash

As already mentioned in Chapter 3, the second production Tu-160 was lost in the course of the manufacturer's flight tests in March 1987, the Tupolev OKB test crew ejecting safely. Apart from that, the *Blackjack* did not suffer accident attrition for more than two decades. On September 18, 2003, however, disaster struck. That day a 121st GvTBAP Tu-160 coded "01 Red" and named *Mikhail Gromov* (c/n 82007617, f/n 7-01) – the first of the type to be delivered new to the Russian Air Force – departed from Engels-2 AB at 1030 hrs Moscow time, heading south-east towards Krasnyy Koot ('Red Corner', Saratov Region). It was making a routine check flight after an engine change (the No.4 engine had been replaced after a chip detector warning light had come on in the previous flight on September 11); there were no weapons on board. The aircraft was captained by 40-year-old Guards Lt.-Col. Yuriy M. Deyneko, the unit's Deputy CO (Chief of Flight Training). The crew also included co-pilot Guards Maj. Oleg N. Fedusenko, navigator Guards Maj. Grigoriy A. Kolchin (the unit's Chief Navigator) and WSO Guards Maj. Sergey M. Sukhorookov.

Everything was normal until the objective had been completed and it was time to return to base. 37 minutes after take-off, when the Tu-160 was approaching Engels from the south-east, an emergency developed with overwhelming speed. According to the preliminary report of the air accident investigation panel: *"as the aircraft descended from 2,100 m [6,890 ft] to 1,200 m [3,940 ft] the airframe started disintegrating, presumably as a result of a strong force applied to it which has not [yet] been determined, with consecutive fire warnings in three of the engines; the hydraulic and electric systems also failed. The emergency arose unexpectedly, without prior indication, and developed as an avalanche process within an extremely brief period (12 seconds)."*

The aircraft behaved abnormally, tending to enter a dive. At mission time 37 minutes 14 seconds the audio warning system indicated a failure of the Nos. 1 and 2 hydraulic system, a surge of all four engines and a fire in both port engines. (According to some reports, the fire warning for the No.2 engine came at 1107:19 hrs; followed by a similar warning for No.1 at 1107:25 hrs.)

In this dire situation Deyneko acted professionally and kept a level head. Getting his bearings, he steered the stricken bomber away from Stepnoye township (located about 45 km/29 miles from Engels-2 AB as the crow flies) and from the nearby subterranean gas reservoir – the largest one in Europe holding about 5 billion cubic metres (176,573,500,000 cu ft) of liquefied natural gas. The crew attempted to extinguish the fire and bring the aircraft under control. The captain advised the tower at Engels of the emergency at mission time 37 minutes 24 seconds. When it became obvious that the bomber was uncontrollable and was losing altitude rapidly, he ordered an ejection, the co-pilot initiating enforced ejection at 576 m (1,889 ft). The back-seaters ejected at 520 m (1,706 ft) and a vertical speed of 104 m/sec (341 ft/sec); the pilots followed suit at 280 m (918 ft) and 154 m/sec (505 ft/sec). A second later, however, the aircraft exploded in mid-air and the crew were caught by the blast which burned up their parachutes, leaving them no chances of survival. The Tu-160 hit the ground with 70° bank 7 km (4.35 miles) from Sovetskoye township, 41 km (25.46 miles) from the base; the second explosion on impact destroyed it utterly.

After this the remainder of the Russian Air Force's Tu-160 fleet were immediately grounded pending investigation. Unsurprisingly,

Алексей
Плохов
Валерий
Чкалов
17

Above: "07 Red" *Aleksandr Molodchiy* after an overhaul at KAPO. The nose flash was reinstated during the repaint but the fin flash was not.

Opposite page: The main flight line at Engels in the late 2000s. Some of the aircraft, including "15 Red" and "18 Red," are still nameless.

Below: Tu-160 "02 Red" *Vasiliy Reshetnikov* refuels from an IL-78 at high altitude.

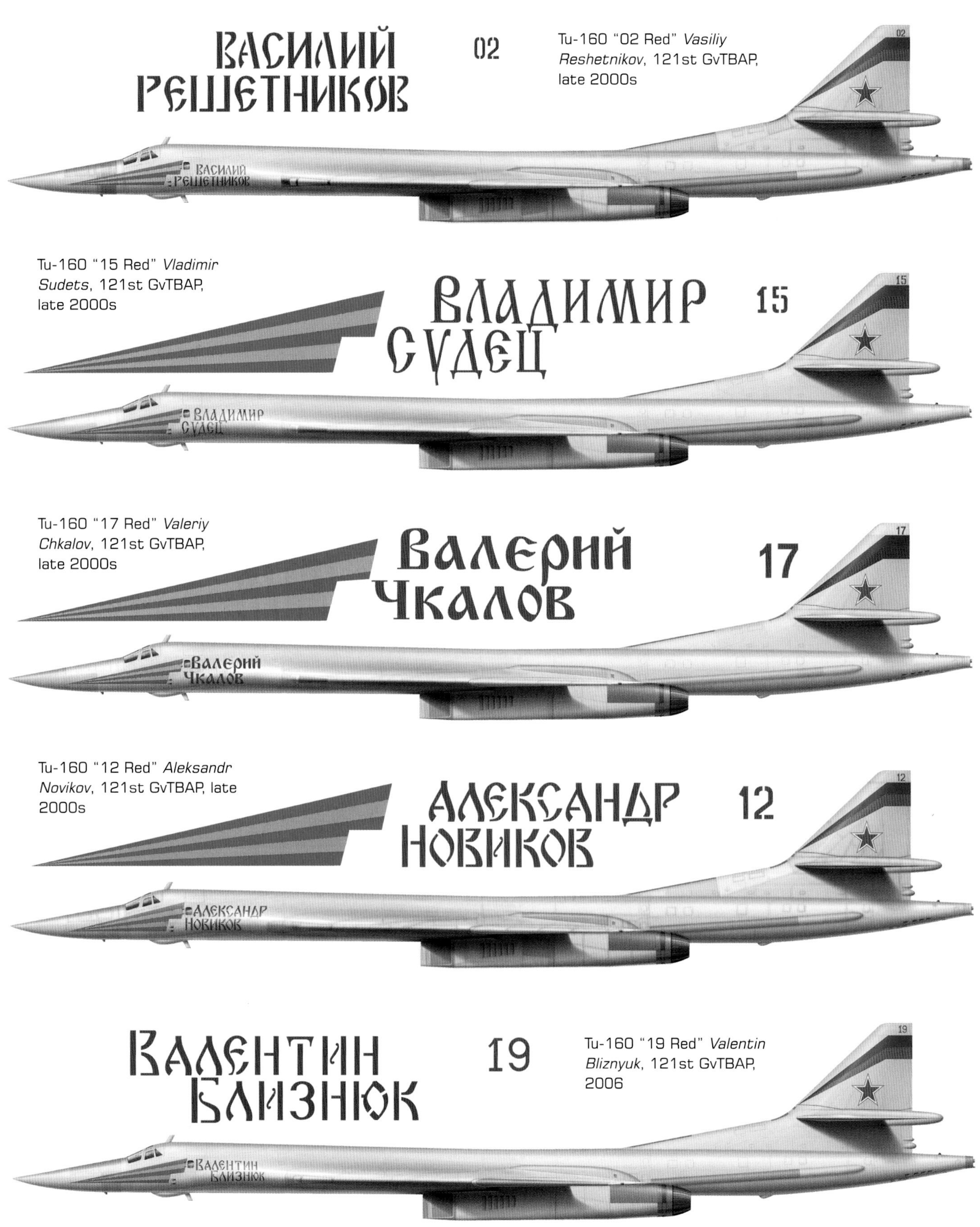

Tu-160 "02 Red" *Vasiliy Reshetnikov*, 121st GvTBAP, late 2000s

Tu-160 "15 Red" *Vladimir Sudets*, 121st GvTBAP, late 2000s

Tu-160 "17 Red" *Valeriy Chkalov*, 121st GvTBAP, late 2000s

Tu-160 "12 Red" *Aleksandr Novikov*, 121st GvTBAP, late 2000s

Tu-160 "19 Red" *Valentin Bliznyuk*, 121st GvTBAP, 2006

Starboard side view of "02 Red"

Starboard side view of "15 Red"

Starboard side view of "17 Red"

Starboard side view of "12 Red"

Starboard side view of "19 Red"

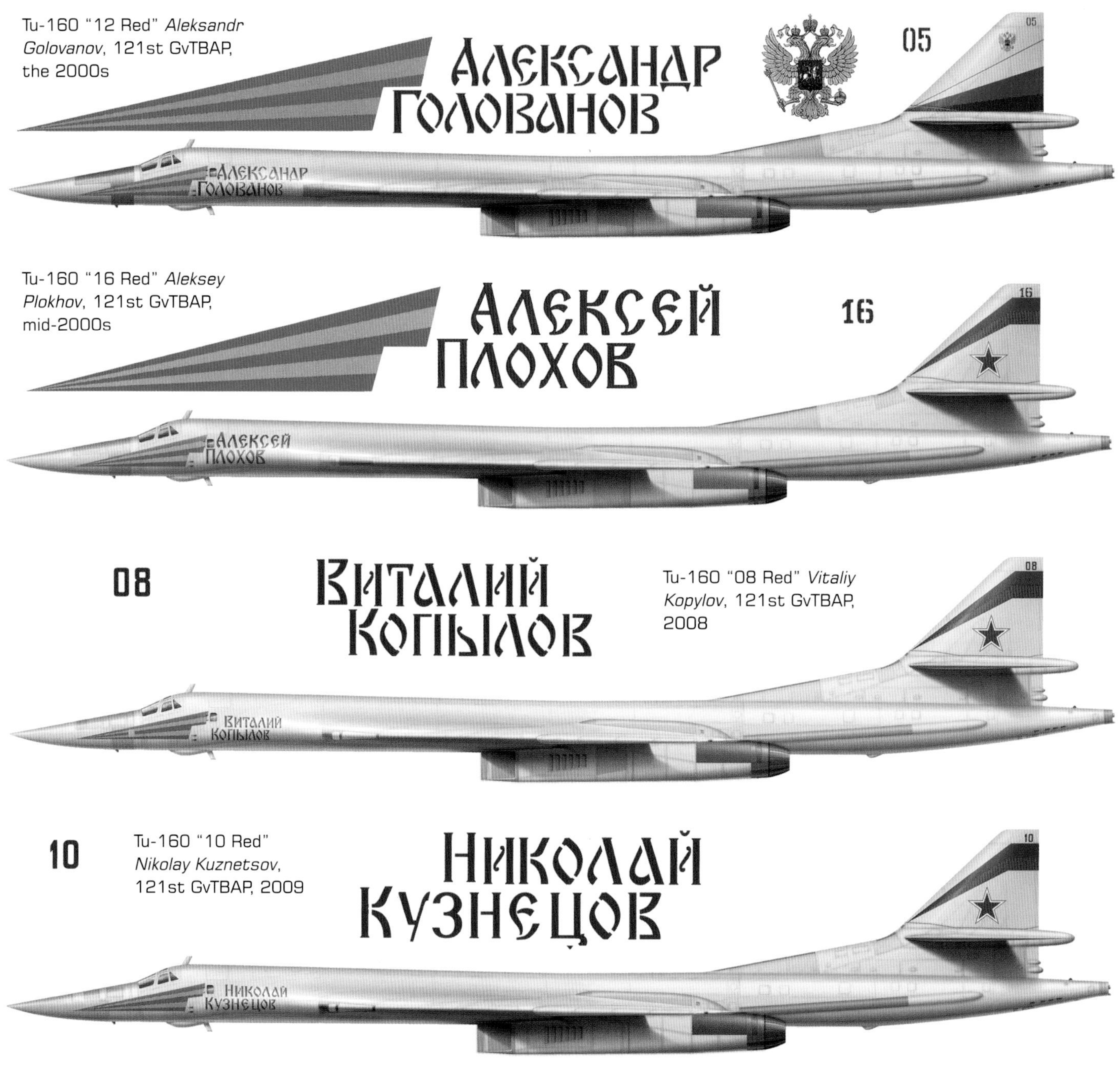

Tu-160 "12 Red" *Aleksandr Golovanov*, 121st GvTBAP, the 2000s

Tu-160 "16 Red" *Aleksey Plokhov*, 121st GvTBAP, mid-2000s

Tu-160 "08 Red" *Vitaliy Kopylov*, 121st GvTBAP, 2008

Tu-160 "10 Red" *Nikolay Kuznetsov*, 121st GvTBAP, 2009

the military were tight-lipped about any details of the accident, which were classified; the abovementioned preliminary report was not released until a couple of months later, and then only because the crash had provoked a public outcry and it was necessary to give the general public some explanation. Meanwhile, given the lack of official information, all manner of rumours and sensationalist theories started circulating, and not only in the yellow press; speaking at a press conference on September 29, Dmitriy F. Ayatskov, the then Governor of the Saratov Region in which Engels is situated, went so far as to suggest the aircraft had been blown out of the sky by a bomb planted by a saboteur! Eventually the cause of the crash was traced to a defect in the fuel tank venting system. With no air coming in as the fuel was burned off, partial vacuum had built up in the Nos. 1 and 2 wing tanks, eventually causing the tanks to implode and fail. Part of the wing skin and the air intake assemblies were ripped off, causing loss of control and engine surge; the escaping fuel came into contact with the engines, causing a massive fire and ultimately an explosion. The scenario was reproduced on a time-expired Tu-160 prototype airframe at Zhukovskiy as part of the investigation: the venting pipelines were blanked off, and the end result was an implosion and structural failure.

The grounding order was partially lifted and Tu-160 operations resumed (with certain restrictions) on November 5, 2003; on January 16, 2004, the restrictions were finally removed after modifica-

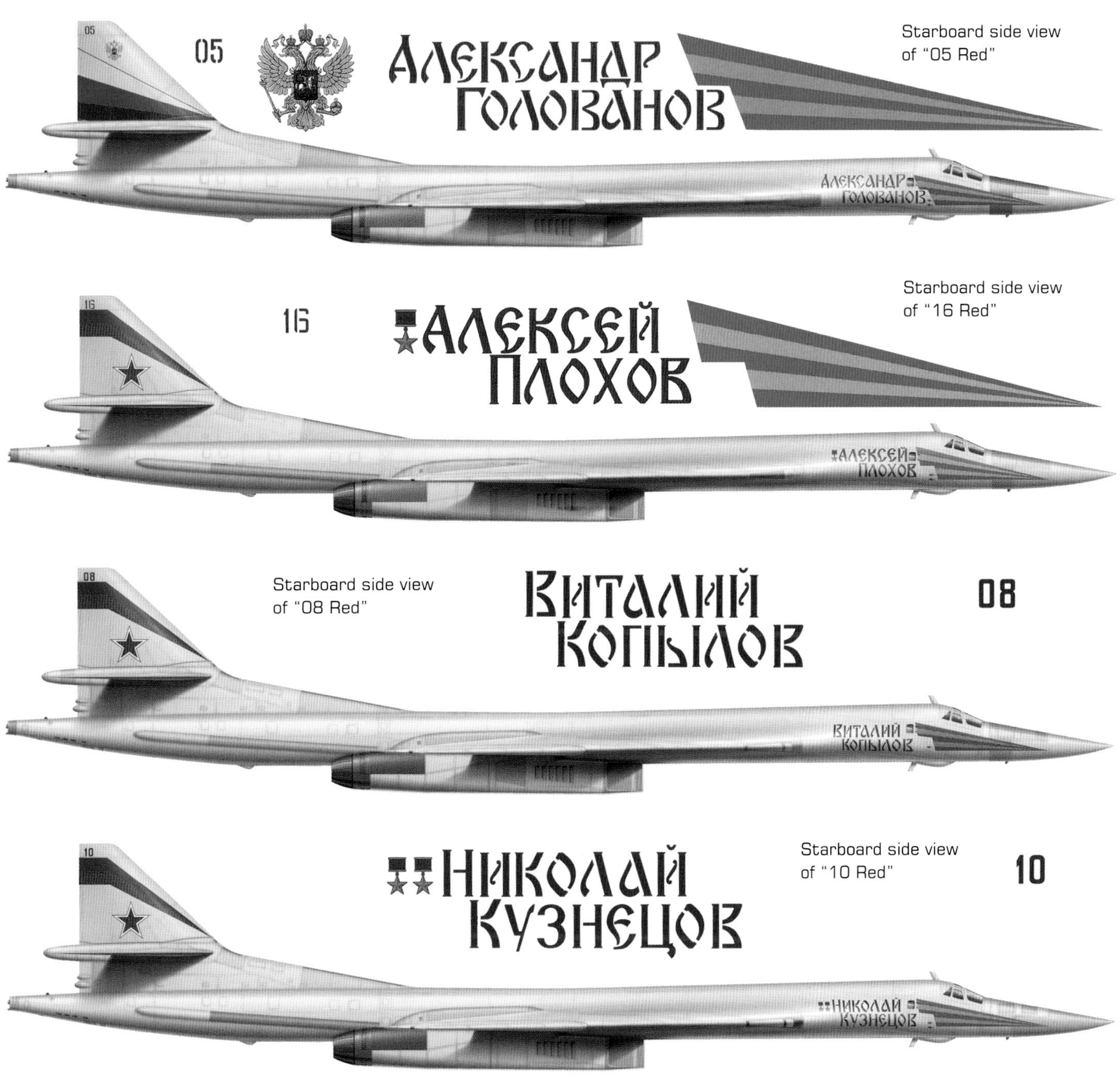

tions had been made to the fuel system and operations were back to normal. On November 22, 2003, Guards Lt.-Col. Yuriy M. Deyneko was posthumously awarded the Hero of Russia title (the modern equivalent of the HSU title) by Presidential decree. By the same decree Guards Maj. Oleg N. Fedusenko, Guards Maj. Grigoriy A. Kolchin and Guards Maj. Sergey M. Sukhorookov were posthumously awarded the Order of Courage.

More Exercises and Reforms

In February 2004, during a strategic command post exercise of Russia's Armed Forces, the crews of Tu-160 and Tu-95MS strategic missile carriers flew close to 20 sorties. During just two days the crews of these aircraft logged a total of some 130-140 hours – an impressive result.

Believe it or not, the *Blackjack* acted as "Air Force One" on a single occasion! On August 16, 2005, Tu-160 "03 Red" *Pavel Taran* left Chkalovskaya AB a short way west of Moscow on a long sortie that included a launch of the latest Kh-555 cruise missile which the 121st GvTBAP had first received in 2004. However, this was not the only unusual thing about the mission – the then President of the Russian Federation Vladimir V. Putin was a passenger on this aircraft. Coming to the base straight from Zhukovskiy after the opening ceremony of the MAKS-2005 airshow, he made a flight in a strategic missile carrier. This was not his first flight in

Left: In August 2005, the then President of Russia, Vladimir V. Putin, was given a ride in a Tu-160 on a mission that was part of an Air Force exercise. Here, he and Anatoliy M. Zhikharev walk towards the aircraft at Chkalovskaya AB.

Above: Putin in the left-hand seat of Tu-160 "03 Red."

Below left: Putin shakes hands with the Tu-160's crew chief before the famous flight. Zhikharev is leftmost

Below: "VVP" receives a model of the Tu-160 as a memento after the flight. The then C-in-C of the Russian Air Force Army Gen. Vladimir S. Mikhailov is on the left.

a combat jet – previously he had flown as a back-seater in a Su-27UB *Flanker-C* combat trainer.

Actually there were three Tu-160s at Chkalovskaya that day, and the planned flight was part of a tactical exercise whose aim was to build up a DA task force covering the north-western strategic direction and accomplish the designated objective. This was not a specially arranged "joyride" – being the Supreme Commander-in-Chief of the Russian Armed Forces, the President simply took the opportunity to witness cruise missile launches, in-flight refuelling, maritime reconnaissance and low-altitude transonic flight.

Prior to the flight Putin was briefed on the mission details by Lt.-Gen. Igor' I. Khvorov, the then Commander of the 37th VA VGK (SN), using maps and placards. Next, the President was given a brief medical check, donned his flight suit and was given a briefing on flight safety procedures and how to use the ejection seat.

Shortly afterwards "03 Red" with the President in the captain's seat took off and headed north to the area where the joint exercise of the DA and the North Fleet was to take place. The aircraft was piloted by the DA's Chief of Staff Maj.-Gen. Anatoliy D. Zhikharev from the right-hand seat, with Col. Vladimir Adamov as navigator and Lt.-Col. Oleg Baranov as WSO. It was closely followed by the other two *Blackjacks*: "05 Red" *Aleksandr Golovanov* captained by Col. Aleksey R. Serebryakov and "07 Red" *Aleksandr Molodchiy* captained by Lt.-Col. Andrey V. Senchurov. Near Nizhniy Novgorod the bombers changed course and went supersonic, then decelerated and descended. During the mission two of the Tu-160s launched four Kh-555 cruise missiles which hit their designated targets at the Pemboy target range near Vorkuta in the Komi Republic. In the course of the mission the "Presidential" Tu-160 was refuelled by an Il-78 tanker. (Speaking of which, by then the 1230th APSZ had moved from Engels-2 AB to Dyagilevo AB, changing its name to the 203rd *Orlovskiy* GvOAPSZ (*Gvardeyskiy otdel'nyy aviapolk samolyotov-zaprahvshchikov* – Guards Independent Aerial Refuelling Regiment), inheriting the number, title and appellation of another former Tu-22KD unit from Belorussia (the 203rd GvTBAP) that had participated in the liberation of the Russian city of Oryol.) After that, the Tu-160s headed to their destination – Olen'ya AB near Olenegorsk, Murmansk Region, making a high-speed dash over the base at 900 km/h (559 mph) before landing.

As a matter of fact, the first case of the Tu-160 carrying a VIP was on August 25, 2003. On that occasion the then Minister of Defence Sergey B. Ivanov was in the left-hand seat of "07 Red" during another command and staff exercise; again, Anatoliy D. Zhikharev did the piloting from the right-hand seat.

As mentioned earlier, Tu-160 operations in the Soviet Air Force had started back in 1987. However, the type was not officially included into the Russian Air Force inventory until late December 2005, when President Putin signed an appropriate decree.

The 37th Air Army again conducted a command exercise on September 26–30, 2006. 93 sorties were flown in the course of this exercise, four regiments dropping bombs on unfamiliar target ranges to replicate a real-life war scenario as closely as possible; three long-range ALCMs were launched, complemented by 48 simulated missile launches. On September 29, a total of 54 "heavies" – Tu-160s, Tu-95MSs, Tu-22M3s and the supporting Il-78Ms – were simultaneously airborne in the northern, southern, western and eastern parts of Russia.

A Long-Range Aviation shoulder patch featuring the Sikorsky S-22 Il'ya Muromets at the bottom and the Tu-160 at the top.

An enamel badge marking the 60th birthday of the 121st *Sevastopol'skiy* GvTBAP, with a Tu-160 occupying centre place.

Another enamel badge released in 2004 on occasion of the DA's 90-year jubilee – again with 'Ye Olde Il'ya Muromets' at the bottom and "The New Il'ya Muromets" at the top.

An important event took place in the middle of August 2007. In response to the growing military-political tension in the world (in particular, as a result of a series of military measures taken by the USA), on instructions from President Vladimir V. Putin the aircraft of the 37th VA VGK (SN) commenced patrol flights outside the territory of the Russian Federation and resumed regular flights over the Pacific and Atlantic Oceans which had not been conducted since 1992. From 0 hours on August 17, 2007, in pursuance of the President's instructions, some two dozen aircraft of the

Above: Tu-160 "10 Red" *Nikolay Kuznetsov* was one of the three involved in the Venezuelan mission – albeit only as a back-up aircraft.

Below: "07 Red" *Aleksandr Molodchiy* tops up its tanks from an IL-78M en route to Venezuela.

37th Air Army, including Tu-160s – backed up in some cases by Mikoyan MiG-31 *Foxhound* heavy interceptors and A-50 AWACS aircraft, carried out 50 sorties over international waters, operating from Olen'ya AB, Vorkuta, Monchegorsk, Tiksi, Anadyr' (Oogol'nyy airport), Engels-2 AB and Shaikovka AB. The Tu-160s and Tu-95MSs were airborne for an average 13 hours. In the course of these flights 21 NATO fighters were observed, shadowing the Russian aircraft for a total of five hours.

On September 6–7 of the same year, Long-Range Aviation aircraft took off from airfields at Engels, Anadyr', Vorkuta and Tiksi to carry out yet another routine patrol in remote geographical regions. According to Deputy Commander of the 37th Air Army Maj.-Gen. Anatoliy D. Zhikharev, the Tu-160s and Tu-95s flew their missions without nuclear munitions. In 2007, for the first time in the course of 15 post-Soviet years, the yearly flying time logged by pilots of Russia's Long-Range Aviation exceeded 80 hours. 37th Air Army Commander Maj.-Gen. Pavel V. Androsov stated that more than 40 crews of strategic bombers and missile carriers received a complete course of training in 2007, and the plan for combat proficiency training was fulfilled 100%. In 2007 more than 50% of the crews were qualified for the participation in air patrols; young crews made up 30% of these, said Androsov.

On August 5–8, 2008, Russia conducted a brief military intervention in Georgia, responding to the latter's aggression against South Ossetia; this operation was officially known as the 'operation for compelling Georgia to peace' but has come to be described as the Russo–Georgian War. The Tu-160 was not involved in this operation because there were no targets that warranted its use. However, the operation was an eye-opener, showing that command and control of the Russian forces was poor; as a result, the objective was attained but with unacceptably high combat losses which could have been avoided.

This triggered a large-scale military reform in 2009–2010 which, among other things, changed the Russian Air Force's order of battle completely. The traditional Soviet/Russian organisation dating back to the 1930s (air army – air division – air regiment – air squadron) was scrapped; the entire order of battle was reshuffled to form Aviation Bases (AvB) and their constituent Aviation Groups (AvGr) – oddly resembling the OrBat of some NATO nations. In so doing, almost every single unit was redeployed and/or merged with other units. The 121st GvTBAP was no exception – despite being a one-of-a-kind unit by Russian Air Force standards, it was pooled with the other bomber unit resident at Engels-2 AB – the new 184th TBAP with 14 Tu-95MSs – to become the 1st AvGr of the 6950th *Donbasskaya* GvAvB (*Gvardeyskaya aviatsionnaya* ***bahza*** – Guards Aviation Base) of the 1st Category. It inherited the honorary appellation and other awards of the disbanded 22nd GvTBAD. The aircraft complement for 2010 was 16 Tu-160s in Sqn 1 and 18 (?) Tu-95MSs in Sqn 2. (As an aside, the supporting 203rd GvOAPSZ became the 6954th AvB.)

Another consequence of the 2009 military reform was the introduction of quasi-civil registrations prefixed RF- ("Russian Federation") on military aircraft as opposed to RA- ("Russian Aviation") for truly civil aircraft. This had nothing to do with the war – the RF- prefix signifies the government aviation register which is not limited to military aircraft; rather, the registrations

Top: A still from a video showing an RAF Panavia Tornado F.3 intercepting a Tu-160 over international waters not far from the British coast.

Above: A similar photo taken by the WSO of a British Tornado.

Below: Royal Norwegian Air Force Lockheed Martin F-16A "277" intercepts a Tu-160 over the Norwegian Sea.

Above left: Tu-160 "04 Red" *Ivan Yarygin* taxies back to the hardstand after landing (note the open brake parachute bay doors).
Left: The same aircraft commences its take-off run.
Below left: "19 Red" *Valentin Bliznyuk* climbs away for an afternoon practice sortie.
This page: Silhouetted against the evening sky, a *Blackjack* is intercepted by an RAF Tornado F.3.

served the same purpose as serials on western military aircraft, allowing positive identification (unlike the tactical codes, which are still used in parallel). The Russian MoD did this to enable checks of aircraft fleet strength for the purpose of checking Russia's compliance with arms reduction treaties. Thus, operational *Blackjacks* were registered consecutively in the same RF-94*** block as the other strategic bombers (specifically, RF-94100 through RF-94115). It was a while before the registrations were applied to the heavy bombers. This led to subtle changes in the Tu-160's colour scheme: the registration caused the star insignia to be moved up and the fin flash in Russian flag colours was deleted to make room for the star.

On October 21, 2009, two Tu-160s and Tu-95MSs from Engels flew a routine practice mission (or, as the Russian Air Force puts it, patrol mission) over the Arctic Ocean. In 2009 the Tu-160 and

Top left: In September 2008 two Russian Air Force Tu-160s paid a much-publicised visit to Venezuela. Here the bombers and the Antonov An-124 support aircraft are seen at Libertador AB.

Top and above: Tu-160 "07 Red" is refuelled by fuel bowsers belonging to the PDV state corporation (Petroleum de Venezuela).

Below: Still-uncoded Tu-160 *Valentin Bliznyuk* departs on a post-overhaul check flight.

Right: Tu-160 "05 Red" resting between sorties.

Below right: Tu-160 "10 Red" *Nikolay Kuznetsov* wears two Gold Star medals indicating that Kuznetsov was twice awarded the Hero of Socialist Labour title, the civilian equivalent of the HSU title.

Tu-95MS strategic bombers also participated in Exercise *Zapad-2009* held jointly with Belorussia.

More long-range practice missions were flown in 2010. Thus, on June 9–10, 2010, a pair of Tu-160s successfully flew a maximum-range mission from Engels-2 AB, staying aloft for nearly 23 hours and covering a distance of some 18,000 km (11,185 miles).

Overseas Visit

Until 2008, the *Blackjack*'s sole visit abroad had been the appearance of Tu-160 f/n 4-01 at the 1995 Paris Air Show in Tu-160SK demonstrator guise. In 2008, however, Russian Air Force Tu-160s made an unprecedented trip abroad, and not just anywhere; the flight took them all the way across the Atlantic Ocean to Venezuela on a goodwill visit. On September 9, three Tu-160s – "07 Red" *Aleksandr Molodchiy*, "10 Red" *Nikolay Kuznetsov* and "11 Red" *Vasiliy Sen'ko* – took off from Engels-2 AB and headed north, "going around the corner" (in Russian Air Force slang this means skirting Northern Europe and heading west across the Atlantic Ocean). Their route lay over the international waters of the Arctic and Atlantic Oceans, taking them towards the South American continent. In the course of the flight the Tu-160 group was twice escorted by NATO fighters. First, a pair of Royal Norwegian Air Force Lockheed Mar-

ВИТАЛИЙ
КОПЫЛОВ

tin F-16C Fighting Falcons put in an appearance when the bombers were over the Norwegian Sea; then in the vicinity of Iceland a USAF F-16C scrambled from Keflavik AFB. The NATO fighters did not undertake any dangerous closing on the Russian aircraft. In accordance with the flight plan, only two missile carriers were to land on the South American continent, the third one was to make a U-turn and return to base. This explains the confusion in some media reports which at first reported this, now that composition of the "pair" of the Russian missile-carriers, mentioning a further aircraft which was not involved ("08 Red" *Aleksandr Golovanov*). Fact is, the Russian media had not been informed of the fact that three aircraft were actually sent on that mission!

On September 10, Tu-160s "07 Red" and "11 Red" arrived at El Libertador airbase near Caracas, Venezuela after a 13-hour non-stop flight. The former aircraft was captained by 121st GvTBAP deputy CO, Pilot 1st Class Lt.-Col. Andrey V. Senchurov, while the other bomber was captained by deputy Commander of the DA Maj.-Gen. Aleksandr I. Afinogentov. Tu-160 "10 Red" returned to Engels. There were no nuclear warheads on board either aircraft. A Russian Air Force official, Lt.-Col. Vladimir V. Drik, pointed out that never before had strategic aircraft approached the equator so close (about 400 km/250 miles were left). The *Blackjacks* were supported by Il-78 tankers and by an An-124 transport from the Russian Air Force's 224th Flight Detachment which carried the ground personnel and support equipment (including a radio beacon) to Venezuela.

Above: Now wearing the code "19 Red," Tu-160 *Valentin Bliznyuk* is seen after a routine landing.

Opposite top: "08 Red" *Vitaliy Kopylov*, The Russian Air Force's youngest Tu-160.

Opposite bottom: Here the same aircraft takes off, showing the distinctively orange-coloured efflux of the NK-32 engines at full power.

Right: A pennant with the DA badge and the legend "Long-Range Aviation, established 1914."

Overleaf: Two views of Tu-160 "02 Red" wearing the current Russian tricolour star insignia and "VVS Rossii" (Russian Air Force) titles.

Tu-160 "06 Red" *Il'ya Muromets* with tri-colour star insignia and Russian Air Force titles

Tu-160 "10 Red" *Nikolay Kuznetsov* with new-style insignia

Here it should be mentioned that in July 2008, the then President of Venezuela Hugo Chávez, a fierce critic of the USA, had visited Russia. He had talks with President Dmitriy A. Medvedev and Prime Minister Vladimir V. Putin on various issues, including co-operation in defence matters. Venezuela is an established partner of Russia in this area, having signed 12 contracts for Russian weapons worth more than $4.4 billion in total in 2005–07. On 1st September Chávez said that Venezuela welcomed the Russian Navy and Air Force on its territory. *"If the Russian Navy arrives in the Caribbean or the Atlantic it may certainly visit Venezuela, we have no problems with that and would warmly welcome it. And if Russian long-range bombers should need to land in Venezuela we would not object to that either. We will also welcome them,"* he said. Well, no sooner said than done.

Tu-160 "02 Red" *Vasiliy Reshetnikov* with new-style insignia

Tu-160 "16 Red" *Aleksey Plokhov* with new-style insignia

In accordance with the pre-arranged plan, within the following few days the *Blackjacks* made two training flights over international waters. Each flight lasted about six hours. The first flight took place over the Caribbean in the direction of Panama, the second one was in the direction of Brazil at some distance from the coastline.

President Hugo Chávez was enthusiastic about the visit of the Russian strategic aircraft. *"You have come to a brother nation, to a people which appreciates Russia and her bravery,"* said Chávez, addressing the Russian crews, as he spoke at the launch ceremony of a new Venezuelan Navy frigate. He went on to say, *"Thanks to the strategic co-operation with Russia and the arrival of the [Russian] aircraft on Venezuelan soil and will be flying sorties over the Caribbean today and in the next few days, we will be informed of even the smallest movements of the [US Navy's] 4th Fleet. [...] Our*

Above: A trio of Tu-160s over the Spasskaya Tower of the Moscow Kremlin during the VE-Day parade on May 9, 2010.

strategic ties with Russia will grow stronger by the day because we are living in a world of free nations," said Chávez.

The *Blackjack* produced an indelible impression on the Venezuelan leader. As a token of solidarity with Bolivian President Evo Moralez, who indeed had reasons to suspect the USA of fanning political tension in the country, on the day of the Russian bombers' arrival Chávez expelled the blameless US ambassador from Caracas and threatened to stop oil deliveries to the USA if the US Navy's 4th Fleet stepped up its activity. (The 4th Fleet had indeed become active in Latin American waters in July 2008, after a five-decade lull.) He described the presence of the two Russian missile carriers in the country as "a warning to the American empire" that Russia supported Venezuela, and that Venezuela was "no longer poor and lonely." Speaking at a press conference shortly after the arrival of the bombers, he said, in Spanish, *"...los bombarderos estratégicos rusos Tupolev-cien-sesenta han aterrizado en Venezuela"* ("...the Russian Tu-160 strategic bombers have landed in Venezuela") and then, after a pause, could not resist the urge to add triumphantly: *"Yessss. The landing of the strategic bombers is an evidence of transition to multi-polarity in world politics. Venezuela is free to develop political, economic, scientific and military-technical relations with those countries, with which she deems it necessary,"* Chávez emphasized. Western correspondents accredited at Caracas noted that it was long since they had seen Hugo Chávez so happy and satisfied.

"I am going to fly one of these birds," Chavez said. *"Yesterday I did not appear in public because I was having a training session in a flight simulator. So, may it be known to you that I will be at the controls! Fidel, I am going to whizz over your island at treetop level!"* However, this was wishful thinking – no Tu-160 flight simulator was available in Venezuela, and Chávez' skills weren't sufficient for him to fly the bomber even as a passenger. Also, he did not speak Russian, and the Russian pilots did not speak Spanish.

Predictably, the Russian bombers' visit caused acute discontent in the West. Russia was then receiving more than enough bad publicity because of the war with US-backed Georgia a month earlier. Also, Moscow was frustrated with Washington's plans to deploy elements of an anti-missile defence system in Europe and by NATO inching closer and closer to Russian borders. In turn, Russia sought to expand its military presence in recent years, up to the point of, *"flexing some muscle in America's backyard"* and *"demonstrating [...] that it has a foothold in a region traditionally dominated by the US,"* as some defence analysts put it.

After a week's stay in Venezuela, the bombers departed from El Libertador AB at 1000 hrs Moscow time on September 18 – three days later than planned because the hospitable Venezuelans would not let the crews go so easily. After following the designated flight route above international waters the *Blackjacks* landed at their home base at 0116 hrs Moscow time on September 19. The crews climbed out into the chilly September night still wearing the light tropical uniforms, which had to be augmented immediately by warm jackets, and received a warm welcome.

Russian Air Force Deputy Commander-in-Chief Aleksandr I. Afinogentov told the RIA Novosti news agency that the Tu-160s had established two world records during their round trip to Venezuela. *"For the first time the duration of flight of a Tu-160 exceeded 15 hours, for the first time the aircraft received 25 tons [55,115 lb] of fuel during an air-to-air refuelling performed in the vicinity of Great Britain* – said he. *The crews of the two bombers spent over ten hours in the textureless area above the ocean with no radio aids whatsoever, so we placed our hopes on the professionalism of the crews and the reliability of the hardware. Building on this experience, we will probably make suggestions on how to improve the aircraft."* According to Afinogentov, in other respects the flights did not differ appreciably from the usual ones, albeit some complications were caused by the weather (when the aircraft were departing from Venezuela, there were powerful thunderstorms in the area, which necessitated a roundabout route). *"Flights in those latitudes have a few peculiarities. This experience will be summed up and used to train young pilots in the future,"* Afinogentov said.

For the Venezuelan mission the participating personnel received Russian government awards. After the award ceremony in the Moscow Kremlin the Long-Range Aviation Chief of Staff Maj.-Gen. Anatoliy D. Zhikharev told the *Izvestiya* daily: *"When this weapons system was being inducted, I was one of the first pilots to master the bomber. Now I am probably one of the "old-timers" still flying these aircraft [from those days]."*

When asked how the idea of the Venezuelan mission came about, Zhikharev replied, *"It was the Supreme Commander-in-Chief's* (President Dmitriy A. Medvedev's – *Auth.*) *decision. We decided to show that the Americans are not the only ones who can perform 'humanitarian' missions near our shores."*

"For the Long-Range Aviation crews this was an invaluable experience – Zhikharev continued. – *For the first time we were flying over unfamiliar territory and still performing our combat training tasks. It's all the more important because in the future such flights may be done on a regular basis. Hugo Chávez has even offered us to use the airfield on Archila Island. Anything is possible, providing the appropriate political decisions are taken."*

The Russian press generally assessed the Venezuelan mission as another high-complexity drill of the DA crews and a show of force in response to the aforementioned NATO exercise in the Black Sea. Some Russian media had been speculating on the possibility of Russian strategic bombers deploying to Cuba long before the *Blackjacks*' Caribbean mission. To date there have been no such deployments, but the CO of the 22nd GvTBAD, Maj.-Gen. Aleksandr Blazhenko, said at the welcoming ceremony after the mission: *"I believe we will be looking for other partners as well – we'll be flying over other areas of the world ocean as well. It's just a matter of time."*

What's In a Name?

Together with the formation of the Russian Air Force's first Tu-160 squadron a long-forgotten tradition was revived. Nose art was generally frowned upon in the Soviet Air Force (except in times of war when it helped keep up the fighting spirit), being broadly regarded as characteristic of the potential adversary and hence unbecoming for the Soviet airmen. Now, however, the operational Tu-160s progressively received individual names. The first two aircraft to be christened ("05 Red" and "06 Red") bore the same name, *Il'ya Muromets*, and markings not seen hitherto on Russian Air Force bombers in the form of blue/yellow nose flashes (a fragment of the Air Force's "sunburst" flag), a fin flash in Russian flag colours and a "double eagle" on the tail in lieu of the red pentastar. This was done at a time when the Air Force experimented with various new insignia before eventually deciding to leave well enough

Russian Air Force Tu-160s with individual names – fleet details

Tactical code/ registration	Name	Notes
01 Red	Mikhail Gromov	Named 22-2-1999. Mikhail M. Gromov (1899-1985) was a famous Soviet test pilot after whom the Flight Research Institute (LII) is named
02 Red/RF-94102	Vasiliy Reshetnikov	Named 23-12-1999. Maj.-Gen. Vasiliy V. Reshetnikov, HSU (born 1919) was a bomber pilot in the Great Patriotic War and, in 1969-1980, Commander of the Long-Range Aviation
03 Red/RF-94101	Pavel Taran	Named 31-7-2002. Lt.-Gen. Pavel A. Taran, Twice HSU (1916-2005) was a bomber unit CO in the Great Patriotic War
04 Red/RF-94112	Ivan Yarygin	Named 6-1-1999. Ivan S. Yarygin (1948-1997) was a Soviet/Russian wrestler who won the gold at the 1972 and 1976 Summer Olympic Games
05 Red	Il'ya Muromets (1);	Named 9-5-1995? See next line
05 Red/RF-94104	Aleksandr Golovanov	Renamed 7-8-1999. Air Chief Marshal Aleksandr Ye. Golovanov (1904-1975) commanded the Long-Range Aviation in 1944-48
06 Red/RF-94105	Il'ya Muromets (2)	Named 9-5-1995. A Russian epic hero; 'Muromets' indicates his origins from the town of Murom
07 Red/RF-94106	Aleksandr Molodchiy	Named 27-6-2000. Lt.-Gen. Aleksandr I. Molodchiy, Twice HSU (1920-2002) was a bomber pilot in the Great Patriotic War
08 Red/RF-94115	Vitaliy Kopylov	Named 29-4-2008. Vitaliy Ye. Kopylov (1926-1995) was the director of the Kazan' aircraft factory in 1974-1994
10 Red/RF-94100	Nikolay Kuznetsov	Named 2009. Nikolay D. Kuznetsov (1911-1995) was a Soviet aero engine designer; the Tu-160 is powered by Kuznetsov engines
11 Red/RF-94114	Vasiliy Sen'ko	Named 15-10-2002. Col. Vasiliy V. Sen'ko (1921-1984) was the sole Long-Range Aviation navigator/bomb-aimer to be twice awarded the HSU title in the Great Patriotic War
12 Red/RF-94109	Aleksandr Novikov	Named 21-12-2000. Air Marshal Aleksandr A. Novikov, Twice HSU (1900-1976), was C-in-C of the Soviet Air Force in 1943-46
14 Red/RF-94103	Igor' Sikorsky	Named 2012. Igor' I. Sikorsky (1889-1972) was a Russian and American aircraft designer who created the world's first four-engine bomber; he is best known for his seaplanes and helicopters designed in the USA
15 Red/RF-94108	Vladimir Sudets	Named 26-10-2004. Air Marshal Vladimir A. Sudets, HSU (1904-1981) commanded various DA units in the Great Patriotic War
16 Red/RF-94107	Aleksey Plokhov	Named 17-4-2003. Aleksey A. Plokhov (HSU) was a bomber pilot in the Great Patriotic War
17 Red/RF-94110	Valeriy Chkalov	Named 2003. Valeriy P. Chkalov (1904-1938) was a famous Soviet test pilot
18 Red/RF-94111	Andrey Tupolev	Named 19-12-2014. Andrey N. Tupolev (1888-1972) was a famous Soviet aircraft designer, the founder of OKB-156 and of Soviet heavy aircraft design
19 Red/RF-94113	Valentin Bliznyuk	Named 5-7-2006. Valentin I. Bliznyuk (born 1928) is the chief designer of the Tu-160

Tu-160 "15 Red"/RF-94108 *Vladimir Sudets*, 6950th AvB, 2010

Tu-160 "17 Red"/RF-94110 *Valeriy Chkalov*, 6950th AvB, 2010

Tu-160 "19 Red"/RF-94113 *Valentin Bliznyuk*, 6950th AvB, 2010

Tu-160 "12 Red"/RF-94109 *Aleksandr Novikov*, 6950th AvB, 2010

Tu-160 "18 Red"/RF-94111 *Andrey Tupolev*, 6950th AvB, 2010

Starboard side view of "15 Red"/RF-94108

Starboard side view of "17 Red"/RF-94110

Starboard side view of "19 Red"/ RF-94113

Starboard side view of "12 Red"/RF-94109

Starboard side view of "18 Red"/RF-94111

alone; after all, the Red Star is immediately recognisable, unlike assorted roundels which often give rise to confusion. Hence later Tu-160s reverted to the red stars, combining them with a different version of the fin flash. One photo showed "05 Red" and "06 Red" parked together, and in 1999 the editors of the *Aviatsiya i Kosmonavtika* monthly (Aviation and Spaceflight) "doctored" the picture a little, altering the name of "05 Red" to *Il'yin Muromets*! This was a practical joke aimed at aviation writer Vladimir Il'yin who was a member of the magazine's editorial board.

Later, however, the Tu-160s were named to honour real people – mostly Soviet Air Force (Long-Range Aviation) airmen who had fought with gallantry in the Great Patriotic War, but also men who were associated with the development of the *Blackjack*. Details of the names are given in the table on page 275.

Showtime

As already mentioned, the Tu-160's public debut took place on August 20, 1989, during the annual Aviation Day display at Moscow-Tushino airfield. The first known display in Zhukovskiy was on August 18, 1991 – again in the form of a low-level flypast over a temporary grandstand on the bank of the Moskva River.

Starting in 1992, the Tu-160 has been an invariable participant in the Moscow airshows at the LII airfield in Zhukovskiy. Mos-Aero-Show-92 and the MAKS airshows (up to 2001) involved company-owned prototypes and initial production aircraft, but in the 21st century the Russian Air Force started putting up operational *Blackjacks* for the occasion – a different aircraft each time. The first time was MAKS-2003 (August 19–24, 2003) where "03 Red" *Pavel Taran* was on display. "04 Red" *Ivan Yarygin* was in the static park at the MAKS-2005 (August 16–21, 2005). The MAKS-2007 show featured two *Blackjacks* – "19 Red" *Valentin Bliznyuk* (on August 20 only) and "11 Red" *Vasiliy Sen'ko*. On August 18–23, 2009, visitors to the MAKS-2009 airshow were able to examine Tu-160 "10 Red" *Nikolay Kuznetsov*.

The latter aircraft was seen at the MAKS-2011 (August 16–21, 2011) as "10 Red"/RF-94100. Tu-160M "12 Red"/RF-94109 *Aleksandr Novikov* appeared both at the MAKS-2013 (August 27 – September 1, 2013) and at the MAKS-2015 (August 25–30, 2015).

The latest occasion when a Tu-160 was displayed statically for the general public was the ***Armiya-2015*** military show held on June 16–19, 2015 (and ostensibly timed to coincide with the Paris Air Show). Part of it took place at Kubinka AB where Tu-160M "12 Red"/RF-94109 was in the static park and the visitors were able to examine the upgraded version at close range for the first time.

The Tu-160 was also represented at other venues. On May 14, 1994, Kubinka AB held its third "open house." Unlike 1992, the static display did not feature any heavy bombers, but the flying programme included a *Bear-H*, a *Backfire-C* and a *Blackjack*. The latter was coded "01 Red" – the aircraft that would be named *Mikhail Gromov* and would be tragically lost in 2003.

On March 28, 2009, Kubinka AB hosted a special aviation display staged for Russia's new President and Supreme Commander-in-Chief of the Russian Armed Forces, former PM Dmitriy A. Medvedev. In addition to the Russian Air Force's latest hardware, such as the Yakovlev Yak-130 *Mitten* advanced trainer/light strike aircraft, the static display included some 'traditional' aircraft, such as Tu-160 "02 Red" *Vasiliy Reshetnikov*.

The grand military parade at Poklonnaya Gora in Moscow on May 9, 1995, on occasion of the 50th anniversary of VE-Day featured a large Air Force component – for the first time in many years; thus was reborn a Soviet tradition. The first fixed-wing aircraft in the flypast (after a quartet of Mil' Mi-8MT *Hip-H* helicopters carrying flags) was Tu-160 "06 Red" *Il'ya Muromets* accompanied by four MiG-29s of the Russian Air Force's ***Strizhi*** (Swifts) aerobatic team from Kubinka AB. The bomber, which was captained by none other than Pyotr S. Deynekin, had flown in non-stop from Engels-2 AB via Kozel'sk, Yookhnov, Vereya and Kubinka. At the latter location it was joined by the fighter escort, approaching the city from the west along Mozhaiskoye Highway.

The general public was treated to a demonstration of the Tu-160 on July 28, 1996, the day when the Russian Navy celebrated its 300th anniversary. The festivities in St. Petersburg, the birthplace of the Russian Navy, included a spectacular flypast over the Neva River featuring, among other things, a Tu-160 escorted by four MiG-29s of the Strizhi team. Piloted by Lt.-Col. Aleksey R. Serebryakov, the *Blackjack* made a high-speed pass at about 500 m (1,600 ft) with the wings at maximum sweep.

Later, after a short break, the Tu-160 continued its participation in the VE-Day parades in Moscow – usually in company with fighters or in line astern formation behind an IL-78M dedicated tanker. Now the parades took place at the usual location – in Red Square; Accordingly the participating aircraft approached the city from the north, flying along Leningradskiy Prospekt (Leningrad Avenue) and Tverskaya Street. For example, on May 9, 2008, the abovementioned "02 Red" *Vasiliy Reshetnikov* was accompanied by two MiG-31B heavy interceptors.

The Long-Range Aviation was heavily involved in the May 9, 2010 parade. The event was a sore trial for the Air Force which put up 127 assorted aircraft, including – for the first time in the history of flypasts over Red Square – three Tu-160s at once in V formation ("02 Red" *Vasiliy Reshetnikov*, "05 Red" *Il'ya Muromets* and "10 Red" *Nikolay Kuznetsov*), plus a further *Blackjack* ("16 Red" *Aleksey Plokhov*) in simulated refuelling formation. The practice sessions for the parade began in early March, and all the DA crews participating in the parade were commended for the spectacular performance. Like most other aircraft in the flypast, the bombers and the tankers wore new-style Russian Air Force pentastars (with a blue outline added inside the usual red/white outline to symbolise the Russian flag) and bold "VVS ROSSIĬ" (RUSSIAN AIR FORCE) titles on the tail (mockingly dubbed "BBC of Russia" by some).

The 2013 VE-Day parade included Tu-160 "17 Red" *Valeriy Chkalov* in simulated refuelling formation. The 2013 VE-Day parade included a similar setup, with Tu-160 "05 Red"/RF-94104 *Aleksandr Golovanov* following Il-78M "80 Blue"/RF-94283. The latest parade on May 9, 2015, is unusual in that, contrary to established practice, a Tu-160M captained by Russian Air Force C-in-C Viktor Bondarev led the way instead of the usual group of helicopters, followed several minutes later by a further *Blackjack* tailing a tanker.

Chapter 8

Blackjack vs. "Bone": Equals or Not?

Some people might be tempted to put the question differently: copy or not? Sure enough, the Tu-160 and the Rockwell International B-1 look quite similar at first glance. Much has been said about the apparent Soviet custom of copying Western designs; this postulate is rooted in a firm conviction that Russia, the old Cold War enemy, cannot produce anything worthwhile. However, it is no surprise that the engineers developing both aircraft chose the same general arrangement, aerodynamic features and internal layout more than 20 years ago. Ideas are borne on the wind, as a Russian saying goes; and indeed, faced with similar general requirements and given basically the same levels of aviation science and technology, the two nations were bound to come up with similar results. However, a closer look at the two bombers reveals that the Tu-160 and the B-1 are not so similar after all.

Originating as the AMSA (Advanced Manned Strike Aircraft) programme in the mid-1960s, the B-1 had a head start on the *Blackjack*. The programme made slow progress under the Lyndon B. Johnson administration but was revived under the new President Richard Nixon; the first prototype of the original B-1A (USAF serial 74-0158) first flew on December 23, 1974, followed by three other prototypes, one of which was originally a structural test airframe. Unlike the Boeing B-52 Superfortress, which was then the mainstay of the USAF's Strategic Air Command fleet, the B-1 was optimised for low-altitude air defence penetration.

However, programme costs kept mounting, and so did unit costs. This, and intelligence reports on the MiG-31 interceptor whose capabilities rendered even low-altitude penetrators vulnerable, worried Nixon's successor President Jimmy Carter (known for his "belt-tightening" policies) so much that he finally cancelled the B-1 on June 30, 1977, the last day of Fiscal Year 1977. Instead, he opted (in addition to ballistic missiles) for upgrading the existing B-52 fleet, allowing it to launch hundreds of Boeing AGM-86B (ALCM) cruise missiles; this was seen as a cheaper option and a more effective way of saturating the Soviet air defences in the event of a war. Also, Carter was informed of the recently launched ATB (Advanced Technology Bomber) programme which was deemed to hold greater promise than the AMSA and eventually materialised as the highly sophisticated Northrop B-2A Spirit stealth bomber.

Seen by the refuelling systems operator of an IL-78, a Tu-160 closes in on the tanker with the IFR probe extended.

A similar perspective of a B-1B (85-0072) about to "hit the tanker" shows the SMCS (Structural Mode Control System) canards, the aerial refuelling receptacle for the "flying boom," the larger glazing area and the generally leaner shape of the aircraft.

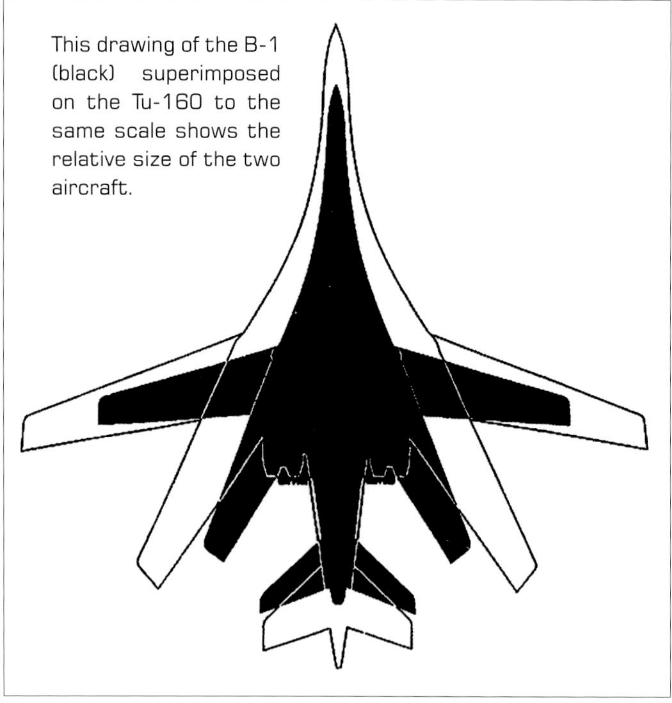

This drawing of the B-1 (black) superimposed on the Tu-160 to the same scale shows the relative size of the two aircraft.

Yet, soon the situation changed. For one thing, the Afghan War began in December 1979; for another, the Americans became aware that the Soviet Union was working on a new strategic bomber. All this prompted the US Department of Defense to revive the B-1 programme, adapting it to changing priorities; the result was the B-1B Lancer – or, as it is popularly known, the Bone (the sobriquet derives from "B-One").

During the transformation from A to B the designers spent a lot of effort on reducing the B-1's RCS; additionally, a more fuel-efficient version of the General Electric F101-GE-100 afterburning turbofan was fitted, and the avionics and armament were revised. The bomber's maximum take-off weight rose from the B-1A's 180,000 kg (395,000 lb) to 217,000 kg (477,000 lb). However, the B-1 lobby and the US Air Force did not succeed in convincing the US Congress that a whole range of costly features needed to be incorporated into the bomber's design and the Congress slashed the funds for the programme. Hence, Rockwell International had to use rather less titanium than originally intended and the engines had simple fixed-area air intakes instead of variable supersonic intakes, restricting the B-1B's top speed from the B-1A's Mach 2.2 to Mach 1.25. The armament was to consist of AGM-86B cruise missiles, Boeing AGM-69A (SRAM) short-range attack missiles and nuclear bombs. When President Ronald Reagan entered office he decided to order the B-1 as a "near term" system to bridge the gap between the B-52 (which would be increasingly vulnerable to new Soviet air defence systems) and the ATB, but the order was reduced from the originally envisaged 244 units to just 100.

Aptly named *Leader of the Fleet*, the B-1B prototype (82-0001, c/n 1) entered flight test on March 23, 1983; it remained a company-owned test aircraft and was never delivered to the USAF. The first production aircraft (83-0065 *Star of Abilene*, c/n 2) took off on October 18, 1984. The final B-1B (86-0140 *Valda J*, c/n 100) left the production line in 1988.

Conversely, the Tu-160 was developed by the world's second superpower at a time when funding issues were of minor importance, if any – in those days the Soviet military got all the money they wanted, as long as the required weapons systems were developed and fielded on time. Hence the Tu-160 escaped the 'vivisection' the B-1 had been subjected to, and the aircraft which entered production and service with the Soviet Air Force was exactly what its creators had wanted it to be – a multi-mode aircraft capable of delivering intercontinental strikes within a wide altitude and speed envelope.

On the other hand, the production line in Palmdale, California, was turning out a steady stream of Lancers on schedule (or ahead of schedule) and the B-1B was already fully operational when Tu-160 production in Kazan' was only just commencing. Today the "Bone," together with the long-serving B-52H and the small number of B-2As, makes up the backbone of the USAF's strategic component. Also, following retirement of the General Dynamics F-111 Aardvark tactical bomber and the Grumman F-14 Tomcat shipboard interceptor, it is currently the only 'swing-wing' aircraft in US service.

After the demise of the Soviet Union the balance of power shifted; Russia had to work hard in order to rebuild its strategic bomber force – at least partly. Despite these efforts, today Russia has only a single regiment of Tu-160s – sixteen aircraft, which is just over 15% of the USAF's B-1 fleet.

An opportunity to make an objective comparison of the two types came on September 23–25, 1994, when the Tu-160 and the B-1B "rubbed noses" (fortunately not literally) for the first time at Poltava AB in the Ukraine during the 50th anniversary celebrations of Operation *Frantic* (the shuttle raids against Germany), to which the USAF sent a large delegation. The flight and ground crews of both bombers had a chance to examine each other's aircraft and make an opinion for themselves.

As already mentioned, outwardly the Tu-160 is very similar to the B-1B; both aircraft share the same general arrangement, utilising the same BWB layout and variable-geometry wing design. Both aircraft have a crew of four, albeit the crewmen's functions differ – instead of a navigator and a WSO, the B-1B has an offensive systems officer (equivalent to the WSO) and a defensive systems officer. However, there are differences. For example, on the B-1 only the horizontal tail is all-movable (the bomber has a conventional fin with a two-section inset rudder for directional control), but the stabilators are augmented by small all-movable canards – the so-called LARC (Low-Altitude Ride Control) vanes, later restyled as the SMCS (Structural Mode Control System) – giving a smoother ride in turbulence at low level. The Tu-160 lacks these vanes, since low-level operations are not its primary operating mode. The landing gear design also differs.

Also, the Russian bomber is rather larger and heavier, which is why the aggregate thrust of its engines is 79% higher – 100,000 kgp (220,460 lbst) versus 42,440 kgp (93,560 lbst). The operating speeds are quite different as well. As already noted, at the insistence of the USAF the B-1B had to do without variable supersonic air intakes. Hence it has an operational limit of Mach 1.2 for structural integrity reasons, which is not ideal from a tactical standpoint. Conversely, the Tu-160 can cruise at Mach 1.5

thanks to its variable intakes, ample engine thrust and slender fuselage having a relatively small cross-section area. Low drag was attained thanks not only to streamlined contours but also to a carefully designed internal layout thanks to which the Tu-160's fuselage height is no bigger than that of the much smaller Tu-22M3.

However, attaining high performance isn't all about aerodynamics. The Tu-160 is designed in such a way as to achieve maximum possible range not only in high-altitude supersonic cruise but also in ultra-low-level flight. The crew is free to choose between these modes or use a combination of them to fulfil the mission with maximum efficiency. This is the Russian bomber's multi-mode design philosophy.

The *Blackjack* has an advantage in offensive capability to a certain extent – its main weapon, the Kh-55SM cruise missile, is well mastered by both the industry and the bomber crews, and the new Kh-555 and Kh-101/Kh-102 cruise missiles are on the way. Conversely, the Americans were unable to adapt the B-1B to take the costly AGM-86B due to budgetary constraints – this would require not only the bomb bays to be modified but also the avionics suite to be substantially altered. The AGM-69A had to be excluded from the inventory in 1994, because the stockpile of missiles had reached the end of their shelf life and the solid propellant had started decomposing. This left the B-1B with only the B61 and B83 free-fall nuclear bombs (although a small number of B28 nukes remained available in 1996). As of 1996 the USAF had plans to integrate the General Dynamics AGM-129A (ACM) advanced cruise missile on the B-1B. The Boeing AGM-131A (SRAM II) was also proposed but was cancelled in September 1991. Later, however, the B-1B was upgraded in stages (so-called blocks) to carry new weapons – the Joint Direct Attack Munition (JDAM) guided bomb, the Wind Corrected Munitions Dispenser (WCMD), the Raytheon AGM-154 Joint Stand-off Weapon (JSOW) and the Lockheed Martin AGM-158 JASSM (Joint Air-to-Surface Stand-off Munition), substantially improving its offensive capability. The Lockheed Martin Sniper XR external laser targeting pod was integrated on the B-1 fleet in 2007. Upgrades were also made to the defensive avionics suite, including the addition of the ALE-50 towed decoy system, and anti-jam radios were fitted.

As for conventional munitions, the Lancer did not receive a conventional capability until after the First Gulf War (true, live weapons tests began in 1991 but the fleet-wide upgrade came too late for the action). Conversely, the Tu-160 was to have a conventional capability from the start, hence the inclusion of the OPB-15T electro-optical bombsight into the targeting suite; on the other hand, it never actually used free-fall bombs.

The approach to weapons carriage is different, too. The B-1B has three weapons bays (two ahead of the wing pivot box and one aft), while the Tu-160 has two bays of larger size. Also, the Lancer has provisions for carrying missiles on six external hardpoints under the forward, centre and rear fuselage, whereas on the *Blackjack* all armament is carried internally. This helps reduce the bomber's RCS and reduce drag, thereby increasing range – albeit this also accounts for the larger size of the Tu-160.

As regards avionics and equipment, the B-1B apparently comes out on top thanks to its avionics suite which includes a Westinghouse AN/ALQ-161 synthetic aperture radar and a comprehensive defensive suite. According to press reports, Russian and Ukrainian pilots rated the Lancer's flight instrumentation as excellent; the flight deck features an electronic flight instrumentation system as opposed to the Tu-160's conventional mechanical instruments. As far as crew comfort and cockpit ergonomics are concerned, the two aircraft are about equal, although the B-1B's flight deck offers somewhat less headroom, being encroached on from below by the nosewheel well. As for the mission avionics, some Russian systems are theoretically more capable than their US counterparts but are not used in full for various reasons (reliability problems and the like); also, some of the *Blackjack*'s avionics are still hampered by operational limits imposed in some flight modes.

The Russian military and many of the world's top aviation experts believe that the combination of the Tu-160's performance and design features theoretically gives it an edge over the B-1B and other American bombers, including the stealthy B-2A – but theory is one thing and real life is another. First, the B-1B was already well mastered when Tu-160 crews were just getting to grips with the aircraft and were hampered by loads of restrictions. Then, due to persistent funding shortfalls the Russian Air Force had serviceability issues with its bomber fleet and suffered from fuel shortages in the 1990s. This, in turn, created the problem of providing enough flying hours for the crews; maintaining proficiency was a sore problem for the Russian airmen. For instance, both the 'Bone' and the *Blackjack* have IFR capability; however, B-1B pilots practiced aerial refuelling almost weekly – something their Russian colleagues could only dream of. In the 21st century the situation started to improve for the Tu-160 crews, with fuel being readily available and numerous exercises giving them a chance to hone their skills.

From an operational reliability standpoint the two types are broadly similar. Both have had their share of powerplant and avionics reliability problems; it was exactly this which prevented the B-1B from taking part in the First Gulf War. As regards flight safety, ten B-1Bs out of 100 have been lost in accidents – a 10% attrition rate, which is higher than the Tu-160's (two of 34 flyable aircraft makes 5.88%).

As for the combat capabilities of the two aircraft, they can be compared only in theory because, whereas the B-1B has seen action on multiple occasions, the Tu-160 has never fired in anger. The Lancer drew first blood in December 1998 during Operation *Desert Fox* in Iraq (the "One-and-a-half Gulf War"). Later it saw action in former Yugoslavia (Operation *Allied Force*, 1999), Afghanistan (Operation *Enduring Freedom*, 2001 onwards) and the Second Gulf War (the US invasion of Iraq in 2003).

Here is the opinion of former 37th VA Commander Lt.-Gen. Mikhail M. Oparin:

"I have a deep respect for the people who charted the development perspectives for the Long-Range Aviation in the 1980s/early 1990s time frame. The structural strength reserves and upgrade potential of the Tu-95MS and Tu-160 strategic bombers allows them to be called aircraft of the 21st century, and with good reason – the missile strike aircraft still have unused potential. These bombers are not only a match for the best Western hardware but excel it in certain respects. I know what I'm saying because I have had a chance to study the strategic aircraft of our 'friends and rivals' firsthand. I had the opportunity to fly a real B-52, and I

made several flights in the B-1 simulator; after this I was enchanted by the Tu-95MS and especially the Tu-160."

It would be best to conclude this chapter, and the book, with the following words from former Russian Air Force C-in-C Army General Pyotr S. Deynekin:

"What do you best compare the 'Il'ya Muromets' (the Tu-160 – *Auth.*) *with? The Tu-95? Or perhaps the An-124?* (The An-124 is the world's heaviest operational military airlifter – *Auth.*) *I guess the correct answer is the B-1B Lancer, the Tu-160's American counterpart. In May 1992, I made three flights in a B-1B over the Nevada Desert, flying the bomber from the left-hand seat, with multiple top-ups from a KC-135 tanker. I have a commemorative picture signed by the Commanders of USAF bomber wings. I dare-say they are both good aircraft and worthy rivals – as, incidentally, are the men who fly them. This is why we'd better be friends than foes, and the Americans are well aware of this."*

Specifications of the Tu-160 and B-1B

	Tu-160	B-1B
Powerplant	4 x Kuznetsov NK-32	4 x General Electric F101-GE-102
Maximum thrust, kgp (lbst)	4 x 25,000 (4 x 55,115)	4 x 10,610 (4 x 23,390)
Length overall	54.095 m (177 ft 5 23/32 in)	45.78 m (150 ft 2½ in)
Wing span:		
at minimum sweep	55.7 m (182 ft 8 29/32 in) @ 20°	41.67 m (136 ft 8½ in) @ 15°
at maximum sweep	35.6 m (116 ft 9 37/64 in) @ 65°	23.84 m (78 ft 2½ in) @ 67°30'
Stabilator span	13.26 m (43 ft 6 in)	13.66 m (44 ft 9 51/64 in)
Height on ground	13.6 m (44 ft 7 7/16 in)	10.24 m (33 ft 7¾ in)
Landing gear track	5.5 m (18 ft 17/32 in)	4.42 m (14 ft 6 in)
Landing gear wheelbase	17.88 m (58 ft 4 25/32 in)	17.21 m (56 ft 5 5/16 in)
Wing area, m^2 (sq ft)	293.15 (3,152.15)	181.2 (1,950)
MTOW, kg (lb)	275,000 (606,260)	216,400 (477,000)
Fuel load, kg (lb)	171,000 (376,980)	88,450 (195,000)
Weapons load, kg (lb)	40,000 (88,180)	34,000 (75,000)
Speed, km/h (mph):		
cruising	1,000 (621)	855 (531)
maximum	2,000 (1,240)	1,270 (789)
Service ceiling, m (ft)	15,000 (49,210)	15,240 (50,000)
Range, loaded, km (miles)	12,300 (7,640)	10,400 (6,459)
Combat radius, km (miles)	7,300 (4,534) *	5,540 (3,444)

* with one top-up

Left: Tu-160 "01 Red" being serviced. The Ural-4320 lorry on the right is an APA-100 GPU; the ZiL-131Ns on the left are oxygen/nitrogen charger or hydraulics test vehicles.

Above: 96th Bombardment Wing B-1Bs at Dyess AFB, Texas, in 1991. In contrast to the all-white anti-flash finish of the Tu-160 the Lancers invariably wear a dark camouflage scheme. Another notable difference is the integral boarding ladder which the Tu-160 lacks.

Below: 121st GvTBAP Tu-160s on the flight line at Engels-2 AB.

Appendix 1

Production List

As of now, the Tu-160's production run stands at 36 – three Moscow-built development aircraft (two prototypes and a static test airframe) and 33 Kazan'-built production examples, including a further static test airframe. These are listed below; the split presentation of the production machines' c/ns is for the sake of convenience only. Crashed examples are indicated by crosses with the date of the accident.

Tu-160 production list

C/n	F/n	Version	Tactical code/registration/name	Manufacture date	Notes
1. MMZ 'Opyt', Moscow					
70-01		Tu-160	no code, 18 Grey	18-12-1981	Tupolev OKB, scrapped
70-02		Tu-160	no code	1982	Tupolev OKB, static test airframe
70-03		Tu-160	no code, 29 Grey	6-10-1984	Tupolev OKB
2. KAPO, Kazan'					
8 3 4 01 5 1 7	1-01	Tu-160	30 Grey	10-10-1984	Tupolev OKB
8 4 4 01 9 2 3	1-02	Tu-160	56 Grey † 6-3-1987	16-3-1985	Tupolev OKB
8 2 5 02 6 1 8	2-01	Tu-160	86 Grey	25-12-1985	Tupolev OKB
8 4 5 02 3 2 4	2-02	Tu-160	87 Grey	24-2-1986	Tupolev OKB. Became, see next line
			Russian AF 19 Red *Valentin Bliznyuk*		121st GvTBAP, 2006. Registered as, see next line
			19 Red/RF-94113 *Valentin Bliznyuk*		6950th GvAvB
8 4 6 02 4 3 8	2-03	Tu-160	Soviet/Ukrainian AF 30 Red		184th GvTBAP, scrapped
8 4 6 03 7 1 2	3-01	Tu-160	Soviet/Ukrainian AF 31 Red	25-4-1987	184th GvTBAP, scrapped
8 2 7 03 6 2 9	3-02	Tu-160	Soviet/Ukrainian AF 32 Red		184th GvTBAP, scrapped
8 * 7 03 * 3 *	3-03	Tu-160	no code		Tupolev OKB, static/fatigue test airframe
8 3 7 03 8 4 5	3-04	Tu-160	Soviet/Ukrainian AF 33 Red		184th GvTBAP, scrapped
8 4 7 03 4 5 3	3-05	Tu-160	Soviet/Ukrainian AF 25 Red		184th GvTBAP, scrapped
8 4 7 04 2 1 7	4-01	Tu-160	63 Grey	16-3-1988	Tupolev OKB. Became, see next line
			'342 Blue', no code (*Boris Veremey*)		Tupolev JSC
8 1 8 04 9 2 1	4-02	Tu-160	Soviet/Ukrainian AF 26 Red#	22-6-1988	184th GvTBAP; preserved Poltava
8 2 8 04 7 3 4	4-03	Tu-160	Soviet/Ukrainian AF 20 Red		184th GvTBAP, scrapped
8 2 8 04 5 4 7	4-04	Tu-160	Soviet/Ukrainian AF 21 Red		184th GvTBAP, scrapped
8 3 8 04 3 5 2	4-05	Tu-160	Soviet/Ukrainian AF 22 Red	14-2-1989	184th GvTBAP. Became, see next line
			Russian AF 14 Red *Igor' Sikorsky*		121st GvTBAP. Registered as, see next line
			14 Red/RF-94103 *Igor' Sikorsky*		6950th GvAvB
8 4 8 05 8 1 3	5-01	Tu-160	Soviet/Ukrainian AF ?? Red		184th GvTBAP, scrapped
8 4 8 05 4 2 5	5-02	Tu-160	Soviet/Ukrainian AF 24 Red	1989	184th GvTBAP, scrapped
8 2 9 05 8 3 6	5-03	Tu-160	Soviet/Ukrainian AF 16 Red	6-6-1990	184th GvTBAP. Became, see next line
			Russian AF 16 Red *Aleksey Plokhov*		121st GvTBAP. Registered as, see next line
			16 Red/RF-94107 *Aleksey Plokhov*		6950th GvAvB
8 3 9 05 1 4 2	5-04	Tu-160	Soviet/Ukrainian AF 17 Red *Priluki*	29-6-1990	184th GvTBAP. Became, see next line
			Russian AF 17 Red *Valeriy Chkalov*		121st GvTBAP. Registered as, see next line
			17 Red/RF-94110 *Valeriy Chkalov*		6950th GvAvB
8 3 9 05 9 5 3	5-05	Tu-160	Soviet/Ukrainian AF 15 Red#	1990	184th GvTBAP. Became, see next line
			Russian AF 15 Red *Vladimir Sudets*		121st GvTBAP. Registered as, see next line
			15 Red/RF-94108 *Vladimir Sudets*		6950th GvAvB
8 4 9 06 2 1 7	6-01	Tu-160	Soviet/Ukrainian AF 10 Red#	1990	184th GvTBAP. Became, see next line
			Russian AF 10 Red *Nikolay Kuznetsov*		121st GvTBAP. Registered as, see next line
			10 Red/RF-94100 *Nikolay Kuznetsov*		6950th GvAvB

8 4 9 06 8 2 6	6-02	Tu-160	Soviet/Ukrainian AF 11 Red	30-12-1990	184th GvTBAP. Became, see next line
			Russian AF 11 Red *Vasiliy Sen'ko*		121st GvTBAP. Registered as, see next line
		Tu-160M	11 Red/RF-94114 *Vasiliy Sen'ko*		6950th GvAvB
8 4 9 06 3 3 5	6-03	Tu-160	Soviet/Ukrainian AF 12 Red[#]	1991	184th GvTBAP. Became, see next line
			Russian AF 12 Red *Aleksandr Novikov*		121st GvTBAP. Registered as, see next line
		Tu-160M	12 Red/RF-94109 *Aleksandr Novikov*		6950th GvAvB
8 1 0 06 7 4 1	6-04	Tu-160	Soviet/Ukrainian AF 14 Red[#]	1991	184th GvTBAP, scrapped
8 2 0 06 4 5 8	6-05	Tu-160	Soviet/Ukrainian AF 18 Red	30-9-1991	184th GvTBAP. Became, see next line
			Russian AF 18 Red *Andrey Tupolev*		121st GvTBAP. Registered as, see next line
		Tu-160M	18 Red/RF-94111 *Andrey Tupolev*		6950th GvAvB
8 2 0 07 6 1 7	7-01	Tu-160	Russian AF 01 Red *Mikhail Gromov*	30-12-1991	1096th TBAP, 121st GvTBAP
			[#] 18-9-2003		
8 3 0 07 5 2 6	7-02	Tu-160	Russian AF 02 Red *Vasiliy Reshetnikov*	30-6-1992	1096th TBAP, 121st GvTBAP. Reg as, see next line
			02 Red/RF-94102 *Vasiliy Reshetnikov*		6950th GvAvB
8 3 0 07 3 3 5	7-03	Tu-160	Russian AF 03 Red *Pavel Taran*	30-9-1992	1096th TBAP, 121st GvTBAP. Reg as, see next line
			03 Red/RF-94101 *Pavel Taran*		6950th GvAvB
8 4 0 07 1 4 2	7-04	Tu-160	Russian AF 04 Red *Ivan Yarygin*	30-12-1992	1096th TBAP, 121st GvTBAP. Reg as, see next line
			04 Red/RF-94112 *Ivan Yarygin*		6950th GvAvB
8 4 0 07 2 5 9	7-05	Tu-160	Russian AF 05 Red *Il'ya Muromets* (1)	21-7-1993	1096th TBAP. Renamed as, see next line
			Russian AF 05 Red *Aleksandr Golovanov*		121st GvTBAP. Registered as, see next line
			05 Red/RF-94104 *Aleksandr Golovanov*		6950th GvAvB
8 4 3 08 2 1 6	8-01	Tu-160	Russian AF 06 Red *Il'ya Muromets* (2)	30-6-1994	121st GvTBAP. Registered as, see next line
			06 Red/RF-94105 *Il'ya Muromets*		6950th GvAvB
8 2 4 08 4 2 7	8-02	Tu-160	Russian AF 07 Red *Aleksandr Molodchiy*	21-3-2000	121st GvTBAP. Registered as, see next line
			07 Red/RF-94106 *Aleksandr Molodchiy*		6950th GvAvB
8 4 4 08 5 3 8	8-03	Tu-160	Russian AF 08 Red *Vitaliy Kopylov*	6-3-2008	121st GvTBAP. Registered as, see next line
			08 Red/RF-94115 *Vitaliy Kopylov*		6950th GvAvB
8 * * 08 * 4 *	8-04	Tu-160			under construction
8 * * 08 * 5 *	8-05	Tu-160			under construction
8 * * 09 * 1 *	9-01	Tu-160			not completed (parts scrapped)
8 * * 09 * 2 *	9-02	Tu-160			not completed (parts scrapped)

[#] Ukrainian Air Force insignia

Russian Air Force Tu-160 "08 Red"/ RF-94115 *Vitaliy Kopylov*, the latest example so far, becomes airborne at Engels.

Appendix 2

World Records Held by the Tu-160

Two and a half years after it entered service the Tu-160 demonstrated its high performance for the world to see when it established an impressive series of world records. On October 31, 1989, a Soviet Air Force crew comprising aircraft captain Maj.-Gen. Lev V. Kozlov, co-pilot Col. Mikhail I. Pozdnyakov, navigator Col. V. S. Neretin and WSO Lt.-Col. S. N. Mart'yanov flew an in-service Tu-160 (f/n 3-04) grossing at 240,000 kg (529,110 lb) to set a total of 21 records in Group 3 under the World Air Sports Federation (FAI – *Fédération Aéronautique Internationale*) classification – that is, turbojet/turbofan-powered aircraft. Two of these were Class C-1 (landplanes with unlimited gross weight) speed records over a 1,000-km (621-mile) closed circuit; the rest were Class C-1r (landplanes with a gross weight of 200,000-250,000 kg/440,920-551,160 lb) altitude and speed records with various payloads.

(Note: Some sources say the aircraft in question was coded "14 Red." However, in the 184th GvTBAP this tactical code was reportedly worn by Tu-160 f/n 6-04, which did not yet exist then, being built in 1991!)

Not to be outdone, on 3rd November 1989 a Tupolev OKB test crew (captain Boris I. Veremey, co-pilot Grigoriy N. Shapoval, navigator Mikhail M. Kozel and WSO Anatoliy V. Yeriomenko) set a further 21 records in the second prototype (*izdeliye* 70-03, "29 Grey") with the maximum take-off weight of 275,000 kg (606,270 lb). Again, two were Class C-1 speed records over a closed circuit but the length of the circuit was 2,000 km (1,242 miles); the other 19 were Class C-1s (landplanes with a gross weight of 250,000-300,000 kg/551,160-661,390 lb) altitude and speed records.

In May 1990, the *Blackjack* continued its conquest of world records. On four non-consecutive days (May 15, May 22, May 24, and May 28) four different Air Force crews set 36 records between them – 18 Class C-1r speed records and 18 Class C-1s speed records over 1,000-km and 5,000-km (3,105-mile) closed circuits. Interestingly, the crews were reduced to three persons in each case: captain Lev V. Kozlov, co-pilot V. P. Rudenko and navigator S. N. Mart'yanov on 15th May; captain Col. Naïl' Sh. Sattarov, co-pilot Maj. Aleksandr S. Medvedev and navigator P. P. Merzlyakov on 22nd May; captain Col. Vladimir I. Pavlov, co-pilot Lt.-Col. Vitaliy P. Selivanov and navigator F. A. Ivlev on 24th May; and captain Col. S. D. Osipov, co-pilot N. N. Matveyev and navigator A. S. Tsarakhov on 28th May. Thus, in Soviet times

World records established by the Tu-160 in 1989-90

Date	Captain	Description	Value	No. of records
31-10-1989	L. V. Kozlov	Speed with payload over a 1,000-km closed circuit	1,731.4 km/h (1,075.4 mph)	2 (Class C-1)
		payload 15,000 kg (33,070 lb)		
		payload 25,000 kg (55,115 lb)		
ditto	ditto	Maximum altitude with payload	13,894 m (45,584 ft)	9 (Class C-1r)
		payload 0 kg		
		payload 1,000 kg (2,204 lb)		
		payload 2,000 kg (4,409 lb)		
		payload 5,000 kg (11,022 lb)		
		payload 10,000 kg (22,045 lb)		
		payload 15,000 kg (33,070 lb)		
		payload 20,000 kg (44,090 lb)		
		payload 25,000 kg (55,115 lb)		
		payload 30,000 kg (66,140 lb)		
ditto	ditto	Altitude in sustained flight with no payload	12,150 m (39,862 ft)	1 (Class C-1r)
ditto	ditto	Payload lifted to 2,000 m (6,560 ft)	30,471 kg (67,175 lb)	1 (Class C-1r)
ditto	ditto	Speed with payload over a 1,000-km closed circuit	1,731.4 km/h (1,075.4 mph)	9 (Class C-1r)
		payload 0 kg		
		payload 1,000 kg		
		payload 2,000 kg		
		payload 5,000 kg		
		payload 10,000 kg		
		payload 15,000 kg		
		payload 20,000 kg		
		payload 25,000 kg		
		payload 30,000 kg		
3-11-1989	B. I. Veremey	Speed with payload over a 2,000-km closed circuit	1,678.0 km/h (1,042.66 mph)	2 (Class C-1)
		payload 15,000 kg		
		payload 25,000 kg		

ditto	ditto	Maximum altitude with payload payload 0 kg payload 1,000 kg payload 2,000 kg payload 5,000 kg payload 10,000 kg payload 15,000 kg payload 20,000 kg payload 25,000 kg payload 30,000 kg	14,000 m (45,931 ft)	9 (Class C-1s)
ditto	ditto	Altitude in sustained flight with no payload	11,250 m (36,909 ft)	1 (Class C-1s)
ditto	ditto	Speed with payload over a 2,000-km closed circuit payload 0 kg payload 1,000 kg payload 2,000 kg payload 5,000 kg payload 10,000 kg payload 15,000 kg payload 20,000 kg payload 25,000 kg payload 30,000 kg	1,678.0 km/h (1,042.66 mph)	9 (Class C-1s)
15-5-1990	L. V. Kozlov	Speed with payload over a 1,000-km closed circuit * payload 0 kg payload 1,000 kg payload 2,000 kg payload 5,000 kg payload 10,000 kg payload 15,000 kg payload 20,000 kg payload 25,000 kg payload 30,000 kg	1,726.9 km/h (1,072.6 mph)	9 (Class C-1s)
22-5-1990	N. Sh. Sattarov	Speed with payload over a 2,000-km closed circuit payload 0 kg payload 1,000 kg payload 2,000 kg payload 5,000 kg payload 10,000 kg payload 15,000 kg payload 20,000 kg payload 25,000 kg payload 30,000 kg	1,195.7 km/h (742.6 mph)	9 (Class C-1r)
24-5-1990	V. I. Pavlov	Speed with payload over a 5,000-km closed circuit payload 0 kg payload 1,000 kg payload 2,000 kg payload 5,000 kg payload 10,000 kg payload 15,000 kg payload 20,000 kg payload 25,000 kg payload 30,000 kg	920.25 km/h (571.82 mph)	9 (Class C-1r)
28-5-1990	S. D. Osipov	Speed with payload over a 5,000-km closed circuit payload 0 kg payload 1,000 kg payload 2,000 kg payload 5,000 kg payload 10,000 kg payload 15,000 kg payload 20,000 kg payload 25,000 kg payload 30,000 kg	1,017.8 km/h (632.17 mph)	9 (Class C-1s)

* TOW 251,000 kg (553,360 lb)

the Tu-160 established no fewer than 78 world records which were officially recognised by the FAI.

That was not the end of it, though. On June 9–10, 2010, two Russian Air Force/6950th GvAvB Tu-160 crews established a distance/endurance record while making a planned ultra-long-range combat patrol flight. One of the two aircraft was "06 Red"/ RF-94105 *Il'ya Muromets* (c/n 84308216, f/n 8-01). It was captained by deputy squadron commander Lt.-Col. Aleksandr I. Khabarov, with instructor pilot Col. Andrey V. Senchurov (a DA Command Flight Safety Department inspector pilot) in the right-hand seat; the crew also included navigator Maj. Dmitriy V. Kirilov and instructor navigator Col. Oleg Yu. Baranov (the 6950th GvAvB's Chief Navigator) in the WSO's seat. The other bomber was "16 Red"/RF-94107 *Aleksey Plokhov* (c/n 82905836, f/n 5-03) which was flown by Lt.-Col. Mikhail N. Shishkin as captain, instructor pilot Col. Andrey A. Malyshev as co-pilot, navigator Maj. Flyur Z. Iskhakov and instructor navigator Lt.-Col. Vladimir V. Sookhodol'skiy as WSO.

This was the second time the Tu-160 had undertaken such an ultra-long-range flight; the first occasion was in 2009 when the *Blackjacks* had stayed aloft for about 21 hours. This time, however, the achievement was bettered. The bombers' route took them along the Russian border over the Arctic Ocean and then out over the Pacific. Care was taken to stay over international waters, not intruding into the airspace of other nations. During the mission the crews practiced lengthy flight over featureless terrain with no landmarks and few navaids. They also practiced IFR techniques, topping up twice from IL-78M tankers; in so doing they achieved another "first" for the Tu-160, twice receiving 50 tons (110,230 lb) of fuel in a single sortie.

The flight went without a hitch, the Tu-160s covering a distance of some 18,000 km (11,180 miles) non-stop; part of it was flown at supersonic speeds. "06 Red" was airborne for 23 hours 32 minutes, while "16 Red" stayed airborne even longer – for 24 hours 22 minutes. The Commander of the DA rated the mission as excellent, and the Russian Air Force is considering an even longer flight.

Rear view of a Tu-160 with two of the spoiler sections open.